Max Shachtman and His Left

REVOLUTIONARY STUDIES
Series Editor: PAUL LE BLANC

Max Shachtman and His Left

A Socialist's Odyssey through the "American Century"

PETER DRUCKER

HUMANITIES PRESS
NEW JERSEY

First published in 1994 by
Humanities Press International, Inc.
Atlantic Highlands, New Jersey 07716

© 1994 by Peter Drucker

Library of Congress Cataloging-in-Publication Data
Drucker, Peter, 1958–
Max Shachtman and his left : a socialist's odyssey through the
"American century" / Peter Drucker.
p.   cm. — (Revolutionary studies)
Includes bibliographical references and index.
ISBN 0-391-03815-X (HB). —ISBN 0-391-03816-8 (PBK)
1. Shachtman, Max, 1903-1972.   2. Communists—United States—
Biography.   3. Socialists—United States—Biography.   4. Communism—
United States—History—20th century.   5. Socialism—United States—
History—20th century.   I. Title.   II. Series.
HX84.S44D78   1993
324.273'75'092—dc20
[B]   93-12763
CIP

A catalog record for this book is available from the British Library

Printed in the United States of America

Contents

Preface

This book attempts to introduce people in the United States not only to an almost unknown man, Max Shachtman, but to the little-known world he lived in: the world of the U.S. left in the 1920s, 1930s, and 1940s.

Shachtman's own words are often used to tell the story. He was a gifted speaker and writer, never happier than when he was showing off his knowledge or ridiculing someone he disagreed with. His words are often eloquent. But they are a product of a time when people read a lot, talked a lot, and never watched television. His audiences were willing to put up with long speeches and long sentences rounded out with extra clauses and adjectives. They also appreciated a higher level of emotion than is fashionable today.

The reaction against "sentimentality" in speaking and writing could be seen as a loss, a reflection of the pervasive sense in our consumer society that every kind of feeling, like everything else, is for sale. But people's taste in prose is what it is. Few readers today would have the patience to wade through Shachtman's unedited words. Enough of his words remain here that readers should be able to appreciate his style.

His audiences were immersed in the doctrines and vocabulary of Marxism, whereas most book-buying, left-leaning people in the United States today are not. This book has to translate Marxist into American English. As the Polish-born Marxist Tamara Deutscher once remarked, no one who has not tried this kind of translation can imagine how difficult it is. But after all, Marxists in the United States have to attempt this same translation whenever we try to explain our politics. We can only hope that our language and our audience's language will eventually converge to create a new one, rich both with what Marxist theory has to offer and with the idiom of people's lives in the United States.

Besides the difficulty of finding a language in which to introduce readers to Shachtman, there is the difficulty of focusing on some of the events and work in his life and leaving out others. The man lived through seven decades, and through most of them his thinking and activity were bound up with developments in half a dozen movements and dozens of countries. A considerable amount of historical background is necessary in order to make his life comprehensible. An "authoritative biography" would take up many volumes. This book is organized around a few threads that were central in almost every period of his life: Leninism; Stalinism; socialism and democracy; national liberation movements; a U.S. labor party.

Coming of age before feminism explained that the personal is political, Shachtman and many socialists of his generation seemed to consider the personal private and irrelevant. In his papers, the two times in his life when a central relationship with one woman ended and another began are marked, if at all, by a note indicating that his address had changed. Almost all the information that could be found about Shachtman's personal relationships has been included. In contrast, the sources contain thousands of pages about faction fights, which are nowhere near as interesting to most people now as they were to the participants. But some account of these fights is necessary to understand what is of lasting importance in Shachtman's thought. As much as possible of the inessential or time bound has been pruned.

Within these limits, this book is the first attempt at a comprehensive examination and evaluation of Shachtman's thought and career as a whole. It tries to learn from and go beyond the valuable accounts that have already been published of different aspects of Shachtman's politics: Eric Chester on his attitude toward the Democratic Party, Maurice Isserman on his relationship with the New Left, Alan Wald on his influence on intellectuals. It also tries to learn from the traditional accounts of Shachtman's political evolution as seen from several current political perspectives, without accepting any of them unexamined. It presents him as a major, sometimes brilliant socialist thinker who made mistakes even at his best moments and had insights even at his worst ones.

The story of Shachtman's political life is rich in lessons for those who are trying to rebuild a socialist movement in the United States today. By unearthing some facts about him and the movement he led, the book tries to help people make their own judgments. At the same time, since I am a socialist myself, I indicate from time to time the lessons I draw from his story. He would disagree with many of my comments, but I imagine that he would forgive me for making them. He cared passionately about politics, was never able to discuss them with scholarly detachment, and would not have been likely to expect such superhuman self-restraint from me.

Reliance on contemporary documents in this book has required flexible standards of quotation. Punctuation that cannot be reconciled with the rules taught today in U.S. schools has been adjusted. Since Shachtman relied on amateur typing and proofreading, spelling errors were common. These errors have been corrected without comment unless there is room for doubt about what word was meant; in these cases, the emendation is in brackets. Italics are always given as in the originals (it would be difficult to find anything to italicize that wasn't italicized already). Ellipses indicate omissions in the middle of quotations but are not shown at the beginning or end.

Upper-case letters have been changed to lower-case and vice versa in order to make clauses flow together.

One detail of punctuation that may require comment is the book's varying system of capitalization. I use capital letters to refer to organizations and their members—e.g., Democratic Party, Socialists (Socialist Party members), Communism (of the Communist parties)—and lower-case letters to refer to political and social systems or perspectives—democratic, socialists, communism. Some readers may find the distinction between "official Communist policy" and "Shachtman's communist vision" confusing. But for Shachtman by the mid-1930s, the first was bureaucratic Stalinism, the second was democratic Marxism, and the two were essentially antagonistic. The difference in punctuation is meant to suggest gently a difference that was passionately felt.

A special problem arises with the people in this book: the use of pseudonyms and nicknames. With the passage of the Voorhis Act in 1940, Shachtman and his friends were committing crimes by being involved in international socialist organizations. U.S. history, from the Palmer raids in 1919 to McCarthyism in the 1950s, made them very much aware of the danger of identifying people in ways that FBI agents could understand. The repression that forced socialists to write in code was reprehensible on any kind of democratic principles. It is also frustrating to later readers who have to break the code.

Luckily there are always sources to say who was who. The names that people were born with are used in both the text and notes (except for a few people such as Abern, Carter, and Howe, whom nobody ever called Abramowitz, Friedman, or Horenstein); real names are put in brackets when the names given in the sources are different. The same policy is used for international institutions, since people in the United States had to refer to the World Congress of the Fourth International, for example, as the "Extraordinary Party Convention." The Abbreviations section of this book contains a list of the pseudonyms and nicknames used. Nicknames rather than formal first names are sometimes used in the text, since no one called Hal Draper "Harold," for example.

The documents of international Trotskyism are not always in English. Translations from French, German, or Castilian (Spanish) are my own unless otherwise indicated.

Another problem is that many documents drafted by Shachtman eventually appeared not as his work but as collective statements of an organization or committee. This practice reflected his conviction that in a socialist organization the whole is greater than the sum of its parts. A document that emerges from collective discussion and decision making is not any individual's property. Although this book attributes such documents to the

committee or the party rather than Shachtman, these documents are taken
as reasonable guides to his own thinking as long as there is no evidence to
the contrary. This is a safe assumption, since Shachtman was generally
acknowledged as one of the two most important leaders of U.S. Trotskyism until 1939 and as *the* most important leader of his organizations from
1940 to 1958. Where there is evidence of disagreements or compromises
involving such documents, this is pointed out. Whenever Shachtman was
explicitly named as at least one of several drafters of a document, the book
tends to assume that his role was the dominant one.

The documents quoted use some conventions that now seem question-
able. They often use "he" and "him" to refer to socialists in general, for
example. (Unfortunately, the male minority in the world at large has
managed to become a majority in the socialist movement, but referring to
all socialists as males seems to add needless insult to the many injuries
women have put up with.) They also use "America" and "American" to
refer exclusively to the United States, thus leaving out all the other inhabitants of the Americas who are too often forgotten (at best) in the United
States. They call the then–Soviet Union "Russia," which avoids the implication that there were any real soviets there but slights the non–Russian half
of the former USSR's population. They include Quebec in "Canada" and Catalonia in "Spain" over many of the inhabitants' objections. These usages in the
sources are not altered or pointed out, but they are avoided in the text.

For all the sources I am indebted to the librarians and libraries that
enabled me to see them, specifically, the Bancroft Library (University of
California at Berkeley), the Butler Library (Columbia), the Houghton
Library (Harvard), the New York Public Library, the Reuther Library
(Wayne State), the San Francisco Public Library (especially the people at the
interlibrary loan desk), and the Tamiment Library (New York University).
Shachtman's and A. J. Muste's memoirs are cited with the permission of the
Columbia University Oral History Research Office, and the Trotsky ar-
chives with the permission of the Houghton Library. The Tamiment
Library in particular has been an invaluable resource, and I am grateful to
Robert Eberwien, Peter Filardo, and Peter Allison of its staff for their help.
The helpfulness of librarians and the wonderfulness of libraries always seem
to contrast strikingly with the factories and stores that are run by the
supposedly more efficient profit motive.

I owe many thanks to many people for my good fortune in being able to
write this book. Encouragement and comments from my mother, Edith
Drucker, were important to the project. The commitment to knowledge
and social justice she encouraged in me while I was growing up was
indispensable. My lover, Christopher Beck, put up with me (or without

me) throughout the work with enormous patience and generosity, in ways that would require a whole book to detail. He also helped me enormously with his keen sense for awkward phrasing and obscure jargon.

Alan Wald encouraged me warmly when I first thought about beginning the work. Glenna Matthews gave me the benefit of her experience as a historian, gave some excellent advice on reorganizing the book, and worked selflessly to help find a publisher. Kent Worcester corrected and suggested improvements to my references to C. L. R. James. Bill Felice helped substantially with the practical task of getting the manuscript ready.

David Hacker and Patricia Friend, who are working on their own biography of Shachtman, generously allowed me to draw on their research, particularly their interview with Michael Harrington. Herman Benson, Hal Draper, Joel Geier, Emanuel Geltman, Albert Glotzer, Gordon Haskell, Tom Kahn, Morris Lewit, and Leo Seidlitz generously allowed me to interview them and filled in many gaps in the written record with their recollections. I am especially indebted to Glotzer and to Julius and Phyllis Jacobson. Glotzer showed extraordinary patience and care in giving me not only many hours of interviews but many pages of corrections. The Jacobsons also gave me many pages of corrections, additional information, and insightful criticisms.

Numberless friends and acquaintances have patiently listened to me babble on about Max. They have even, through occasional questions, pointed out what I had failed to explain or failed myself to understand.

I owe the most to those who taught me my Marxism through long years of collaborative efforts at building the socialist movement. Several of these comrades—Sam Farber, David Finkel, Michael Löwy, Ernest Mandel, Joanna Misnik, Charlie Post, Alan Wald—were generous enough to read drafts of the book and give me the benefit of their insightful (though at times conflicting) opinions. Michael Löwy generously read two different drafts and highlighted several crucial historical and theoretical issues for me. I have been uniquely fortunate in having a series editor, Paul Le Blanc, with an extraordinarily broad knowledge of U.S. leftist history and an acute sensitivity to unfair or unsubstantiated criticism. I am grateful as well to my Humanities Press production editor, Cindy Nixon, for her enthusiasm and help.

Although the book that came out at the end cannot be seen as a collective document (historical and theoretical judgments being too fluid and tentative to be voted on by groups), the thought that went into it certainly was collective. For this reason I have no honorable choice but to dedicate the book to my comrades in Solidarity and the Fourth International and to revolutionaries around the world. Their struggles made it possible, and I hope that their struggles will be informed by it.

Abbreviations

UAW   United Auto Workers (founded 1935)

WP   Workers Party ("Musteites" and Trotskyists, 1935–36;
           "Shachtmanites," 1940–49)

YPSL   Young People's Socialist League (Socialist Party youth
           group until 1972; also SWP youth 1938–40 and WP
           youth 1940–41)

YSL   Young Socialist League (youth group linked to ISL,
           1954–58)

ABBREVIATIONS IN NOTES

Some frequently cited sources and terms are referred to in the notes by the
following abbreviations:

b   box

BR   *Bureaucratic Revolution* (collected *New International* articles)

DW   *Daily Worker* (Chicago to Jan. 1927, then New York)

f   folder

ISM   Independent Socialist Mimeographia (Hal Draper, ed.)

LA   *Labor Action* (New York)

LD   *Labor Defender* (Chicago to Sept. 1927, then New York)

M   *Militant* (New York)

MSC   Max Shachtman Collection, Tamiment Library,
           New York University, New York, New York

n   number

NA   *New America* (New York)

NI   *New International* (New York)

OHAL   Oral History of the American Left Collection,
           Tamiment Library, New York University, New York,
           New York

PMA   The Papers of Martin Abern, John Dwyer Collection,
           Archives of Labor and Urban Affairs, Walter P. Reuther
           Library, Wayne State University, Detroit, Michigan

r   microfilm reel

RMS   The Reminiscences of Max Shachtman (1963), Oral
           History Collection, Butler Library, Columbia
           University, New York, New York

s   side(s) of an interview tape

SA   *Socialist Appeal* (New York)

TA   Trotsky Archives, Houghton Library, Harvard
            University, Cambridge, Massachusetts
v   volume
W   *The Worker* (New York until July 1923, then Chicago)
YW   *The Young Worker* (Chicago)

Full publication data for books cited can be found in the bibliography. The tapes of all the interviews conducted by the author and cited in the notes are now available to the public in the Oral History of the American Left collection at the Tamiment Library, New York University.

Pseudonyms/Nicknames

The following list gives real names of people or institutions (used in the footnotes) on the left; the pseudonyms or nicknames often used in original sources on the right.

Abern   Harry Allen, Stone, Marty (born Martin Abramowitz)
Benson   Ben Hall
Bernick   Paul Bern, Charnis, Robert Nevis, Izzy
Burbank   H. D. Coleman
Burnham   Kelvin, John West
Calverton   (born George Goetz)
Cannon   Legrand, Martel, Martin, X, Jim
Carter   Walsh, Joe (born Joseph Friedman)
Coser   Europicus
Draper   Philip Coven, Bernard Cramer, H. D. Spectre, Paul
               Temple, Hal
T. Draper   Ted
Dunayevskaya   Freddie Forest, Rae Spiegel
V. R. Dunne   Jones, Ray
Erber   Erickson, Ernest Lund, Ernie
Fernandez   Munis
FI   The Movement
Geltman   Emanuel Garrett, Manny
Genecin   Milton Alvin, Milt
Glotzer   Albert Gates, Al
Goldman   Morris, Morrison, Al (born Albert Verblen)
Gordon   J. Stuart

Gould	Acton, Anton, Natie
Hansen	Stern, Joe
Harrington	Eli Fishman, Mike
Haskell	Larry O'Connor, Gordon, Smith
Howe	Theodore Dryden, R. Fahan, R. F. Fangston (born Irving Horenstein)
IEC	Committee in Charge, CIC
Jacobson	Julius Falk, Julie
P. Jacobson	born Phyllis Garden
James	J. R. Johnson, CLR, Jimmy, Nello
Kahn	Tom Marcel
Lee	Ria Stone
Lewit	Stein
Lipset	Martin Lewitt
Mandel	Ernest Germain, Walter
Martinson	Robert Magnus
McKinney	David Coolidge, Courtney, Mac, Dave
Morrow	Cassidy, George Cooper, John C. Wilson (born Felix Mayorwitz)
Novack	John Marshall, William F. Warde (born Y. M. Novograbelski)
Pedrosa	A. Lebrun
Plastrik	Henry Judd, Sherman Stanley, Rajah
Rader	Jack Brad
Raptis	Archer, Gabriel, Michel Pablo, Robert, Smith
Sard	Frank Demby, Walter S. Oakes, T. N. Vance, Ed
Selznick	Sherman (born Philip Schachter)
Shachtman	Michaels, Pedro, S-n, M. N. Trent
Sterling	Scopa
Stuart	James Fenwick
Trotsky	Crux, Hansen, LD, Leo, O'Brien, Old Man, OM, W. Rork, Wolfe
Widick	Walter Jason, Jack Wilson
World Congress	Extraordinary Party Convention, EPC

Chronology

1904	Shachtman born in Warsaw
1905	Moves with his mother to join his father in New York
1916–20	Attends DeWitt Clinton High School
1917	United States enters First World War Bolsheviks take power in Russia
1918	Civil war begins in Russia Armistice ends First World War
1919	Communist International founded in Moscow Socialist Party splits in United States; Communist groups formed Allies impose Versailles peace treaty on Germany
1919–20	Many U.S. radicals rounded up, jailed, deported
1920	Shachtman enrolls in City College; withdraws because of illness Sacco and Vanzetti tried and convicted of murder
1921	Civil war ends in Russia with defeat of Kronstadt uprising Shachtman drops out of City College again Joins Workers Party (new, legal Communist party)
1923	Moves to Chicago at Abern's request to edit *Young Worker* Joins Foster-Cannon fight against Ruthenberg-Lovestone Meets Billie Ramloff, his first wife Trotsky defeated in faction fight in USSR Communist uprising fails in Germany Glotzer joins Young Workers League
1924	Lenin dies Glotzer meets Shachtman Communist International ends Communist support for LaFollette
1925	International turns U.S. Communist Party over to Ruthenberg

Shachtman and Cannon break with Foster group
Shachtman visits Moscow for first time

1926   Becomes *Labor Defender* editor
British general strike fails

1926–27   Trotsky relaunches fight in USSR; is defeated and expelled
Shachtman's second visit to Moscow

1927   Moves back to New York with Communist headquarters
Chiang Kai-shek massacres Chinese Communists in Shanghai
Sacco and Vanzetti executed
Ruthenberg dies; Lovestone takes over party

1928   At Moscow congress, Cannon becomes secret Trotsky supporter
Cannon returns to New York and wins over Shachtman and Abern
All three expelled from Communist Party, publish *Militant*

1929   Trotsky deported from USSR to Turkey
Trotskyist Communist League of America founded
Stalin starts collectivizing Soviet agriculture
Communist International turns left, breaks with Lovestone
Worldwide depression begins

1930   Shachtman travels to Turkey and meets Trotsky
Glotzer comes to New York to edit *Militant*

1931   Shachtman founds Pioneer Publishers
Republican revolution in Spain

1931–32   Shachtman travels to Britain, France, and Spain

1931–33   Shachtman, Abern, and Glotzer fight inside CLA against Cannon

1933   Hitler takes power in Germany
Roosevelt launches "first New Deal"
Trotsky declares need for Fourth International
Shachtman travels with Trotsky from Turkey to France
Glotzer moves back to Chicago with Edith Harvey

1934   Dollfuss crushes socialists in Vienna
Edith Harvey leaves Glotzer and moves to New York

Trotsky moves from France to Norway
New International founded, with Shachtman as editor
CP and Musteites lead San Francisco and Toledo general strikes
Shachtman edits Minneapolis general strike newspaper
Trotskyists in United States merge with Musteites to form WP
Kirov killed in Leningrad

1935   Roosevelt's "second New Deal" (Wagner Act, Social Security)
            CIO founded
            Communist International calls for Popular Fronts

1936   Socialist Party's right wing ("Old Guard") leaves
            Shachtman and Cannon convince WP to join Socialist Party
            Popular Front wins French elections
            Civil war breaks out in Spain
            Shachtman visits Trotsky in Norway
            Works with Trotsky to expose Moscow trials
            Trotsky calls for violent revolution in USSR

1937   Shachtman greets Trotsky on his arrival in Mexico
            Spanish Republic crushes anarchists and Marxists in Barcelona
            Sit-down strikes in Detroit, Flint, and Pontiac auto plants
            Thomas withdraws in favor of LaGuardia in New York
            Shachtman moves in with Edith Harvey, his second wife

1937–38   Trotskyists, expelled from SP, form Socialist Workers Party
            Carter and Burnham call USSR "bureaucratic collectivist"

1938   Trotsky's son Sedov dies under suspicious circumstances in Paris
            Shachtman discusses new SWP course with Trotsky in Mexico
            Presides over Fourth International's founding congress
            Britain and France capitulate to Hitler at Munich

1939   Shachtman and Harvey's son Michael born
            Germany and USSR invade Poland, starting Second World War

Shachtman and others in SWP reject "defense" of USSR
USSR invades Finland

1940   Shachtman's faction expelled from SWP, forms Workers
        Party
        German army overruns France, which surrenders
        Trotsky murdered in Mexico City
        Shachtman decides USSR is "bureaucratic collectivist"

1941   Germany invades USSR, begins mass murder of Jews
        Shachtman refuses to support USSR in war
        Shachtman's mother dies
        Japan attacks Pearl Harbor; United States enters World
        War

1942   United States and Britain invade North Africa

1942–43 USSR defeats Germans at Stalingrad

1943   United States and Britain invade Italy; Mussolini falls
        Resistance forces grow in occupied Europe
        Shachtman predicts Soviet domination of Eastern Europe

1944   United States and Britain invade France
        Auto Workers Rank and File Caucus fights no-strike
        pledge

1944–45 Soviet Union occupies Eastern Europe
        Yugoslav Communists seize power

1945   Germany defeated and occupied
        Labour Party wins British elections
        United States drops atom bombs on Japan, which
        surrenders

1945–46 Wave of "pressure valve" strikes led by General Motors
        strike
        SWP minority pushes unsuccessfully for SWP-WP unity

1946   Reuther becomes UAW president
        Shachtman calls for "all-inclusive revolutionary party"
        Backs Mikolajczyk in Poland

1947   Urges Trotskyists in Europe to join Socialist parties
        Raptis visit launches SWP-WP unity talks, which fail
        Truman pledges to "contain" Communism in Greece
        Proposes Marshall Plan aid to Western Europe
        Taft-Hartley Act passed
        Shachtman backs Reuther over Addes in UAW

	Glotzer moves from New York to Akron, then Los Angeles
	Draper moves from Los Angeles to New York
1948	Communist coup in Czechoslovakia completes division of Europe
	Shachtman attends Fourth International's second congress
	Fights Geltman's support for Marshall Plan
	Workers Party breaks with Fourth International
	Tito's Yugoslavia breaks with Stalin
	Erber and Goldman quit Workers Party
	Communists back Wallace for president against Truman
	Shachtman's father dies
1949	Mao's Communists win civil war in China
	Workers Party changes name to Independent Socialist League
	Haskell and Benson move to New York
	Shachtman decides peaceful, legal path to socialism is possible
	Backs CIO's expulsion of left-wing unions
	Pushes to support labor candidates in Democratic Party
1950–53	Korean War
1951	Controversy over "defeatism" in ISL
	Shachtman leaves Edith Harvey for Yetta Barsh, his third wife
	Edith and Michael move to California
	Shachtman has first heart attack
1952	Howe and Geltman quit ISL
1953	Stalin dies
	Workers revolt in East Germany
1953–54	YPSL breaks with Socialists and merges with ISL youth group
1954	Geneva accords partition Vietnam
	Howe and Geltman found *Dissent*
	Shachtman wins ISL to idea of backing labor Democrats
	Shachtman and Barsh move to Floral Park on Long Island, NY
1955	Montgomery bus boycott begins civil rights movement

1956   Khrushchev denounces Stalin's crimes
Soviet tanks crush Hungarian revolution
Crisis in U.S. Communist Party

1957   Shachtman rejects idea of separate revolutionary groups

1958   Independent Socialist League joins Socialist Party

1959   Castro's July 26 Movement takes power in Cuba

1960   Shachtman leads SP "realignment tendency"

1961   Cuban exiles backed by CIA invade Cuba at Bay of Pigs
Shachtman refuses to condemn invasion; breaks with Draper

1962   Faction fight tears YPSL apart
SDS clashes with Harrington over Port Huron statement

1963   Rustin organizes March on Washington for civil rights

1964   Draper ends activity in SP
Free Speech Movement in Berkeley
Shachtman backs Johnson for president

1965   YPSL reconstituted under Shachtman's control
Shachtman baptizes Freedom Budget
Johnson escalates U.S. troop presence in Vietnam
SDS calls first big anti-war march

1968   Police riot and beat protesters at Chicago Democratic Convention
Shachtman backs Humphrey for president

1970   Shachtman refuses to back U.S. withdrawal from Vietnam
Breaks with Harrington and Howe

1971   Praises Hillquit and Roosevelt

1972   Refuses to back McGovern against Nixon
Socialist Party splits
Shachtman dies in Floral Park from a heart attack

PART I

"The Working Class of This Country . . . Will Yet Be the Living Vindication of Marxism"

The end of the Cold War is a propitious time to remember Max Shachtman, a radical who predicted the Cold War and did his best to explain and chart it. But there are at least two Shachtmans to remember. One is the Cold War Shachtman: a socialist who became a decreasingly critical supporter of U.S. foreign policy. The other is an earlier, pre–Cold War Shachtman: a radical of the 1920s, 1930s, and 1940s.

By the time he died in 1972, the Cold War Shachtman was a figure of some importance behind the scenes of U.S. politics. He was a builder and breaker of coalitions inside the Democratic Party. He was seen as an intellectual gray eminence behind AFL-CIO leaders George Meany and Albert Shanker. He was a mentor for African-American leaders such as Bayard Rustin and socialist intellectuals such as Michael Harrington and Irving Howe. He even influenced young people who would become prominent in the neoconservative right—influential essayist and editor Irving Kristol and Reagan UN representative Carl Gershman.

This Cold War Shachtman is closest to us chronologically, but he already seems remote from us historically. He made his reputation at a time when the Soviet Union could still be portrayed as the greatest enemy to freedom in the world. The AFL-CIO could still be portrayed as a powerful force that, operating through the Democratic Party, could reshape U.S. society. Today, with the USSR gone and the AFL-CIO rapidly losing what social base and influence it has left, Shachtman's world of the 1950s and 1960s is almost unrecognizable.

1

Paradoxically, in some respects the pre–Cold War Shachtman of the 1920s, 1930s, and 1940s now seems startlingly contemporary. To understand why, we have to reimagine the world of the left in the United States in its heyday. Thanks to the successful destruction of the U.S. left by McCarthyism, that world is remembered today only in patches. But the more clearly we conjure up the picture of that pre–Cold War world, the more unsettlingly familiar it looks.

Before the Cold War, as well as in its aftermath, the United States emerged as the world's clearly preeminent power. But U.S. power was threatened in the 1930s by both the economic crisis at home and the growing strength of Germany and Japan overseas. Within U.S. society, the superficial prosperity and speculative boom of the 1920s failed to paper over the glaring disparity between rich and poor. Then as now, many of the people who produced the country's wealth in its factories and sweatshops were immigrants (then mostly from Southern or Eastern Europe rather than from Asia or Latin America). They were often poor, often ununionized, often denied democratic rights that most U.S. citizens would later come to take for granted.

These immigrants' languages, cultures, and political traditions were seen as alien and threatening by the cultural elite and much of the "native" working and middle classes. Sometimes they identified with radical movements, even radical labor movements, that were fighting against dictatorships in their original countries, just as many Haitians, Filipinos, and Salvadorans did in the United States in the 1980s. Many of them viewed the U.S. government, despite its democratic constitution, as a North American counterpart of the repressive governments it supported abroad. Sometimes they worked alongside African-American migrants from the South, whose recent arrival in northern cities had fueled racial tensions and clashes. Even in the midst of the 1920s boom, most African Americans and immigrants were denied the affluence they had dreamed of. With the onset of the Great Depression, even native-born white workers felt that the promises of the "American dream" had been broken.

Max Shachtman grew up in this familiar-seeming, pre–Cold War world in an immigrant, working-class community that was more or less consciously, more or less consistently resisting pressures to adapt, conform, and resign itself to the existing U.S. order. Shachtman's boyhood neighborhood, Jewish Harlem, like many other neighborhoods in the 1920s, had its own embattled working-class values that were opposed to those of the dominant culture represented by Henry Ford and Calvin Coolidge. The politics Shachtman developed in the 1920s and 1930s were rooted in his community's oppositional values. Through his education in the Communist Party and Trotskyist movement and his own creative adaptation of Marxism, he harnessed those values by the 1940s to a vision of a different United States and a coherent, original strategy for getting there.

When Shachtman talked about the working class in those years he was neither spouting Marxist jargon nor glorifying union officials. He was talking about his parents and neighbors. In his Harlem neighborhood, his decision at age seventeen to join the Communist Party was, if not typical, commonplace. Although Communists in their 1920s immigrant ghettos were almost as marginal as the socialist left of the 1990s, they were sustained by the subcultures that surrounded them. The people Shachtman knew when he was young were not necessarily Communists or socialists, but most of them shared his elemental alienation from and suspicion toward those who controlled the government and economy.

The class identity and class antagonism Shachtman took for granted was not unique to Jews or New Yorkers. It was common to many of the people who lived and worked in industrial centers in the 1920s and 1930s. Most of them were immigrants or children of immigrants who felt that bosses, senators, judges, and professors belonged to a different and hostile group of people. Working-class identity and language united not only the whole left but much of the working class in the 1920s, 1930s, and 1940s. Only later, in the 1950s, did the dogma take hold that the United States is a classless society.

Shachtman's politics grew out of his community's sense of alienation and tried to create an alternative to the alien society it rejected. Out of his particular Jewish immigrant experience, he developed a personal solution, never explicitly articulated, to the conundrum of being a radical internationalist in the United States. In a sense he overcame the tension between being "American" and being radical that has bedeviled the U.S. socialist left throughout its existence—a tension that permeates two apparently opposite main currents in U.S. radicalism.

One main current among U.S. radicals, rooted ultimately in the radicalism of the War for Independence, found particular expression in the agrarian populist side of Debsian socialism. This current has stressed "American exceptionalism." Its partisans have argued that U.S. socialism should derive primarily from its own native roots in our "New World." They have often seen Marxism as an alien European import that at the very least needs to be infused with "American" democratic values before it can be applied to the United States. Sometimes they have singled out the Marxist idea of revolution as particularly alien. Though they believe that the United States must be transformed, they argue that the democratic revolution that took place two centuries ago in the United States enables us to avoid the bloodshed and class hatred that has often characterized "Old World" radicalism.

An apparently diametrically opposed current has tended to stress the backwardness of the U.S. left and our need to learn from more advanced European, Asian, or Latin American traditions. The first partisans of this current were German immigrants in the 1870s and 1880s who introduced Marxism to the United States but frustrated Marx and Engels by their proud self-isolation from the rest of the U.S. working class. Their attitude was duplicated later by immigrants from tsarist Russia who appointed themselves the bearers of U.S. communism after 1917; some New Leftist who wrote off most U.S. workers as irredeemably co-opted and considered Ho Chi Minh, Mao Zedong, and/or Fidel Castro the fonts of revolutionary doctrine; and academic Marxists since the 1970s who have specialized in popularizing sophisticated "neo-Marxist" and "post-Marxist" theories from France and Germany. Though superficially these radicals are much more internationalist than U.S. populists, they have nonetheless accepted the populist assumption that Marxism is something alien to the United States.

Shachtman diverged from and transcended both these approaches to being a radical in the United States. As a Jew born in Eastern Europe, he identified deeply with the European workers' movement and its theoretical heritage. As a child of parents who chose to come to the United States and believed in its potential for freedom, he also identified with and was fascinated by all things "American." For him, Marxism became something that naturally fits the United States, makes sense of this country, and can enable it to live up to its own best possibilities. Acknowledging that "the working class of this country is the 'living refutation' of Marxism," he was nonetheless confident that it would "yet be the living vindication of Marxism."*

---

*Shachtman, "Under the banner of Marxism" (misdated 19 Mar. 1949), WP bul v 4 n 1 (Jan. 1949), ISM v 10, 2202.

Without ever fully articulating this attitude, Shachtman exemplified it in his political practice. As a young Communist organizer reaching out to other working-class teenagers in the years before federal child labor laws, he appealed to a spirit of rebellion, nonconformity, and countercultural experimentation—a striking foreshadowing of the 1960s New Left. As a leader in the fight to save anarchists Nicola Sacco and Bartolomeo Vanzetti from execution in 1927, he voiced the suspicion and anger that poor immigrants felt toward police, judges, officials, and the rich, as well as a sense of entitlement to freedom and justice.

As a commentator on international events for the Communist press and then as the exiled Trotsky's "commissar for foreign affairs," he expressed the identification that U.S. radicals felt with Augusto Sandino fighting the U.S. Marines in Nicaragua and with Chinese trade unionists striking against foreign bosses in Shanghai. As a labor journalist, he helped put out the newspaper that made the difference between victory and defeat in the 1934 Minneapolis general strike, one of the big strikes that cleared the ground for the CIO.

Later, in the course of the New Deal and Second World War, most of the U.S. left abandoned Shachtman's 1920s-style radicalism. Most Communists and Socialists tried to throw off their immigrant marginality and become part of the cultural and political mainstream. The CIO began the process by joining native-born and immigrant, white and nonwhite workers into a single, militant, "Americanized" movement. Its New Deal and wartime patriotism prefigured the later patriotic, anti-Communist, not-so-militant, even pro-capitalist consensus of the AFL-CIO. The Communist Party, which for a short time in the 1930s and 1940s became the dominant force on the U.S. left, often accepted and even exaggerated this trend—with slogans like "Communism Is Twentieth-Century Americanism"—only to find late in the 1940s that twentieth-century "Americanism" was viciously hostile to communism.

Shachtman thought that the choices made by most of the U.S. left in the 1930s and 1940s unwittingly helped prepare the division, defeat, and dispersal of the left during the 1950s. He made different choices that were rooted in the intransigent radicalism he had learned in the 1920s. He refused to jump on the bandwagon of Franklin Roosevelt's presidency and opposed the New Deal and the Second World War. His small Workers Party organized workers during the war to fight against the no-strike pledge, led wildcat strikes, and nearly won official United Auto Workers renunciation of the no-strike pledge over the combined opposition of union leaders and the U.S. government. Through innovative activism in the American Labor Party, he worked to give the union-based ferment of the mid-1940s independent political expression.

Shachtman saw his movement in the United States as part of a worldwide movement that united diverse people in diverse struggles: U.S. strikers, the French resistance to the Nazis, the Irish Republican Army, the Vietminh fighting both Japan and France in Indochina. He and his movement predicted the United States' rise to empire and opposed it, while others on the left acquiesced in it. Some of his prewar and wartime prophecies were impressive in their accuracy.

At the same time, Shachtman wrestled with the connection between democracy and socialism, an issue that has concerned and perplexed later radicals. He had a standard for democracy different from any available to latter-day socialists; it was derived from the grassroots democracy of U.S. radicals and their international co-thinkers in the years immediately before and after the Russian Revolution. This standard enabled him to reject the idea of supporting "democracy" as the U.S.

government practiced and championed it, because he saw how distorted and hollow that democracy could be when used as an adjunct of imperial power. But his vivid sense of what real democracy in action could be saved him from dismissing democratic freedoms as empty. He fought for several decades against the destruction of democratic freedoms, without settling for democratic capitalism as democracy's highest embodiment. He argued that radicals could not only support fights against fascism and McCarthyism but also lead and transform those fights.

Shachtman's commitment to the democratic radicalism of the early 1920s made him a harsh critic and perceptive analyst of Stalinism. He seconded Leon Trotsky's criticisms of Stalin's policies in the 1930s, campaigning full time to expose the 1936–38 Moscow purge trials. In 1939–40 he opposed the Soviet government even more sweepingly than Trotsky could accept, rejecting any support for Soviet military advances into Eastern Europe. He built his own Workers Party into the democratic antithesis of bureaucratized Communism, priding himself on the freedom and openness of its debates.

This is the pre–Cold War Max Shachtman whose story this book tries to tell. The book is written in the hope that it can provide a bridge between Shachtman's pre–Cold War U.S. socialism and the post–Cold War socialism that we can now begin to create.

In light of the dangers—homelessness, crumbling cities, ecological disasters—now threatening the United States that the New Deal and Second World War gave birth to, Shachtman's intransigent radicalism of the 1920s, 1930s, and 1940s deserves a fresh hearing. Not that the answers he came up with can be applied mechanically to today's problems. In many ways we live in a different world from his. The people around us no longer live in the same neighborhoods, speak the same languages, or have the same hopes as people in Shachtman's time. In other ways we are aware of dimensions of our world—ecology, sexuality—that he hardly dealt with in his politics. But the decades that separate us from the 1930s and 1940s have not erased the problems he faced then. On the contrary: Facing the unresolved problems of Shachtman's "American century" is a prerequisite to meeting the challenges of the twenty-first century.

1

A Communist from Harlem

Max Shachtman grew up between two worlds. Born in Warsaw (then part of the Russian Empire) on 10 September 1904 to Jewish parents, he inherited their "hatred and contempt for the czarist regime," their working–class identity, their sense of being victims and adversaries of power. But Max himself had no experience of life under tsarism. He grew up in New York City, where his father, Benjamin, moved from Warsaw soon after Max was born, and where Max's mother, Sarah, and he moved when he was eight months old.[1] His early life was the life of an urban North American teenager. His language (although he was fluent in Yiddish) was English with a New York accent. Many of his values and beliefs were not his parents' but rather the mainstream American values he was taught in elementary school and high school.

The Russian Revolution disrupted Max's smooth assimilation into the U.S. mainstream and pulled his attention back to the Eastern Europe he had come from. He did not follow the path his parents and teachers had mapped out for him: a City College education and a professional career. Instead he dropped out of college in 1920–21, joined the Communist movement, and spent the years from 1923 to 1927 in Chicago as a full-time Communist organizer.

The Communist movement he joined in the 1920s was an overwhelmingly immigrant movement, largely Russian, Finnish, East European Jewish, and Yugoslav. It was struggling to reach a broader U.S. audience, speak in English, and "Americanize" itself. Yet at the same time it tried to "Bolshevize" itself and integrate itself into an international movement. Its attention was continually drawn to the drama of revolution and counterrevolution in Europe and Asia. Shachtman spent his late teens and early twenties trying both to "Americanize" and "Bolshevize" himself. He worked as a young working–class North American reaching out to other young working–class North Americans; at the same time he trained himself as an expert on Marxism, Russian bolshevism, German social democracy, British miners, and Nicaraguan guerrillas. He threw himself into an effort

6

to reconcile an American identity with a radical internationalist politics.

U.S. communism in the 1920s was a relatively youthful movement, and it turned Shachtman into a lifelong admirer of radical youth. As an organizer for the Communists' Young Workers League and editor of its newspaper, he became part of a circle of young Communists in Chicago, some of whom would be his intimates for decades. Martin Abern, the Young Workers League's first leader, brought him to Chicago, groomed him as his heir as the League's leader, and became his ally in the first of several joint factional battles. Albert Glotzer, a younger Jewish Chicago teenager, became Shachtman's follower and friend. Billie Ramloff, a young Latvian Communist, became Shachtman's first wife. They were bound together in a peculiar, exhilarating life in which bouts of intense work alternated with organizational intrigue, arguments about fine points of Marxism, and outings to vaudeville shows. Shachtman later remembered his Chicago years as "one of the most pleasant periods of my life."[2]

During the Chicago years, Shachtman matured from a somewhat self-centered, excitable teenager into a writer, speaker, thinker, and leader. His chief teacher and model was Communist leader James P. Cannon. Cannon shared and reinforced his desire for a Marxism rooted in the U.S. working class. Thanks to Cannon, Shachtman took on his second major role in the Communist movement when he moved on from the Young Workers League in 1925–26 to work in the organization Cannon headed, the International Labor Defense. As editor of the newspaper *Labor Defender*, Shachtman campaigned for U.S. working people who were victimized because of their union activism or radical politics. He helped develop a movement for democratic rights that exposed the limits instead of perpetuating the myths of U.S. democracy. As a leader in the fight to save Sacco and Vanzetti from execution, he powerfully evoked the sense of alienation and persecution that U.S. immigrant radicals of the 1920s shared.

Cannon's and Shachtman's efforts to shape U.S. communism in a mold that was American as well as revolutionary and internationalist were brought to an abrupt halt in the mid-1920s. They were shocked to discover that the Communist International's guiding lights in Moscow disagreed with their perspective and suspected their loyalty. Shachtman's dreams of bringing the two worlds he grew up in into harmony turned into a frustrating experience of conflict between his understanding of his country and his internationalist commitment. The conflict would turn out to be unresolvable within the Communist Party.

Max Shachtman's father, Benjamin, lived the life of a typical immigrant Jewish tailor in New York. He went back and forth between the shop (where he did his share in union organizing and strikes) and (for a few brief periods, when he had accumulated some savings) "a little two-by-four business of his own," which somehow never quite earned him a living. "We didn't starve, nothing of the sort," Max later remembered, "but neither were we affluent."[3]

Max grew up on East 100th Street in Harlem between First and Second Avenues in an overwhelmingly working-class, East European Jewish community. Only twenty years or so before, East Harlem had been a sparsely settled village an hour and a half's journey by horse-drawn trolley from downtown Manhattan. But since the early 1890s it had been home for thousands of East European Jews pushed out of the overcrowded Lower East Side. By 1910, with 100,000 Jews living in East Harlem and a housing shortage pushing rents up and conditions down for everyone, poor East Europeans flooded west across Lexington Avenue from the neighborhood's east end where the Shachtman family lived.

East Harlem was a crowded corner apart from the rest of uptown Manhattan. Its streets were lined with "landsmanshaft" synagogues (i.e., those whose congregations were drawn from a single Russian province), Jewish schools (religious, Zionist, secular Yiddish, or English-language socialist), and innumerable coffee shops to sit and argue in—for those who had time after their exhausting workdays.

Not particularly rebellious as either a child or a teenager, Max stayed happily enough in his parents' Harlem home until he was eighteen. His father "doted on Max." Max had a very affectionate relationship with his mother: "He'd hug her and kiss her and hug her and kiss her, just incessantly." He was not very fond of his younger sister Tilly, but Tilly was never a serious rival for their parents' love.[4]

The whole family assumed that Max would lead a better life. Naturally they would all sacrifice so he could go to high school and college and become some kind of professional. His secure childhood may have given Max the sense of self-confidence, even cockiness, that always seemed to stay with him. He always seemed to expect that he would be loved and admired—and he usually was. He always seemed to expect that he would be taken care of—and thanks to his followers and wives, he usually was.

Max crossed the bridge between his parents' East European background and his new country without much pain or difficulty. Most of the people he grew up with were making the same transition. Obviously and unashamedly a New York Jew, he nonetheless felt himself to be as American as anyone. He never gave much thought to being Jewish, since most of the people around him were Jewish; he was apparently equally indifferent to Judaism, Zionism, and assimilationism. He never thought that being American meant being for the government; like most of the people he lived among, he thought of the government as an alien institution that belonged somewhere else. His distinctive "American" identity—an identity bound up with being working class, an immigrant, a Jew—found a natural expression in his joining the Communist Party at age seventeen.

Socialist politics was an accepted but not terribly important part of Shachtman's world during his childhood. His father read the *Forward*, the Yiddish socialist daily published downtown, and generally voted Socialist. Max, like most of his neighbors, was not particularly interested. Before the First World War, East Harlem's sentimental socialism rarely stopped it from electing whatever Democrats Tammany Hall picked to represent it. But Max would hang around with his friends listening to socialist speakers on street corners. Branch Number 2 of the Workmen's Circle, the Jewish left's ecumenical gathering place and benefit society at 100th Street and Lexington Avenue, was a couple of blocks from his home. He even knew socialist students at DeWitt Clinton High School who organized a student strike against overcrowding and compulsory military training. But the strike fizzled out without capturing his imagination.

Like many other bright students, Shachtman was won to socialism not through activism but through his studies. Thanks to a gifted high school teacher, he became fascinated by history at a time when history seemed to be shaking the world. After a century of relative peace, Europe was torn apart from 1914 to 1918 by the First World War. The empires that Shachtman's parents had hated—Russian, German, Austro-Hungarian—were shattered. The United States, no longer a bystander, entered the war in April 1917. U.S. soldiers sent to fight in the trenches made the difference for Britain, France, and Italy between winning and losing. When people in the United States looked at the peace treaties imposed by the victors in 1919 and 1920—treaties that turned over Germany's African and Pacific colonies to the Allied colonial powers, demanded billions of dollars in reparations from the defeated countries, and replaced the hated old Central European empires with new, French-sponsored republics almost as ethnically jumbled and far less stable—many felt that they had been tricked into fighting so that European empires could plunder one another.

In this atmosphere of disillusionment, the socialist movement in the United States looked like an appealing alternative. Even before the war Eugene Debs's Socialist Party had been growing fast. In the 1912 presidential elections, Debs had won 897,000 votes, 6 percent of the total. Unlike many European Socialist parties, U.S. socialists opposed the war, at least on paper. Despite fierce repression that put many socialist and anti-war activists in jail in 1917, 1918, and 1919, the party kept up its membership, losing support in the agrarian Midwest but winning over eastern immigrants. With the end of the war, over four million workers went out on strike across the country, including the 1919 general strike that paralyzed Seattle.

East Harlem too experienced socialism's growing appeal. In 1916, 1918, and 1920 Morris Hillquit, the grand old man of New York Jewish socialism, made a dent in Democratic control of Harlem with repeated congressional campaigns. Though Hillquit never won the election, he came in first in Jewish precincts every time.[5]

Most important, for the first time socialists had a real socialist government to point to: the Russian Bolshevik government that took power in November 1917. It pulled Russia out of the war, gave land to the farmers, and nationalized the factories. It fought a desperate civil war against Russian monarchists and fourteen capitalist governments (including the United States) that banded together to crush it. By late 1920 the civil war was almost won. Enthusiasm for the Russian Revolution was enormous among U.S. socialists in those years, especially among immigrants from Eastern Europe. Shachtman remembered later the Bolsheviks' prestige among socialists "whose hearts and hopes lifted at the thought that the first socialist revolution was now an established success."[6]

Shachtman was not distinguished in his student days by enthusiasm for the Russian Revolution or indignation at the war. On the contrary, he was ready at first to soak up the public schools' pro-war indoctrination. He later remembered sarcastically how indignant he had been at the kaiser's supposed atrocities (most of them invented by Allied propagandists). But his history teacher, Abraham Lefkowitz, cured him of his gullibility. Lefkowitz's radicalism was obvious not only to his brighter students but also to the school authorities, who had no doubts that he was subversive. But because Lefkowitz was careful, he spent years on the verge of being fired before they managed to get rid of him. Shachtman loved his "subtle and ironical way of bringing the ideas of socialism into history."[7]

Socialism allowed Shachtman to see the tension his parents had felt between their working-class world and the world outside as a conflict being fought on a world scale. It also enabled him to reconcile two impulses he had inherited from his childhood. Socialism allowed him to use his intelligence, feel part of a broader world than East Harlem, and play a part in that broader world. Yet at the same time it allowed him to stay loyal to East Harlem and the working-class immigrants he had grown up with. Unlike second-generation Jews who would feel torn between their desire to succeed and a reluctance to abandon their Jewishness, Shachtman saw a way to satisfy his ambition without sacrificing his identity. He chose socialism over integration into the middle-class U.S. mainstream. He withdrew from City College, where he had just enrolled, in the fall of 1920 (because of illness, he said later). Although he enrolled again in the fall of 1921, he dropped out in two or three months. He later said that he had become absorbed in the radical movement and put everything else aside for it.[8]

Unfortunately for Shachtman's radical dreams, the radical wave began to subside before he was ready to ride it. The Russian Revolution, which had first brought new energy and enthusiasm into the international socialist movement, soon brought new divisions. Lenin and other Bolshevik leaders saw these divisions as unavoidable. They had built the Bolshevik Party, the instrument through which the Russian Revolution was made, through fifteen years of fierce factional battles. Looking toward Western Europe, where most of the Socialist parties had supported the war and socialist leaders had achieved a comfortable, legal existence as journalists, lawyers, union officials, members of parliament, and even ministers in capitalist governments, Bolsheviks concluded that a hard fight would be necessary there as well in order to create parties that could lead revolutions.

In March 1919 the Bolsheviks proclaimed a new Communist International that would be the organizing center for new revolutionary parties. They called it the Third International to emphasize that it was replacing the Socialist Second International that had fallen apart in 1914 as well as the First International of the 1860s and 1870s. In August 1920 they drew up twenty-one conditions that parties would have to meet to gain admission to their International. Parties that wanted to join would have to put their newspapers, union officials, and members of parliament under tight (though democratic) central control, prepare to work illegally in case capitalist governments resorted to repression against them, and purge themselves of leaders who resisted this revolutionary course. Socialist parties around the world were given three months to accept or reject the conditions. Through these measures the Bolsheviks hoped to help socialists in other countries learn from the Russian experience and create in a few years the kind of revolutionary party the Bolsheviks had needed two decades to build in Russia.

Leaders of the new International saw no reason to make the United States an exception in their plans for reconstructing the world socialist movement. True, socialist leaders in the United States had opposed the World War, unlike most of their European counterparts. Eugene Debs even ended up in jail for his anti-war activity. But not many socialist leaders could equal Debs's fervor. Shachtman later said that few of the mainstream socialist leaders ever allowed their anti-war declaration "to leave the paper it was written on."[9] The fact that the tsar had been overthrown and a Russian republic established just before the United States declared war in 1917 increased some socialists' sympathy for the Allies' "war for democracy." Hillquit, who ran the party behind the scenes while Debs carried its banner in public, set a cautious tone.

Like Western European socialist groups, the U.S. Socialist Party was mostly an electoral machine. Alongside Debs's famous presidential campaigns the party ran candidates for every office from Congress down to the most lowly local offices. Many were elected. Once in office, few devoted themselves to building up militant radical movements. Instead they became champions of "sewer socialism," trying to prove that socialists could provide more honest and efficient local governments even under capitalism.

Victor Berger, leader of the moderate German American Socialists of Milwaukee, typified this brand of socialism. He also led Socialists into a modus vivendi with Samuel Gompers's American Federation of Labor (AFL). The AFL concentrated on organizing skilled craft workers, who were a small, better paid, disproportionately native-born minority of the work force. It treated radical politics and the great mass of unorganized, unskilled immigrant workers with indifference. Most socialists who supported the more militant Industrial Workers of the World, which combined industrial organizing with complete opposition to electoral politics, were pushed out of the party in 1912, when a party convention excluded anyone who favored violent or illegal action.

For a time in 1917 and 1918 the differences in the Socialist Party were covered over by common opposition to the war and common enthusiasm for the Russian Revolution. But the party peace was soon broken by socialists who wanted not only to admire the Russian Revolution from a distance but to work toward emulating it, at least someday, in the United States. Socialists' old emphasis on electioneering and peaceful reform seemed ludicrous in the face of the repression that was sending so many radicals to jail and breaking so many strikes.

By early 1919 the revolutionary left wing of the party won a majority of the membership and twelve out of fifteen seats on the Socialists' National Executive Committee. The old, defeated National Executive Committee annulled the elections, expelled more than half the party's members, and kept control of the party convention with the help of the Chicago police. The split between the Socialist right wing and Communist left wing was an accomplished fact by the time Shachtman became politically active.

Many such splits took place around the world from 1918 to 1921. For Shachtman, all the impulses that led him to socialism in the first place dictated that he choose the Communist side. The AFL craft unionism and municipal politics the right-wing socialists were committed to had little to do with the working class he knew. Although the right-wingers said in the early 1920s that they too supported the Russian Revolution, they had a weakness for the U.S. Constitution and political institutions that could not be squared with the Bolsheviks' revolutionary example. The Bolsheviks appealed to Shachtman's sense of drama in a way that the right-wingers could not match.

For radicals like Shachtman, "social democrat," the term used for socialists who refused to join the new Communist movement, became and remained a virtual synonym for sellout. The bitterness spawned when most

European socialist leaders supported the war in 1914 hatched afterwards, when they tried to contain or bloodily crush Communists' attempts at revolution after the war. The lasting symbol of this bitterness was the murder of Communist leaders Rosa Luxemburg and Karl Liebknecht in Berlin in January 1919 by right-wing military officers supported by a social democratic minister of the interior. Shachtman summed up young Communists' reaction: "Already stained with the blood of their brothers, the social democrats burned into their own foreheads, irrevocably, the mark of Cain which they bear to this day." The memory of that crime and others like it cut Shachtman off from social democrats. For the first thirty years of his socialist career he would dismiss any organization trying to unite social democrats and real radicals as "an impossible marriage." He saw the events of 1917–19 as "a huge steel wall" between Socialists and Communists.[10]

This "huge steel wall" separated Shachtman from the teacher who had won him to socialism, Abraham Lefkowitz. Lefkowitz's talents got him elected as a vice president in the New York teachers' union. Like most left-leaning union officials, he found the Socialist Party a more comfortable home than the Communist Party. Soon he was trying to exclude Communists from labor conferences, while Communists angrily demanded, "Abraham Lefkowitz—whom do you represent?"[11]

In some European countries where the socialist movement was strong and Communists won over much of it—France, Germany, Poland—strong new Communist parties resulted from the 1918–21 splits. But in the United States socialists had barely begun to win mass influence, were deeply divided by language and geography, and had barely begun to grasp the international issues. Here the split threw the entire left back into marginality. Communists did not even manage to hold together in a single organization; instead they formed several groups that fought among themselves.

Most Communists had belonged to Socialist Party "foreign language federations," semi-independent groups that carried on their work in Russian or other languages instead of English. Several foreign language federations were expelled en masse from the Socialist Party. They were cut off by language from U.S. workers they wanted to recruit. Facing deportation and repression from the U.S. government, and more knowledgeable about Russia than the United States, these Communists identified with Bolsheviks who had responded to tsarist repression by organizing underground. Their focus on underground organizing and their neglect of opportunities for public work and recruitment cut them off even more from English-speaking working people. As a result of all the quarrels and disappointments, membership fell: In early 1919, the Socialist Party had 109,000 members, but by late 1920, the Socialist and Communist groups together had only 36,000 members.[12]

Shachtman's attempts to join this flailing movement frustrated him completely. He could not find a Communist group to join, although he haunted the meetings held at 110th Street and Fifth Avenue (the Central Park corner known as "Trotsky Square"). Ironically he was too Americanized and spoke English too well to find his way into the overwhelmingly immigrant Communist circles.

> I would try to express from the periphery of the crowd my sympathies with the Communist movement in the hope that they would attempt to recruit me. [But] the more pronounced I was in support of the Communist wing against the Socialist wing, the more it seemed that they were suspicious of me. . . . I had no foreign accent, of course. And given their intense suspicion and fear of outsiders, I was never recruited into the Communist party, although I made every attempt to get in. [13]

Only as the Communists began to find their way out of their dead end did Shachtman find his way into their ranks. In 1920 the Communist International forced U.S. Communists to form a united organization. In 1921, again under pressure from Moscow, Communists began to form aboveground groups that could work publicly. At the same time the Communist International continued to win support inside the Socialist Party. A new call to accept Moscow's twenty-one conditions gained 1,301 votes at a Socialist convention, but the hostile leadership managed to barely defeat it with 1,339 votes. Many in this new minority—largely in the Socialist Yiddish-language, German, and Finnish federations—left the Socialist Party. A few of them formed a new organization called the Workers Council. Shachtman found this organization not through activism but by hanging around the Rand School Library, where he could read radical publications. There he met two of its leaders, Alexander Trachtenberg and Benjamin Glassberg. Shachtman was one of the first people to receive a Workers Council membership card. [14]

The Workers Council "didn't amount to very much," Shachtman said later. Its leaders were "timid"; their attitude toward the Communist International was ambivalent. [15] It didn't matter. In December 1921 the Workers Council merged with other aboveground Communists to form the Workers Party. This party quickly became the real Communist party of the United States, although it took more pressure from the Communist International (particularly Trotsky) to get U.S. Communists to dissolve their underground organization. Finally Communists had a reasonable public presence and could consolidate their public following. Soon the new party outstripped the Socialists in many immigrant communities, including East European Jews. Even Shachtman's father switched from reading the Socialist *Forward* to the new Communist *Freiheit*. Shachtman, at age seventeen, began his career as a revolutionary.

Joining the party was a great step for Shachtman. Like the Lenin of his glowing imagination, he considered the party "sacred and above everything." Years after he had left this particular party he would insist, "The ingenuity of man has produced no better vehicle for realizing [social and even individual] aspirations than the political party."[16] He would be a member of some kind of socialist organization until he died.

Shachtman gradually realized that the Communist Party that had so much appeal for him had little appeal for most other people in the United States. The language of Marxism was often spoken with a foreign accent, or at least a New York accent, which made most U.S. workers uncomfortable with it. Many immigrant Marxists in the United States since the 1860s had reacted to this disheartening realization by barricading themselves in immigrant Marxist ghettos. Shachtman, who did not think of himself as an immigrant, reacted differently. He did not believe that the U.S. working class, composed mostly of immigrants and their children, was much different from the working class he had known in East Harlem. If Marxism seemed foreign to Americans, he would help Americanize it.

Although he had given up on upward mobility by becoming a Communist, he had gained outward mobility: out of his old immigrant neighborhood. He may have realized that the East Harlem he left behind was crumbling. Building restrictions and overcrowding during the First World War had made New York's older Jewish areas more slumlike. Jewish Harlem was the first to fall apart. The proximity of rising Jewish neighborhoods to the north in the Bronx, and the even more overcrowded tenements of Puerto Rican, Italian, and Black Harlem spurred Jews to begin leaving Harlem in the early 1920s. In 1921 there were 178,000 Jews in Harlem. By 1930 all but 5,000 would be gone. The synagogues and socialist clubs picked up and followed their fleeing members, Shachtman's parents among them, to the Bronx. As the exodus got under way, Shachtman began spending his time at Communist Party headquarters downtown on Broadway.

A high school education and fluency in English were enough to give him a racing start in the Communist movement. He spoke at street-corner meetings "on practically everything and anything with an absolutely sure knowledge." He helped out on the party's new English-language weekly, the *Worker*, writing what he later called "fillers."[17]

Communists still had an easier time publishing in Yiddish, Slovak, and Lithuanian than in English. Just the same, they must have been very hard up for English-speaking writers to use as much of Shachtman's material as they did. He wrote on anything: a strike of laundry workers; the fortieth anniversary of Karl Marx's death; a millionaire murderer unjustly freed by a capitalist court. Many of his early contributions seemed dedicated to proving that he had been to college. Perhaps some of his working-class readers agreed with him that "the workers are not so cultured as they might be; their lives are drab, monotonous." Perhaps, like the Russian workers he wrote about, they yearned for "cultural advancement."[18] What they made of his references to impressionist painters and symbolist poets one can only guess.

Mostly Shachtman soaked up the atmosphere of his new party and met its leaders. Most important, he met party chairman James P. Cannon, who pointed the way forward to the Americanization of Marxism that Shachtman was looking for. Barely thirty years old, Cannon was party chairman largely because he had an authentic midwestern background (and blue eyes) that few U.S. Communist leaders could match. His commitment to the legal organization won the trust of Communists who were suspicious of the shadowy underground party. The son of an Irish socialist worker in Kansas City, he had started work in a meat-packing plant when he was twelve, had been an organizer for the Industrial Workers of the World, and was one of the Communist Party's few links to the world of prewar U.S. socialism.

In the early 1920s, Cannon's was one of the strongest voices in the party calling for a serious commitment to aboveground organizing, to the union movement, to breaking out of the party's eastern immigrant ghetto. He knew how to operate in the unions too, as well as in the tight little world of the party. Another early Communist leader later remarked that Cannon's skill and pleasure at inner-party politics were made possible by his humor, wit, and "charming personality, when he chose to be charming."[19] Years later Shachtman remembered Cannon with admiration. "He made an enormous impression upon me. . . . He was known as an excellent orator, a very smooth writer, an exceedingly intelligent and shrewd politician," Shachtman remembered. "He knew what the American worker was, how he lived, how he thought, what he aspired to." Above all, "I felt from the very beginning of my acquaintance with him that he was by far the ablest and the best of the leaders of the Communist party," Shachtman said. "I learned more about speaking from Cannon—not just from watching Cannon but by being told by him how to plan a speech, how to work it out; until then, I never dreamed that a speech had to be planned; I thought you just talked on and on and on and on—than I did from anybody else."[20] Shachtman's relationship with Cannon began with admiration for the political leader. It developed to the point where Cannon and his second wife, Rose Karsner, almost became his surrogate parents. He remembered even in his last years how he was "warmed by the friendship and the affection and the understanding of Rose and Jim."[21]

The teenager from Harlem formed another friendship with Martin Abern, national secretary of the Young Workers League. Abern was in his early twenties, closer to Shachtman's age, and like him a Jew born in

Eastern Europe. He was the youngest member of the Communist Central Committee, a shy, gruff man, broad-chested and bullnecked, whose "sleeves were always rolled up for the 'menial' work."[22]

Shachtman found a new outlet for his writing in Abern's *Young Worker*. He wrote in praise of "flapperism": "a defiant sloughing off of carefully and painfully instilled laws of proper behavior . . . a mass revolt of Youth." To begin with he was not very interested in the Young Workers League as an organization. But in the summer of 1923 when Abern invited him to come to Young Workers League headquarters in Chicago and edit the *Young Worker*, Shachtman jumped at the chance. Not yet nineteen, he hitchhiked from New York to Chicago to take up his first "official appointment."[23]

The move to Chicago marked Shachtman's coming of age as a writer, speaker, and organizer. In months—even weeks—references to Cézanne and convoluted syntax dropped away from his articles. The improvement was startling. The move was also important for the Communist Party, whose headquarters followed the Young Workers League to the then capital of the industrial Midwest. The move symbolized the changes Cannon wanted to see in the party. Shachtman became a partisan of Cannon's ideas: rooting the Communist Party in the U.S. labor movement and operating in harmony with the rhythms of the U.S. working class. He and Abern tried to lead the Young Workers League in that spirit, making it a voice for young rank-and-file workers in their conflicts with AFL officials. His enthusiasm for Cannon's strategy soon made him a participant in a bitter faction fight.

Chicago had a strong trade union left wing with which Cannon wanted to consolidate the party's ties. It was also the center of the movement for a national Farmer-Labor Party. Many people in the labor movement agreed in the early 1920s that the Republican and Democratic parties were committed to capitalism and dead ends for working people. With the socialist movement divided and in disarray, Eugene Debs's old answer—vote Socialist—was no longer as convincing as it had been. Support grew for the idea of a single Farmer-Labor Party that included all existing socialist groups and was broader than any of them. By June 1922 the Communists, who could see that they did not have the electoral influence the Socialists had had, came out in support of it. The majority of Communists believed that if they could participate from the beginning in building a working-class alternative to the Republicans and Democrats they would have good prospects for winning over many of the new party's supporters to communism.

U.S. Communists' support for a labor party fit in initially with the "united-front" tactics that the Communist International adopted in December 1921. Bolshevik leaders saw that in many countries their policy of splitting the socialist movement had created isolated Communist groups rather than the strong revolutionary parties they had aimed at. Capitalist economies and governments had stabilized. Bolsheviks were confident that the new stability would be short-lived, and the 1929 crash would prove them right. But while waiting for new revolutionary prospects to take shape, they wanted Communists to put themselves in a better position to lead masses of discontented people when the time came. They suggested that Communists propose united actions for common goals to other social- ist organizations and, if leaders of the other organizations were unwilling to cooperate, appeal over their heads to the rank and file for joint action. Even where social democratic parties were stronger than the Communists, the International was confident that Communists would turn out to be better fighters even for limited reforms; they did not shy away from revolution, and they were less ready to make pointless compromises. The International expected many workers who were not yet Communists to be won over to communism through united actions.

Since a U.S. labor party was meant to be a united front, Communists had to work with non-Communist allies to build it. Their first important ally was Chicago AFL leader John Fitzpatrick. Together the Communists and Fitzpatrick began organizing a convention that would found a Farmer- Labor Party. Yet no sooner did the convention assemble in Chicago in July 1923 than the Communists and Fitzpatrick fell out. Fitzpatrick felt that the forces gathered at the convention were too weak to launch a serious national party. Other delegates—representing Sidney Hillman's Amalgamated Clo- thing Workers; labor councils from West Virginia, Detroit, Buffalo, and Minneapolis, and the Washington Farmer-Labor Party—wanted to go ahead. Carried away with their dream and the apparent backing of a significant segment of labor, Communists joined the nine-tenths majority for proclaiming the party. Fitzpatrick and his supporters walked out.

Shachtman arrived in Chicago in time to attend the conference and root for the Communists. He dismissed Fitzpatrick's opposition as "quibbling."[24] More experienced Communists saw that they had made a false start. One by one the organizations represented in Chicago repudiated their delegates' commitments. Soon the only force left in the new party was the Commun- ists, who controlled a slightly enlarged carbon copy of their own organiza- tion with the name "Federated Farmer-Labor Party" plastered onto it.

Cannon saw what had happened right away. He got William Foster, the Communist Party's most prominent trade unionist, hero of the 1919 Little Steel strike, and head of the party's Trade Union Educational League, to see it too. Cannon and Foster decided that Communist leaders around Charles Ruthenberg were out of touch with U.S. realities and that the party needed a new leadership rooted in the native working class. They won over two-thirds of the delegates to the Communists' December 1923 convention.

Shachtman supported the party's new majority. Although Cannon and Foster were challenging the party's control by eastern immigrants, the chief leaders of the Jewish Communist federation were on their side. The Jews were, "by far, more assimilated in American life" than the other immigrant groups, Cannon later explained.[25] For Shachtman, his allegiance to Cannon reflected his identity with the working class he had grown up in.

Soon Communists faced a new wrinkle in their work for a labor party. By early 1924 most of the sentiment for a third party had found a focus in Wisconsin Senator Robert LaFollette. LaFollette was a Republican, but he had populist agrarian roots. He opposed the Coolidge administration's pro-business policies. As the election drew near it became clear that Coolidge would be the Republican candidate, and the Democrats would not choose a candidate to appeal to workers' or farmers' discontent. LaFollette decided to run as an independent. The Socialist Party, railroad unions, and local Farmer-Labor parties decided to support him.

Communists could not deceive themselves that LaFollette was building a labor party. He had more support among small farmers than among urban workers, and his platform in no way challenged capitalism. Most important, his campaign was not an initiative taken by trade unions or any other popular organizations, and he was not under any control from below. This placed the LaFollette campaign outside the limits of the united-front tactic, because it prevented Communists from proposing their own slogans and trying to win over the rank and file.

Almost everyone in the United States who was interested in a labor party in 1924 was supporting LaFollette, however, so Communists went along at first with their Farmer-Labor allies' support for him. Ruthenberg championed a theory that LaFollette was going to lead a "people's revolution" in the United States and Communists should join a "third-party alliance" to support him. Cannon and Foster acquiesced, but Trotsky called the third-party alliance a "senseless and infamous adventure," an abandonment of the working-class political independence that was the cornerstone of Communist politics.[26] The International ordered U.S. Communists to drop their support for LaFollette immediately.

At almost the same moment, LaFollette announced that he would have nothing to do with the Farmer-Labor Party convention that Communists were helping Minnesota Farmer-Laborites to organize in St. Paul. LaFollette's attack kept many radicals away from St. Paul and left the Communists once more as a dominant force. Communists pushed a decision through the Farmer-Labor National Executive Committee to endorse Foster for president. With a convert's zeal, Foster filled his campaign speeches with attacks on LaFollette. Shachtman helped fill the *Daily Worker* with LaFollette baiting. "The workers must realize that LaFollette's anti-monopolism is a double-edged sword which may some day—which *will* some day—be pushed into their back," he wrote. A real labor party could "only be achieved over the political dead body of LaFollettism."[27] LaFollette got almost five million votes, but Foster's campaign was a fiasco. He got only 33,000 votes.

After 1924 the Farmer-Labor Party movement fell apart. LaFollette did not try to build an enduring, grassroots organization, and the Farmer-Labor organization that Communists had helped build was isolated and discredited by Foster's anti-LaFollette campaign. Although the International was largely to blame for the debacle, U.S. Communists did not dare to say so. Instead the failure of Foster's campaign gave new life to the factional conflict that Cannon and Foster had begun against Ruthenberg in 1923. Ruthenberg proposed to keep campaigning for a labor party and run Communists on "labor party" tickets. Foster and Cannon were still committed to a labor party in the long run, but they could see that just using the labor party label to build the Communist Party would discredit Communists in the eyes of independents. Cannon and Foster argued that the idea of a labor party would become credible again only when unions and other broad organizations showed fresh interest in it.

The prosperity of the mid-1920s made a breakthrough toward political independence by those broad organizations unlikely. Although many working people lived in poverty, many others were caught up in the previously unheard of dream of buying their own Fords and houses. Coolidge was popular. In these circumstances, Shachtman argued, it would be absurd for the Communists to build a "rival party" that would compete with it for the same small constituency.[28]

U.S. Communists did not yet expect their disputes to be settled for them in Moscow. They fought out their differences among themselves without inhibition. "Everybody was free to say just about anything that he had in his heart, and he said it," Shachtman said later.[29] Often a third of the six-page *Daily Worker* was taken up with long factional debates. Since each faction in the party had a junior faction in the Young Workers League, Shachtman and Abern led the junior Foster-Cannon faction. Shachtman used his post as editor of the *Young Worker* without scruple to promote Cannon's politics.

The real issues at stake in the debate were often obscured both by personal rivalries and hostilities and by the taboo against questioning the International's authority. The Foster-Cannon group did draw one important lesson from the experiences of 1923–24: the importance of working together with non-Communist unionists who favored independent political action, without using them to set up isolated Communist front groups. But a key, thorny question was left unresolved. Since LaFollette's campaign did not rest on a national, democratic, grassroots organization, it was not an independent labor party. How could Communists have avoided trailing helplessly behind LaFollette and at the same time avoided cutting themselves off from the thousands of LaFollette's pro-labor party supporters? In the mid-1940s Shachtman would take another look at this issue of the role of ephemeral third-party campaigns in the creation of an independent labor party.

The politics Shachtman picked up from Cannon were crucial to his own political education. In Chicago he began educating himself as a serious Marxist. The novels that had filled his bookshelves at first were discarded and replaced with the beginnings of a comprehensive Marxist library. A careless, one-paragraph review of James Joyce's *Ulysses* in the June 1924 *Liberator* (impressive to younger Communists around him) was his last foray into literary criticism. His hunger for Marxist classics reached the point where he acquired a reputation for stealing books—not "wholly untrue either." His knowledge narrowed as it deepened. He was never at a loss in later years for a quotation from Marx or Lenin, but when he had to debate someone who could quote the Bible or Shakespeare, he would have to thumb through *Bartlett's Quotations* beforehand in order to find quotations of his own.[30]

His bonds to Cannon and Abern were personal as well as political, and the friends he made among young Communists in Chicago became part of Cannon's circle. One new friend, Albert Glotzer, had also been born in the Russian Empire and had come to the United States as a young child to join his father, who was first a butcher and then a milkman. One of Glotzer's uncles was a socialist, a leader in the 1910 clothing workers' strike and later (briefly) a Communist who tried to organize a communal dairy farm in Russia in the early 1920s. At his uncle's urging, Glotzer would go around his Chicago neighborhood stuffing mailboxes with Socialist campaign leaflets and attend socialist meetings at the neighborhood's Old Style Inn. On his fifteenth birthday in November 1923, he joined the Young Workers League, just as Abern was preparing to move on to the adult movement and leave Shachtman in charge.[31]

Glotzer began volunteering in the League office. He enjoyed Shachtman's company. He would listen to Shachtman talking and "telling jokes three, four days a week," Glotzer remembered, "and on the fifth day he'd write the *Young Worker*."[32]

Glotzer took his communism seriously, however. At sixteen or seventeen he quit high school and went to work for International Harvester in Chicago, working on a punch press that punched holes in chunks of steel, earning almost as much money as his father and recruiting another young worker to the League. Then he went to southern Illinois and spent six months there organizing miners into a Save the Union Movement that challenged John L. Lewis's dictatorial rule of the United Mine Workers. For a while Glotzer directed the League's school in New England on a Finnish Communist cooperative farm. Then he left that oasis to strengthen the Cannon faction in Detroit, working nine hours a day in a Ford plant all summer, polishing auto bodies by hand until he was exhausted. He had become a good soldier in Shachtman's army, and he would remain one.[33] The two friends were caught up in their common enthusiasm and all-absorbing work.

The move to Chicago brought Shachtman new freedom as well as responsibilities. For the first year in his new job he lived and slept in the back room of the League's office, sharing it with another staffer. He cooked his meals there on a small burner. But these primitive conditions did not last long. His father sent him money and handmade suits from New York. Then he met and married Billie Ramloff, a young, non-Jewish Communist from a Latvian family. Ramloff worked so that Shachtman could organize. She and Glotzer became good friends: She was a lighthearted person, "without any guile," he said later. The three of them would often go off together to vaudeville shows. Soon Shachtman could even buy a used, fire engine–red Stutz Bearcat convertible.[34] He may have been a professional revolutionary, but he still managed to live as an up-to-date young American.

A couple of years as a Communist youth organizer stripped away some of Shachtman's determination to be an adult Communist among adults. He acquired a lasting commitment to youth movements, even idealizing them at times. Communists were younger, on average, than social democrats, and Shachtman associated youth with true radicalism. Adopting Lenin's explanation that a conservative wing had arisen in the labor movement because some union officials and members were corrupted by colonial spoils, he argued that young workers did not share in the spoils. Instead they had to do the dirty work of conquering and defending colonies. Their different circumstances and rebel instincts separated them from the "grayhaired party theoreticians and bureaucrats." Shachtman adopted the principle that young socialists should organize independently of adults whenever possible, to train themselves as fighters and activists. He implicitly likened himself to Lenin, who, according to Shachtman, loved arguing socialism with youngsters in the middle of bicycling or swimming expeditions.[35]

In the 1920s the Young Workers League was what its name implied. It organized young workers who lived in conditions similar to those found in third-world countries today. The Labor Department estimated in 1924 that there were over a million children between ten and fifteen years old in the work force, and thousands as young as five or six.[36] Congress had passed the first federal child labor law after the war only to have the Supreme Court strike it down as unconstitutional—leaving little doubt in Communists' minds whose Constitution and whose court they were.

Unions, driven back to the wall after the brief postwar strike wave, did little to protect the young. Samuel Gompers's American Federation of Labor ignored a Communist call to set up a youth bureau. Teenagers were often used as strikebreakers. "Even the smallest can be organized," Shachtman insisted. Teenage workers had the "spirit of the 'gang,' 'stick-to-itiveness.'"[37] But a special approach and special groups were needed.

Communists were already warning about the danger of another world war. Shachtman worked to safeguard young people from the gullibility toward war propaganda that he had shown in school. He warned teenagers away from the Citizens' Military Training Camps, Reserve Officers' Training Corps, and the Boy and Girl Scouts. Communists were implacably hostile toward them all. Even if Communists had to march off to war with the rest, they hoped to have as many conscious anti-militarists in the army as possible. They wanted soldiers who would be ready to turn their bayonets around when the time came. Communist parents who allowed their sons to join the Boy Scouts, where they would be indoctrinated and drilled by the enemy, were rebuked.

The Young Workers League had its own alternative to the Scouts: the Young Workers League Junior Section (later the Young Pioneers). Nothing summons up better the libertarian, iconoclastic spirit of the Communist movement of the early 1920s (before it was submerged by Soviet-imposed "Bolshevization") than Shachtman's account of the Junior Section. Not until the 1960s would U.S. radicals again declare such sweeping war on the society around them.

For Shachtman, not only Boy Scouts but also teachers and parents were potential agents of the hated system. The Communist children's movement aimed to turn capitalist values upside down, he declared in the *Daily Worker*. Children should not be discouraged from scribbling on walls; they should be encouraged to scribble Communist slogans. Children sent home for being rude to their teachers should be praised, not punished. The Young Workers League Junior Section would *teach* children to interrupt their teachers, start unwanted discussions, fight back against corporal punishment, even organize school strikes. "In America the minds of the youth are filled with a greater proportion of capitalist poison per square brain cell than in any other country," Shachtman said. Schoolchildren were taught to despise the working class and aspire to a middle-class life. Communist children's groups would counteract the school's worldview by taking children on tours of both working-class and upper-class neighborhoods so that they could see the truth of their society.[38]

The children's groups would not replace the lockstep discipline of the school with the lockstep discipline of the movement. In the Communist children's movement, Shachtman said, "the method of education and leadership is a symbol of the methods that will be followed in the classless society." Communists would "develop the initiative of the children, stimulate the spirit of freedom and solidarity." Even games should be free-spirited and encouraging for each child. Communists should fight to replace school administrators with "children's councils." Children would run the children's movement. Although the junior groups did have assigned leaders who were not children, Shachtman believed that they should be younger Communists who would not look too much like authority figures. Junior group leaders should never give orders, but keep in the background. The Young Workers League Junior Section was prefiguring the education of the future, and "the future brings the free teaching of free children."[39]

Between the children and their glorious tomorrow stood their too often recalcitrant parents. Shachtman chided Communist parents who kept their children out of the Junior Section. Perhaps remembering his own parents, he complained about working-class parents who "sacrifice all to make a business man" out of their son. Too many apologized for their children's troublemaking instead of being proud. Too many beat their children. Even worse, parents used their "economic power . . . to tyrannize over their children." Shachtman pleaded with the parents not to "exercise the big stick" on their children. "The 'love' which parents ordinarily bestow upon their children is a relationship based on the child's meekness, upon ignorance, upon imposed authority," he said. "True love of children depends upon an understanding of their problems and battles."[40] He implied that the truest love would be found outside the family, among fellow young Communist activists.

The libertarian Communist children's movement existed more in Shachtman's imagination than in reality. Manny Geltman, who joined a junior group as a ten-year-old in 1924, remembered an organization far removed from Shachtman's program. In his memory, Communist children's groups spent most of their time putting up posters and dragging literature and speakers' platforms back and forth for street-corner speakers.[41] But the left of the 1960s was not able to translate its ideas about child rearing into reality too well either. The fact that the *Daily Worker* published Shachtman's ideas showed that Communists had a libertarian spirit, even as their practice became more authoritarian.

Shachtman in 1923–25 saw the young, militant, libertarian movement he was helping to build in the United States as one small detachment of a worldwide movement whose headquarters were in Moscow. In March and April 1925 he got his first opportunity to see up close the revolution he idealized; he was entrusted with the responsibility of representing the U.S.

Communist Party at a meeting of the Communist International in Moscow. The trip "made an indescribably powerful impression" on him. [42]

When compared with Shachtman's feelings in 1925, the enthusiasm of 1960s radicals for China or Vietnam or Cuba seems to have almost a defensive undertone. Communists in the 1920s were at one with many working people around the world in their enthusiasm for the Soviet Union. And compared with Maoists of the 1960s or even Communists in the 1930s, Communists in Shachtman's day felt less need to keep quiet about the poverty, difficulties, and restrictions on freedom they saw there. The pages of the *Daily Worker* were full of descriptions of Russian famines and hardships, which in no way detracted from Communists' enthusiasm for all things Russian: Russian songs, Russian shirts, anything. For Shachtman, the USSR was "a brilliant red light in the darkness of capitalistic gloom." [43]

He remembered years later seeing a Red Army soldier at the frontier "parading up and down with his rifle right under the big arch that's marked in four languages: 'Proletarians of the world unite!'" He recalled, "You're as much at home—indeed, much more at home—there than you are in your party back home—perhaps in your own country back home." The young delegates from the United States "could hardly speak for delight" when they visited a regiment of horse artillery. Shachtman did his best to maintain his sense of comradeship with the Russian cavalrymen by riding alongside them on horseback. Unfortunately, horseback riding was not a skill he had mastered in Harlem or Chicago, and he fell off. [44]

The trip to Russia seemed to propel Shachtman toward the top leadership of the Communist Party. The party was beginning to take advantage of his talents as a speaker. When its major leaders spoke at its May Day rally in Chicago about their Russian experiences, the *Daily Worker* put his name alone alongside Ruthenberg's in one headline announcing the rally. [45] He and his friends Cannon, Abern, and Glotzer felt that they were moving their party out of its first immaturity, developing a Marxism that would work for the United States and advance the world revolution.

But in the summer of 1925, Shachtman's and his friends' confidence in the future was suddenly shaken. Stalin wanted above all to have a U.S. leadership that would support him in the International. He was suspicious of the arguments Foster and Cannon were making about the course of U.S. communism. Although Foster and Cannon won another two-thirds majority at the August 1925 party convention and their supporters, Shachtman among them, took over the *Daily Worker* building with a few pistols to safeguard their control, the International's hostility doomed them to defeat. When a cable from the International backing the minority was read to the convention, Glotzer sat looking at his faction's leaders. "They were just white. They just didn't believe it!" [46]

Foster wanted to withdraw from the party leadership in protest against the International's decision. Cannon insisted on accepting the International's decision and working with the minority. The Foster-Cannon group split. Although a majority of the caucus went along with Cannon on the immediate issue, most of its embittered members soon rallied to Foster's side. Loyal to Cannon, Shachtman found himself a supporter of the smallest of the three Communist factions. But his loyalty to the International did nothing to save his position in the Young Workers League. He had used the *Young Worker* for two years to attack Ruthenberg's supporters, not even allowing them a right of reply. Now they took their revenge. By November he was off the masthead.[47] His first "official appointment" was over.

To Cannon's and his followers' bewildered surprise, their leaders in Moscow had deposed them from leadership of U.S. communism. The Communist Party was in the hands of their adversaries. Shachtman and the others, who had believed that their Americanized Marxist movement would be the best U.S. ally of bolshevism, found that their goals and the Soviet leaders' goals were in conflict. Their attempts to understand the conflict would end in a few years with Cannon's and Shachtman's break with Moscow.

For the time being Shachtman gave up most of his work with youth, leaving Glotzer to struggle on alone. He joined Cannon and Abern in running the Communist-controlled International Labor Defense, the last Cannonite stronghold in the Communist movement. His work with International Labor Defense, a kind of civil liberties union for the left, exemplified his Cannonite convictions even more than his stint with the Young Workers League had. His beliefs in mobilizing working people, in organizing them in opposition to AFL officials and every kind of middle-class liberal, and in asserting immigrants' claim to power in their new country all found expression in his efforts on behalf of radical prisoners.

The Labor Defense was founded to defend "*all workers persecuted on account of their activity for the workers,*" whatever their politics. It fought for prisoners' release, exposed abuses, paid for lawyers, sent five dollars each month and a special gift at Christmas to prisoners and their families, and joined in protests against repression anywhere in the world. It defended foreign-born workers when the government tried to deport them for their radical activities, often to countries "where jail . . . would be the best they could hope for." To Shachtman, the Labor Defense was not defending civil liberties and democracy in the abstract but defending the working class against the "class persecution and justice" that was used against them each time they fought for their rights.[48] That meant that it belonged to the whole working class, not just Communists. Despite the fact that Communists openly controlled it, the Labor Defense under Cannon's leadership provided a rare center of socialist ecumenism. At Labor Defense meetings a young Communist like Glotzer could hear old socialist heroes like Eugene Debs.

In 1926 Cannon asked Shachtman to help out Tom O'Flaherty, editor of the new International Labor Defense newspaper *Labor Defender*. O'Flaherty, an old friend of Cannon's, had a drinking problem, as did Cannon on occasion. Glotzer remembered older Communists' being called several times to come to a speakeasy at three in the morning to pay O'Flaherty's bill and take him home.[49] By July 1926 Shachtman's name replaced O'Flaherty's on the masthead and stayed there until 1928.

Shachtman gave credit to German Communist magazines he had seen for the *Labor Defender*'s appealing format, which broke with the U.S. radical tradition of unbroken columns of small print. He showed a "unique flair for typography." Earlier radical publications like the prewar *Masses* had used drawings, but the *Labor Defender* was the first to give photographs and graphics almost as much space as the text. As a result, *Labor Defender* became by far the most popular of U.S. Communists' publications, with a circulation of 22,000 by mid-1928.

Putting out the magazine turned Shachtman, who was good with his hands, into an enthusiastic amateur photographer and camera specialist. He would spend hours "shmoozing" with camera store clerks. Cannonites would joke that Shachtman had lost interest in politics and opened a camera store instead. Shachtman would retort, "Yeah, it's right above Cannon's saloon."[50]

The high point of the Labor Defense's work was its campaign to save anarchists Nicola Sacco and Bartolomeo Vanzetti from execution. Although the Sacco-Vanzetti case began several years before the Labor Defense was founded, Communists took on a major role in organizing to save the two men's lives in the two years before their execution in 1927. Cannon and Shachtman had ideas about how the fight should be waged and disagreed with others who had been waging it before they came along. After Sacco and Vanzetti died, Shachtman wrote a book, *Sacco and Vanzetti: Labor's Martyrs*, that not only denounced the injustice that had been done but defended Communists' tactics. He laid out an entire theory of prisoners' defense in keeping with Communists' emphasis on grassroots organizing; their suspicion of liberals, union officials, and the legal system; and their commitment to immigrants' rights.

The crimes for which Sacco and Vanzetti were convicted were two holdups near Boston: an unsuccessful holdup of a shoe company payroll truck in December 1919 in Bridgewater, and a second holdup, which led to the deaths of a shoe company paymaster and guard, in April 1920 in South Braintree. After Vanzetti was tried, convicted, and sentenced to fifteen years for the Bridgewater holdup, he and Sacco were put on trial for the

South Braintree murders. Many witnesses testified that Sacco was in Boston applying for a passport during the South Braintree holdup and that Vanzetti was peddling fish and eels as usual in Plymouth, miles away, during both. The prosecution's witnesses were hesitant and contradicted themselves and one another. Nonetheless both defendants were found guilty, and Judge Webster Thayer sentenced both to death.

New evidence of the two men's innocence began coming out right away. An eyewitness in South Braintree who was never called during the trial said that neither Sacco nor Vanzetti were in the getaway car as it sped away five feet from him. The main expert witness called to prove that a fatal bullet was fired from Sacco's gun said that his testimony had been misconstrued, since he had no way of knowing whether the gun was Sacco's or not. Judge Thayer's partiality was exposed when he turned out to have spoken to an acquaintance of "those bastards down there. . . . I'll get them."[51] Finally in November 1925 a young Portuguese criminal confessed that he had taken part in the South Braintree holdup and that Sacco and Vanzetti were not there. But each time Thayer ruled that the validity of the verdict was not affected. He said in the end that the jury had found Sacco and Vanzetti guilty on the basis of the "consciousness of guilt" the two men had shown at their arrest, and that no new evidence would make any difference.

Sacco and Vanzetti's original conviction had come in the midst of a frenzied witch-hunt after anarchists, Communists, and immigrant radicals of all kinds. By the mid-1920s the frenzy had died down, and many liberals and even conservatives wanted to show their lack of prejudice. The campaign to save Sacco and Vanzetti became fashionable. Felix Frankfurter, a Harvard law professor who later became a Supreme Court justice, called for their release. So did the Uruguayan congress, the municipal council of Rio de Janeiro, and town councils in Switzerland. Liberals signed petitions and prominent citizens, particularly jurists and technical experts, made statements.

Communists had their own ideas about how to save Sacco and Vanzetti. "All of us . . . spoke scores of times at scores of meetings for Sacco and Vanzetti," Shachtman remembered. "Many of the meetings that I spoke at . . . were broken up systematically by police in squad cars who followed me around from one street corner to another, breaking up the meetings, tearing me down from platforms, tearing up the literature, threatening us with arrest." Although Sacco and Vanzetti were anarchists, Communists were better organized than any anarchist group to fight for their freedom. The Labor Defense claimed (probably with exaggeration) to have over two million people organized into Sacco-Vanzetti committees in the United States and millions more organized in other countries through International Red Aid. Vanzetti wrote to the *Labor Defender*, "The echo of your campaign in our behalf has reached my heart."[52]

Tensions mounted between Communists and liberals over tactics until accusations were being thrown back and forth publicly. Shachtman had little use for petitions and dignified statements, which he belittled in ways that appealed to Communists' poor, largely immigrant constituency. "Sacco and Vanzetti were so doggedly persecuted, from the very beginning, because of their radical beliefs, and not on the basis of the ridiculous charges of robbery and murder," he argued. They had every reason to be afraid of the police, who had killed one of their anarchist comrades only weeks before their arrest. Their so-called consciousness of guilt was simply consciousness of the government's readiness to harass and persecute radicals. Otherwise, why, in a supposedly straightforward criminal case, did the judge wave "the red, white and blue almost into tatters"? Why did the prosecutor question Sacco and Vanzetti about their politics?

> Why did he insinuatingly ridicule their foreign accent . . .? Why was it necessary to incite the patriotic feelings of the provincial jurymen? . . . If a Republican is on trial for bigamy, does the prosecuting attorney expose his attitude toward the tariff?[53]

This basic truth about the Sacco-Vanzetti case made it ridiculous to treat them like ordinary defendants, victims of a simple judicial mistake. Yet their non-Communist defenders did exactly that, Shachtman charged. He described Boston Defense Committee members as people "with the tragic dignity of gnomes" handed the leadership of the movement to save Sacco and Vanzetti by a "quirk of fate." They did everything according to the law books, dissociated themselves from protesters, and "sold the class birthright of the Sacco-Vanzetti case for a mess of liberal milk and pap."[54] Liberals, union officials, and Socialist leaders all wanted to restore people's faith in the legal system.

Although infighting helped weaken the movement to save Sacco and Vanzetti, Shachtman still credited it with keeping them alive for several extra years and bringing about a lasting gain in organization and understanding. "It was no longer a simple matter of railroading two Italian Reds," he said. "Instead, a jury of constantly growing thousands in every part of the world was sitting in judgement against the persecutors of Sacco and Vanzetti." International solidarity was "wrapped around the two prisoners like a warm cloak" to protect them.[55]

Obviously the cloak did not protect them well enough. Any socialist or union activist could be faced with Sacco and Vanzetti's fate in a month or a year. At least the Labor Defense could ensure that a whole new defense campaign would not have to be set up each time.

The important task after Sacco and Vanzetti's death was not to prove and re-prove their innocence, an exercise interesting only to "those uncertain

Hamlets who are always trembling on the fine needle point of doubt," Shachtman said.* The Labor Defense's goal was to protect future Saccos and Vanzettis and ultimately win victory for the cause for which they died.

> The history of Sacco and Vanzetti was a dramatic episode in the class struggle. Not to understand this today is not to understand anything. . . . The Sacco-Vanzetti case tore away every veil that covers the fact that the ruling class of this country, the bankers and business men, pulls the strings to which a million dignified puppets dance; that theirs is really the voice that seems to issue from the throats of presidents, governors, mayors, justices of the supreme court . . . —all of the well-bred, well-dressed and right-thinking gentlemen and ladies who tortured the two Italian immigrants, seated and strapped them in the chair, polished the electrodes and threw the switch.[57]

The Labor Defense's work helped carve out a space in which it was safe to be a radical in the United States. Radicals today can hardly imagine the attacks that were a constant part of the left's life before the breakthroughs of the 1930s. There were only a few safe corners in a few socialist immigrant neighborhoods: the corner of 110th Street and Fifth Avenue in New York, the corner of Division and Washaw in Chicago, another corner in St. Louis. Those were the years in which the mayor of Duquesne, Pennsylvania, said that Jesus himself could not speak for the union there, in which a man could be sentenced to six months in jail for calling the queen of Romania a bitch. Communists felt that the persecution of radicals in the United States was only one part of a worldwide wave of persecutions. During 1925–27 alone International Red Aid attributed 86,591 deaths to right-wing terror in Southern, Central, and Eastern Europe. In the United States, Glotzer remembered,

> it was a different country then. You had no trade union organization. . . . You could not hold a street meeting in those days without having a free speech fight. Every time you went out for a meeting the cops were there to break it up. You knew you were going to jail. . . . In those days you were alone.[58]

---

*The argument over Sacco and Vanzetti's guilt or innocence did continue, of course, and still continues today. Two months after their execution in 1927, an examination of the four fatal bullets with the newly invented comparison microscope proved that one of them, bullet III, had been fired from Sacco's Colt automatic. Many accounts of the case since then have concluded that though Vanzetti was innocent, Sacco was guilty. Sacco's defenders argue that since only three shells were found near the victim's body, and since bullet III was visibly and improbably different from the other three bullets, bullet III had to have been fired from Sacco's Colt *after* the police confiscated it. Sacco's detractors retort that respectable, upstanding police officers and prosecutors cannot be suspected of such a frame-up.[56] The issue still comes down to a choice between immigrant, working-class radicals and respectable, middle-class government officials.

Despite Shachtman's work for *Labor Defender*, 1926–28 were years of frustration for him and Cannon. Their ideas for a Communist Party that would be rooted in the U.S. working class and attuned to U.S. realities had come to nothing. The party's new leaders were loud in their loyalty to Moscow and servile in carrying out its directives. They gave symbolic expression to their loyalty when Charles Ruthenberg died in 1927: They decided to send his ashes to Moscow for burial under the Kremlin wall. Cannon and his associates were scornful, saying, "An American revolutionist should be buried in the United States."[59]

Ruthenberg's death left Jay Lovestone, a New Yorker who had been to City College, in charge of the party. Soon party headquarters moved back to New York. Although Cannon had felt at home in Chicago in a milieu of Communist trade unionists, he and Rose Karsner and Shachtman and Billie Ramloff moved back to New York too. Each time the Cannonites' understanding of U.S. politics impelled them to resist the Communist International's orders, their sense of loyalty to the Russian Revolution and the International tripped them up and led them to submit.

Notes

1. RMS 2.
2. RMS 20.
3. RMS 2–4, 6.
4. Interview with Glotzer (28 Mar. 1989), s 4.
5. Jeffrey Gurock, *When Harlem Was Jewish*, 75–80.
6. Shachtman, "Foreword to the new edition," in Leon Trotsky, *Terrorism and Communism*, ix.
7. Shachtman, "From cover to cover," W n 272 (28 Apr. 1923), 5; RMS 4–5.
8. RMS 6.
9. Shachtman, "The Second International in the war," NI v 1 n 2 (Aug. 1934), 46.
10. Shachtman, *Lenin, Liebknecht, Luxemburg*, 10, 15; Shachtman, "Lovestone and the Russian revolution," M v 2 n 21 (21 Dec. 1929), 6.
11. "Abraham Lefkowitz—whom do you represent?" W n 274 (12 May 1923), 2.
12. James Weinstein, *The Decline of Socialism in America*, 232.
13. RMS 10.
14. Branko Lazitch and Milorad Drachkovitch, *Lenin and the Comintern*, v 1, 469; RMS 12–13.
15. Shachtman, "The right wing liquidators and the S.P. 'Militants,'" M v 4 n 5 (1 Mar. 1931), 5.
16. Shachtman, *Lenin, Liebknecht, Luxemburg*, 28; Shachtman, *The Fight for Socialism*, 4.
17. RMS 14.
18. Shachtman, "In the world of books," W n 248 (11 Nov. 1922), 5; Shachtman, "The Moscow Art Theater," W n 261 (10 Feb. 1923), 4.
19. Alexander Bittelman, *Memoirs*, Tamiment Library, New York University, cited

in Paul Le Blanc, ed., *Revolutionary Principles and Working Class Democracy*, 10; M v 2 n 1 (1 Jan. 1929).

20. RMS 24, 26, 324–25, 61.
21. Shachtman to Dobbs (9 Mar. 1968), MSC b 28 f 31A (r 3378).
22. Shachtman, "Martin Abern," LA v 13 n 19 (9 May 1949), 1, 4.
23. Shachtman, "A thought provoking situation," YW v 2 n 4 (Apr. 1923), 20–21; RMS 13.
24. Shachtman, "Two conferences," YW v 2 n 8 (Aug. 1923), 4.
25. James P. Cannon, *The First Ten Years of American Communism*, 91.
26. Leon Trotsky, *The Third International after Lenin*, 120, 122.
27. Shachtman, "LaFollette, labor and the business men," DW v 2 n 113 (30 July 1924), 6; Shachtman, "Clothing workers back Communist campaign," DW v 2 n 129 (18 Aug. 1924), 2.
28. Shachtman, "How shall we make the united front?" YW v 3 n 23 (1 Dec. 1924), 4.
29. RMS 24, 94.
30. Interview with Glotzer (28 Mar. 1989), s 4; interview with Geltman (22 Mar. 1989), s 1.
31. Interview with Glotzer by Bloom (13–21 Dec. 1983), OHAL 1–7; Glotzer to Drucker (6 Jan. 1990), 2.
32. Interview with Glotzer (24 Mar. 1989), s 1.
33. Interview with Glotzer by Bloom, 10–12; Glotzer to Drucker (6 Jan. 1990), 2.
34. RMS 67, 16; interview with Glotzer, s 1, 4.
35. Shachtman, *Lenin, Liebknecht, Luxemburg*, 5, 29; Shachtman, "Why Liebknecht turned to the youth," DW v 3 n 4 (16 Jan. 1926), 6.
36. Shachtman, "America's 3,000,000 child slaves," YW v 3 n 13 (1 July 1924), 2.
37. Shachtman, "Organize the young workers!" YW v 2 n 10 (Oct. 1923), 2; Shachtman, "Gompers fails nation's youth," W n 284 (29 Sept. 1923), 5.
38. Shachtman, "Keeping them young and red," DW v 2 n 204 (15 Nov. 1924); Shachtman, "The cradle of the giants," *Liberator* v 7 n 10 (Oct. 1924), 15.
39. Shachtman, "Leading the junior groups," DW v 2 n 210 (22 Nov. 1924); "Keeping them young and red," DW v 2 n 204.
40. Shachtman, "Parents and children," DW v 2 n 215 (29 Nov. 1924).
41. Interview with Geltman (22 Mar. 1989), s 1; interview with Glotzer (24 Mar. 1989), s 2.
42. RMS 467–69.
43. Shachtman, "The sixth anniversary of the Bolshevik revolution," YW v 2 n 11 (Nov. 1923), 2.
44. RMS 71, 73, 75, 77.
45. DW v 2 n 93 (30 Apr. 1925), 1, 4.
46. RMS 88, 92; interview with Glotzer, s 1.
47. "Resolution of the convention," YW v 4 n 35 (17 Oct. 1925), 3.
48. "What is International Labor Defense?" [nd], PMA b 11 f 15; RMS 448–49; Shachtman, "International Labor Defense in action," DW v 4 n 229 (8 Oct. 1927).
49. Interview with Glotzer (24 Mar. 1989), s 2; Glotzer to Drucker (6 Jan. 1990), 2.
50. RMS 115–16; Sam Gordon, in Les Evans, ed., *James P. Cannon as We Knew Him*, 61; James P. Cannon, *James P. Cannon and the Early Years of American Communism*, 537; interview with Geltman (22 Mar. 1989), s 1; Haskell, "Max Shachtman," 7; interview with Glotzer (28 Mar. 1989), s 6.
51. Shachtman, *Sacco and Vanzetti*, 36.
52. RMS 114–15; Vanzetti to LD (23 May 1926), LD v 1 n 7 (July 1926), 114.

53. Shachtman, *Sacco and Vanzetti*, 15, 31–33; Shachtman, "Life and freedom for Sacco and Vanzetti," DW v 4 n 129 (12 June 1926).
54. Shachtman, *Sacco and Vanzetti*, 58, 40.
55. Shachtman, *Sacco and Vanzetti*, 35, 48.
56. Russell, "Clinching the case," *New York Review of Books* v 33 n 4 (13 Mar. 1986), 32–36; Kaiser and Russell, "Sacco and Vanzetti," *New York Review of Books* v 33 n 9 (29 May 1986), 52–56.
57. Shachtman, *Sacco and Vanzetti*, 78, 75.
58. Shachtman, "One for all and all for one," LD v 3 n 4 (Apr. 1928), 84; interview with Glotzer by Bloom (13–21 Dec. 1983), OHAL 12–13.
59. RMS 130.

2

Trotsky's Commissar

At the end of 1928, Shachtman and Cannon freed themselves from the frustrating conflict between their internationalism and their U.S. working-class identity when they discovered Trotskyism. Trotsky's criticisms of Stalin's policies gave them an explanation for Communists' defeats in the United States and around the world in the 1920s. Shachtman suddenly realized that his and Cannon's loyalty to the Soviet leadership had been misguided. The increasingly reluctant follower of U.S. and international Communism became a leader of U.S. and international Trotskyism. Shachtman would remain a Trotskyist through the 1930s and 1940s and contribute to the shaping of Trotskyist thinking and strategy.

Trotskyism dovetailed with Shachtman's and Cannon's desire for a Marxism rooted in the U.S. working class. In the mid-1920s they had subordinated their own convictions about what was best for the U.S. movement to their loyalty to Communists in Moscow, who presumably knew what was best for the whole world movement. Now Trotsky convinced them that what was wrong in the United States was also wrong internationally. He convinced them that Communists who were loyal to Stalin were maneuvering with alien forces around the world: unreliable trade union officials in the United States and Europe, technocrats in Soviet factories, middle-class nationalists in Asia. They set out to rescue authentic working-class politics from Stalin internationally and from Lovestone and his supporters in the United States.

Many of Cannon's followers broke away from Communist orthodoxy along with Cannon and Shachtman. Cannonite malcontents developed into open Trotskyist heretics, and they were expelled by the dozens from the Communist Party in 1928–29. Once U.S. Trotskyists were out of the party, Shachtman became a key organizer of Cannon's new group, the Communist League of America; editor of its newspaper, the *Militant*; and founder of its publishing house, Pioneer Publishers. Its tiny ranks gradually expanded to a hundred, then two hundred Trotskyists.

Shachtman blossomed at first in this small, isolated, embattled group.

34

The Communist Party had frustrated his ambitions and neglected his talents; the Communist League gave more scope to both. While Cannon led the Trotskyists, Shachtman became his second-in-command and "idea man." He became one of the Trotskyists' star speakers, with a flair that even non-Trotskyists paid grudging tribute to. As a theorist he was second to no one among U.S. Trotskyists, as he showed in a long 1933 analysis of African-American oppression and struggle.

Although Cannon and Shachtman had been dragged back to New York against their will by the Communist Party, Shachtman was at home as a Trotskyist leader in his native city. A younger, Jewish Trotskyist milieu began to form around him in New York. Al Glotzer moved to New York in 1929 to help out in the Communist League office, cementing his friendship with Shachtman. Max and his wife, Billie, and Glotzer and his companion Edith Harvey were an intimate foursome. Max's parents in the Bronx welcomed them all into the Shachtman family circle. Shachtman became a mentor and model for New York teenagers, many of them Jewish, who were attracted to the Trotskyists.

In the same years that Shachtman settled down in his hometown, he became a world traveler and international Trotskyist leader. In February 1930 he visited Trotsky at his home in exile on the Turkish island of Büyük-Ada and began a decade as Trotsky's close disciple and collaborator. He became Trotsky's emissary to Trotskyists in several countries and an interpreter of Trotsky's ideas. He combined insights gleaned from Trotsky's analysis of Guomindang-Communist clashes in China with insights he had begun to develop himself in his account of Augusto Sandino's guerrilla war against the marines in Nicaragua. He became one of the chief exponents of Trotsky's theory of permanent revolution. He contributed analyses of opportunities opened up by Palestinian Arab resistance to Zionism, the Indian independence movement, and the 1931 Spanish republican revolution.

Yet Shachtman and other Trotskyists failed in the early 1930s to change the course of the Communist Party or the Communist International. Although they were right to fear that democracy was being eliminated in the USSR and the Communist movement, and right to suspect that Soviet foreign policy was overriding every other factor in the International's decisions, their analysis of Stalin's policies turned out to be wrong in some other basic ways. Stalin surprised them by collectivizing Soviet agriculture, rapidly building up Soviet industry, and turning Communists outside the USSR in ultraradical directions. A concerted Communist campaign of abuse and attacks frustrated Trotskyists' efforts to influence rank-and-file Communists. Trotskyists took out their frustrations on one another in a 1931–33 faction fight in which impatient young New Yorkers around Shachtman battled older trade unionists around Cannon.

While Trotskyists remained isolated in their small group, the Communist Party began to grow again as the Depression radicalized thousands of working people. As democracy was virtually extinguished in the Communist ranks, Communists grew more self-confident and more impervious to outside criticism. Even Stalin's disastrous policy in Germany, which facilitated the Nazis' rise to power in 1933, hardly shook U.S. Communists' monolithic unity, although Trotsky internationally and Shachtman in the *Militant* wrote eloquently and insightfully about the catastrophe Stalin helped bring about. Trotskyists came to the reluctant conclusion that the Communist movement could not be saved. They would have to use their tiny forces to help build a new movement separate from and opposed to official Communism.

U.S. Communists were surprisingly ignorant about Trotsky's ideas in the 1920s. Beginning in 1924, at the International's insistence, they passed resolutions against Trotskyism—as quickly as possible—so they could return to the issues they cared about. "We knew, to put it most bluntly, nothing about the real issues," Shachtman remembered. However many times they condemned Trotskyism, U.S. Communists in the 1920s never really saw Trotsky as a force for evil. They developed a virtual split personality about him, denouncing Trotskyism on certain occasions and praising Trotsky as the organizer of the Bolshevik insurrection and commander of the Red Army on other occasions. The *Daily Worker* weighted its coverage of the Soviet faction fight overwhelmingly against Trotsky, yet published article after article by him on international issues. During a 1926–27 visit to Moscow, where he attended a meeting of the International's Executive Committee in Cannon's place, Shachtman met a follower of the Trotskyist opposition who explained Trotsky's point of view. Shachtman listened to him intently but made sure not to be convinced.[1]

Shachtman's eventual conversion to Trotskyism resulted from an accident that put Cannon on the Program Commission at the International's sixth congress in Moscow in June 1928. Cannon sat sullen and silent through the commission meetings, which he had been assigned to because other U.S. Communists had no interest in them. But he was one of the few congress delegates to read Trotsky's attack on the draft program submitted to the congress. Cannon's outlook was transformed. "It was as clear as daylight that Marxist truth was on the side of Trotsky," he said.[2] He cast his lot with Trotsky, a Soviet dissident who had just been stripped of his job and party membership and sent into internal exile in central Asia.

By another fluke, Maurice Spector was serving on the Program Commission along with Cannon. An engaging, well-educated, and independent-minded Canadian Communist leader, Spector had begun to have misgivings about the attacks on Trotsky years before. When Spector had heard about Cannon's general disgruntlement from Shachtman and Marty Abern during a visit to New York in February 1928, he had sought Cannon out and got Cannon to confide in him. At the June meeting in Moscow, Cannon and Spector promised each other that when they got back to North America they would both speak out in Trotsky's defense.

No sooner had Cannon returned to the United States than he began looking for allies in his new fight. He talked first to his wife, Rose Karsner. The second person to whom he showed his precious copy of Trotsky's critique of the draft program was Shachtman. The document did not make for easy reading, Shachtman remembered. The translation was poor, and whole sections of Trotsky's work had been chopped out. But Shachtman was convinced. He remembered years later the document's "absolutely shattering effect upon my inexcusable indifference to the fight in the Russian party, upon my smug ignorance about the issues involved, upon my sense of shame." He also remembered the "explosive effect the *Critique* had in lighting new horizons . . . and pointing out new roads to tread."[3] In only two or three days Shachtman was one of Cannon's converts.

The Trotskyism to which Shachtman became a convert defined itself above all by its internationalism. Trotskyists believed that they, not the official Communists, were the true internationalists as well as the best U.S. revolutionaries. They saw internationalism not just as a bond of loyalty among Communists but as an inescapable necessity for socialism, Shachtman explained, because socialism "arises directly out of the development of the world economy."[4] Building socialism as an international movement had to come first, even if it sometimes conflicted with the short-term interests of the Soviet Union. Trotskyists believed that Communists were putting narrowly defined Soviet interests above the needs of international socialism, with disastrous results.

One defeat cited by Trotsky as an example of the International's upside-down priorities was the British general strike of 1926, which was called by the Trades Union Congress to support striking coal miners. The International, which had put together a joint trade union committee of British and Soviet union leaders to guard against a British attack on the Soviet Union, hailed Trades Union Congress officials as leaders of the coming British revolution. In fact, the officials called off the general strike after nine days. The British working class won virtually nothing from its mobilization, the British Communists still less. Bewildered U.S. Communists hailed the strike settlement as a "partial victory," only to turn around the next day and denounce it as a "betrayal."[5] Now Shachtman had an explanation for the confusion: Stalin had looked to British union leaders instead of Communist workers because union leaders would protect embryonic Soviet socialism from British attack—even though the union leaders stood in the way of socialism in Britain.

Shachtman and Cannon saw the same upside-down priorities and fruitless maneuvers at work in U.S. communism: for example, in Ruthenberg's enthusiasm for LaFollette in 1924. They came to think that the International, lacking confidence in the possibility of a strong working-class movement in the United States in the near future, was trying to squeeze the U.S. party arbitrarily into its shifting, short-term quest for allies. In breaking with official Communism, Cannonites returned to much of the perspective they had held in 1923–25: looking to build a broad, working-class radical movement in the long term, but skeptical of coalitions in the short term.

For example, Trotskyists were skeptical in the late 1920s and early 1930s about seeing a U.S. labor party anytime soon. Cannon had switched to a pro-labor party line in 1925, reversing his own position in obedience to the International's desire to find new friends for the Soviet Union in the labor movement. Shachtman had loyally gone along. But Chicago Trotskyists led by Al Glotzer and Tom O'Flaherty pushed reconsideration of the issue in 1929, and Trotsky said in 1930 that he was not sure that there would ever be a labor party in the United States. In 1931, thanks in part to Shachtman's pushing, Cannon's followers returned to their old rejection of labor party campaigns.[6] The Communist Party, by contrast, had decided in 1928 to continue campaigning for a labor party "only from below": by attacking every other tendency that might help form it.

Trotskyists believed that the mind-set that accounted for most of Communists' mistakes was crystallized in Stalin's theory of "socialism in one country." On its face, the theory was a purely hypothetical proposition: Even if new revolutions did not give Communists power in other capitalist countries, Soviet Communists would still be able sometime in the indefinite future to create socialism on their own. For Stalin, the theory was an expression of confidence in Soviet workers and peasants, and Trotsky was a defeatist for insisting that only several advanced countries working together could create socialism. Trotskyists thought that Stalin was the defeatist. The fact that Stalin made socialism in one country the "very axis" of his whole policy proved for Shachtman that Stalin had no confidence in socialist victory anywhere outside the USSR for decades to come.[7] Even from the standpoint of Soviet defense, Shachtman said, a strong Communist movement was the best guarantee against capitalist attacks.

Above all, Trotsky argued, to define socialism as a goal attainable by backward Russia was to debase the idea of socialism. Socialism was supposed to be a society of freedom, equality, and abundance. Shachtman summed up the Trotskyist viewpoint: "The proletarian revolution in the West is far closer . . . than . . . the establishment of a socialist society in Russia. If it is not closer, then the proletarian revolution is doomed!"[8]

Cannon and Shachtman began working in the fall of 1928 to win other Communists over to their new perspective. Although they dared to approach only members of their own faction whom they trusted—and even then tried only obliquely to raise doubts about the condemnations of Trotsky—in a matter of weeks they and Abern were facing a formal investigation. Party leaders' first move was to test the suspects by proposing a fresh resolution condemning Trotskyism. Abern voted for, Cannon abstained, and Shachtman voted against. Shachtman later explained that the division was partly "tactical guile," but it also reflected real differences of opinion among them. "I felt absolutely uncompromising by that time," he said. "I was for Trotsky's position and I was not going to hide it."[9]

As the investigation wore on day after day, all three found their convictions hardening and their patience diminishing. On 27 October they presented a joint statement of their support for Trotsky. The vultures descended on the three with gusto—Cannon bore the brunt of their attack, Abern faced only a few questions, and Shachtman virtually none. That day they were expelled from the Communist Party.[10]

"We set about without a nickel in our pockets" and no followers, Shachtman remembered, to organize a Trotskyist group outside the Communist Party. He "plunged into it with the greatest enthusiasm."[11]

In the first days after their expulsion, Shachtman, Cannon, and Abern received help from a small group of survivors loyal to the shrunken Industrial Workers of the World who remembered Cannon from the union's great days before the First World War. An Italian immigrant in that group provided the Trotskyists with the print shop to issue their new paper, gave them credit for costs of printing it, and even suggested its name: the *Militant*. Within a week of their expulsion, the handful of Trotskyists took their new publication down to Communist headquarters and began to hawk it on the party's doorstep. Soon they had bought their own linotype, learned to use it, and did their own printing in the back of their office.

Although Shachtman, Cannon, and Abern were ridiculed as "the three generals without an army," Communist leaders soon provided them with troops. Worried that the Trotskyist heresy had spread further than it really had, the leadership set about extirpating it by introducing resolutions in every cell condemning the three expelled Trotskyists by name. Whenever members voted no or even demanded more evidence before voting yes, they were expelled on the spot. Of course former Cannon supporters were most likely to balk at the vote. In this way, scores of party members who knew nothing about Trotskyism were expelled as Trotskyists. Once freed from party discipline, most of them were curious to know what it was they had been expelled for and went to seek out the three Trotskyists, who were only too happy to explain.

Shachtman's young Chicago friend Al Glotzer heard rumors about his leaders' heresy even before their expulsion. He wrote to Cannon asking him "what the hell was going on." One morning he received Cannon's answer: galley proofs of Trotsky's document. Glotzer and Chicago Cannonite leader Arne Swabeck read the proofs. Glotzer found them "hair raising"; he was "aghast," even "sick." But he was influenced by what he read. When Glotzer and Swabeck listened to a party leader who had just returned from three years at the Lenin School and had supposedly learned all about Trotskyism, they found that the expert's expertise amounted to less than they knew from one pamphlet. They stuck with the Communist leaders they knew and trusted, and they were expelled. To their surprise, two or three others voted against their expulsion and were expelled with them— not Trotskyists, just old comrades who could not countenance what they were seeing.[12]

Most of the first hundred recruits to Trotskyism in the United States were Cannonites who had been expelled in this way—a dozen in Chicago, a dozen in New York, two dozen in Minneapolis, scattered twos and threes elsewhere. "Our initial success was due to [CP leaders'] narrow and stupid and vindictive factionalism—not any effort on our part," Shachtman reflected. The Trotskyists' access to Communist Party members that had been grabbed away with one hand was being given back with the other. The first handful of expelled Trotskyists had been driven away from Communist headquarters by Communist furriers (i.e., members of the Communist-controlled Fur Workers Union) screaming insults, while they looked "in utter disbelief" at how their comrades of the day before were treating them. Communists went on to burglarize Cannon's home and beat up *Militant* vendors. But the first few Trotskyists recruited others. Soon they had groups in New York, Chicago, Minneapolis, Cleveland, Boston, Pittsburgh, and Youngstown; Greek Trotskyists, Italian Trotskyists, and Hungarian Trotskyists. In May 1929 the first hundred Trotskyists founded the Communist League of America.[13]

Shachtman found himself a leader of the new movement. He had been the most junior of the Trotskyists' three "generals." He had become an alternate member of the Communist Central Committee only in 1927. But force of circumstances now pushed him forward. He was young, totally convinced that Trotsky was right, and eager to prove himself. Cannon was willing to let Shachtman try his new wings. In October 1929 Cannon was replaced as editor of the *Militant*—in theory by a five-member board, but in actuality mostly by Shachtman.[14]

At the time of his expulsion from the Communist Party, Shachtman was twenty-four years old. He had spent his seven years in the party under the shadow of more prominent figures, above all Cannon and Abern. With his emergence into the smaller circle of Trotskyism, Shachtman took on new stature. Not only was he a bigger fish in a smaller pond but he also began thinking more independently and creatively. His apprenticeship was over, and he had become a leader in his own right. Although he had begun as Abern's protégé, Abern was now the junior partner in the relationship. Glotzer felt in hindsight that he as well as Shachtman had "outstripped" Abern.[15]

Though Shachtman never overshadowed Cannon, he was no longer overshadowed by him either. People were soon linking their names automatically. They made a good team because they complemented one another. Alongside his undeniable strengths Cannon also had his weaknesses, and Shachtman made up for them. When times were hard, Cannon could sometimes get depressed, drink too much, and work too little. Shachtman, despite a lazy streak, could work through the night for days in a row when he felt impelled to. Cannon did not know any foreign languages and was held back by this lack in international work. Shachtman was more or less fluent in French, German, and Yiddish, could struggle along in Spanish, and picked up a few words of Russian. He came to enjoy frequent trips and a lively correspondence that made him the best-known U.S. Trotskyist in the international movement.

Cannon respected committed intellectuals. But he was aware of his own shortcomings as a theorist, which reinforced his doubts about middle-class theorists in the radical movement. Shachtman, facile with ideas himself, was much more at ease with the intellectuals who cautiously circled around the movement because of the allure of Trotsky's fame. He became Cannon's 'idea man,"[16] while Cannon kept the greater authority.

Although Shachtman learned much of what he knew about public speaking from Cannon, he developed his own style. Trotskyists valued him above all for his skill and verve as a debater. Shachtman confessed that he "always had a weakness and a fondness for debates and polemics," and never could "get the polemical style out of my speaking or writing." Cannon commented sourly that Shachtman's "extraordinary literary facility" went together with "a no less extraordinary literary versatility, which enabled him to write equally well on both sides of a question."[17] But Shachtman never defended a position he did not believe in strongly, at least at the moment. He could not understand how serious opinions could be defended without passion. Many times when he could not summon up emotion or conviction he refrained from taking part in a major debate. When he did take part, he had emotion and conviction to spare.

Shachtman's speeches became famous. He "had very mordant wit. He knew words; he knew how to fire your imagination; he was a great mimic." He "excelled in destroying an opponent's use of citations from holy text by restoring them to their proper context; he was devilish in his mockery of pretension and false learning." He had an impressive memory for quotations, names, and statistics. He was masterful at preparing a good line in advance and producing it at just the right moment, so that it seemed completely spontaneous. He also had a gift for long, dramatic buildups, starting from soft whispers and ending in powerful (though high-pitched) crescendos. Occasionally, early on in a Shachtman speech, someone would shout "Louder!" The speaker would look up and say, to the amusement of those who had heard him before, "Don't worry." In the end his voice would "burst forth, with powerful resonance, filling up the room and tingling your spine."[18]

In their thoughtful moments, even Shachtman's admirers saw that his oratory had its limitations. Gordon Haskell, a recruit of the 1930s, remembered Shachtman as a "great *inside* speaker." He could always draw a crowd because people knew that they would "have a good time at the expense of the Stalinists or whoever. . . . But we didn't attract new people with that." Although Shachtman often kept people riveted to their seats for three or four hours, he could also be long-winded. Glotzer once complained to him about his "infernal non-stop gab." He always went over the time allotted to him, and his audience always voted him extensions. "Stalin expected to create socialism in one country," Trotskyists joked, "and Shachtman in one speech."[19]

In one other respect Shachtman had an advantage over Cannon: He had more appeal for bright young Trotskyists. His hair and pencil mustache were still black when Cannon's hair was already graying. He was outgoing, at a time when Cannon was often moody and withdrawn. He "would talk to anybody anytime," Glotzer said. "His youth would sit around, five, ten of them and talk all afternoon." People found him easy to talk to. Often they would discuss fine points of socialist theory and practice with him over meals while he indulged his "truly Rabelaisian appetite for food."[20] He also had a crude, bawdy, often scatalogical sense of humor that delighted most of his followers, even when he amused himself by inventing obscene nicknames for them.

Shachtman did not take on any practical responsibility for organizing younger Trotskyists. In the early 1930s youth work was still Glotzer's particular field. But given how few Trotskyists there were, dedicated young recruits got to know Shachtman easily. Among them was Joe Carter, a bright, neurotic City College student who had been expelled from the Socialist youth for Communism at eighteen and expelled from the Communist youth for Trotskyism at nineteen. Emanuel (Manny) Geltman, a Jewish longshoreman's son from Coney Island, joined the Trotskyists after he was denied admission to the Young Communist League at age fourteen for reading the *Militant*. Glotzer brought other young leaders like Nathan (Natie) Gould into the organization in Chicago. Glotzer, Carter, and Geltman started a Trotskyist youth newspaper, *Young Spartacus.* "The life was very intense and very close," Geltman remembered. Shachtman fed this sense of intensity and closeness by his physical affection for his followers. He would hug them and kiss them. He would pinch both their cheeks, hard, in a habit that some felt blended sadism and affection. "I think I still have scars" from Shachtman's pinches, one remembered. "Tears would come down your eyes."[21]

Young people who became close to Shachtman could learn an enormous amount from him about Marxist theory and history. Despite his own careless streak he rarely condescended to young followers or let their efforts go unnoticed or their errors uncorrected. If one of them said something he objected to, "Max would say, 'You stupid son of a bitch. Are you listening to what you're saying?' Then he would sit down and explain it to you, point by point." He *"loved* to explode fallacious arguments." He taught his followers to value intellectual discipline and to delight in catching obscure historical references in his speeches. He also encouraged them to write, although he did not have much patience for working with aspiring young writers. In this respect Geltman felt that he "was closer to Shachtman but . . . learned more from Cannon."[22]

Shachtman's way of training new recruits had a particular appeal for his young followers who were Jews. Cannon's young followers were often Jewish too, as were many Trotskyists in the 1930s. But young Jews around Cannon were likely to imitate his blue-collar, midwestern earthiness, while youngsters around Shachtman made little effort to hide their New York background or intellectual skills and tastes. Years later they could still hear Shachtman's voice in one another's speeches.

During the 1930s and 1940s, Shachtman would be one of the most gifted thinkers and writers of the Trotskyist movement. He acquired great and often justified confidence in his ability to see the shape of things to come before almost anyone else and to see drastic changes the movement would have to make in its thinking and practice in order to keep pace with events. He grew bitingly and ironically impatient with those who did not see the changed reality and the need for changed practice as quickly and thoroughly as he did. Into his disdain for these doubters there sometimes crept the intonation of a teacher picking on a slow student. But in the 1930s Shachtman's impatience was counterbalanced by his encouragement, even zest, for no-holds-barred debate. He valued lively discussion and a critical-minded membership enough to accept even the defeat or dilution of his own positions.

As Shachtman's self-confidence and impatience grew, another part of his personality came into focus: a certain secretiveness, an occasional unexpected reserve. He even had a "sort of vindictiveness belied by his surface bonhomie."[23] But in the 1930s his enthusiasm and humor still cast any occasional flashes of temper in shadow.

Shachtman became a mentor to many young Trotskyists not only because of his impressive speeches and lively arguments with his protégés but also because of his role as a leading Trotskyist thinker and writer. In the late 1920s and early 1930s, he focused his intellectual work on an idea that became a Trotskyist hallmark: the theory of permanent revolution.

The phrase "permanent revolution" was first used by Marx in a discussion of the German Revolution of 1848, which he said would begin as a revolution to create a German democratic republic and should continue uninterruptedly to the creation of socialism. Trotsky picked up the idea in 1906 as he analyzed the Russian Revolution of 1905 and predicted another revolution to come. The next revolution, he said, would not only begin the creation of socialism in Russia but give the signal for socialist revolution in the rest of Europe. Without working-class victories elsewhere in Europe, the Russian revolution would be doomed to give way to reaction. Trotsky thus described a revolution that would have to be "permanent" in a double sense—expanding beyond the limits of a narrowly democratic revolution as well as beyond the boundaries of a single country.

The first half of Trotsky's prediction was vindicated by the Russian Revolution of 1917, which virtually wiped out capitalism in the urban centers by the summer of 1918. But no other socialist revolution was victorious in the 1920s. By 1924 Stalin, with his theory of socialism in one country, was challenging Trotsky's attempt to link the Russian Revolution in a single dynamic with international revolution. Trotsky fought against the idea of socialism in one country. But he fought it with arguments that had been common to all Bolsheviks until 1924, not with his distinctive catchword of permanent revolution. He revived and generalized his theory of permanent revolution only in debates over the defeated Chinese Revolution of 1927. In these debates Trotsky began to argue for the first time that *no* backward country could win true national independence or self-propelled economic development except under working-class rule, and working-class rule could not survive anywhere unless it spread relatively soon to several advanced countries.

Trotsky rejected Stalin's strategy for China: that the working class should ally not only with peasants but also with middle-class democrats to create a democratic, independent, but still capitalist republic. Only peasants' self-interested urge to produce for the market and spend in the market could create a big enough internal demand for a country like China, Trotsky argued. Development required land reform. Capitalists and the middle classes had interests intertwined with landlords that kept peasants living in isolation at a mere subsistence level; they would not push through the necessary agrarian transformation. Only the working class could ally with peasants to carry it out.

The Chinese Communist Party started small but exploded into a powerful mass movement in 1925 and 1926. The International encouraged Chinese Communists to rely not on their own working-class and peasant constituencies but on the nationalist Guomindang led by Chiang Kai-shek. As Chiang led his armies northward to unify the country under Guomindang rule, Moscow ordered Communists not to support strikes, not to form soviets, not to help peasants seize land. Communists in industrial Shanghai led a working-class revolt in April 1927 that won control of the city, then welcomed in Chiang's army without a fight, gave up their guns to Chiang's soldiers, and were massacred almost without resistance.

At the time, Shachtman presented the official Communist response in the *Labor Defender*: After the massacre the Chinese supported the Guomindang "in even greater numbers," he said. Presumably he stuck to the same improbable account in an illustrated lecture tour on "Revolution and Counterrevolution in China," which he took to twenty-eight cities in early 1928. But he changed his mind after reading Trotsky's critique, charging, "*The Chinese proletariat was prohibited by . . . the leadership of the Communist International . . . from fulfilling the role imposed upon it by history.*"[24]

Trotsky's theory of permanent revolution gave Shachtman a tool with which he could better understand events around the world. He was eager to use it. He published, interpreted, and defended Trotsky's writings about the Russian and Chinese revolutions. He also kept up the habit from his days at the *Daily Worker* of reading foreign newspapers. Every now and then he ventured to give his own Trotskyist analysis of events abroad. However fragmentary the information he had, Shachtman did more than apply Trotsky's theory mechanically to every country he looked at. He arrived at independent conclusions that can still inform our understanding of history.

Many U.S. Communists in the 1920s who were not very clear about what Trotskyism was were unconscious Trotskyists when they wrote about the third world. Several of Trotsky's works were printed and circulated by the Communist press; they were bound to have an influence on Communist readers who had not yet been thoroughly inoculated against Trotsky's ideas. Shachtman himself seems to have leaned toward the idea of permanent revolution even before he saw it explained in print: for example, in an article he wrote in praise of Nicaraguan revolutionary Augusto Sandino in March 1928.[25] Sandino was not a Communist but a leader who had emerged from the Nicaraguan Liberal Party to command a guerrilla war against U.S. marines. U.S. Communists backed him enthusiastically. Like U.S. radicals generations later, they showed their support by a medical aid campaign for the Central American rebels.

Contrary to the Communist orthodoxy of the day, Shachtman did not expect that Sandino's war could stay limited either to Nicaragua or to a program of independence and democratic reforms. "In Nicaragua particularly, one who leads must lead either into the arms of Wall Street or lead with arms against Wall Street," he said. Sandino was leading with arms against Wall Street, with considerable success. The Nicaraguan climate and terrain were deadly for marines. U.S. planes, unchallenged in the air, had to fly so low to see through the forest cover that Sandino's rebels could down them with rifles. But Shachtman did not believe that Sandino could win a lasting victory within Nicaragua alone. Sandino's war, cheered on by Latin Americans everywhere, would be "a hundred times more effective" if it spread to other Central American countries, Shachtman said. Sandino's ultimate victory would come when he "carved out a new historical epoch for the oppressed peoples of the two American continents." Although Anastasio Somoza's National Guard would betray and kill Sandino in 1934, Shachtman would continue to develop his vision of a Pan-American revolution in more detail later in the 1930s.

Shachtman made conscious use of the theory of permanent revolution for the first time during an upheaval in Palestine in 1929. Jewish settlement had provoked opposition from the Arab population of the British colony. The tension finally sparked riots in which Arabs killed Jewish settlers in Hebron (still a focal point of Jewish-Arab conflict on the Israeli-occupied West Bank today). Reaction to the riots in the U.S. Communist press was confused. At first the Yiddish Communist *Freiheit* condemned the killings as a "pogrom." This line was abruptly countermanded by party leaders, and the *Freiheit* turned around to hail the birth of an anti-Zionist "national revolutionary movement." Prominent Jewish writers left the party in protest.

The notion of a "national revolutionary movement" was bound to make Trotskyists suspicious. They had seen this concept used to justify Communist support for the Chinese Guomindang in 1927, with disastrous results. Shachtman pointed out that the social composition of the Palestinian Arab movement was even less promising than the Guomindang's had been. The Guomindang at least included middle-class and capitalist elements. The Palestinian movement was led in 1929 almost entirely by Arab landowners and Muslim religious figures, who had scant claims to lead opposition against the British. Many Arab landowners had been responsible for the sale of land to Zionist settlers and the resulting eviction of Arab peasants. During the attacks on Jews, Shachtman did not know of a single shot having been fired at British troops. He even argued (as Trotskyists argued consistently throughout the 1930s and 1940s) that the call to restrict Jewish immigration to Palestine was reactionary. Marxists had to try to unite Arab peasants with Jewish workers who were fleeing persecution in

Europe. Supporting the riots, which diverted Palestinians' anger "*into Pan-Islamic and anti-Semitic channels and out of its natural current against British imperialism,*" was a typical Stalinist evasion of Marxist responsibility.

But Shachtman refused to accommodate too far to Jewish anger at the Communist line. The riots did not constitute a "national revolutionary movement," but neither were they a mere "pogrom," he argued. Despite their wrong actions, they were "an uprising of the down-trodden [Arab] masses." Any reliance on the British to suppress them was ruled out.[26]

Early in 1930 Shachtman turned his attention to India, a country that would be crucial to his vision of the third world in the 1940s and 1950s. Here a well-developed nationalist movement did exist, led mainly by Mohandas Gandhi's Indian National Congress. It gained support from the "land hunger of the Indian peasants . . . as acute as it is remediable," since nearly a quarter of India's agricultural land was not under cultivation.[27] There was also a significant industrial working class in India, concentrated in the Bombay textile factories. The Communist International's strategy of backing middle-class nationalism seemed feasible in India if it was feasible anywhere.

But Trotsky had warned that the methods Stalin used in China would have even worse consequences in India, and Shachtman could draw on a wealth of evidence that Gandhi and his Congress were not leading a resolute fight for Indian independence. Already in the early 1920s Gandhi had called off a tax boycott that was shaking British rule. Gandhi was dismayed by the violence the boycott encouraged. He condemned the burning of police stations, for example, and gave it as a reason for calling off his campaign. To Shachtman, Gandhi's pacifism, which was widely praised then and later, expressed the timidity of native landowners and capitalists who feared peasants' land hunger and workers' discontent. Under their domination the Congress was willing to accept dominion status, which Shachtman saw as a way for Congress leaders to get government jobs without the dangers of a war for independence. (Dominion status gave a country significantly less independence before the 1931 Statute of Westminister, which gave dominions control of their own foreign policy.)

In Shachtman's eyes, war or at least large-scale confrontation was a prerequisite to winning true independence. He could not imagine that anything else would make Britain grant freedom to India—the heart of the British Empire and a source of "almost inexhaustible loot." If the Congress would not lead a revolutionary war for independence, the task should logically fall on an Indian Communist Party. But in 1930 no Indian Communist Party had been organized "because Stalin has been too busy playing with Indian nationalism."[28]

Shachtman's faith in this analysis was shaken after the Second World

War, when the Congress succeeded in making India (minus Pakistan) not only a dominion but an independent republic within the Commonwealth. Yet independence has not solved the problems of landlessness in the Indian countryside, poverty in the cities, and economic dependence on Europe and the United States. Much of Shachtman's 1930 criticism of Gandhi and the Congress leaders stands up better than the hero worship Gandhi has often received, which in any event has been more uncritical in Europe and North America than in India.

Shachtman's first efforts to apply Trotsky's ideas to international events were made using whatever fragments of Trotsky's writings he could get hold of. Soon, however, Shachtman was able to collaborate with Trotsky. In January 1929 Stalin expelled Trotsky from internal exile in Soviet central Asia and shipped him to Turkey, where he settled on the little island of Büyük-Ada near Istanbul. Although Shachtman fretted about Trotsky's safety—Istanbul "swarms with counterrevolutionary, White Guard vermin," he said—Trotsky could now help his supporters abroad far more. From then on, whatever formal structures the Trotskyists set up, Trotsky himself was always their real organizing center. In March 1929, U.S. Trotskyists made contact with him.[29] Soon they relied on him for information and advice. For his part, Trotsky wanted his U.S. followers to bear some of the burden of building up the movement in other countries, particularly English-speaking countries.

Among the available U.S. Trotskyists, Shachtman was the logical candidate to work as Trotsky's assistant for international affairs. He was more interested in other countries than Cannon, who did not even visit Trotsky until 1934. Shachtman was also willing to beg money from anyone to keep the *Militant* going, since U.S. Trotskyists could not sustain a weekly with their own resources. Their leaders were financing the *Militant* out of their own pockets, even though they had never been paid their back wages when they were fired from the International Labor Defense after their expulsion. They could barely afford their dingy Third Avenue office with the old elevated railway "roaring in the window." So in February 1930, partly to help with international work and partly to ask for money, Shachtman went to visit Trotsky, who was living on Büyük-Ada with his wife, Natalia Sedova, and their son Lyova "a few blocks from the ferry slip, in an old and somewhat dilapidated mansion."[30]

Shachtman had seen Trotsky only once before, in 1925 in Moscow as Trotsky's car was driving by. Now for the first time the two of them met and spoke. Shachtman was overwhelmed at meeting the man he still described in his last years as "the captain of the Bolshevik Revolution," "the most audacious and sweeping revolutionary theoretician of the century," "the most scintillating, the most elegant and the most eloquent orator-writer . . . of the age," a man whose ideas "opened the minds and lifted the hearts of the best of a whole generation." Although Shachtman was received warmly he was "overawed."

> Trotsky always seemed to give the impression of being very tall although actually he was not. He was a very solid figure of a man, large-framed, large-chested. And that together with the leonine head that everybody commented upon made him look much bigger than he actually was.[31]

In his years of exile Trotsky was surrounded not only by his family but by secretaries, messengers, and Trotskyist leaders from different countries, sacrificed by their own organizations to the needs of the international movement. His house was never so much a home as a headquarters. For Shachtman his stay on Büyük-Ada was a new education in work. He had worked hard before, but he was a little sloppy, notorious for missing deadlines and appointments. "He could write well when he *chose* to write well, when you could *push* him to write." He once said apologetically to an ill-treated correspondent, "You know (a) how it is and (b) how I am. Too late to change."[32] Trotsky judged work not by what was enjoyable or easy or even possible but by what was historically necessary. Since the Trotskyist movement set itself historical tasks far beyond its means, Trotsky drove himself and everyone around him always to do more.

Despite malarial attacks, headaches, and continual pestering by reporters who wanted his opinions on religion or art, Trotsky worked on a rigid schedule. His sweater was always buttoned, his tie was never loosened, his posture was always erect. He set his followers to work answering his mail by day and patrolling the grounds with a flashlight by night. He had no time for idle speculation or gossip—although he would go so far as mild teasing of his younger followers, and was often sarcastic. He also had time for long talks with Shachtman of which Shachtman said, "I am learning more for myself and our movement by my daily talks with him on a thousand different subjects than I could learn from a thousand books."[33]

Trotsky could be warmly appreciative and even affectionate toward those who he felt had earned it, but his judgments almost always rested (or so he thought) on some objective basis. When he decided that his regard was no longer merited, he withdrew it. Shachtman was struck at not finding "a trace of personal animosity or personal bitterness or personal hatred of Stalin in anything that Trotsky said or did." Shachtman, for his part, took his politics personally and sometimes a little lightly. Trotsky dismissed the streak of frivolity that sometimes leavened Shachtman's politics as "clownishness." He also distrusted Shachtman's occasional freewheeling speculations: "Shachtman plays with ideas," he complained.[34]

Trotsky had only two forms of relaxation on Büyük-Ada, characteristically productive ones: hunting and fishing, which he enjoyed immensely. Shachtman would dutifully set out with him "at the ungodly hour of five in the morning, which in those days was just about the time I was falling asleep in my room." Occasionally on hunting or fishing expeditions Trotsky would run into local farmers or fisherpeople, and he would question them for hours about how they made a living, their customs, their politics. When he went fishing he would set up the nets with military efficiency under the guidance of a local fisherman and haul in quantities of fish or the lobster-like shellfish called langouste. None of it was wasted. "We used to have langouste for breakfast, lunch, tea, and dinner, day in and day out . . . until I thought I would never want to look at a langouste again for the rest of my days." But no one who entered Trotsky's household dared to quibble over minor matters like food. About one Trotskyist who had come to Büyük-Ada a vegetarian, Shachtman joked, "Ah, that Büyük-Ada air! It makes the tamest men carnivorous."[35]

Shachtman won Trotsky's confidence during that first visit to Büyük-Ada. Trotsky could forgive a lot in a person who was loyal and committed to the cause, and Shachtman had loyalty and commitment in abundance. Trotsky decided that he could use Shachtman in his dealings with the various Trotskyist groups. When the Trotskyist movement set up its first International Bureau in 1930, Shachtman became its only non-European member. Every year or two Trotsky would ask him to come to Europe to visit, and after talking at length with Trotsky, Shachtman would set off on missions that could keep him away from the United States for months.

One of these missions brought Shachtman in 1931–32 to the new Spanish republic, which had been proclaimed in the spring of 1931 after dictator Primo de Rivera had been overthrown and the king had abdicated. With the beginning of the Spanish Civil War in 1936, the Spanish republic would become the favorite cause of Communists and leftists around the world, and Trotskyists' criticisms of the republican regime would cut them off from the mainstream of international socialist opinion. All these later criticisms can be found in Shachtman's account of politics in the republic's first months.

Repression against the left and the workers' movement did not begin with General Francisco Franco's 1936 revolt. There was harsh repression even under the left-leaning coalition that first governed the republic, as Shachtman saw during his visit. In the new regime's first weeks, the government suppressed a general strike and imposed martial law in the Catalan working-class center of Barcelona. The hated Civil Guard was used to break strikes, beat up demonstrators, and even fire on peaceful rallies. The government required people to carry internal passports, sent police into union meetings, and jailed its opponents for months at a time without trial. Once again for Shachtman Trotsky's theory explained the republic's "brutally anti-labor character": "The Spanish bourgeoisie now in power is bound by a thousand threads to the old monarchical system and the semi-feudal relationships on the land."

The Spanish Socialist Workers Party led by Francisco Largo Caballero was complicit in all these repressive measures, since three Socialist ministers sat in the first republican government. Largo Caballero had been a Councilor of State even under the dictator Primo de Rivera. The Socialists were incapable of improving people's living standards, Shachtman said. The main working-class opposition to the regime came from the anarchists, strong in the Catalan east. But anarchists' opposition was made fruitless by their refusal to set working-class conquest of power as a goal, he argued. Refusing to recognize the state, anarchists were "completely discomfited and checkmated when the 'social myth' of the state turns up at every corner." Anarchists' refusal to organize workers for insurrection resulted in "bleeding them slowly in futile skirmishes."[36]

Spanish Communists, divided into three different groups, were far weaker than either Socialists or anarchists. The official Communists who were loyal to Stalin had discredited themselves, first by taking no part in the republican revolution, then by calling immediately for its overthrow and replacement by soviets, without even pausing to put forward democratic demands that the government's opponents could rally around. "The Stalinists acted throughout like the man who has come too late for his train and then, after going home because 'there is still time for the next one,' misses that one too," Shachtman said.[37] He already suspected that Stalin preferred not to run the risk of a Spanish socialist revolution, which might set off a European war that would be dangerous to the Soviet regime.

The weakness of Socialists, anarchists, and official Communists left an opening for Catalan and Spanish Trotskyists. Shachtman met and liked the Trotskyist leaders Andreu Nin and Juan Andrade. He was excited at the prospects open to them. "A successful proletarian revolt in Spain . . . is an 'absurdity' only to such people as regarded a Bolshevik victory as absurd in the early part of 1917," Shachtman said.[38] If Trotskyists could push aside the floundering Stalinists, build up a strong communist party, and lead a revolution, international Trotskyism would get the same powerful momentum behind it that bolshevism had gotten from the Russian Revolution.

Trotsky and his followers were convinced in the late 1920s that Stalin and his faction were heading to the right. Trotsky attacked Soviet leaders for making too many concessions to farmers and merchants and doing too little to collectivize agriculture and build up industry. He believed that even if the bureaucrats running the Soviet Union put up episodic resistance to capitalist forces, they would always end by making more concessions. He still saw capital and labor as the two fundamental forces in conflict in Soviet society and thought that the bureaucracy was only a vacillating, fragmented force between the two important ones. He expected the bureaucracy to be torn apart between capital and labor as the conflict between them intensified. Within the International in the late 1920s, Trotsky attacked the leadership for its softness and its misplaced faith in trade union leaders and middle-class nationalists. Shachtman and Cannon pointed to the rightward course of U.S. Communists under Jay Lovestone. Trotskyists were convinced that U.S. capitalism was headed for severe storms that would show the foolishness of Lovestone's strategy. They expected rank-and-file Communists to grow more discontented and listen more attentively to Trotskyist criticisms.

But Trotskyists were wrong in some important ways about the Soviet Union, wrong about the Communist International, and wrong about the U.S. Communist Party. Above all, Trotsky drastically underestimated the dynamism of the Stalinist bureaucracy and the solidity of the social system it was creating. No sooner had Shachtman become a Trotskyist than he had to begin a rethinking of Trotskyism that lasted throughout the 1930s and 1940s.

New developments began to diverge from Trotsky's predictions almost as soon as he was expelled from the party in November 1927. That winter the wealthier farmers (*kulaks*) in the Soviet Union, discontented with grain prices and with the shortage of industrial goods for them to buy, failed to sell enough grain to the cities, where the workers were dependent on it for their survival. Stalin resorted to forced requisitions of grain for the first time since the civil war years of 1918–21. The requisitions were often brutal, and moderates in the party leadership were outraged. But the same crisis recurred with the 1928 harvest, and the balance in top party circles shifted in Stalin's favor. Stalin began repeating Trotsky's warnings about the threat from the party's right wing. By 1929 Stalin, willingly or unwillingly, was heading for the confrontation with farmers that he had been avoiding throughout the 1920s.

Stalin ended up carrying out a far more rapid and violent transformation of Soviet society than Trotsky had ever dreamed of. In the space of a year Stalin herded most of the USSR's rural inhabitants into collective farms. By 1930, as farmers slaughtered the livestock and resisted working the land they felt had been stolen from them, the Soviet Union faced chaos and starvation. Epidemics of cholera, dysentery, and typhoid swept the country. People ate the bark off trees or even one another. Stalin retreated, allowing many farmers to regain their private plots. But in 1931 Stalin again reversed direction and speeded up collectivization. Meanwhile he kept pushing up the rates of industrial growth demanded by his first Five Year Plan—up to the 20 percent rate of growth he had ridiculed when Trotsky suggested it and higher still. Hours and days of work were stretched, real wages were cut to provide funds for investment, and output in heavy industry skyrocketed.

The zigzags in Stalin's policy allowed Trotskyists to say at first that he would never stick to his program, or at least that he would face challenges in the party and be forced to welcome the Trotskyists back. Shachtman argued that Stalin's anti-*kulak* slogans could not be taken at face value.[39] But Trotsky gradually shifted the main thrust of his criticisms. Without denying the gains the Soviet Union was making, he pointed out that Stalin's policies were driving the country further from socialism in at least as many ways as they were moving it closer. The limited role workers had played in managing the economy at the end of the 1920s had been taken away from them. The Communist Party had ceased to be a workers' party in almost anything but name, since workers were swamped and manipulated by government bureaucrats. As real incomes fell and incentives to make people work harder grew, the economic gap between bureaucrats and workers and the inequalities among workers widened. The undemocratic character of the regime grew more pronounced.

Stalin's new course had important consequences outside the USSR as well. By 1929 Stalin was imposing a "panic-stricken, chartless ultra-radicalism" on the world's Communists.[40] According to the International's analysis, capitalism in the early 1930s had entered a "third period" of imminent collapse. In this situation the main enemy of Communists everywhere was not the rising fascist movement or conservatives but social democrats, who would combine guile with repression to distract workers from revolution and were labeled "social-fascists." The tactics dictated by this "third period" line were endless ideological attacks on other leftists, street fighting, and splits in non-Communist-controlled unions.

In the United States, Lovestone was deserted by most of his supporters and expelled from the Communist Party when he resisted "third period" tactics. By 1930 an old friend of Cannon's from prewar Kansas City, Earl Browder, emerged as the party's new general secretary. Communists ordered all their trade union supporters into futile splits and weak Communist-controlled unions.

Shachtman said that the theory of "social-fascism" had "brought the Communist movement to its knees." He warned that trade union splits and heavy-handed party control of the new unions were decimating the Communists' base: "The workers are not chessmen that can be moved about unresistingly by 'master strategists.'" The Communist Party could not be saved from isolation without a rebirth of democracy in its ranks, he said. But Communists' change of course confused Trotskyists, he said later.[41] They had foreseen the party's going further and further to the right, and it was not.

Meanwhile the sneaking admiration that most U.S. Communists had had for Trotsky withered under an intensive campaign of accusations and physical attacks. Lovestone's replacement by Browder made no difference. To Trotskyists' shock, one of the first public meetings they tried to hold was broken up by Communists with "blackjacks, knives, lead pipes, brass knuckles and other subtle political arguments." Although Trotskyists ("female as well as male!" Shachtman said) somehow managed to defend their meetings from disruption, the attacks went on unremittingly for two or three years. Shachtman marveled years later at Communists' "extraordinary hostility" toward Trotskyists.

> The source of this hostility was deep and it was strong: the over-whelmingly passionate attachment that every Communist had to the Soviet regime, to its leadership as the incarnation of the Bolshevik Revolution . . . which was under constant siege from a hated encircling capitalist world.[42]

The Communist attacks solidified Shachtman's conviction that he and other Trotskyists were right. Why else would Communist leaders be so defensive and resort to such outrageous lies? He could see that those who stayed in the party were forced to accept absurdities. In an otherwise respectful obituary for German Communist leader Klara Zetkin, he said that the best of Communists were suffering from "a gag in the mouth . . . a terrible spiritual degradation."[43] He was all the more convinced that disseminating the facts and promoting free discussion would guarantee Trotskyists victory in the end.

Meanwhile the Trotskyists tacitly began to function as an independent group rather than as a Communist faction. They focused on what little work in the unions and among the unemployed they could manage with their small forces. Shachtman assembled a small staff that kept the Communist League going. Al Glotzer, who had moved to New York to run the office while Shachtman went to Europe, stayed in New York after Shachtman came back, working in the subway nine hours a day, sometimes seven days a week, and helping out in the office in his free hours. Maurice Spector, the Canadian Trotskyist sympathizer, also moved to New York after being expelled from the Communist Party of Canada. Spector easily fit into the group around Shachtman, since he too was a young Jew born in Eastern Europe. Often after putting the *Militant* to bed the group would go off to an Italian restaurant on Second Avenue.

Trotskyists were involved less in activism than in propaganda for Trotsky's views. Shachtman founded a small Trotskyist publishing firm. In 1929 they issued Trotsky's critique of the Communist International's program, their "bible," as a pamphlet. In 1930 Shachtman got hold of a German edition of the previously unknown, missing second section, which he translated and published as a second pamphlet. He went on to translate Trotsky's book on permanent revolution from German (which he modestly remarked was "easy for me"), and told Trotsky that the Trotskyists were "proud and happy to have been able to issue the book in our own name."[44] To publish his and others' translations he founded Pioneer Publishers. Its list grew: a pamphlet on the situation in Germany, one on Stalin's Five Year Plan, one on the Spanish Revolution, one on French trade unions. Ownership of their own linotype machine allowed Trotskyists to put out a newspaper in Yiddish and one in Greek with a simple change of character sets.

Shachtman could count on his family to ease the hardships of a revolutionary organizer's life. On Friday nights he and Billie Ramloff would have dinner with his parents and sister. Often Glotzer would come along. Soon Glotzer was bringing along a companion of his own: Edith Harvey, still legally married to a man who had worked alongside Shachtman as the *Young Worker*'s business manager. Ramloff and Harvey, an intelligent, strong-minded woman a little older than Glotzer, were best friends. They completed a warm little circle around the Communist League office.

Yet the work got harder, not easier. Shachtman had come back from Büyük-Ada with political guidance and inspiration but not the money the Trotskyists needed. Trotsky urged him to save the weekly *Militant*, but the only practical help Trotsky could offer was the profits from the Yiddish edition of his autobiography. Shachtman was utterly discouraged.

> I am essentially responsible for . . . everything under the sun. I suppose it would have been the better part of self-satisfied wisdom and caution to have retreated, and continued to retreat, at the very beginning. Unfortunately, I cannot yet, in spite of everything, get it into my thick, stubborn head that such a course was more correct than the one decided upon. . . . It is with difficulty that I turn away from this subject, because in less than two hours it has become like a gargoyle fixed before me and mocking me.

By the end of July 1930, Shachtman had to admit failure in the effort to keep the *Militant* a weekly. It became a semimonthly again.[45]

Shachtman's frustration resulted inevitably from the constraints Trotskyists worked under in the early 1930s. They were still trying to reach and recruit Communists, yet the Communist movement was one of the last places they could expect to get a hearing. Communist League membership reached about a hundred in the year of its foundation; it barely reached 200 during the next three years. During those same years, with the impetus of the Depression, the Communists began a spurt of growth that gave them something approaching mass influence. In the history of the U.S. left, only the Socialist Party in the 1910s had a greater impact on U.S. political life than Communists did in the 1930s. Communists' success made them even less disposed to question their leaders and doctrines. By the early 1930s, the idea of the Trotskyists' gaining readmission to the Communist Party seemed farfetched. "I think that we all knew in our hearts that it was just about impossible, short of a miracle, and there were very few of us trained to believe in miracles," Shachtman said.[46] The Trotskyists were in a dead-end alley.

Their difficulties took a toll on their handful of leaders, whose hard jobs building the movement did not always give them enough money to eat or pay the rent. For Cannon, who had years of radical activity behind him and had led far more impressive organizations, the toll showed in resignation and a tendency to hoard his energy for a time when it could be spent more fruitfully. When his first wife died, Cannon and Karsner had two more children to take care of, and he was forced to take a job with the *New York Tribune* circulation department. He drank more. He talked about moving to Kansas City and getting a job in a hotel with his brother there.[47]

For Shachtman, trying his wings as a leader, the toll showed in impatience and resentment toward Cannon, who he felt was not pulling his weight. As Shachtman struggled to keep putting out a weekly *Militant*, he wrote to Spector, "Pardon me if I sound bitter, but when [Cannon] proposes at this date that *we return to a semi-monthly* . . . I cannot but entertain a harsh resentment."[48] Abern, Glotzer, and Spector joined in Shachtman's criticisms. Cannon, stung, accused Shachtman of wanting to squander Trotskyists' limited resources on extravagant, hopeless projects. Soon long-time allies of Cannon's, midwestern trade unionists such as Arne Swabeck in Chicago and Ray Dunne in Minneapolis, lined up against the younger leaders in the New York office. From these petty beginnings arose charges and countercharges that divided the Trotskyists through most of the 1930s and 1940s.

Cannon argued that he had been the leader of the Communist Party's "proletarian kernel" and was still the leader of the "proletarian kernel" in the Communist League. He seemed to imply that he had an ironclad claim to leadership. He dismissed his critics as middle-class journalists and intellectuals who did not understand working-class politics in their bones the way he did. Many rank-and-file workers who came around the group sympathized with his demands for loyalty and his impatience with intellectual discussion. The U.S. working class has often been suspicious of intellectuals for good reasons, since people with education have often used it to manipulate or domineer over working people. Cannon trusted and appealed to these working-class instincts.

But this egalitarian strength of U.S. working-class culture has also been a weakness for revolutionary working-class politics. The countries where Marxism has been strongest—Germany and Russia before 1917, France and Italy after 1945, and more recently Latin American countries—have each had a strong philosophical tradition that gave Marxism a cultural context. Working-class radicals in these countries have identified with this intellectual tradition. They have been willing to work hard to master it and, as a result, have acquired the self-confidence to challenge middle-class leaders in debate. Lack of this intellectual climate among U.S. workers has often left them at the mercy of trade union officials with a superficial, often procapitalist outlook and of middle-class intellectuals who show little interest in working-class struggles. Shachtman's eagerness to promote debate and theoretical discussion among U.S. Trotskyists showed a conviction of their importance that Cannon did not fully share.

Shachtman wanted to claim Communist traditions as "*our* traditions." But he kept an open, critical mind about the traditions of the Cannon faction. He later said that "nine-tenths" of the Cannon group's platform, such as the pro-labor party position it adopted in 1925, was wrong. He and his allies charged that Cannon could not abide critics and wanted to impose on the Communist League a "SPURIOUS AND STRANGULATING 'MONO-LITHISM.'" This was the beginning of complaints about the Cannon "regime" that would persist in U.S. Trotskyism even after Cannon's death. Shachtman's followers warned against giving old Cannonites special status and creating an atmosphere of "hereditary succession."[49] They encouraged younger Trotskyists' ambitions and pushed to add young recruits to the National Committee.

In international Trotskyism Shachtman showed the same desire for freewheeling discussion and tolerance for differences that raised Cannon's hackles in the United States. He strained his friendship with Trotsky by questioning Trotsky's intervention in fights among German and French Trotskyists. Shachtman, who had come to believe that he could say whatever he thought to Trotsky, was hurt and bewildered. He was also afraid that Cannon would use Trotsky's reproaches against him. But he never dreamed of breaking with Trotsky. "I could wish for nothing more ardently" than reconciliation, he told Trotsky. He condemned his own second thoughts about Trotsky's stands. Trotsky expressed "great relief" that Shachtman had given in and their friendship could "now develop unhurt."[50]

Trotsky exerted himself to reconcile Shachtman with Cannon. He chided Cannon's allies for their "intransigence" and Shachtman for his "impatience." By the summer of 1933, Shachtman was ready to give up the dispute. He urged his allies to follow Trotsky's advice. "If your estimate of Cannon and his group is correct," he added, "you have only to wait."[51]

Shachtman ventured to disagree with Trotsky on one more issue in the early 1930s: the Black movement. Communists and Trotskyists were unique among pre-1950s U.S. white radicals in the attention they paid to injustices perpetrated against African Americans. Their awareness of racism resulted from pressures put on them by comrades abroad, particularly by Lenin on the Communists and later Trotsky on the Trotskyists. Before they experienced these pressures, Communists were happy enough to continue in the tradition of Debsian socialism, which saw racism as a shame and something that should be banished from the socialist movement but not as one of its particular concerns. Lenin's vision of a revolutionary party as a "tribune of all the oppressed" forced Communists to give African-American struggles a higher priority than any white radicals had since Reconstruction.

Lenin and Trotsky saw African-American oppression and liberation in the same framework as other oppressed people's struggles around the world. They tended to define African Americans as an "oppressed nation" or "oppressed national minority" within the United States, fighting for its national rights. This approach reached a kind of culmination in the early 1930s when the Communists called for a "Black Belt republic" in Black-majority areas of the South.

Most Trotskyists, like most radicals outside the Communist Party, thought that the Black Belt position made no sense. Although the September 1931 Communist League convention reached no formal decision on the issue, the delegates had an informal consensus that the slogan should be rejected. Among Trotskyists, Shachtman was one of the most eager to repudiate it and develop an alternative strategy. By the end of 1932 he was speaking for the League and posing the alternative: "the Negroes in America: national or proletarian revolution?"[52]

Trotsky was not attached to the Black Belt position, but he would never frame the issue as working-class revolution or African-American national revolution. He saw the African-American movement in the United States as an autonomous movement that over the course of time would make its own particular demands: if not a separate state, then African-American community institutions in some other form. Shachtman did not share Trotsky's interest in a separate African-American movement, which seemed to him to have value only in limited struggles against segregation and discrimination. African Americans' already striking integration into the U.S. working class seemed more important to him in the long run. "Tens of millions of

American workers and poor farmers" suffered under the same system that African Americans did, he said. The whole U.S. labor movement was "inseparably connected with the position and interests of the black millions." He came to realize that he was headed outside the framework of Trotsky's approach. In April 1933 he told Trotsky that he could not agree with Trotsky's analysis of African-American struggles in the United States. He laid out his own viewpoint in an eighty-page document on "Communism and the Negro Question."[53]

The situation of African Americans in the modern United States was the consequence of events after the Civil War, Shachtman said, and especially of the fact that the northern capitalists who won the Civil War were willing to give African-American freedmen "the short end of the stick" afterwards. The democratic revolution in the South advocated by Radical Reconstructionist Republicans never occurred. Instead the old slaveholders became the rulers of the new South and used their power to reduce African-American tenants to "unspeakable" misery. As a result, after the turn of the century, African Americans migrated from the southern countryside to mostly northern industrial cities. African Americans had fallen from 36 percent of the southern population in 1880 to 24.7 percent in 1930, Shachtman pointed out, and the urban African-American population had risen from a million and a half to five million. The 1930s was "the epoch of the industrial Negro, the leader of his race, the comrade in arms of the white proletarian."

The capitalist response to African-American problems was "the rope or torch of the lynching mob." For that reason the first fight African Americans had to wage was against the racism that isolated and cowed them, against Jim Crow. But Shachtman had little use for the policies of either the mainstream Black movement or most of the white left. Middle-class African Americans lived off of segregation and the separate Black market that segregation created. They wanted better lives for African American "roughly in the same sense that the Standard Oil Company favored the adoption by the Chinese of the kerosene lamp." They were willing to cooperate with white liberals in running groups like the National Association for the Advancement of Colored People, which opposed African Americans' fighting "belligerently" or "offensively."

Shachtman was just as opposed to the color blindness of the Socialist Party and its leader Norman Thomas. He quoted African-American socialist W. E. B. Du Bois against Thomas, but went on to criticize Du Bois's scheme for African-American cooperatives. All these reformist schemes were bound to fail because they remained within capitalist limits. Shachtman was sure that capitalists would never "even attempt half as much in the emancipation of the Negro" as was attempted during Reconstruction.

He said that the Communist program for a Black Belt republic was also wrong. African Americans do not constitute a nation any more than Jews do, he argued; neither has a distinct language, a distinct territory (any boundaries drawn for the Black Belt would be arbitrary and exclude most African Americans), or a common culture. The demand for a separate African-American nation had never been raised in the Communist International under Lenin. The whole idea was the result of Communists' abandonment of permanent revolution and their search for halfway solutions that they hoped would be palatable to middle-class people, he said. But there was no halfway solution for African Americans. "The Negro will not only be liberated from the wage slavery of today, but the survivals of feudalism and slavery will be exterminated, as a 'by-product' of the military-political struggle of the last progressive class in American society—the class of black and white proletarians—to establish a socialist nation."

The real workers' movement had always tried to unite with African Americans against racism, according to Shachtman—from the National Labor Union of the 1860s to the Industrial Workers of the World, Communist Party, and United Mine Workers. There should be no wall dividing African-American struggles from workers' struggles. "The two flow together in a single movement." Shachtman acknowledged that white workers bore the main responsibility for the choice between unity with African Americans and victory or division and defeat. But he was unclear in laying out how this unity should be achieved. He said only that whites should join in "the uncompromising demand for full and equal rights for the oppressed Negro."

U.S. Trotskyists turned away from Shachtman's distinctive approach in 1939, when they adopted a position worked out by Trotsky and Black Trinidadian Trotskyist C. L. R. James that looked toward an independent African-American struggle. Even in the 1940s Shachtman's followers never formally abandoned Trotsky's views for his. But stands they took over the years illustrate the positive and negative consequences of his approach. They fought together with African-American workers to increase African-American participation in the unions and keep prejudice out of the factories during the Second World War. But when soldiers came back from the war in 1945 and many African Americans were fired to make way for returning whites, Shachtman and his fellow leaders came out against the idea of African-American "super-seniority" to protect African-American gains. They said that such a proposal would "sow discord."[54] Sending African-American women who had seized wartime opportunities to escape from poorly paid and demeaning domestic work back into it at the war's end apparently did not sow discord. Racism caught Shachtman's attention mainly when it disrupted working-class unity in some obvious way.

During the 1930s, 1940s, and 1950s, all Communists and Trotskyists were united in their support for African-American struggles against racism, struggles that the great majority of other whites viewed with hostility or indifference. The differences between Shachtman and other U.S. radicals on African-American issues seemed relatively unimportant.

If Trotsky is remembered for one contribution he made after he fell from power in the Soviet Union, that contribution is undoubtedly his warning about the danger of German fascism. After the Nazis got six million votes in 1930, Trotsky said that whoever did not see the danger of fascism was "either blind or a braggart." While German Communists were still treating Social Democrats as their main enemy and saying that after Hitler's day theirs would come, Trotsky urged them repeatedly to unite with Social Democrats to stop the Nazis' rise to power. German Trotskyists energetically distributed Trotsky's writings in hopes of changing Communist policy. In response, Al Glotzer found when he visited Europe in 1931–32 that Communists were "denouncing Trotsky every day."[55] The vindication of Trotsky's warnings lifted his and his movement's prestige. But the failure to stop Adolf Hitler set back European socialism for years. Trotskyists saw official Communism as an obstacle not only in the fight for socialism but even in the defense of basic democratic freedoms under capitalism.

Shachtman joined in Trotsky's warnings. As early as 1929, Shachtman, accepting Trotsky's characterization of the United States as the "basic counterrevolutionary force of the modern epoch," warned that U.S. policies were spreading war and dictatorship. In the Western Hemisphere, the U.S. government was the direct source of violence and repression, as when President Herbert Hoover sent marines to Nicaragua and Haiti. In Europe, U.S. policies had equally deadly, though indirect, results. The United States tried to extract reparations from Germany and war debt payments from the Allies. Shachtman said that U.S. capital was trying to find a way out of the "maelstrom of world economics" at Germany's expense. Even before the Nazis' rise he predicted that Germany's rulers would squeeze the working class hard in order to get the money that the United States, Britain, and France demanded. The political result of these economic pressures was a movement for a "naked dictatorship."[56]

Back from his visit to Europe at the beginning of 1932, Shachtman warned of the Nazis by name with redoubled urgency. A Nazi victory would not only "exterminate the flower of the German proletariat, but would inaugurate a prolonged period of reaction throughout Europe," he said. Yet Communists not only rejected unity with Social Democrats but watched the Nazis' rise "without firing anything more deadly than a manifesto . . . from exile."[57]

Shachtman explained that the preservation of German capitalist democracy was in the interest not only of the working class but also of at least part of the capitalist class. In a country with a well-organized working class, he said, the ruling elite would usually prefer to conciliate and co-opt the left rather than attack it frontally. As long as order could somehow be maintained by constitutional means, the state would keep the fascists "in reserve." But the pressure to increase profits at workers' expense was growing because of the Depression. German unions and socialist organizations were the main obstacle.[58] Divided and weakened as they were by Communist and Social Democratic policies, they made a tempting target. Shachtman was not surprised that in these circumstances Germany's ruling and middle classes turned to Hitler.

Hitler's appointment as chancellor in January 1933 galvanized Trotskyists into a frenzy of activity. They argued that fascism could still be stopped in Germany if only German Communists changed course and acted decisively. No effort could be spared: Even pressure from the remote United States had to be brought to bear. Over 500 people turned up in Manhattan to listen to Shachtman and Cannon talk about the German events, and another 500 in the Bronx, in February 1933. Official Communist spokespeople even showed up and took the floor, but there was nothing they could do to stop the wave of criticisms that rolled at them from Communist sympathizers in the audience.[59] Although Trotskyists had been managing to put the *Militant* out once a week again through most of 1931 and 1932 only by struggling and begging, they seized on people's eagerness to read about Germany by putting it out three times a week now.

Shachtman wrote lead articles about Germany under front-page banner headlines in almost every issue. He had predicted the worst outcome in Germany over a year before, but he spared no effort now to prove himself wrong. A victorious Hitler, he said, would "crush every semblance of organized strength and [militancy] in the German working class, beginning with the Communist party, the spearhead of the proletariat, following with the social democracy and the big trade union movement." He insisted, "Whoever even hints to the working class that there is no real difference between the 'democratic' rule of the bourgeoisie and the Fascist rule by torch and sword . . . is playing the game to the best interests of Fascism!" Expressing his hopes rather than his true conviction, he said, "It is entirely unthinkable that the German working class, millions strong, trained in the school of the class struggle for years, having at its head the most powerful Communist party in the world outside of the Soviet Union, will permit the Nazi assassins to remain in power without a violent struggle." A general strike could still topple Hitler's coalition government, as a general strike had stymied a military coup attempt in 1920. "It is not too late!" he urged. "But the time to act is now!"[60]

At the end of February, after the German Reichstag building was set on fire (an action Nazis used even if they did not plan it), Nazi terror began in earnest. The German Communist newspaper *Rote Fahne* was shut down. All 100 Communist deputies were arrested, along with thousands of other Communists across Germany. All Communist and Social Democratic election activity was prohibited. *"For what is the party waiting before it acts?"* Shachtman asked. *"Until the streets of Germany run red with the blood of an unprepared, disunited, demoralized working class?"*[61]*

He blamed Social Democrats—who had counted on authoritarian right-wingers like German President Paul von Hindenburg to stop Hitler—even more than Communists for what was happening. Shachtman breathed contempt for Social Democrats who looked toward the Reichstag elections Hitler called for in March as the moment to save democracy. The decisive battle in the streets would be over by then, he was sure. When the Yiddish Socialist *Forward* in the United States told its readers that Hitler would be a "constitutional Chancellor," Shachtman raged, "Everybody has his role. That of the social democracy is base treason." "To talk about 'struggle on the basis of the Constitution' at a time like this is deliberately to surrender the German working class, bound and gagged, to the butchers of Fascism," he said. Shachtman called on Communists to expose Social Democrats' *"sham, verbal* opposition" to fascism by demanding that they act and not just talk.[63] One of his criticisms of Communist leaders was that their failure to make any proposal for a common fight-back made even social democratic passivity look good to workers, as shown when the Communist vote fell 20 percent in the March elections and the Social Democratic vote rose slightly.

Trotskyists acknowledged their failure to save the German left when the *Militant* became a weekly again on 18 March. Shachtman got ready for a trip to Europe, where Trotskyists would gather to reassess their politics in light

---

*In the midst of this crisis Shachtman had one last factional dispute with Cannon that foreshadowed later, major disagreements. Cannon suggested that Trotskyists call on the Soviet army to come to the rescue of the German working class. Shachtman denied that the Soviet army could make up in this way for German Communists' failure to fight fascism. Soviet intervention could only be a weapon in the hands of an already mobilized working class, not a foreign substitute for action by native workers. He pointed out that in July 1920, when a Red Army counteroffensive against a Polish attack reached the frontiers of ethnic Poland, Trotsky alone of top Bolshevik leaders had insisted that the army could not create a revolution in Poland by conquest. Trotsky had again opposed using the Red Army to overthrow the social democratic government of Georgia in February 1921. Shachtman quoted Trotsky's words: "Soviet Russia does not by any means intend to make its military power take the place of the revolutionary efforts of the proletariat of other countries."[62]

of the German disaster. By the time he reached Europe in May, German Communists were in jail or exile, their newspapers banned, their party virtually destroyed.

Social Democrats' share in responsibility for the rollback of democracy in Europe was confirmed for Shachtman by the triumph of Engelbert Dollfuss's dictatorship in Austria in February 1934. Dollfuss did not crush the Austrian left effortlessly, however, unlike in Germany. Because the Austrian Communist Party was insignificant, the Austrian left was united. Vienna was a Socialist stronghold, complete with a miniature welfare state, strong unions, and a Socialist militia. When Dollfuss attacked Vienna's working-class institutions, the workers fought back fiercely for several days.

For Shachtman, Austrian social democrats' unchallenged prior leadership only compounded their responsibility for the left's defeat. He rejected the social democratic movement's attempt to "restore its exploded prestige by a parasitic association with the heroism of the Austrian rebels." Socialist leaders had sat back passively while their militia was dissolved, the Communist Party banned, the Socialist newspaper closed, and the constitution abrogated, without giving any signal for resistance. They had talked about a general strike but failed to organize one. They had offered to join Dollfuss's cabinet and grant him the right to rule by decree for two years. In short, Shachtman said, they "hung pathetically at the coat-tails of Dollfuss until they were contemptuously kicked away." The ill-prepared, leaderless Vienna revolt "sounded the death knell of the once mighty Austrian Social Democracy."[64]

The spread of dictatorships and both Communists' and Social Democrats' failure to resist effectively made Trotsky determined to leave Turkey for a more central European country, from which he hoped to play a more active role in reshaping the left. In the summer of 1933 he managed to get a visa for France, which he foresaw would become the pivot of European working-class politics after the German left's defeat. Trotsky had chosen Shachtman, "a good, one hundred per cent American with a good, one hundred per cent American passport," as his "commissar for foreign affairs" to handle the trip. Trotsky traveled secretly, which complicated Shachtman's life somewhat in making the travel arrangements. Shachtman booked the passage under his own name, adding only, "and party."

> I remember the agent was very curious as to who the party was made up of, and when I explained to him with a wink that the man and woman involved were foreigners in a very difficult situation, the French manager of the steamship office—I remember this with real hilarity—returned my wink very significantly and said, "Ah, monsieur, I understand perfectly."

The boat left Istanbul in July 1933, and for the whole week of the voyage

Shachtman stood guard over Trotsky's cabin with a couple of pistols. "What I would have done if there had been a real attack," he commented later, "I don't pretend to know." But luckily his nonexistent military skills were not called upon. Trotsky was taken off the boat in the Marseilles harbor by his son Lyova, and Shachtman did not see Trotsky again in France.[65]

Notes

1. RMS 23, 118, 120.
2. James Cannon, *The History of American Trotskyism*, 50.
3. Shachtman, "Twenty-five years of American Trotskyism," NI v 20 n 1 (Jan.– Feb. 1954), 16.
4. Shachtman, *Genesis of Trotskyism*, 25.
5. DW v 3 n 104 (13 May 1926), 1; DW v 3 n 105 (14 May 1926), 1.
6. Interview with Glotzer (24 Mar. 1989), s 4; Shachtman, "A visit to the island of Prinkipo," M v 3 n 19 (10 May 1930), 4; M v 4 n 26 (10 Oct. 1931), 3.
7. Shachtman, "Introduction" (15 Mar. 1936), in Leon Trotsky, *The Third International after Lenin*, xii–xiii.
8. Shachtman, *Genesis of Trotskyism*, 21.
9. RMS 160–61, 165.
10. CP PC (27 Oct. 1928), MSC b 1 f 28 (r 3345); Cannon, Abern, and Shachtman, "For the Russian opposition" (27 Oct. 1928), M v 1 n 1; (15 Nov. 1928), 1–2.
11. RMS 167–68.
12. Interview with Glotzer by Bloom (13–21 Dec. 1983), OHAL, 17–25; Glotzer to Drucker (6 Jan. 1990), 3.
13. Theodore Draper, *American Communism and Soviet Russia*, 371–72; RMS 191, 176; M v 1 n 3 and v 2 n 1 and 2 (15 Dec. 1928, 1 and 15 Jan. 1929); "The organization of the Communist opposition" (18 May 1929), PMA b 11 f 43.
14. DW v 4 n 203 (8 Sept. 1927), 1; M v 2 n 16 (15 Oct. 1929), 2.
15. Interview with Glotzer (24 Mar. 1989), s 3.
16. Interview with Glotzer (4 Apr. 1989), s 9.
17. RMS 69; Cannon, *The History of American Trotskyism*, 214.
18. Jacobson, "The two deaths of Max Shachtman," *New Politics* v 10 n 2 (Winter 1973), 95; interview with P. Jacobson (21 Apr. 1984); Maurice Isserman, *If I Had a Hammer*, 41; Irving Howe, *A Margin of Hope*, 54; Haskell, "Max Shachtman," 1; Kahn, "Max Shachtman," NA v 10 n 22 (15 Nov. 1972), 4.
19. Interview with Haskell (15 July 1983), Isserman, *If I Had a Hammer*, 42; Glotzer to Shachtman [note, nd], MSC b 29 f 7 (r 3378); Novack, "Max Shachtman," *International Socialist Review* v 34 n 2 (Feb. 1973), 27.
20. Interview with Glotzer (4 Apr. 1989), s 9; Jacobson to Drucker (10 Sept. 1992), 7.
21. Interview with Geltman (22 Mar. 1989), s 1; interview with Glotzer (24 Mar. 1989), s 2; interview with Kahn (7 Apr. 1989), s 1.
22. Interview with Kahn (7 Apr. 1989), s 1; interview with Geltman (22 Mar. 1989), s 1.
23. Jacobson, "The two deaths," 96.
24. Shachtman, "American imperialism shall not throttle the Chinese revolution, "

LD v 2 n 7 (July 1927), 104; Shachtman, "Introduction" (7 Aug. 1931), in Leon Trotsky, *Problems of the Chinese Revolution*, 4–5.

25. Shachtman, "How long can Sandino hold out?" DW v 5 n 67 (20 Mar. 1928), 6.
26. Shachtman, "Palestine—pogrom or revolution?" M v 2 n 15 (1 Oct. 1929), 5.
27. Shachtman, "The proletariat and peasantry in the Indian revolution," M v 3 n 6 (8 Feb. 1930), 6.
28. Shachtman, "The Indian revolution at the cross-roads," M v 3 n 5 (1 Feb. 1930), 3; Shachtman, "MacDonald's assault on India," M v 3 n 20 (17 May 1930), 1.
29. Shachtman, "Trotsky's deportation," M v 2 n 3 (1 Feb. 1929), 1, 6; M v 2 n 7 (1 Apr. 1929), 1.
30. Cannon, *The History of American Trotskyism*, 55, 59, 182; RMS 351–52; Isaac Deutscher, *The Prophet Outcast*, 476, puts Shachtman's visit in "early 1929" and RMS says "1929 or 1930," but I have found no evidence for a visit before 1930.
31. RMS 252–53; Shachtman, "Radicalism in the thirties," in Simon, ed., *As We Saw the Thirties*, 43–44; Shachtman, "The end of socialism," NI v 20 n 2 (Mar.–Apr. 1954), 67.
32. Interview with Geltman (22 Mar. 1989), s 2; Shachtman to Novack (21 Sept. 1963), MSC b 30 f 32 (r 3381).
33. Shachtman to Abern (22 Mar. 1930), PMA b 11 f 41.
34. RMS 361; Deutscher, *Prophet Outcast*, 476; Trotsky to Glotzer (3 June 1932), Leon Trotsky, *Writings*, supplement v 1, 118.
35. RMS 354–56; Shachtman to Trotsky (2 May 1930), TA 5035.
36. Shachtman, "The recent outbreaks in Spain," M v 5 n 5 (30 Jan. 1932), 4; Shachtman, "Spain's bourgeoisie on the offensive," M v 5 n 6 (6 Feb. 1932), 4.
37. Shachtman, "The Spanish Communist Party in the revolution," M v 5 n 10 (5 Mar. 1932), 4.
38. Shachtman, "The theory of Stalinism and the revolution in Spain," M v 4 n 9 (1 May 1931), 5.
39. Shachtman, "Slogans for today," M v 1 n 1 (15 Nov. 1928), 8.
40. Shachtman, "Introduction" (15 Mar. 1936), in Leon Trotsky, *The Third International after Lenin*, xxiv.
41. Shachtman, *Genesis of Trotskyism*, 46; Shachtman, "Left wing needle trades crisis," M v 3 n 21 (24 May 1930), 3; RMS 206–8.
42. Shachtman, "Twenty-five years of American Trotskyism," NI v 20 n 1 (Jan.–Feb. 1954), 12; Shachtman, "Radicalism in the thirties," in Simon, ed., *As We Saw the Thirties*, 17.
43. Shachtman, "The death of com. Klara Zetkin," M v 6 n 36 (22 July 1933), 4.
44. Shachtman to Trotsky (17 Dec. 1930), TA 5040; Shachtman to Trotsky (17 June 1931), TA 5046.
45. Shachtman, "A visit to the island of Prinkipo," M v 3 n 19 (10 May 1930), 4; Shachtman to Abern (22 Mar. 1930), PMA b 11 f 41; M v 3 n 27 (26 July 1930), 1.
46. Breitman to Wald (17 July 1985), cited in Alan Wald, *The New York Intellectuals*, 110; RMS 197.
47. Wald, *NY Intellectuals*, 171.
48. Shachtman to Spector (8 Feb. 1930), MSC b 6 f 22 (r 3353).
49. Shachtman speech to New York membership [1932], MSC b 6 f 15 (r 3353); "Twenty-five years," NI v 20 n 1, 15–16; Abern, Glotzer, and Shachtman, "The situation in the American opposition" (4 June 1932), TA 17238 [also MSC b 39 f 24 (not microfilmed)].
50. Shachtman to Trotsky (13 Mar. 1932), TA 5059; Shachtman to IS (17 June

1932), TA 15412; Trotsky to Shachtman (4 July 1932), TA 10306.
51. Trotsky to Swabeck (7 Mar. 1933) and Trotsky to Shachtman (8 Mar. 1933), in Leon Trotsky, *Writings*, supplement v 1, 212–14; Shachtman to NC minority (9 June 1933), PMA b 11 f 42.
52. M v 4 n 26 (10 Oct. 1931), 3; M v 5 n 49 (10 Dec. 1932).
53. Shachtman to Trotsky (15 Apr. 1933), TA 5070; Shachtman, "Communism and the Negro" [1933], TA 17244.
54. Leon Trotsky, *Writings*, supplement v 1, 407; WP PC statement (16 July 1945), WP bul (29 Oct. 1945), ISM v 5, 784; WP PC, "Resolution on the Negro question" (1 Feb. 1949), WP bul v 4 n 3 (2 Feb. 1949), ISM v 10, 2265, 2263.
55. Leon Trotsky, *The Turn in the Communist International*, 11; Interview with Glotzer by Bloom (13–21 Dec. 1983), OHAL, 31.
56. Trotsky, *The Third International after Lenin*, 8; Shachtman, "Weekly International Reviews," DW v 3 n 250 (4 Nov. 1926), 3; Shachtman, "A new Dawes Plan," M v 2 n 7 (1 Apr. 1929), 3.
57. Shachtman, "Is Stalin preparing new 1923 in Germany?" M v 5 n 3 (16 Jan. 1932), 1, 4.
58. Shachtman, "Hitler in power," M v 6 n 5 (4 Feb. 1933), 1.
59. M v 6 n 1 (7 Jan. 1933), 1.
60. "Hitler in power," M v 6 n 5, 1, 4; Shachtman, "Why is the Comintern silent on Germany?" M v 6 n 6 (11 Feb. 1933), 4.
61. Shachtman, "Fascists frame-up the Communist Party" (28 Feb. 1933), M v 6 n 14 (1 Mar. 1933), 1.
62. Shachtman, "Statement on the dispute over the Red Army and the German situation," CLA bul n 10 (18 Mar. 1933), PMA b 12 f 8.
63. Shachtman, "Hitler lays new trap for workers" (12 Feb. 1933), M v 6 n 7 (13 Feb. 1933), 1; Shachtman, "Hitlerites shut down headquarters of the Communist Party" (26 Feb. 1933), M v 6 n 13 (27 Feb. 1933), 1; Shachtman, "Fascists command police: Shoot the reds!" (21 Feb. 1933), M v 6 n 11 (22 Feb. 1933), 2.
64. Shachtman, "Austrian workers fight historic battle" (1 Feb. 1934), M v 7 n 8 (17 Feb. 1934), 1–2; Shachtman, "Collapse of Austro-Marxism," M v 7 n 9 (24 Feb. 1934), 1.
65. RMS 363–67; Deutscher, *Prophet Outcast*, 260.

3

The New International

Trotsky and Shachtman watched from Büyük-Ada with disbelief in the spring and summer of 1933 as the German Communist Party, the largest revolutionary organization in Europe, collapsed unresisting in the face of the Nazi takeover. German Communist leaders crumbled in the face of the fascist attack; rank-and-file Communists accepted their leaders' disastrous policies almost without protest. By the time Shachtman left Büyük-Ada in July, Trotsky had given up hope of reforming the Communist parties. He called for a new revolutionary party, first in Germany to replace the one that had been destroyed, then in every country in the world outside the Soviet Union. The Communist International was bankrupt, he said. In Shachtman's words, the Third International, once "the revolutionary Phoenix arising out of the ashes of the Second," had become an "ossified frontier patrol of the Soviet Union." A new international, a Fourth International, had to be built.[1]

"The tremendous historical significance of the step we are taking so boldly leaves one almost breathless upon reflection," Shachtman wrote. But he was ready for it. Back in New York in August, he began working out a strategy for building a new revolutionary organization in the United States. He dismissed the U.S. Communist Party as a "sieve," which attracted new members radicalized by the Depression only to lose them because of its misguided policies. It was weighed down by a large proportion of members who depended on the leadership for their salaries: In New York, capital of the party apparatus, about 1,000 out of 3,000 Communists were paid functionaries. Prospects were better for Trotskyists outside the Communist ranks, he said.[2] He exuded optimism about the prospects for a new party in the United States.

His optimism was borne out in the spring and summer of 1934, when general strikes in Toledo, San Francisco, and Minneapolis ended the quiescence of U.S. workers in the face of the Depression. By leading the Minneapolis general strike, which Shachtman helped to victory with an innovative daily strikers' newspaper, Trotskyists gained new stature for themselves on the left. They used their new prominence to rally other radicals, particularly leftists around A. J. Muste, who had led the Toledo general strike, to the idea of a new party and a new international. Shachtman predicted that the U.S. working class was headed for a "speedy revolutionary development" that would put it "in the very front ranks of the world's working class" and that a new U.S. revolutionary party could be formed "in advance of most of the other countries in the world."[3] In December 1934 Trotskyists took a step toward their goal by merging with Muste's followers to form the Workers Party of the United States.

Trotsky said in 1933 that the "revolutionary center of gravity" of the capitalist world, which had moved eastward toward Russia with the revolutions of 1905 and 1917, had now shifted westward.[4] At first he looked toward France, where he expected the next big battles between fascism and the working class to be fought. The 1934 strike wave in the United States made him look hopefully toward the United States as well. Building revolutionary parties in the United States and France became Trotskyists' highest priority. Trotskyism ceased to be a movement based mainly in the Soviet Union, as it had been in the 1920s and early 1930s. For several decades after the mid-1930s, the United States and France would be its two centers.

Trotskyism's turn westward released Shachtman from the dead end in which he had been trapped in the early 1930s, when Trotskyists had been waging a hopeless fight for reinstatement in the Communist Party. New vistas began to open up for him as a writer, editor, activist, and leader. "This is a time for the joy of living," he said.[5]

To reach the growing ranks of new radicals, the new party needed tools: books, pamphlets, a cheaper and more popular newspaper, a high-quality magazine. Shachtman's talents as translator, writer, and editor were in demand. The task that excited him most and demanded most of his time was the Trotskyists' new magazine, the *New International*. One of his assistants, George Novack, remembered decades later the feeling of exhilaration "as the freshly inked pages of the early issues, with a two-colored cover, came off the wheezy press."[6]

The *New International*'s rejection of the "bombast, exaggeration, self-praise and tricky headlines and stories" that Shachtman saw more and more of in the *Daily Worker* impressed independent leftists. Musteite philosophy professor James Burnham contributed further to its intellectual prestige when he joined Shachtman as co-editor. Orders came in from Glasgow, Rotterdam, Capetown, Buenos Aires, Athens, Shanghai, Antwerp, and India. Writers John Dos Passos and Max Eastman praised it. A report in the late 1930s said, "Everyone in Europe reads it, friend and foe alike within revolutionary circles." As editor of the foremost Trotskyist theoretical journal in English, Shachtman became the main exponent of Trotsky's ideas in the English-speaking world. Trotsky chided him jokingly, "Since you have become editor of the best Marxist publication you don't answer old friends' letters any more."[7]

Putting out the monthly *New International* along with the weekly *Militant*, the youth newspaper, the newspapers in Yiddish, Greek, and Polish, and Trotsky's writings "took Herculean efforts," Shachtman said later. "Outsiders simply could not believe that all this was being done by only a few hundred people."[8] Throughout the 1930s there were never more than a few hundred people to do it. The new Workers Party was not a serious rival to the rapidly growing Communist Party, which had tens of thousands of members, let alone a serious threat to the Democrats and Republicans.

After the 1934 Minneapolis strike, James Cannon suggested that Trotskyists use the old Communist call for a labor party to translate their organizing success into the broader political influence they obviously still lacked. The Toledo radicals backed the idea as they helped found the United Auto Workers in 1935–36. The call for a labor party won a short-lived majority at the auto workers' July 1936 convention. Shachtman helped convince the Workers Party to reject it. But in 1938, when Trotsky convinced his U.S. followers to campaign for a labor party after all, Shachtman began a decade-long effort to find tactics and demands that would give the idea reality.

Meanwhile, the political appeal of Democratic President Franklin Roosevelt's New Deal helped ensure that the working-class activism of the mid-1930s did not flow into independent working-class politics. Instead the Communist Party and many trade unionists leaving the Socialist Party swung to support the Democrats in 1936. While European Fourth Internationalists joined mass labor and social democratic parties, U.S. Fourth Internationalists reacted to their new party's isolation by dissolving it and joining the remnant of the Socialist Party, now posing as a broad left-wing alternative to both Democrats and Communists. Trotskyists inside the Socialist Party rejected the idea of building a broader labor party that might have appealed to the growing, militant ranks of the CIO.

Despite the radical ferment of the 1930s, Shachtman and his fellow Trotskyists found themselves swimming against the mainstream of the left. They rejected the New Deal and the Democratic Party, which most radicals embraced. They were even more starkly isolated in their criticisms of the Soviet government. In fact, mainstream leftists in this time of growth and confidence were contributing to the left's later virtual destruction in the Cold War years. The patriotism they espoused in hopes that the U.S. government would be a bulwark against fascism helped foster the uncritical Americanism that would be used against all radicals in the 1950s. The enthusiasm many of them expressed for Stalin's rule in the Soviet Union facilitated the branding of radicals as enemies of democracy.

Shachtman rejected both the broader left's flirtation with patriotism and its identification with Stalinism. He was with Trotsky in Norway in 1936 when Stalin began putting most of bolshevism's foremost leaders on trial and arresting and sometimes executing large numbers of Communists. Shachtman helped Trotsky plan an international campaign against the purge trials. In his book *Behind the Moscow Trial* and in dozens of speeches he gave as he toured the United States, Shachtman pleaded with U.S. leftists to speak out in defense of persecuted Soviet radicals. As the massacre continued, he denounced what he saw as the betrayal of the original communist vision. He began to distance himself emotionally and theoretically from the Soviet Union.

The already fierce antagonism between Trotskyists and Communists grew worse in response to Soviet and Western European events, particularly the Spanish Civil War. While most of the U.S. left rallied to the republican government threatened by General Francisco Franco's fascist-backed revolt, Shachtman and other Trotskyists argued that the way to defeat Franco was to continue the radical assertion of working-class power that had begun in 1936–37. They hoped that a socialist revolution would arise from the civil war and give new impetus to revolutionary politics worldwide, as the Russian Revolution had in 1917. They denounced the republican government's killing of anarchists and independent Marxists in Barcelona that helped bury their hopes in May and June 1937. Trotskyists' intransigent criticism of Socialist leaders' equivocations about the Barcelona events helped bring about their expulsion, along with hundreds of new recruits, from the Socialist Party.

The new Socialist Workers Party that U.S. Trotskyists formed in early 1938, with barely a thousand members, was the largest Trotskyist group in the world. Shachtman was second only to Trotsky as a leader of their international movement. Together the two men had prepared the first conference of the movement for the Fourth International in July 1936, which in turn prepared for the formal founding congress of the Fourth International in September 1938. Shachtman presided over the founding congress and wrote several major documents for it. Looking beyond the defeats of the 1930s, he foresaw the emergence of the United States as the world's hegemonic, counterrevolutionary power and outlined a strategy for resisting it. He foresaw that the United States would secure its international domination through victory in the Second World War, which loomed on the political horizon as the unavoidable test for the radicals of the 1930s.

The Fourth International was launched in the United States with a Trotskyist breakthrough in 1934. The breakthrough came unexpectedly: with a truck drivers' strike that led to a citywide general strike in Minneapolis. That same year an auto workers' strike led by radicals in Toledo (called "Musteites" after their leader A. J. Muste) and a longshoremen's strike led by Communists in San Francisco also became general strikes. Together these three strikes captured the attention not only of radicals but of millions of working people across the country. They foreshadowed the great industrial strikes on which the CIO was founded. They also established the Trotskyists and Musteites as the Communists' rivals for leadership in the labor movement.

The three strikes—almost simultaneous outbreaks of pent-up working-class frustration—paralleled each other closely. The Toledo strike began on 23 February 1934 among auto parts workers, the San Francisco strike on 9 May among longshore workers, the Minneapolis strike on 15 May among truck drivers. In each city strikers succeeded in rallying the great majority of workers to their side and matched strikebreakers' and police force with force. Police efforts to break picket lines resulted in police shooting down dozens of unarmed strikers in each city. On 24 May in Toledo, the police wounded twenty-eight strikers and killed two; in the 5 July "Battle of Rincon Hill" in San Francisco, police wounded 109 and killed two; on "Bloody Friday," 20 July in Minneapolis, police wounded sixty-seven and killed two. The bloodshed gave state governors a pretext to send in the National Guard and strike leaders the support to call citywide strikes.

Only the outcomes of the three strikes differed. The Toledo radicals and Minneapolis Trotskyists fought their strikes through to victory and joined forces in their aftermath to form a new, united Workers Party. Union leaders in San Francisco were forced by craft divisions between sailors and stevedores to call off their strike and agree to arbitration, so that another year's hard struggle was needed to win union hiring halls on the West Coast docks.

Trotskyists' success in Minneapolis was due to their willingness to stand together with working people against employers and the whole union hierarchy, their skill at mobilizing an entire community around the strike, and their instant recognition of the strike's importance. As it grew violent in late May, Cannon took the unusual and expensive step of traveling by plane from New York to Minneapolis, but soon returned to New York during a temporary lull. When a resumption of the strike seemed likely, every Communist League member was asked to give a full day's pay to help. Cannon set out again on 5 July for Minneapolis, and Shachtman was "to be in readiness to follow shortly."[9] By the time the strike broke out again on 16 July, half a dozen Trotskyist leaders from out of town were on the spot.

Trotskyists distinguished themselves by their quickness to learn from others' experience and the creativity of their tactics. They led a strike in a city where no strike had been successful for a decade, where a third of the labor force was unemployed, where strikers' families were hungry. They overcame these difficulties by opening the union to anyone who wanted to join it, organizing an unemployed league and a women's auxiliary, and forming an alliance with the Minnesota Farmers' Holiday Association. They encouraged strikers to fight back against police with baseball bats and banisters but took on the thankless task of taking away strikers' guns even after police had shot their friends down in the street. They even set up a union hospital to avoid awkward questions from the police when wounded strikers needed medical care.

Communist League leaders worked as a well-coordinated team almost throughout the strike. Shachtman played the central role in one of their most important innovations. Teamsters Local 544 had begun to publish its special strike newspaper, the *Organizer*, as a weekly before Shachtman arrived. But it was Shachtman who turned it into the world's first strike daily. Teamster Farrell Dobbs, who joined the Communist League only in March 1934, was listed on the masthead as its editor, but Shachtman wrote most of it and actually put it out. "A weekly paper would have been utterly inadequate to deal with the fast-moving events," Dobbs said, but "the daily *Organizer* packed a wallop and the working class of the city soon came to swear by it." Cannon said,

> For the first time in the history of the American labor movement, strikers were not left dependent on the capitalist press, were not befuddled and terrorized by it. . . . The *Daily Organizer* covered the town like a blanket. . . . The power of that little paper, its hold on the workers, is indescribable. . . . Of all the contributions we made, the one that tipped the scale to victory was the publication of the daily paper. Without the *Organizer* the strike would not have been won.[10]

The *Organizer* reached a circulation of 10,000 and paid its bills out of workers' voluntary donations, despite the fact that one printer after another refused to print it. It also survived Shachtman's and Cannon's 25 July arrest on criminal syndicalism charges. Cannon later blamed their arrest on Shachtman's decision to wear a ten-gallon cowboy hat around Minneapolis. Shachtman may have thought that this headgear was common west of Chicago, but it might have helped the police pick the Trotskyists out of a crowd. Dragged to a police station at ten o'clock at night, fingerprinted, denied the right to a lawyer or to know the charges against them, the two leaders were released by a judge two days later—warrantless searches of their hotel rooms having produced no damning evidence against them— only to be put under immediate military arrest. A sergeant with a submachine gun and a dozen Guardsmen with automatics and rifles took them in a truck to a National Guard Armory, where their guards were told, "Shoot to kill if they make a move to escape!"[11]

Shachtman and Cannon may have had a few nervous hours in the armory as they remembered Rosa Luxemburg's and Karl Liebknecht's fate. After six hours they were released and told to leave the city. An appeal to the state's Farmer-Labor governor—the man who had declared martial law against the strikers—got the illegal expulsion order revoked the next morning. But soon Shachtman had to go back to New York anyway. The *New International*'s second issue was already running behind schedule. Another Trotskyist took over his job at the *Organizer*. Shachtman was not in Minneapolis on 22 August to see the strikers' victory.

Before the Minneapolis strike, the Trotskyists were widely seen, despite or because of their high-quality publications and their campaign against German fascism, more as intellectuals than as activists. They attracted mainly students, "intellectuals good and bad, very few workers, even fewer active trade unionists," Shachtman remembered. Minneapolis changed the group's profile. Its authority was "immensely enhanced."[12]

With the momentum of the Minneapolis victory behind them, Trotskyists took their first big step toward forming a new U.S. revolutionary party. As in 1928, Shachtman was eager to escape from a narrow, faction-ridden existence to a new organization based on principles. He suggested that the Communist League unite with Muste's American Workers Party. Muste, a pacifist preacher turned socialist leader, had begun by organizing Massachusetts textile workers in 1919, set up a labor college called Brookwood in 1921, and then formed a new socialist group around it. This loose group of radicals, many of them refugees from the Communist Party, had been talking since 1931 about building a new party in the United States that was more revolutionary than the Socialists and less sectarian than the Communists. Trotskyists' leadership in Minneapolis made Musteites view them with respect, and Musteites won Trotskyists' respect by leading the Toledo strike. After several months of negotiations, Musteites accepted Trotskyists' conception of the Fourth International. In December 1934 the two groups merged into the new Workers Party.[13]

In the process of moving toward a new party, Shachtman restored his working relationship with Jim Cannon but strained and broke off his friendships with Marty Abern, Al Glotzer, and Maurice Spector. From 1931 to 1933, Shachtman had led them against Cannon because he thought that Cannon was holding back the Communist League, for example, by opposing the weekly *Militant*. Now, as Cannon had a new surge of energy and threw himself into the Trotskyists' new endeavors as enthusiastically as Shachtman, Shachtman became Cannon's ally. Abern, Glotzer, and Spector felt that he had deserted them. Abern resisted merger with the Musteites.

Glotzer, who went back to Chicago with Edith Harvey in the summer of 1933 because he could not find a job in New York, felt ill-informed, neglected, and personally slighted by Shachtman, whom he had thought of as a close friend. "You were disappointing to me and to all the other comrades with whom you were associated in the past," he told Shachtman.[14]

Shachtman felt that if his critics were to prevail, the Fourth International would never get "off paper and into life" in the United States. He lost patience in particular with Abern, who had developed a habit of writing letters to his particular friends in the organization, giving his own slant on issues and events. At the end of 1934, to his old friends' shock and surprise, Shachtman joined Cannon in attacking them, singling out Abern for forming a "clique" with a "destructive, negative and spiteful position."[15]

Although Shachtman lost old friends by uniting with the Musteites, he found new allies among them. James Burnham, a Musteite professor of philosophy at New York University, now became Shachtman's fellow editor of the *New International*. Shachtman was impressed but ill at ease with his new colleague. He had never met anyone like Burnham, a tall, conservatively dressed graduate of Princeton and Oxford whose father was a British-born railroad executive. Burnham was logical, polite, reserved, dry. He rarely argued or gossiped. Al Glotzer remembered him as a "cold fish." Burnham insisted on keeping his job at New York University while going back and forth to his editing job. He resisted all his comrades' urgings that he come work in the party office. Everyone "felt that although he was with us and with us thoroughly, he was not, so to say, of us," Shachtman remembered.[16]

Another Musteite Shachtman would later work closely with was Ernest McKinney, the only African American among the new party's leaders. McKinney grew up in West Virginia, where his grandfather fought to organize miners and his father was principal of a Black school. He joined the National Association for the Advancement of Colored People and the Socialist Party before the First World War. He came back from the war a Communist, worked with African-American Socialist A. Philip Randolph to organize Pullman car porters, then became a national leader of the Musteite-organized unemployed movement.[17] In the new party, McKinney was looked to as an authority on unemployment, labor, and African-American issues.

Trotskyists emerged from the Minneapolis strike and unification with the Musteites with a glowing sense that the future would be theirs. The *New International* voiced their sense of the limitless possibilities ahead. "Once started on the road of radicalization, the American workers will move with seven league boots," it predicted. They would "accomplish miracles of progress that would bring the United States well towards the top in the list of revolutionary succession."[18] But events soon dimmed their optimism.

Despite the excitement of Minneapolis and Toledo, Trotskyists and Musteites were unable to channel their strike victories into a serious, national political impact. Trotsky had suggested in 1933 that "two or three thousand members" would suffice to get a new revolutionary party going. The Workers Party fell short of this modest goal. Even the Communist Party was fifty or a hundred times its size. By August 1935, Shachtman admitted that it was "only the beginnings of a party." Creating a mass revolutionary party in the United States would require even more flexibility and a greater variety of tactics than creating new Communist parties after the Russian Revolution had, he said. After all, one victory in Minneapolis hardly outweighed the defeats Trotskyists had suffered in the Soviet Union and Germany. "We have only our ideas, practically no organization, no state power (just the contrary)," he said. "If we do not break out of our sectarian existence, we are doomed!"[19]

The Communist Party of the mid-1920s, trapped in a sectarian ghetto itself, had come up with a tactic to help it break out: campaigning for a labor party. The Minneapolis and Toledo victories would have made a broad labor party a more plausible medium-term goal for the Workers Party in the mid-1930s than it had ever been for Communists in the 1920s. Some of the Workers Party's experienced unionists floated the idea. After the Minneapolis strike, Cannon cautiously suggested that a labor party based on reinvigorated unions was "not out of the question." But Shachtman opposed him. Shachtman helped formulate a Workers Party policy that allowed branches to support labor party campaigns only in exceptional circumstances. The idea of Marxists organizing "*another party for the 'second-class citizens,' for the 'backward workers'*" had been "shelved with a sigh of relief" years before, he said.[20]

But the rise of the CIO made the movement for a labor party impossible for Shachtman to dismiss. Encouraged by the 1933 National Recovery Act, one million people joined unions in 1932–36, an unprecedented influx that split apart the narrow, craft-dominated American Federation of Labor. Several dissident AFL leaders formed the Committee for Industrial Organization to take control of new organizing drives. Meanwhile the Toledo Musteites who had led the 1934 Auto-Lite strike went on to organize the General Motors Chevrolet plant there in April 1935. Their early leadership in Toledo enabled them to play a significant role in founding the United Auto Workers—and forced them to deal with auto activists' eagerness to translate newfound economic strength into political power.

Roosevelt's New Deal had not reversed the fall in workers' living standards, which had been cut in half between 1929 and 1932. Because capitalists were investing in new machinery, only part of the increase in output in 1935–36 created new jobs. Though there were now unemployment benefits, they were low, financed by workers' contributions from their wages, and administered without any say from workers' own organizations.

Strikes were still being "broken in a subtle fashion by government mediation boards or brutally by private gangsters, police, or National Guard without effective rebuke from the 'liberal' administration," Trotskyists noted. Despite the spread of strikes, increasingly aggressive strike tactics, and the increased public willingness to fight alongside workers against strikebreakers and police, organizing drives had been beaten back. Though the 1937 Flint and Pontiac sit-downs would win union recognition from General Motors, most industries remained unorganized.[21] Many auto workers were ready to support a party that, unlike the Democrats, would unequivocally back their organizing efforts.

At the July 1936 convention of the United Auto Workers, the Toledo radicals led a delegation, commanding 17 percent of the votes, that was seated over the opposition of CIO leaders. Despite the old Workers Party position to the contrary, Toledo delegates joined Socialists and Communists in a unanimous convention vote calling for a national Farmer-Labor Party. Then they fought—successfully when the vote was first taken, unsuccessfully when the leadership forced a second vote—against CIO leadership pressure for an endorsement of Franklin Roosevelt's reelection campaign.[22] Around the country CIO leaders were forced to camouflage support for Democrats as a temporary exception to their commitment to labor's political independence. They called the political action group they founded in April 1936 Labor's Non-Partisan League, and its New York affiliate—formed to divert Socialist and Communist votes to Roosevelt— the American Labor Party.

Trotskyists' flexibility in the UAW at first made no dent in their official position. Neither did the flexibility of Minneapolis teamster Trotskyists in the spring of 1937 in supporting Minneapolis's Farmer-Labor mayor against a Communist-backed challenge. But in 1938 discussions in Mexico City with Shachtman, Cannon, and other leaders of the new party, Trotsky convinced them that the CIO's rise had made Trotskyists' opposition to a labor party obsolete. The creation of a labor party based on the CIO in the midst of the Depression and an escalating strike wave would mean "a terrible sharpening of forces," he said. A revolutionary group that did not jump into it would "doom itself to isolation."

Trotsky warned that trade union officials would try to tame the labor party movement. Radicals should not take any responsibility for a labor party while such leaders controlled it. Instead they would have to challenge the leaders with their own program of "transitional demands" designed to push the movement beyond the limits union officials set for it. "The further sharpening of the revolutionary situation," Trotsky said, "will inevitably break the shell of the Labor Party." To push Trotskyists forward in this tricky situation he drew up a program of transitional demands, which he called "The Death Agony of Capitalism and the Tasks of the Fourth International."[23] This document was nicknamed "the transitional program." Under that name it became the Trotskyists' single most important document.

Once Shachtman had digested Trotsky's reasoning, he became one of the main interpreters of the new labor party policy. He stressed the need to adapt Trotsky's document to the United States and sort out the demands in it that the party could act on right away, the ones it should raise in broader movements, and the ones it could use only as propaganda. He urged support for union affiliation to Labor's Non-Partisan League, the Minnesota Farmer-Labor Party, and the American Labor Party and advocated work inside these groups for a real labor party instead of a new "bourgeois liberal party." He borrowed many of Trotsky's statements word for word on how transitional demands could bridge the gap between the objective possibility of overthrowing capitalism and workers' unreadiness to do it. But he added his own cautious emphasis on the need "to advance or on occasion to retreat, altering the emphasis and utilization of slogans and shifting tactics through which the program is presented."[24]

By the logic of the Trotskyists' new strategy, Cannon had been right to suggest more openness to independent electoral campaigns in 1934. Shachtman's hostility to the idea might have made Trotskyists miss opportunities to give the 1934 and 1937 strikes independent political expression. Their belated change in orientation was made at least temporarily fruitless by the slowing of working-class radicalization. After a rhetorical leftward swing that helped Roosevelt win reelection in 1936, the administration turned to conservative economic policies that sent the country back into the depths of the Depression by late 1937. The monthly average of strikes declined from 395 in 1937 to 231 in 1938 to 192 in 1939.[25] At the same time, the AFL broke the momentum of CIO organizing by launching a virtual civil war in labor's ranks, signing sweetheart agreements with employers that the CIO had laid siege to and walking out of the local quasi-labor parties.

Shachtman's failure in the mid-1930s to find a way forward to a new mass party left him reacting against more powerful political actors. Franklin Roosevelt captured most working people's imagination and thirst for change with his "second New Deal" of 1935–36. At the same moment the Communist Party's "Popular Front" strategy led them to support Roosevelt. The Communists, not the Trotskyists, became the major radical force of the 1930s and 1940s. In later years the idea of a labor party would be central to Shachtman's effort to put his kind of socialism on the U.S. political agenda. Meanwhile he was left to articulate a hypothetical alternative to the New Deal and Popular Front.

From the late 1920s on, Democrats like Alfred Smith had turned the Democratic Party toward an urban base and a reform program. Both Smith and Franklin Roosevelt pioneered some reforms as Democratic governors of New York. After the 1934 strikes, Roosevelt's commitment to reform deepened. Movements born of the strikes were fueling the growth of socialist groups as well as a broader Farmer-Labor movement. He had reason to fear that a major opponent in the 1936 election might come from the left. He responded with a major policy shift.

Roosevelt's "first New Deal" of 1933 had little appeal for the left: It aimed mostly to help business by relaxing anti-trust laws, bailing out banks, and keeping up prices. The "second New Deal" of 1935 was a stronger bid for labor support. Its highlights were the Wagner Act, which authorized and regulated union organizing, and the Social Security Act, which created the first national system of old-age pensions and unemployment benefits. Roosevelt also pumped up the economy with public spending so that unemployment eased a little.

Roosevelt's reforms posed a challenge to the left that it might have been able to meet by uniting into an independent party with its own more radical program. But at this critical juncture, the growing Communist Party chose to cement rather than weaken working people's dependence on Democrats. Stalin had been shocked to find that as Hitler headed toward confrontation with Britain and France after 1933 he simultaneously broke off the decade-old German-Soviet rapprochement. Looking frantically for allies in a possible German-Soviet war, Stalin sent Communists in a new direction in 1935 with the policy of the Popular Front. The Communist International told Communists to ally with socialists and to support liberals who would oppose fascism, favor reforms, and push for a pro-Soviet foreign policy.

Communists took the fight for socialism in the United States, and then even the fight for a labor party, off their immediate agenda. They tacitly supported Roosevelt's 1936 reelection campaign. They began supporting U.S., British, and French military budgets on the grounds that these governments were "peace-loving." They "discovered an affinity for the Spirit of '76, for George Washington, for the American Flag, and the National Anthem," Shachtman said.[26]

For Trotskyists, the Popular Front confirmed their prediction that building "socialism in one country" would mean hobbling the Communist movement as a revolutionary force. In Shachtman's eyes, Communists were putting themselves through "contortions" to prove that they were "housebroken."[27] But while Stalin's foreign policy provided the initial impetus for the Popular Front, Communists benefited by association from the enthusiasm working people and radicals felt for the New Deal. Many socialists believed that Roosevelt, though no socialist, was bringing socialism closer in the United States. Many of them joined the Communist Party. The belief took hold on the left that reform, not revolution, was the road to U.S. socialism.

Shachtman responded by showing how state intervention in the economy reinforced rather than undermined capitalism. He gave an analysis of the class dynamics behind the New Deal (articulated most fully later in the 1940s) that would have done credit to an academic Marxist of the 1980s or 1990s, with a clarity that few latter-day academic Marxists could match. He exemplified his conviction that the Marxism he had learned from Lenin and Trotsky could be easily and thoroughly "Americanized."

In Shachtman's words, since the capitalist state works "to *maintain the conditions of capitalist production,*" it also has to "regulate the conflict within the capitalist class which is united, as a rule," only against the working class. The New Deal preserved capitalism from collapse and the capitalist class from fragmentation—by countering the shortsightedness of individual capitalists and winning over most of the working class. "For every scratch they suffered under [Roosevelt's] administration," Shachtman concluded, "he saved them a bone that would otherwise have been broken."[28]

Many Communists and social democrats in the 1930s felt that even if the New Deal did save capitalism, it was a far preferable alternative to fascism. They reasoned that the alliance of pro–New Deal capitalists with most of the left represented the overall best interest of U.S. society. Shachtman responded, "There is *no such thing* as 'society as a whole' and there has not been for hundreds and thousands of years." The New Deal was no more an instrument of "society as a whole" than Nazism, which together led to the Second World War. The fact that Nazism required a harsh dictatorship, while the New Deal did not only showed that U.S. capitalism was richer and more powerful than German. As Hitler said, "Democracy is a luxury of rich nations." The New Deal was the luxury of rich U.S. capitalism.

> Did that operation bring Roosevelt and the New Deal state into conflict with certain sections of the capitalist class? Of course! . . . Did it force them to seek support in the ranks of the working class? To be sure! . . . The bourgeois state can come into conflict with the bourgeoisie, and . . . the working class can extract economic and political concessions from the bourgeois state, especially from the bourgeois-democratic state. It is an important discovery. At any rate, it was important when it was first made, a century or two ago.[29]

The reason that most leftists saw such reforms as being in the interests of "society as a whole," Shachtman said, was that they had fallen victim to the ruling confusion of every unjust society: the confusion of the rulers' interests with the people's. Once the overthrow of the existing order seems an unreal prospect, then patching it up in such a way that people can somehow survive under it inevitably *seems* to be in their interests—though it is far more in their rulers' interests than in theirs. Similarly, Communists' defense of U.S. democracy only convinced Shachtman how thoroughly they had forgotten the original communist vision of a more thoroughgoing, working-class democracy. They no longer saw clearly how U.S. democracy really functions: how it keeps third parties off the ballot, limits freedom of the press to those that own one, and denies the vote to immigrants, migrant workers, and the majority of the world's population, over whom the United States "rules by sheer force."

> Of all the bourgeois democracies, the American is the most reactionary and the least responsive to the will of the masses. No other bourgeois democracy has a political system so cunningly calculated to thwart the will of the people: with its states' rights, its division into a bicameral legislative body, its enormously bureaucratized executive with unprecedented powers, its appointed judiciary with law-making and law-breaking powers, its outrageously undemocratic system for amending the Constitution, its broken-field system of electing Congressmen every two years, Presidents every four and Senators every six, with its boss-patronage political machine which parallels and mocks the legal government machinery from top to bottom—to mention only a few of the *traditional and fundamental* characteristics of our bourgeois democracy.[30]

Even when Communists were only proposing joint action with Socialists, Shachtman warned that they were putting too much emphasis on deals in Congress and unions and not enough on action in the streets. When Communists moved to ally with liberal Democrats, he rejected this kind of unity altogether. Communists had only traded in the disastrous policy they had followed in Germany until 1933 for the disastrous policy the Social Democrats had followed in Germany until 1933, he said. Just as social democratic appeals to liberals had weakened, not strengthened, resistance to fascism, so would Communist appeals to liberals now. Social democratic appeals to liberals, Shachtman said, had reflected

> a deeply-felt desire to protect the mighty organizations and institutions of labor. . . . The Stalinists have adopted the same line out of just as deep a desire to protect the proletarian institutions and the foundations of socialism which are being laid in the Soviet Union. . . . Such a line must ultimately lead—as it already has in Germany—. . . to the wiping out of these institutions and conquests.

The only way to preserve democratic rights even under capitalism was to mobilize those who could be counted on—working people—and only radical ideas would mobilize them.[31]

But Shachtman's logic was powerless against the tangible benefits and potent rhetoric of the New Deal. The Popular Front policy of supporting it attracted many people to Communism. Though the proportion of workers in the Communist Party fell in the later 1930s, it recruited widely among students and progressive-minded middle-class people. Shachtman later estimated that 95 percent of the people who became radicals in the 1930s were under Communist leadership or influence.[32]

Support for the New Deal and Popular Front extended into the Socialist Party's ranks. More diverse than the Communists and lacking the unity imposed from above on the Communists, the Socialist Party grew more slowly and was weakened by internal battles. The Socialist "Old Guard," rooted in New York's largely Jewish garment unions, was fiercely anti-Communist and increasingly drawn toward Roosevelt. Younger Socialists were attracted to the more radical-sounding "Militant" group, whose radicalism was tempered by desire for unity on the left. Ironically, after their own disastrous mistakes had helped bring fascism to power in Germany, Communists could successfully appeal to other socialists to unite against the fascist danger. With the Communists' turn away from revolutionary politics, the old barriers between them and Socialists seemed less important.

Shachtman and Cannon worried that the growth of the Socialist left wing could "*be swallowed up, and consequently, vitiated and destroyed*" by the Communists.[33] The result would be a left turned into almost unanimous cheerleaders for the Democratic Party, wasting all the potential for independent politics created by the Depression. Shachtman and Cannon had hardly established themselves in their new Workers Party before they began to wonder how something might be saved from the Socialist Party.

Tensions built up in 1934 and 1935 between the Socialist Party's leadership, controlled by the "Militants," and the increasingly pro-Roosevelt "Old Guard." In early 1936 the Old Guard walked out of the Socialist Party. Soon the Old Guard, joined by the Communists, would create the pro-Roosevelt American Labor Party in New York State. Shachtman would later help convince Trotskyists to work in the ALP to try to turn it into a truly independent party. But in 1936–37, Trotskyists refused to have anything to do with it. Instead, in May 1936, the Workers Party dissolved itself so that its members could join the Socialist Party and build with the remaining Socialists an alternative to both the Old Guard and the Communists.

Al Goldman, a Trotskyist lawyer from Chicago, had joined the Socialist Party in 1934 and started a newspaper for its far left wing, the *Socialist Appeal*. Now he welcomed his old comrades into the Socialist Party. The

Appeal became the new Trotskyist paper, and Trotskyists called themselves "the Appeal group." Armed only with the *Appeal* and their political skills, they won new recruits among Socialists. Growth and merger with the Musteites had increased their numbers from about 200 in early 1933 to 400–500 in early 1936. By winning over the left wing of the Socialist Party they doubled their ranks again[34]—and Shachtman enlarged his circle of admiring younger followers.

Young Trotskyists like Nathan Gould and Manny Geltman joined the Young People's Socialist League, the Socialist youth group, and won over its major leaders. Al Goldman had already won over Ernest Erber, a soft-spoken, even-tempered, blond midwesterner who had become YPSL national chairman. Hal Draper was perhaps the most prominent new supporter, a twenty-two-year-old high school teacher from Brooklyn and left-wing leader in New York who had begun to accumulate an impressive Marxist erudition. Another YPSL left-winger, Herman Benson, who was working as a laborer after being expelled from City College for taking part in a demonstration, remembered Draper as "a stickler for formulations and principles, . . . socially sort of awkward, a guy of absolute integrity." Before the Trotskyists joined the Socialists, Draper became friends with Joe Carter. Draper also knew Geltman from Brooklyn College. Soon the Appeal group made Draper YPSL national secretary.[35]

By mid-1937 the Appeal group had won over the overwhelming majority of the Young People's Socialist League: many hundreds of new supporters of the Fourth International, in addition to the hundreds of adult Socialists newly convinced of Fourth Internationalist politics. The young socialists would be Shachtman's most loyal constituency. One of them, Julius Jacobson, remembered, "When Max spoke at a 'big meeting' at Irving Plaza or Webster Hall we were always there. It was not merely that we were entertained by his razor-sharp wit, his polemical skills, his sense of irony, his robust humor but primarily because we were clearly in the presence of an exceptional political intelligence."[36]

Jacobson and his crowd respected Cannon, but "knew him as Cannon. Shachtman was Max. We could joke and banter with him." Jacobson remembered Shachtman as "a young man's person. . . . He was fun to be with." Shachtman's followers had "special feelings" for him; they were "Shachtmanites in a political and personal sense"—"Max's boys." In the late 1930s some of Max's boys would take midnight hikes across the Bronx together, drawn into "a kind of male bonding: a retreat from the pressures of politics and sex."[37] Today, in a world grown conscious of homoerotic undertones, the intense bond between Shachtman and his young male followers might not have the same feel of simplicity and innocence it had for them.

Meanwhile Shachtman's relationships with older Trotskyist leaders grew more complex. Shachtman's already cool relations with Al Glotzer became more distant in some ways in the late 1930s. Glotzer's relationship with Edith Harvey had been difficult; Harvey still "carried a torch" for her husband John Harvey, whom she had married in her teens and never divorced. In the spring of 1934 she left Glotzer and moved back to New York. The move brought her closer to Shachtman, who "always had a soft spot" for her. In 1937 he left Billie Ramloff and moved to the Grand Concourse in the Bronx. Harvey lived with him there. With Shachtman and Harvey sharing an apartment, Harvey "couldn't tolerate my being there," Glotzer remembered. He visited their home once in ten years.[38]

Harvey rarely welcomed any of Shachtman's Trotskyist friends into their house. She had no "real vital interest" in politics. Whether because of Harvey's feelings, Shachtman's own desire for privacy, or both, his life at home became a realm apart that his political associates rarely glimpsed. Although quite a few Trotskyists lived in the South Bronx, which was still "sort of fresh, open country" in the 1930s, they rarely knew what he did "outside working hours."[39] He had hardly any social ties with Cannon, who lived in Greenwich Village, a neighborhood with a working-class as well as bohemian character in those years. Shachtman did not regain the personal closeness he had had with Cannon in the 1920s or with Glotzer in the early 1930s.

Whatever the state of their personal relationships, Trotskyist leaders were pleased at the headway they had made among Socialists. But the same issues that had led them to join the Socialist Party—Stalin's policies, the Popular Front in Europe, the New Deal at home—would make their time inside it stormy and short.

By the mid-1930s, Trotskyists saw the fate of socialism as dependent on the battle they were waging with Stalinists for leadership of the left. The Trotskyists were by far the weaker force. Their weakness was most obvious in the Soviet Union, where they were almost all in concentration camps. Although U.S. and Western European Trotskyists were now more focused on prospects for socialism in their own countries, their attention was continually pulled back to the fate of the original Soviet Trotskyists and the first workers' revolution. They were helpless to hinder Stalin's reshaping of Soviet society, which was taking forms they had never expected.

Stalin was burying the egalitarian principles of the Bolshevik Revolution. He increased wage disparities, eliminated days off, set up special stores for officials, reestablished ranks and titles in the army, and gave managers absolute power in the factories. He banned abortion and recriminalized homosexuality. He enforced these inequities with savage repression. "A 12-year old who commits a theft is now punishable by death in Stalin's 'socialist' society," Shachtman said: "*No* country on the face of the earth has such a barbarous piece of legislation on its books."[40] Worse than the new penal legislation were the purges of the late 1930s, which killed off Stalin's Communist critics and completed the accumulation of power in the bureaucracy's hands. The new privileges and repression amounted in Trotskyists' minds to a bureaucratic counterrevolution. By 1936 Trotsky gave up any hope of putting the Soviet Union back on course toward a genuine socialist order without violent upheavals. He expected a civil war against Stalinism in the Soviet Union and a prolonged fight against official Communism almost everywhere in the world.

For Shachtman the battle with Stalinism became a continual preoccupation. Although his internationalist commitment remained as strong as ever, he began to shed the identification with the Soviet Union that had been central to his internationalism in the 1920s. By the end of 1936 he saw Stalinism as the main obstacle to socialism within the labor movement.

> Stalinism does not represent our conception of socialism. It oppresses men instead of liberating them. It debases and humiliates and demoralizes men, instead of raising them to the lofty level of a new dignity and freedom and independence. . . . The struggle against Stalinism is . . . the struggle for the honor of the movement and for its future.[41]

With the dramatic growth the Communist Party was enjoying in the late 1930s, Shachtman and his comrades had a fight on their hands.

The more Shachtman focused on the fight against Stalin's regime, the more important it was for him to understand it. At first he worked together with Trotsky to explain the Soviet counterrevolution without giving up his loyalty to the Soviet state. He insisted that the Russian Revolution was still "filled with life, potentialities, resources that merely need touching off to re-assert themselves."[42] But for Shachtman this optimistic analysis of Soviet society was only a first attempt at a new understanding. The purges shook his optimism. Trotsky's willingness to modify the analysis in subtle ways in order to deal with new issues, such as the need to organize new revolutionary soviets and the need to support Ukrainian resistance to Russian rule, increased Shachtman's willingness to reconsider. Other Trotskyists were challenging Trotsky's analysis openly by the end of 1937. Shachtman's adherence to it would not outlast the 1930s.

The position Trotsky took in 1936 was already a qualification of his old explanation of Stalinism as a short-lived regime wavering between capitalism and the working class. Stalin's success in crushing all his enemies put in question Trotsky's belief that once "the proletariat springs into action" the Soviet bureaucracy could be pushed aside by "measures of a police character." In October 1933, Trotsky admitted that real communists could no longer hope to recapture the Soviet Communist Party. The July 1936 Trotskyist world conference finally said that since state coercion in the USSR had become "concentrated, open and cynical," the opposition had *"been robbed of the last possibility of a legal reformation."*[43] Violent revolution would be necessary.

But Trotskyists still valued the nationalization of industry, economic planning, and independence from the world capitalist market brought about by the Russian Revolution. They still wanted to defend the Soviet Union in a war with any capitalist state, so that these gains of the revolution would not be lost. In order to preserve these principles, Trotsky developed a position that called for both overthrowing Stalin's regime and defending the Soviet state. The key idea in this argument was that although Soviet society was not socialist and the state had "degenerated," it was still a "workers' state," and the revolution Trotskyists wanted in the USSR was a "political revolution," not a "social revolution."

Trotskyists explained this stand with an analogy between the Soviet Union and a gangster-controlled labor union. Socialists should never support employers even against a gangster-controlled union, they said, but neither should they stop trying to get rid of the gangsters who were robbing and weakening the union. Similarly, Marxists should simultaneously defend the Soviet workers' state against its external, capitalist enemies and the internal enemies ruling it and speaking in its name. "When the union is engaged in direct struggle with the capitalist enemy," Shachtman said, "the truest defenders of the workers' interests will be those who combat, inside the union, those reactionary or corrupt leaders whose continued domination of the union is just the thing that paralyzes it." He said that the Soviet bureaucracy still defended working-class interests, "distortedly and decreasingly," though he suggested that it might become "so corrupted that it cannot or does not fight for its class even though the latter's defeat means the wiping out of the bureaucracy itself."[44]

Trotsky's insistence that the Soviet Union was still a workers' state was undermined by events only weeks after the 1936 Trotskyist world conference endorsed his position. Shachtman was with Trotsky in Norway when news reached them of a new trial in Moscow for the murder of S. M. Kirov, a Communist politburo member who had been killed in Leningrad in December 1934. There had already been a secret trial for the killing, in which at least a hundred of Stalin's opponents were charged with complicity in a "White terrorist" plot; 114 had been executed. "A plot has indeed been hatched," Shachtman had said: a plot by Stalin "to dispose of revolutionists under the guise of combatting counter-revolutionists." Now Stalin staged another, public trial. On 15 August 1936 the Soviet state prosecutor announced the indictment of sixteen Soviet leaders for Kirov's murder as well as plots to murder Stalin and other high officials. Trotsky's name figured prominently in the indictment. The trial opened on 19 August. It consisted mostly of the defendants' confessions. On 24 August it was over: All the defendants were sentenced to be shot. On 25 August the Soviet press announced, "The verdict has been carried out."[45]

This trial was only the beginning of an assault by Stalin on the ranks of the Communist Party. He began with Trotskyists and ex-Trotskyists, moved on to anyone who had ever opposed him, and finished with most of the leaders who had supported him through all the faction fights. In the end he killed the great majority of the members of Lenin's Central Committee, the great majority of those who had been delegates to his triumphal party congress in 1934, and a million or more rank-and-file Communists. By the time the purges ended, most of the Bolsheviks who had created the Soviet state had been eliminated from its ranks. The underlying continuity Trotsky had seen between the state of 1917 and the state of 1936 was shattered.

In his book *Behind the Moscow Trial*, finished in November 1936, Shachtman stressed the discontinuity in Soviet society that the purges symbolized and completed. Stalin was killing "the whole Leninist Guard, the men who directed the Russian movement, who directed its destinies through the civil war," Shachtman said. Stalin had "dug the grave of the Third International, its founders, its traditions and literally filled it with corpses." The Moscow defendants symbolized "a different epoch, a different tradition, a different ideology, than that of the new ruling caste which could not, and would not, assimilate the old into the new."[46]

Stalin was using the trials to discredit the Bolshevik tradition, by depicting long-time Bolshevik leaders as terrorists and fascists. Shachtman responded by telling the defendants' political history and explaining their communist principles. He told the story of the debate on terrorism carried on for four decades in Russia, in which the defendants had unanimously argued against it. He told the story of Trotsky's fight to unite the left against Hitler in 1931–33. Without denying the possibility of fascist infiltration in Trotskyist ranks, he pointed out that there were known and admitted cases of Gestapo agents in Communist parties and none in Trotskyist groups. It was Stalin who was imitating Hitler's 1934 blood purge, not Trotsky. It was Stalin's victory that fascist newspapers hailed as "a victory of political reason over revolutionary romanticism."[47]

Why then had the Moscow defendants confessed? Shachtman pointed out that none of the defendants was still a Trotskyist. Each had renounced his opposition to Stalin more than once, some five times. They still believed that they were somehow serving socialism by serving the Soviet state. Shachtman analyzed with great psychological insight the thought processes of such men under the secret police's treatment: strict isolation, extremes of heat and cold, inadequate food and clothing, nothing to read, nothing to do, all of which could be ended simply by agreeing to perform one more service for the USSR. He did not call the defendants cowards. But he said that they had been fatally misguided in believing their jailers' promises of clemency, and fatally misguided in imagining that there could be any compromise between socialism and Stalinism.

Despite their weakness and isolation, Trotsky and his followers tried to broadcast the truth about the trials. Trotsky was still capable of an "utterly staggering" amount of work, Shachtman remembered, but he was under tremendous strain, shocked by his old comrades' degrading confessions and "cooped up" by the Norwegian government. Soon it interned him, destroying his ability to respond to the charges against him. It assigned an official known to be a fascist to censor his ingoing and outgoing mail. At the end of 1936 it expelled him from Norwegian soil. Shachtman got Trotsky a Mexican visa and was delighted when Trotsky accepted. He drove down from New York to Mexico with fellow Trotskyist George Novack, so that when Trotsky's boat arrived in Tampico in January 1937 Shachtman was there to meet him at the dock. Trotsky and Shachtman took a train from Tampico to Mexico City, where Trotsky moved in with radical artists Diego Rivera and Frida Kahlo.[48] The move untied Trotsky's hands for his defense against Stalin's accusations. In April 1937 Glotzer went down to Mexico to record a Trotskyist-organized commission of inquiry, chaired by philosopher John Dewey, which declared the Moscow trial a frame-up.

Shachtman threw himself into the task of exposing the trials, which was tailor-made for him. He drew on his skills as a publicist by making a new effort to make Trotsky's writings known to the public, preparing a new edition of Trotsky's *Selected Works*. Trotsky praised Shachtman's "extraordinarily good edition" with "your so weighty and informative introduction."[49] Shachtman's gifts of invective and irony could be given full rein in his own speeches and articles about the trials. After his return from Mexico he set off on a speaking tour from New York to Hollywood and back, again and again exposing the same lies, denouncing the killings.

One of Shachtman's speeches against the trials was a godsend to Trotskyists at City College. The three lone Trotskyist students there at the beginning of 1936 shared "murky" Alcove 1 in the vast, "slummy and smelly" college cafeteria with various Socialists and Old Guard social democrats. Occasionally a young Trotskyist would climb onto a cafeteria table and start speaking in an effort to gather a crowd. But all the denizens of Alcove 1 put together had perhaps a fifth of the drawing power of the Communists in Alcove 2, until Shachtman came to City College to debate. Irving Howe, a storekeeper's son noted for his own skill at cafeteria oratory, remembered years later how Shachtman turned his Communist opponent's comparison of Trotsky with Benedict Arnold inside out, pointing out that if Arnold's plot had succeeded he could have put Washington, Jefferson, Madison, and Franklin on trial as traitors just as Stalin had tried and executed all the other leaders of the Russian Revolution. The debate broke the City College Communists' "impenetrable armor."[50]

Shachtman saw that the executions were bound to continue in the Soviet Union for years unless international pressure put a stop to them. "The conscience of the labor and revolutionary movements would be stone if it did not reply to this summons," he said. But his plea for the international working-class movement to "ring out in such a mighty protest" that the trials would end went mostly unheeded. "Only a few thousand who escaped the influence of Stalinism responded," he said later. "The others were indifferent or clearly antagonistic." The trials continued; the deaths continued. Shachtman was bitter, particularly at the spectacle of writers— safe, respected, and prosperous in the United States—who thought that they could prove their radicalism by apologizing for Stalin. These writers carried out "the dirtiest hack work, the most shameful and sophisticated apologetics" for Stalin, he later remembered. He was also afraid of more attacks to come. "Stalin is out to 'get'" Trotsky, he said, "and he will not rest until he does."[51]

Anyone who claimed the heritage of the Russian Revolution now had to choose between Stalin and the Communists he was killing. Those who chose Stalin, openly or through their silence, were separated from his victims and their supporters by a sea of blood. Communists escalated their attacks on Trotskyists to new heights of vilification. In the 1920s Trotskyists were dismissed as disguised social democrats. By the early 1930s they were denounced as objective allies of fascism. By the late 1930s the rulers in the Kremlin and their U.S. followers made grotesque accusations: Trotskyists were and always had been a ring of conspirators in Hitler's pay, spies, saboteurs, poisoners, assassins. Trotskyists were often embattled even in their own families, since young Trotskyists like Hal Draper and Gordon Haskell had Communist brothers. Just as Shachtman's commitment to Trotskyism had been reinforced by Communist leaders' lies about it in the early 1930s, bolder lies fed his revulsion from Stalinism. "Falsehood is the weapon of reaction and truth the weapon of socialism," he said.[52] But there were not many who acknowledged the truth.

Trotskyists became more willing to question their loyalty to the Soviet Union and their conviction that it was a workers' state. Their sense of loyalty was strong: They had seen themselves as the real champions of the Red Army and Soviet state, while Stalin was subverting and endangering them. Jim Cannon had told his Communist inquisitors in 1928, "Trotsky will be fighting for the Soviet Union when many of those who are hollering against him will be on the other side of the barricades." Facing the prospect of a war in which the Soviet Union would be allied with U.S., British, and French empires, Trotskyists had reaffirmed in 1934 that they would do everything possible to rush aid to the Soviet Union for its defense even as they opposed Western countries' war efforts.[53] But now they could not avoid the question: Why support a state that was betraying socialism internationally and at home?

Some Trotskyists began to say that the counterrevolution had overthrown the Soviet workers' state. Joe Carter was the first to challenge Trotsky's position that a workers' state still existed, followed by James Burnham and Manny Geltman. The Soviet bureaucracy was in fact destroying the nationalized economy, Carter said, recreating private property and consolidating itself as a new propertied class. "The class rule of the proletariat, however carried out—through full soviet democracy, the revolutionary party, several workers' parties, or through a distorting but still proletarian bureaucracy—is an essential aspect of a Workers' State," he argued.[54] Since workers were no longer ruling the Soviet Union in any sense, it was no longer a workers' state.

Shachtman disagreed with Carter and delivered the majority report at the Trotskyists' 1938 convention against him. Geltman remembered that in 1938 Shachtman and he "were thrown out of a café in Paris because we were arguing so loudly." But Shachtman could hardly consider Trotsky's 1936 position as sacrosanct when Trotsky himself was modifying it in subtle ways. In the summer of 1938, Trotsky called for the expulsion of all bureaucrats from democratized soviets. In the spring of 1939, when Hungary seized the Ukrainian-speaking part of Czechoslovakia, Trotsky began calling for an *independent* Soviet Ukraine. He reasoned that calling on Ukrainians outside the USSR to rebel and unite with the Soviet Ukraine was useless, because Ukrainians would not throw off Hungarian or Polish oppression in order to submit to Stalin's oppression. Calling for a *"united, free and independent workers' and peasants' Soviet Ukraine,"* on the other hand, could spark not only Ukrainian rebellions against Hungary and Poland but revolution in the Soviet Ukraine, which might lead to the overthrow of the bureaucracy throughout the Soviet Union.[55]

Shachtman accepted Trotsky's innovations but began to have doubts about the positions Trotsky was leaving unchanged. When Carter and Burnham proposed in September 1938 that the founding congress of the Fourth International table Trotsky's innovative paragraph on the soviets pending fuller discussion, Shachtman and Cannon agreed that more discussion was needed. Lenin had said that even capitalists should not necessarily be excluded from soviets, Shachtman pointed out at the congress. Could there be no exceptions for bureaucrats? The discussion showed the confusion and dissension in the Trotskyist ranks. Each of the delegates who spoke up to defend Trotsky's idea had a different argument. One said that bureaucrats had to be expelled from the soviets because they were a class; another said that they had to be expelled because they were not a class; a couple claimed that the point was minor, and another said that Trotskyists should *call* for excluding bureaucrats but not necessarily do it. "The great variety of views expressed," Shachtman summed up, "showed clearly that a further discussion and clarification were necessary."[56]

He began to rethink his position. In November 1938 he pointedly avoided open agreement with either Carter or Trotsky. In December he proposed to open a free discussion on the issue throughout the Socialist Workers Party.[57] He rejected Carter's idea that the bureaucracy was restoring private property in the Soviet Union, a notion he would never find plausible. Carter's idea that workers' political power was an essential characteristic of a workers' state, however, was one that he found interesting. He was beginning to combine Trotsky's ideas and Carter's into a distinct position of his own.

The mutating Soviet state shaped the Communist movement in the 1930s to fit its requirements. The initial impetus behind Communists' Popular Front policy came from Stalin's desire for an alliance with Britain and France against Germany. U.S. Communists therefore backed not only Roosevelt's domestic reforms but his pro–British, pro–French foreign policy. Breaking with the Communist perspective of the 1920s, they identified the United States as a pacific power standing up to warmongers.

Trotskyists disagreed. They continued to see the United States as an imperial power that needed room to expand and would cause war to get it. "American imperialism cannot expand further, or even maintain its existing world position, without cutting deeply into the share of world power now in the hands of other imperialist nations," they said. "The economy and politics of the United States depend upon crises, wars, and revolutions in all parts of the world." Shachtman pointed to the soaring military budget Roosevelt had gotten from Congress—over a billion dollars by 1936. He called Roosevelt "the agent of American imperialism in its gigantic war preparations."[58]

The whole idea of distinguishing between "peace-loving" and "aggressive" capitalist governments was fraudulent for Shachtman. They were all aggressive, "just as lions are by their very nature carnivorous and diplomatists are by their very nature liars." The United States, Britain, and France already had their empires and were clinging to the status quo. "Hitler has yet to match the American record in Haiti, Nicaragua, Cuba, Mexico," Shachtman said. "The record of imperialist France in Northern Africa and in Asia is far more atrocious than anything done to date by Hitler and Mussolini."[59] Neither the United States nor Britain nor France had slowed the pace of the arms race or the momentum toward war.

The most important test of Communists' international policy came in Spain. Spain had been in turmoil since 1930–31 when the dictator Primo de Rivera had been overthrown and a republic established. Early in 1936 elections installed a Popular Front government uniting liberal republicans, Socialists, and Communists. Rightist generals including Francisco Franco, backed by fascist Germany and Italy, reacted in July by trying to overthrow the republic. The coup attempt plunged the country into civil war. The republic survived only in the Madrid region, the Basque country to the north, and Catalonia to the east.

The generals' coup was temporarily thwarted not by the government but by working-class organizations, above all anarchists and the independent communists of the Workers Party of Marxist Unification (POUM). The anarchists and POUM, especially strong in independent-minded Catalonia and its industrialized capital, Barcelona, founded their own people's militias that bore the brunt of the fighting in the civil war. Landlords' estates were seized, factories occupied. The situation resembled the "dual power" that existed in Russia before November 1917, with the government and workers' organizations, neither completely in control, jockeying for power.

The government was under pressure to restore order and reassure the country's capitalists and landowners (though they overwhelmingly supported Franco). Pressure came above all from the Soviet Union, which saw the Spanish war as its chance to get democratic Britain and France to ally against Germany. At first Stalin went along with the British-French farce of agreeing with Germany and Italy not to intervene—and overlooking blatant German and Italian aid to Franco. No Soviet aid arrived in the summer of 1936 except some food and bandages, which Shachtman called "alms given with a sneer."[60] Stalin did eventually opt out of the farce of nonintervention and provided the republican side with precious weapons (duly paid for with Spanish gold). In return he urged the republican government to ensure as quickly and dramatically as possible that there would be no Spanish socialist revolution to frighten Britain and France out of cooperation with the USSR.

In May 1937 the republican government made its move, seizing the anarchist-occupied Barcelona telephone exchange. After some fighting the anarchists and POUM, who wanted to avoid confrontation while the civil war was on, agreed to withdraw. The government responded in June by sending in its army and jailing and slaughtering the disarmed anarchists and POUM members.

Trotskyists had been critical of the anarchists and POUM before 1937.

POUM leaders Andreu Nin and Juan Andrade were former Trotskyists who had rejected Trotsky's urging to go into the Spanish Socialist Party, shocked Trotsky by signing the Popular Front program, and expelled the remaining loyal Trotskyists in their ranks. Trotsky believed that the anarchists and POUM had ruined Spain's chances for a socialist revolution by failing to take power in Barcelona when they had the chance. But Trotskyists everywhere united in condemning the repressive actions of the Spanish republican government backed by the Spanish Communist and Socialist parties. Shachtman declared that the Barcelona events revealed the Communist International as "the fiercest protagonist within the labor movement of the monstrous fraud known as bourgeois democracy and the most brutally aggressive guardian . . . of capitalist private property."[61]

If anything could deepen the divide between Trotskyists and Communists after the Moscow trials began, the Barcelona events did it. The Spanish republic's soldiers and leaders were Communists' most beloved heroes in the late 1930s. Many U.S. Communists and sympathizers joined the Lincoln Brigade that fought alongside the republican army. Many died in the sincere belief that they were fighting for democracy. Yet even in the Lincoln Brigade there were people who took part in attacks on the anti-Stalinist left. Communists and liberals who supported the republic did not want to know. They were eager to believe that anyone repeating such stories was a fascist.

The Spanish war even divided Trotskyists from other Socialists, in particular from Socialist leader Norman Thomas. Thomas, a clean-cut son of an Ohio Presbyterian minister, had been a religious pacifist and Woodrow Wilson supporter before becoming the Socialists' presidential standard-bearer in 1928. He was obviously no Marxist. Trotskyists believed that his calling himself a socialist was a result of some kind of misunderstanding. As early as 1924, when Thomas ran for governor of New York, Shachtman poked fun at him in the *Daily Worker*: "Every evening before he dons his nightie he lights a lamp and says a prayer for clean government and hopes that the workers will forget that there is or should be or might be such a thing as a class struggle." Even as Thomas's ally decades later, Shachtman spoke of his timidity: He "thinks ten times before he steps on anyone's toes."[62]

Thomas had drifted leftward with the tide in the early 1930s, but by 1937 he was drifting back. He visited Spain in 1937 and met with Francisco Largo Caballero, leader of the Spanish Socialist left wing, who had been prime minister in the government that suppressed the May 1937 Barcelona uprising. Largo Caballero had not ordered the repression—he had resigned as prime minister less than two weeks after the fighting broke out—but neither had he supported the uprising. Thomas came back defending Largo Caballero.

The Appeal group could not stand for this equivocation. The Spanish Revolution in 1936–37 was the best argument for revolutionary Marxism since 1917. It was an opportunity to explain revolutionary politics that they could not pass up. They fought hard to have Socialists repudiate Thomas and condemn the Spanish Popular Front, which they blamed for the Barcelona killings.

It was a hard debate. Young recruit Leo Seidlitz later commented that he did not feel isolated on any other issue: not on opposing Roosevelt, not on opposing LaGuardia; but "Spain—that was isolating. . . . That we were a freak minority on." To even Shachtman's and Cannon's initial disquiet, Trotsky insisted that his followers oppose any aid to the republican government—which was, after all, killing socialists—and instead support aid to the left-wing militias. Understanding this position required a high level of political sophistication. Appeal supporters acquired this sophistication—joining Appeal meant enrolling in a course of "hothouse learning"—and were soon vigorously condemning other Socialists' confusion. But other Socialists proved stubborn. The line between Appeal and the rest hardened.* Spain became "*the* touchstone issue."[64]

Shachtman and Cannon had predicted that the Socialist Party would be a far easier organization to recruit from than the Communist Party, but they had also warned that once revolutionaries gained strength within it Thomas's vaunted commitment to an "all-inclusive party" would crumble. Years before going into the Socialist Party, Shachtman had called the Militants around Thomas "a lightning rod for grounding truly revolutionary sentiment in the party into the safe soil of reformism." In normal times they were "quiet office boys of the Right Wing bureaucracy," he said; in times of crisis they were "the emergency brake on the advance of the workers." In March 1937 Thomas had persuaded an emergency party convention to ban the *Socialist Appeal* as a "factional organ."[65] Although Shachtman and Cannon convinced Trotskyists to abide by the resolution, the debate over Barcelona aggravated the tensions.

Trotsky believed that only the lack of a revolutionary Marxist party in Spain and Catalonia had prevented a socialist revolution. Victory there would have given Trotskyists the same overwhelming impetus around the world that Communists had received from the Russian Revolution. Now the chance was lost. The defeat was bitter, but Trotsky believed that new revolutionary opportunities would arise in other countries, and he was

---

*The debate over Spain underlined A. J. Muste's break with the Trotskyists. Having fought in alliance with Abern and Glotzer against going into the Socialist Party, he had joined it once the Trotskyists voted to; but unlike Abern and Glotzer, he had not stayed within the Appeal group. The Spanish war pushed him still further from Trotskyism. The prospect of a world war made him revert to his early religious pacifism.[63]

determined that the next one would not be missed. The experience with POUM had shown the futility of waiting for forces vacillating between reformism and revolutionary politics to make up their minds, he said. Revolutionary parties should be set up in every country as soon as possible. In April 1937 Trotsky told Al Glotzer in Mexico that U.S. Trotskyists should leave the Socialist Party. In late May he gave Cannon and Shachtman the same advice. "We suddenly found ourselves under irresistible pressure, and that pressure came from Trotsky himself," Shachtman remembered.[66]

Trotskyists' position in the Socialist Party became still more precarious when a debate broke out over the 1937 New York mayoral election. Thomas had been the Socialist candidate against Fiorello LaGuardia, the incumbent liberal Republican who had pro-Roosevelt union leaders solidly behind him. Encouraged by the Militants, Thomas withdrew from the race in favor of LaGuardia. Trotskyists criticized Thomas harshly. Shachtman, who had argued at first that Trotsky was pushing for too early a split, sent out a joint statement with Cannon at the end of June calling a "speedy split" inevitable.[67]

Fed up with criticism, New York Socialist leaders expelled over fifty Trotskyists at one stroke in August 1937. The Socialist National Executive Committee condemned the New York expulsions, then legalized them retroactively because the expelled Trotskyists had begun publishing the *Appeal* again. A steady wave of expulsions flowed through the party over the following weeks. "We welcomed the expulsions," Shachtman remembered. "We were enormously enthusiastic." The Trotskyists walked away with the majority of Socialists in New York, California, Chicago, Ohio, and Minnesota. The Socialist Party continued on a downward, rightward spiral. From 17,000 members at the end of 1935 and 11,000 in mid-1936, it fell to about 6,000 members at the end of 1937, barely 3,000 in mid-1938, and under 2,000 by the end of 1940.[68]

Trotskyists emerged from the split with over a thousand members. In addition, the Young People's Socialist League broke its ties to the Socialist Party and took the name Young People's Socialist League (Fourth International), adding hundreds more to the ranks of U.S. Fourth Internationalists. Still dwarfed by the Communists, the Trotskyists were now at least comparable in strength to the couple of thousand ineffectual Socialists.[69] In January 1938 they founded the Socialist Workers Party. Its foundation was a prelude to the official proclamation of the Fourth International.

Shachtman's highest recognition in the Trotskyist movement came on 3 September 1938. On that day he presided in the village of Périgny outside Paris over the founding congress of the Fourth International, an attempt to prepare the world's Trotskyists for daunting tasks ahead. Trotsky had said since 1933 that another world war was inevitable unless socialist revolutions averted the danger. After the Barcelona events of 1937, war rather than revolution was the immediate prospect. Trotsky counted on the congress to solidify and invigorate his following so that it could hold together and make a breakthrough during the war, which he thought would make or break Trotskyism.

By September 1938 the most dynamic political force in the world, to all outward appearances, was fascism. Hitler had crushed the German Social Democratic and Communist parties, the central bulwarks of the European labor movement. He treated with contempt every rule that governed the European order between the wars—the peace treaties, the disarmament requirements, the requirements for German reparations, the League of Nations, the intricate structure of loans and deals—and the rules faded as if they had never been more than diplomats' daydreams. In 1936 the German army, barely reconstituted, occupied the previously demilitarized Rhineland. In March 1938 it occupied Austria. As the Fourth International's congress met, the Germans were preparing to march into Czechoslovakia, an attack on a French ally that the British and French governments would meet with ignominious surrender.

People's faith in the capitalist world order had already been shaken by the First World War. To the extent faith survived in the 1920s, it rested largely on the illusion that Wilsonian liberalism—benevolent preparation of colonies for independence, free trade, the League of Nations—could reform the world order and guarantee peace. But free trade was destroyed by the Depression; movements for national independence in India and Nicaragua were suppressed; and the League of Nations was a joke once it had failed to stop Italy's conquest of Ethiopia. Liberal illusions were propped up in the late 1930s by those unlikely crutches, the Communist International and the Soviet Union. Communists preached "collective security" as the salvation of democracy. As war impended over Czechoslovakia, Stalin vowed to defend it against Germany if France would.

Trotskyists were set apart from Stalinists by their rejection of all illusions about the status quo and peace. They were fervently anti-fascist; in February 1939 they would organize a protest by tens of thousands of people against a Nazi rally at Madison Square Garden, with Shachtman and other leaders speaking eloquently and standing firm at the head of the march as police attacked it. With their rally front-page news and their leaflet reproduced by the millions in the daily papers, Trotskyists' anti-fascist credentials were secure. But Shachtman attacked Communists' defense of Czechoslovakia, a country which he called a "synthetic product of an abominable peace treaty," a "pawn of French imperialism" that oppressed

Slovaks, Germans, Hungarians, and Ukrainians. He ridiculed Communists in Dublin who before Munich "ran up and down the city calling upon all good Irishmen and true to rally to the defense of that institution so deeply beloved by Erin—British Democracy."[70] Like Trotsky, Shachtman expected that once war began, discontent with it would grow rapidly—and Trotskyists' moment would come.

Given the weakness of the scattered Trotskyist groups, unity behind a clear program would be crucial to their survival and ability to seize new opportunities. Although Trotsky had originally meant the Fourth International to be founded with larger forces than his own small following, the Popular Front's appeal had pulled European socialists away from his movement. Even some of the Trotskyist groups had deserted him. The unifications and splits of the mid-1930s seemed to many to lead "to nothing more positive than the constant churning up of stagnant water," Shachtman said. Although congress organizers talked about Trotskyist groups in thirty-one countries, when the congress assembled it claimed to represent only eleven. The Socialist Workers Party, the largest of them, had about a thousand members, well below the two or three thousand Trotsky had originally set as a minimum; the Belgian, French, and Polish groups had several hundred each; most of the Germans were in jails or concentration camps. The rest counted their members in handfuls. Trotsky counted on Shachtman to help make the congress a success and end the movement's retreat. Shachtman's "work not only during but after the conference will be of the greatest value," he said.[71]

The few dozen delegates—including three from the United States, Shachtman, Cannon, and Nathan Gould—gathered in secrecy in a little village on the outskirts of Paris. They met in pleasant surroundings, a converted barn belonging to an old French radical leader in the middle of a beautiful garden. But the mood, as the young Greek delegate Michel Raptis remembered it, was somber. The delegates were weighed down by a sense of their responsibility. Even Cannon, whom Raptis thought of as jovial and outgoing, seemed subdued. The delegates were afraid to let anyone else know about their meeting place for fear of giving Stalin's agents a chance to attack. They met for only a single day, beginning at 9:30 in the morning and continuing until late at night, all of them sitting around one long table.[72]

The delegates spent much of the day discussing how to prepare for the war, expose the war plans of the United States and its allies-to-be along with Hitler's, and move toward a transformed postwar world. Shachtman's biggest contribution was a "Thesis on the World Role of American Imperialism." Much of it restated what Trotskyists had been saying since their anti-war manifesto of 1934. It repeated the verdict that the United States was "the principal motive force in propelling the capitalist world towards

another war and the firmest brake upon the revolutionary movement."[73]
But Shachtman's resolution went beyond orthodoxy to prophecy, foreseeing a postwar world ruled from Washington and New York. It went
beyond mere prediction too, to plot a joint fight after the war by U.S.,
Latin American, and Asian rebels against the new empire.

In Europe, the resolution said, the only capitalist alternative to postwar
German domination was postwar U.S. domination. Trotsky had warned as
early as 1926 that the United States was consolidating its hold over Europe,
though both Communist and anti-Communist opponents ridiculed the
idea. The resolution accepted Trotsky's analysis that U.S. isolationism of
the 1920s and 1930s was only a façade and U.S. passivity in Europe had
only been a measure of its supremacy there. The resolution said that U.S.
rulers were now about to drop their isolationist mask, which belonged to
"an epoch of the past."

> It is out of the question for the United States to remain a passive observer
> of the coming war. Quite the contrary. Not only will it participate
> actively as one of the belligerents, but it is easy to predict that it will enter
> the war after a much shorter interval than elapsed before its entry into the
> last world war. . . . The United States will dictate the terms of the
> imperialist peace after emerging as the victor. Its participation will not
> only determine the victory of the side it joins, but will also determine the
> disposition of the booty, of which it will claim the lion's share.[74]

The U.S. call for an "open door" in China and east Asia was as deceitful
as its isolationism in Europe. Both stances cloaked U.S. designs for mas-
tery, which Japan blocked in the Pacific as Germany did in the Atlantic.
"Behind this 'pacific' slogan is the half-drawn sword—against both Japan
and England for an increasing right to exploit China." U.S. war preparations were already visible in reinforcements of its Aleutian and Guam bases
and Roosevelt's demand for the highest peacetime naval budget ever.
Already these war preparations were helping the United States supplant
Britain in Canada and Australia, which turned to the United States for
protection against Japan.[75] U.S. socialists had to respond by demanding
U.S. withdrawal from the Pacific and independence for U.S. colonies there:
Hawaii, Samoa, and the Philippines.

The U.S. government's democratic and peaceful masquerade was nowhere so obviously fraudulent as in Latin America. There Roosevelt had
devised a new form of sugarcoating—his "good neighbor" policy, which
meant only that "the policy of the iron fist in Latin America is sheathed in
the velvet glove of demogogic pretensions of friendship and 'democracy.'"
Roosevelt's real policy was revealed by his loyalty to Anastasio Somoza,
"our son of a bitch" in Nicaragua.

The Monroe Doctrine has been uniformly interpreted by all the Washington administrators as the right of American imperialism to the dominant position in the Latin American countries, preliminary to the conquest of the position as their exclusive exploiter. In the Central American, Caribbean, and upper-South American countries in particular, this has signified . . . the imposition, often by the most naked use of force, of governments which are the merest puppets in the hands of Wall Street. . . . The real character of "democratic" American capitalism is best revealed by . . . the bloodthirsty despots under whose oppressive rule the millions of workers and peasants of Latin America suffer.[76]

Shachtman's interest in linking Latin American and North American struggles dated back to the mid-1920s. He had been acting secretary of the Communist-backed All American Anti-Imperialist League, which had published a Spanish-language monthly called *El Libertador* in Mexico and claimed to have sections in eleven countries. In 1933 he had said, "For the masses in Latin America, the struggle for liberation from Yankee oppression is bound up by a thousand invisible threads with the movement of the American working class."

Although Shachtman's call for a "union of the Latin American peoples" recalled Trotskyists' 1934 slogan of a "Soviet United States of South and Central America," he now pushed Trotskyists toward a more Pan-American strategy. His resolution declared that U.S. revolutionaries were bound to Latin American rebels by more than ordinary ties of international solidarity. The Socialist Workers Party should organize protests against U.S. intervention in Latin America, try to keep U.S. troops north of the Rio Grande, and demand independence for Puerto Rico and the Virgin Islands. In a prevision of "borderlands" battles, refugee organizing, and resistance to the U.S.-Mexico free-trade pact decades later, the resolution said that U.S. radicals had to organize Mexican, Caribbean, and Latin American working people *within the United States*, to link them not only with U.S. unions but also with "revolutionary movements in the countries from which these workers originally came." Latin American and U.S. revolutionary struggles would join to create "the United Socialist Republics of the Americas."[77]

Shachtman summed up the case against supporting the Allies in an anti-war manifesto he drafted for the congress. Fascism and war were simply the "poisons" emitted by "mortally wounded" capitalism, the manifesto said. Shachtman scoffed at Communists and social democrats who swore that the war would be fought not "for spheres of influence, sources of raw materials, colonies and markets" but "for the Great and Honorable Cause of smashing fascism. . . . The garbage which these social-democratic war missionaries spread before the workers is not new; it is the same foul stuff with which they poisoned the European masses twenty-five years ago," he said. "*The mothers of the people are called upon to become brood sows . . . fields will be transformed into blood-soaked trenches and cities into devastated tombs—so that the imperialists may preserve their profits and their colonies, or acquire new ones.*" Only the Fourth International, the manifesto concluded, offered a way out.[78]

Trotskyists did not delude themselves that they had anything like the strength necessary to save the world. Polish Trotskyists in particular pointed out the movement's weakness. Before and during the congress, the Poles made a strong case against proclaiming an International on this feeble basis. They pointed out that each of the previous Internationals (the First, founded in 1864; the Second, founded in 1889; and the Third, founded in 1919) had had thousands of working-class people in several countries behind it at its foundation. Each, by the act of its foundation, was staking a plausible claim to international leadership. The Trotskyist claim had no such plausibility. In these circumstances the Poles saw proclaiming the Fourth International as "a gesture, . . . a folly."[79]

Trotsky insisted that his followers had to push forward alone. "This International will become strong by our own action, not by maneuvers with other groups," he said. "We have no reason to boast that we are strong, but we are what we are." Shachtman supported Trotsky before and during the congress. But unlike the Brazilian Mario Pedrosa and other delegates who attacked the Poles with bluster and called them "Mensheviks," Shachtman looked carefully at their historical analogies before concluding that they were wrong. Lenin had not waited for the Russian Revolution before calling for a new international, he pointed out, nor for communist parties to be built outside Russia before proclaiming it. He declared the need for it in 1914 when the need became clear. Then he delayed proclaiming it for five years "because he hoped to win over various vacillating and centrist groups," just as Trotsky delayed from 1933 to 1938. But there was no reason to delay any longer. "All the centrist organizations have either disintegrated or evolved away from us," Shachtman said. "The path is thus clear for the proclamation of the Fourth, and it is necessary to constitute it definitively."[80]

The Poles' defeat in the final vote was a foregone conclusion. But Shachtman went out of his way to stand up for them later in the session. Stalin had just decreed the dissolution of the Polish Communist Party on the fantastic pretext that it was controlled by Trotskyists and Gestapo agents. Trotsky proposed that Polish Trotskyists proclaim a new Polish communist party. Again the Poles resisted. To proclaim a party with their 350 people would be a "useless and dangerous . . . fiction," they said. Emboldened by the earlier victory over the Poles, several delegates condemned them for their lack of revolutionary zeal and said that they should be ordered to found a party. But Shachtman shrank from imposing policy on a national group. He said that the Polish group should "concentrate from the present moment 90 percent of its energy toward the creation of a new communist party." But it should not "rush into proclaiming the new party without the necessary preparation." Shachtman's face-saving compromise passed.

Several times at the congress a proposal by Shachtman ended a discussion. One theme reiterated again and again in the minutes shows how great his authority in the International had grown. Delegates said unanimously and repeatedly that Shachtman had to stay in Europe as a permanent member of the International Secretariat. The French delegates said that unless Shachtman came to Paris they would insist that the International's center be moved to New York. The congress as a whole voted unanimously that he should stay in Europe.[81] Many of the delegates must have wondered afterwards if Shachtman's life or the International's would have been different if he had obeyed the summons. None of them could have guessed that when the International held its next conference he would not even be allowed to attend.

Shachtman did not move to Paris. Instead several of the International's leaders moved to New York. One of them was C. L. R. James, a Black Trotskyist intellectual from Trinidad who was three years older than Shachtman, and already well known as a novelist, historian, Pan-African leader, and cricket writer. James left London and became one of Shachtman's collaborators on the *New International*. He began assembling a devoted personal following among U.S. Trotskyists who were drawn by his passionate speeches, tall, muscular handsomeness, and charisma. For some of them he was "a figure of physical grace and the veritable symbol of revolutionary promise."[82] For the Trotskyist movement as a whole, James was one of a handful of leaders who gave the Fourth International intellectual distinction, a man who wrote confidently about a wide range of subjects including Plato, Lenin, Africa, Herman Melville, cricket, and the comics.

The foundation of the Fourth International was a defiant gesture in the face of overwhelming odds. By the normal ground rules of political life in 1938, the proclamation of this tiny movement seemed senseless. But it made sense in Trotsky's mind and his followers' minds, because they saw that normal ground rules were about to be suspended by a world war. In those last months before the war broke out, thinking people saw it opening up in front of them like an abyss. Trotskyists believed that they were laying the foundations for the bridge that would allow humanity to get across the abyss.

Notes

1. Shachtman, "The League and the new party" (Aug. 1934), MSC b 7 f 15 (r 3356).
2. Shachtman to Glotzer (7 Sept. 1933), MSC b 6 f 26 (r 3354); Shachtman, *Genesis of Trotskyism*, 3; Shachtman, "A stupendous bureaucracy," NI v 1 n 3 (Sept.–Oct. 1934), 80.
3. "The League and the new party," MSC b 7 f 15 (r 3356).
4. Leon Trotsky, *The Soviet Union and the Fourth International*, 28.
5. "For the Fourth International!" NI v 1 n 1 (July 1934), 1.
6. Novack, "Max Shachtman," *International Socialist Review* v 34 n 2 (Feb. 1973), 26.
7. Shachtman to Abern (22 June 1933), PMA b 11 f 42; NI v 1 n 3 (Sept.–Oct. 1934), NI v 1 n 4 (Nov. 1934) and NI v 1 n 5 (Dec. 1934), back inside covers; Sard to NI (Aug. 1938), NI v 4 n 11 (Nov. 1938) (also MSC b 8 f 12 [r 3358]); Trotsky to Shachtman (18 Sept. 1935), TA 10317.
8. Shachtman, "Radicalism in the thirties," in Simon, ed., *As We Saw the Thirties*, 22.
9. CLA NC (5 and 9 July 1934), MSC b 6 f 10 (r 3353).
10. Farrell Dobbs, *Teamster Rebellion*, 149–50; interview with Dobbs (Dec. 1977); Alan Wald, *The New York Intellectuals*, 105; James Cannon, *The History of American Trotskyism*, 158–60.
11. Cannon, *History of American Trotskyism*, 162; Shachtman, "Frame-up against League leaders," M v 7 n 31 (4 Aug. 1934), 4.
12. Shachtman, "Twenty-five years of American Trotskyism," NI v 20 n 1 (Jan.–Feb. 1954), 18; RMS 217.
13. RMS 221; interview with Muste by Yorburg (31 May 1965), Oral History Research Office, Butler Library, Columbia University, NY, 6; M v 4 n 18 (18 Aug. 1931), 1; "Discussions between American Workers Party and the Communist League" (26 Feb. 1934), PMA b 14 f 1; CLA NC (28 Aug., 12 and 21 Sept., 22 Oct., 19 Nov. 1934), MSC b 6 f 10 (r 3353).
14. Interview with Glotzer (24 Mar. 1989), s 3; Glotzer to Drucker (6 Jan. 1990), 4–5; Glotzer to Shachtman (22 Oct. 1934), MSC b 6 f 28 (r 3354) (also PMA b 14 f 2).
15. Shachtman, "Report on the international resolution" (12 July 1935), MSC b 6 f 39 (r 3354); Cannon, Swabeck, and Shachtman, "Resolution on the organizational report" (Nov. 1934), MSC b 7 f 11 (r 3355).
16. Wald, *NY Intellectuals*, 176–79; RMS 336–39; interview with Glotzer (28 Mar. 1989), s 6.
17. Feeley, "Fighter for the unemployed," *Socialist Action* (Feb. 1984), 10.
18. "Prospects for a new party in America," NI v 1 n 3 (Sept.–Oct. 1934), 65–66.
19. Shachtman to Abern (6 July 1933), PMA b 11 f 42; Shachtman, "Report on theses for attitude towards SP and CP" (late 1935), MSC b 7 f 19 (r 3356); Shachtman, "The road to the Fourth International" (10 Aug. 1935), MSC b 7 f 19 (r 3356).
20. CLA NC (24 Sept. 1934), MSC b 6 f 10 (r 3353); WP PC (13 Jan. 1935), MSC b 7 f 1 (r 3355); WP NC, "Statement on labor party question" (16 Mar. 1935), MSC b 7 f 8 (r 3355); Shachtman, "The problem of the labor party," NI v 2 n 2 (Mar. 1935), 36; Shachtman, "'People's Front'—new panacea of Stalinism," *New Militant* v 2 n 2 (11 Jan. 1936), 3.

21. FI International Conference, "The situation in the United States" (29–31 July 1936), *Documents of the Fourth International*, 132–35.
22. Art Preis, *Labor's Giant Step*, 37–38, 52, 48; Eric Chester, *Socialists and the Ballot Box*, 68–69.
23. "Labor party discussion" (1938) and Trotsky, "The problem of the labor party" (1938), MSC b 8 f 4 (r 3357).
24. SWP NC (22–25 Apr. 1938), MSC b 8 f 4 (r 3357); SWP PC (7 July 1938), MSC b 8 f 7 (r 3358); Shachtman, "For a labor party" (1938), WP Basic Documents 2 (1946), ISM v 16, 679–81 (also in NI v 4 n 8 [Aug. 1938] and MSC b 8 f 16 [r 3358]).
25. Preis, *Labor's Giant Step*, 72.
26. Shachtman, "Introduction" (15 Mar. 1936), in Leon Trotsky, *The Third International after Lenin*, xlii.
27. Shachtman, "The Stalinist convention," NI v 4 n 7 (July 1938), 203.
28. Shachtman, "Under the banner of Marxism" (misdated 19 Mar. 1949), WP bul v 4 n 1 (Jan. 1949), ISM v 10, 2126; Shachtman, "FDR—a capitalist statesman," LA v 9 n 17 (23 Apr. 1945), 4.
29. Shachtman, "Under the banner of Marxism," ISM v 10, 2120–21, 2124–26.
30. Shachtman, *The Fight for Socialism*, 90; "Under the banner of Marxism," ISM v 10, 2157.
31. Shachtman, "'People's Front'—new panacea of Stalinism," *New Militant* v 2 n 2 (11 Jan. 1936), 3.
32. Shachtman, "Radicalism in the thirties," in Simon, ed., *As We Saw the Thirties*, 27, 37.
33. Shachtman and Cannon to Trotsky (4 Jan. 1936), TA 5077.
34. Breitman to Wald (17 July 1985), cited in Wald, *NY Intellectuals*, 110; Bernard Johnpoll, *Pacifist's Progress*, 190–91.
35. Wald, *NY Intellectuals*, 283, 181; interview with Benson (6 Apr. 1989), s 1; interview with Draper (13 Feb. 1989), s 1.
36. Jacobson, "The two deaths of Max Shachtman," *New Politics* v 10 n 2 (Winter 1973), 96.
37. Interview with J. Jacobson (21 Apr. 1984); Maurice Isserman, *If I Had a Hammer*, 41; Jacobson, "The two deaths," 96; Irving Howe, *A Margin of Hope*, 45.
38. Interview with Glotzer (24 Mar. 1989), s 1; Glotzer to Drucker (6 Jan. 1990), 4–5; MSC b 6 f 28 (r 3354); interview with Glotzer (4 Apr. 1989), s 10.
39. Interview with Glotzer (4 Apr. 1989), s 1; Haskell, "Max Shachtman," 7 (unpublished manuscript); interview with Seidlitz (16 Jan. 1989), s 3.
40. Shachtman, *Behind the Moscow Trial*, 119–24.
41. Ibid., 130–31.
42. Shachtman, "Nineteen years of the Russian revolution," SA v 2 n 10 (1 Nov. 1936), 5.
43. Trotsky, *Soviet Union and Fourth International*, 25; FI International Conference, "The Fourth International and the Soviet Union" (29–31 July 1936), *Documents of the Fourth International*, 104–5 (also PMA b 14 f 28).
44. "The Fourth International and the Soviet Union," 107; Shachtman, "Introduction" (23 Mar. 1937), in Trotsky, *In Defense of the Soviet Union*, 3; Shachtman, "Introduction" (15 Mar. 1936), in Trotsky, *The Third International after Lenin*, xvii–xviii.
45. Shachtman, "Behind the Kirov assassination," NI v 2 n 1 (Jan. 1935), 5–6;

Shachtman, *Behind the Moscow Trial*, 30, 7.
46. Shachtman, *Behind the Moscow Trial*, 124, 117; Shachtman, "Introduction" (1 May 1937), in Leon Trotsky, *The Stalin School of Falsification*, xxvi.
47. Shachtman, *Behind the Moscow Trial*, 105–6, 71–72.
48. RMS 371–74, 379–83; Shachtman to Trotsky (8, 11, 13 Dec. 1936), TA 15426; Isaac Deutscher, *Prophet Outcast*, 356–58.
49. Trotsky to Shachtman (18 June 1936), TA 10318.
50. "The legacy of the Workers Party, 1940–49," ed. Paul Buhle, OHAL, 19; interview with Seidlitz (16 Jan. 1989), s 1; Irving Kristol, *Reflections of a Neoconservative*, 5, 8, 7; Howe, *Margin of Hope*, 12–13, 28, 64, 34; Wald, *NY Intellectuals*, 312–13.
51. Shachtman, *Behind the Moscow Trial*, 142, 126; Shachtman, "Radicalism in the thirties," in Simon, ed., *As We Saw the Thirties* 40–41; RMS 287; Shachtman to Dunayevskaya (28 Feb. 1938), TA 7100.
52. Interview with Haskell (8 July 1989), s 1; Shachtman, "Introduction" (1 May 1937), in Trotsky, *Stalin School of Falsification*, xxviii.
53. CP PC (27 Oct. 1928), MSC b 1 f 21 (r 3345); IS, *War and the 4th International*.
54. Interview with Geltman (22 Mar. 1989), s 1; interview with Glotzer (24 Mar. 1989), s 2; Burnham and Carter, "Amendment to draft resolution," Organizing Committee for the Socialist Party Convention bul n 2 (Nov. 1937), 13 (SP Papers, Duke University Library, Durham, North Carolina [r 129]).
55. SWP convention (31 Dec. 1937–3 Jan. 1938), MSC b 8 f 1 (r 3357); interview with Geltman (22 Mar. 1989), s 1; Trotsky, "The problem of the Ukraine" (22 Apr. 1939), SA v 3 n 31 (9 May 1939), 2.
56. SWP PC (4 Aug. 1938), MSC b 8 f 7 (r 3358); FI 1st congress, *Documents of the Fourth International*, 291–94.
57. SWP NC (19–20 Nov. 1938), MSC b 8 f 5 (r 3357); SWP PC (12 Dec. 1938), MSC b 8 f 7 (r 3357).
58. FI International Conference, "The situation in the United States" (29–31 July 1936), *Documents of the Fourth International*, 132, 134, 136.
59. Shachtman, "In this corner," SA v 3 n 25 (18 Apr. 1939), 4.
60. Shachtman, *Behind the Moscow Trial*, 117.
61. Shachtman, "Introduction" (20 Sept. 1937), in Leon Trotsky, *Stalinism and Bolshevism*, 3.
62. Shachtman, "The tale of the Socialist Party," DW v 2 n 157 (22 Sept. 1924), 4; RMS 463, 293.
63. Interview with Muste by Yorburg (31 May 1965), Oral History Research Office, Butler Library, Columbia University, NY, 16.
64. Interview with Seidlitz (16 Jan. 1989), s 1; Abern, Bernick, Burnham, and Shachtman, "Where is the petty bourgeois opposition?" (9 Mar. 1940), NI v 6 n 5 (June 1940), 111.
65. Shachtman, "The 'Left': saviors of reformism," M v 4 n 4 (15 Feb. 1931), 6; Shachtman, "Right face in the Socialist Party," NI v 1 n 5 (Dec. 1934), 131; Shachtman to Spencer (9 Apr. 1937), PMA b 14 f 29.
66. Trotsky to Cannon and Shachtman (25 May 1937), PMA b 14 f 13; RMS 294.
67. RMS 298; Cannon, Shachtman, and Trimble to Appeal members (29 June 1937), PMA b 14 f 34.
68. Shachtman, "Supporting LaGuardia betrays socialism," SA v 1 n 5 (11 Sept. 1937), 2; RMS 299–300; "The convention of the new party," NI v 4 n 1 (Jan. 1938), 5; Johnpoll, *Pacifist's Progress*, 171, 190–91, 222.

69. James, "The roots of the party crisis" (late 1939), PMA b 16 f 19; Breitman to Wald (17 July 1985), cited in Wald, *NY Intellectuals*, 165.

70. Interview with Seidlitz (16 Jan. 1989), s 1; SA v 3 n 10 (24 Feb. 1939), 1, 3; NI v 4 n 7 (July 1938), 197; FI 1st congress, "Against imperialist war!" (3 Sept. 1938), *Documents of the Fourth International*, 171; Shachtman, "Introduction" (15 Mar. 1936), in Trotsky, *Third International after Lenin*, xlii; "The 4th International is launched," NI v 4 n 11 (Nov. 1938), 326.

71. Shachtman, "The 4th International is launched," NI v 4 n 11 (Nov. 1938), 326; IS circular n 2 (11 June 1938), MSC b 8 f 12 (r 3358); FI 1st congress (3 Sept. 1938), *Documents of the Fourth International*, 284, 289; Mandel to Drucker (9 May 1989); Trotsky to Cannon (25 May 1938), TA 7533.

72. Raptis, "Le 3 sept 1938," *Sous le drapeau du Socialisme* n 108–9 (Nov.–Dec. 1988), 30–32; FI 1st congress, 284–85, 287.

73. Leon Trotsky, *Germany: The Key to the International Situation*, 19; Shachtman to Kerry (8 July 1969), MSC b 29 f 37 (r 3380); FI 1st congress, "Thesis on the world role of American imperialism" (3 Sept. 1938), *Documents of the Fourth International*, 248–49.

74. "Thesis on the world role of American imperialism," 249, 246–47.

75. Ibid., 247–48.

76. Ibid., 244, 242–43.

77. James P. Cannon, *James P. Cannon and the Early Years of American Communism*, 386 n; Shachtman, "Communism and the Negro" (1933), TA 17244; IS, *War and the 4th International*, 11; "Thesis on the world role of American imperialism," 250–51.

78. Shachtman to Kerry (8 July 1969), MSC b 29 f 37 (r 3380); "Against imperialist war!" *Documents of the Fourth International*, 171–73; Shachtman, "Old garbage in new pails," NI v 5 n 6 (June 1939), 180.

79. FI 1st congress (3 Sept. 1938), 296–97.

80. "International Conference" (Apr. 1938—discussion with Trotsky), MSC b 8 f 4 (r 3357); SWP NC (22–25 Apr. 1938), MSC b 8 f 4 (r 3357); FI 1st congress, 297–98. Deutscher, *Prophet Outcast*, 422, attributes harsh attacks on the Polish delegates to Shachtman, particularly the charge that they were "Mensheviks." Not only did Shachtman emphatically deny ever having said this (Shachtman to Naville [6 Nov. 1963], MSC b 30 f 24 [r 3381]), but the minutes Deutscher himself relied on attribute that comment not to Shachtman but to the Brazilian Mario Pedrosa (FI 1st congress [3 Sept. 1938], 298).

81. FI 1st congress, 289, 298, 301, 288, 299–300.

82. Paul Buhle, *C. L. R. James*, 12, 69; interview with Zeluck by Buhle (15 Dec. 1982), OHAL, s 1; interview with Glotzer (24 Mar. 1989), s 5.

4

War

By 1939, the approach of the Second World War cast a shadow over political discussions in the United States. Trotskyists were as foresighted as anyone in making out the shape of the approaching conflict. But the actual outbreak of the war in September showed that Shachtman disagreed with many other Trotskyists about how to respond to it. In the spring of 1940 he still saw himself as a Trotskyist, but others no longer saw him as an "orthodox" Trotskyist. He became a leader of his own organization, with his own distinctive vision and strategy.

Shachtman agreed with other Trotskyists in seeing the Second World War as an attempt by different national capitalisms to solve their crises at one another's expense, an attempt in which U.S. capitalism was also culpable. The government that had sent its marines to Haiti and Nicaragua was now warding off German influence in South America; the government that had tried to forcibly impose an "open door" for U.S. investment in China now tried to resist Japanese encroachment there; the government that had helped extract reparations and profits from Germany now resisted Germany's aggressive independence. But Shachtman differed from other Trotskyists in the strategy he put forward, a strategy based on solidarity with movements of resistance that might arise against any of the warring empires. Unlike others, he put the Soviet Union among the empires that had to be resisted.

After the British and French capitulation at Munich, Trotsky predicted that Stalin would try to make a deal with Hitler. The result would be another world war and the "physical extermination" of Eastern European Jews.[1] The Socialist Workers Party was so convinced of war's inevitability that it held a special party convention in July 1939 devoted almost entirely to preparing for it.

On 23 August Trotskyists were vindicated and liberals and Communists thrown into confusion when Trotsky's prediction came true. Germany and the Soviet Union signed a nonaggression pact that guaranteed that the Soviet Union would not go to war with Germany even if Germany attacked

Poland. Secret clauses of the agreement guaranteed a Soviet sphere of influence in eastern Poland (inhabited mostly by Belorussians and Ukrainians) and the Baltic states of Lithuania, Latvia, and Estonia. The colonels who ruled Poland managed to drag Britain and France into war behind them despite the pact. But British and French armies stood by almost inactive as the German army crushed Poland and the Soviet army marched in to claim Stalin's share.

In hindsight, the events of late 1939 seem more like a prologue to world war than the war itself. The main acts of the war came later: the first act in May–June 1940, when the German army attacked through Belgium, cut apart the French army, and occupied Western Europe; the second in June 1941, when the German army attacked the Soviet Union; the third in December 1941, when Japan attacked British, Dutch, and U.S. forces in Asia. Only after all these deals, betrayals, and attacks did the alignments of the war solidify: the United States, Britain, and the Soviet Union on one side, Germany and Japan on the other.

The war that broke out in September 1939 looked different: The Soviet Union was aligned with Germany against Britain and France. In November 1939 Stalin moved to protect his northwestern flank by demanding that Finland turn over bases and territory to the Soviet Union. When Finland refused, the Soviet army attacked. Finland had been a base for British and French intervention against the Bolsheviks in 1918–21; it seemed likely to become a British and French base again for an attack on the Soviet Union. And Trotsky, as foresighted as ever, predicted that the bargain between Hitler and Stalin would break down and war would break out between Germany and the USSR.

The Soviet wars against Poland and Finland were analyzed by Trotskyists in different ways. Sometimes the wars were seen primarily as conflicts between capitalist powers—Germany against Britain and France—with the USSR as a German ally. Sometimes they were seen as wars to expand the Soviet bureaucracy's own territory and power. Sometimes they were seen as preventive wars in defense of nationalized property, which could be threatened by either an Allied intervention in Finland or the expected German invasion. The Soviet wars were also entangled in other wars: the defensive war China had been fighting since Japan attacked in 1937; the war of resistance Europeans would soon be waging against German occupation; wars of colonial liberation Asians would be fighting against both the Allies and Japan. Most Trotskyists spent the war years trying to unravel these strands so they could deal with them separately.

Shachtman, instead of dealing with the war piecemeal, tried to do what communists had done in the First World War: characterize the war as a whole. His attitude toward the Second World War owed much to Lenin's earlier analysis. Although working people's hatred of fascism made this war seem different, he said that it was, at bottom, "*a direct continuation of the war of 1914–1918.*"[2] Socialists' attitude toward it should be a continuation of Lenin's fight against the war of 1914–18. Lenin had opposed any socialist complicity in the First World War so that socialists could lead a potentially revolutionary movement for peace. He had opposed the war as a whole. He even opposed Serbia's war of self-defense against Austria in 1914. However wrong the Austrian attack was, Lenin argued, Serbian resistance was a tool of Russian imperial ambitions in the Balkans.

Shachtman looked at the Second World War with the same basic concerns as Lenin and made the same basic choices. He resisted any tactic that would lead socialists to support German, British, or U.S. imperial power, even critically or indirectly. The chief issue of the war was "who is going to get the major share of the swag," the *New International* said. "The blood stains all of their hands alike." From the onset of the war the *New International* resisted any attempt to portray it as a conflict between the "democratic West" and some alien force.

> Hitler is not Attila. . . . The Nazis are neither barbarians from the North nor infidels from the South. They are flesh of Europe's flesh and bone of Europe's bone. They represent a stage in the development of capitalist society, the epoch of its decay.[3]

In short, all the capitalist armies represented barbarism. Shachtman believed in the possibility of a third force arising, a force for civilization that could defeat Nazism without upholding U.S. or any other capitalism.

The idea of a third force, a "third camp," was common to all Trotskyists when the Second World War broke out. But Shachtman put the "third camp" at the center of all his arguments, while other Trotskyists focused on a different slogan: the "unconditional defense of the USSR." With the Soviet invasion of Poland, the two slogans conflicted for the first time. The third camp in Poland, the camp of revolutionary opposition to all the imperial powers, could only be an independent Polish resistance. Whatever independent Polish resistance there was—actual or potential—the Soviet Union in alliance with Germany was at war with it. Shachtman decided that the Soviet Union could not be defended in this war. He denied that the international working class had more to gain from a Soviet victory than from a German, British, or French victory. Once Shachtman staked out this position, he came into conflict with Trotsky, ended his alliance with Jim Cannon, and formed a new current within international Trotskyism.

In the course of a fierce debate over the war in the Socialist Workers Party from September 1939 to April 1940, Shachtman unearthed and sharpened differences with Cannon, half-buried since the early 1930s, about Marxism as a way of thinking and organizing. Like Cannon's, Shachtman's Marxism was intransigently internationalist, included a commitment to building the Fourth International, and held its adherents to a high standard of political education and activity. But the Marxism Shachtman argued for was a body of thought still expanding and developing, being continually reshaped through constant discussion both inside the Marxist movement and with working people outside it.

Shachtman wanted to add innovations to this body of thought, beginning with a new look at the Soviet Union. He could not accept Cannon's emphasis on preserving unchanged the substance of what Marx, Lenin, and Trotsky had handed down. As Cannon's orthodoxy won support from a majority of the SWP, Shachtman fought for the right to present his own ideas to a broader public, first through the Trotskyists' publications, then through an independent publication that he demanded the right to publish. In response, Cannon insisted that the revolutionary party must have one clear public voice, the voice of the majority.

In April 1940 Shachtman left the Socialist Workers Party and founded his own Workers Party on the basis of his own conceptions. But both before he created the Workers Party and afterwards, he had to defend his open version of Marxism from another side, against radicals who challenged basic Marxist axioms. In early 1939 and again in 1940–41, he wrote at length to uphold a core set of Marxist ideas that were still central to his worldview. He defended the heritage of the Russian Revolution and a Marxist understanding of Stalinism and fascism. He continued, in a critical and democratic spirit, to try to adapt Leninism to the United States. In the process he attacked leading radical intellectuals such as Sidney Hook, Max Eastman, Dwight Macdonald, and his former ally James Burnham.

He set out to weld his followers into a strong, cohesive force by following the "really best traditions of the Marxist movement" of pre–First World War Germany and Russia.[4] He renounced the dogmatic and conservative habits Trotskyists had picked up in the Communist International of the 1920s but defended the idea of a disciplined, activist organization. He succeeded in giving the Workers Party the identity he wanted: a Trotskyist identity, but one that stressed the critical and democratic strains within Trotskyism and pushed the group outward toward the working class. He took a group consisting largely of students and unemployed ex-students and helped turn them into organizers.

In the early 1940s Shachtman saw the new Workers Party as *the* U.S. revolutionary party, the force that would win workers away from capitalist ideas and organize them to take power. It was the radical movement's "repository of socialist consciousness" and "organized memory," which joined "yesterday with today" and "today with tomorrow."[5] As he mourned the loss of Trotsky's friendship, made permanent by Trotsky's assassination in August 1940, he said that he was doing what had to be done in the United States to build Trotsky's International. All his independent thoughts that had been germinating through the 1930s reached fruition in the Workers Party's "third-camp" Marxism of the early and mid-1940s.

The most enduring aspect of his evolving third-camp Marxism was his theory of "bureaucratic collectivism" in the USSR, which he laid out for the first time in November 1940. The theory justified his abandonment of unconditional loyalty to the USSR. It borrowed not only its phraseology but much of its content from the theory Burnham and Joe Carter had come up with in 1938. Like Carter and Burnham, Shachtman said that there can be no socialism and no workers' state without some form of working-class political power. Like them, he rejected Trotsky's characterization of the USSR as a workers' state. Like them, he said that the Soviet state had become the instrument of a new, bureaucratic ruling class.

But Shachtman did not turn his back completely on the Soviet experiment and dismiss it as a failure. By synthesizing some of Carter's and Burnham's insights with some of Trotsky's, he continued to maintain that the Russian Revolution had not yet been entirely undone. Like Trotsky, he still said that collective property in the Soviet Union, though bureaucratically mismanaged, was an advance over capitalism, a necessary condition for the dramatic Soviet economic growth of the 1930s, and a sign that the world had entered an epoch of transition toward socialism. The Soviet Union's bureaucratic class relations were in contradiction with its collectivist property forms, he said. Socialists should save Soviet collectivism by overthrowing the bureaucracy and reestablishing the workers' democracy of the revolution's first months.

The Workers Party spent the spring and summer of 1941 immersed in debates over Shachtman's new theory. A few of its members still upheld Trotsky's position that the USSR was a workers' state. More supported Joe Carter or C. L. R. James, whose alternative theories denied that there was anything positive remaining in the USSR from the Russian Revolution. In the midst of these debates, in June 1941, Germany invaded the Soviet Union. Shachtman disconcerted his supporters in the Workers Party and heartened his critics by refusing, contrary to his theory's apparent implications, to give any kind of support to the Soviet Union's defense.

Shachtman got a formal majority of his organization to endorse his theory, and an overwhelming majority supported his "plague on all their houses" attitude toward the war. The Workers Party had closed ranks by the time the United States entered the war in December 1941. Its members united in rejecting not only Nazism but the U.S. fight for world supremacy and in upholding a Marxism they defined as internationalist but completely independent of Soviet Communism.

The Nazi-Soviet pact and Soviet intervention in Poland took Communists outside the USSR completely by surprise. They had anticipated none of these events and were at a loss to respond to them. Before the German-Soviet pact, U.S. Communist leader Earl Browder said, "There is as much chance of Russo-German agreement as of Earl Browder being elected President of the Chamber of Commerce." As late as 11 September, with Soviet troops poised to invade, Browder urged the U.S. government to aid Poland. Only a cable from Moscow installed a new party line: that Britain, France, and Poland were at least as responsible for the war as Germany, probably more. As Shachtman had predicted a year before, Communists discovered once more "that the Versailles Peace Treaty and the *status quo* are viciously reactionary and bourgeois democracy a hoax and a snare."[6] Thousands of the Communist Party's members left it in protest, but few of its major leaders resigned or even demurred.

Trotskyists, by contrast, who had foreseen almost everything, were wracked by debates. Prediction is one thing in politics; action is another. Trotskyists had been happily united behind Trotsky's prediction of a deal between Hitler and Stalin; they were divided about what to do about the Soviet attack on Poland. Some wanted to support it, some to oppose it, some to take no position. They were divided again about how to respond to the Soviet attack on Finland in November 1939. Shachtman emerged in these debates as the leader of a distinctive current with a distinctive attitude toward the war.

The fault lines in the Trotskyists' ranks took time to crack open. In the first days of the German-Soviet pact, the Socialist Workers Party was united in condemning it. On 22 August 1939, the day before the pact was signed, Shachtman successfully pushed the Political Committee for a strong campaign against it. In a speech on 25 August he said, "Stalin has given Hitler the go-ahead signal, the green light, to invade Poland." He made the same argument at length in a series of articles in the *Socialist Appeal*, which were to be collected into a party pamphlet. "The mask is off, at last," he and Burnham said in the *New International*. "The blood-stained, monstrous face of Stalinism is exposed, now, for the whole world to see."[7] On 1 September, German troops invaded Poland and the Second World War began.

When Soviet troops marched into Poland in mid-September, Shachtman and Burnham proposed to denounce Stalin for having joined in Hitler's invasion. Now many Socialist Workers Party leaders hesitated to back Shachtman's stand. The fact that Hitler and Stalin had carved up Poland in advance was still a secret. Thousands of Polish Jews were glad enough of Soviet intervention and fled from German-occupied Poland to Soviet-occupied Poland. Many Ukrainian and Belorussian peasants were willing to be incorporated into the Soviet Ukraine and Soviet Belorussia if the alternative was German occupation.

Al Goldman proposed to support the Soviet intervention as a way of "preventing Hitler from getting control of all of Poland" and "defending the Soviet Union against Hitler." Cannon reserved judgment on it in order to wait for Trotsky's opinion. The party leadership reaffirmed Trotskyists' basic analysis of the Soviet state and their call for an independent Soviet Ukraine but said nothing about the invasion. Only when Trotsky denounced it did U.S. Trotskyists fall in line behind him.[8]

Shachtman was too sure of his own opinion to wait to hear Trotsky's. He was sure that Stalin had struck a deal with Hitler to expand his dictatorship in the east in return for Hitler's expanding his dictatorship in the west. He dismissed Cannon's and Goldman's failure to see the deal as an inability "to believe their own eyes." He had begun to have doubts about the orthodox Trotskyist line on the Soviet state, he said later, but in any event the orthodox line did not tell Trotskyists what they should *do*.[9] Many party members shared Shachtman's sense of frustration.

Trotskyist leaders' hesitation stemmed from disorientation. They had been united before the invasion in the assumption that Stalinism would compromise with capitalist states, connive with them, surrender to them, but not confront them head-on. Stalinism might stumblingly defend the conquests of the revolution but never extend them. Its foreign policy was bound to be timid, conservative, even cowardly. In his first statement on the German-Soviet pact, two weeks before Soviet troops invaded Poland, Trotsky still stressed, "I *never* predicted that Stalin would conclude an *aggressive* pact with Hitler."[10] Yet Stalin did act aggressively, not only in Poland but elsewhere, not only at Hitler's initiative but at his own.

First Stalin forced the Baltic republics of Lithuania, Latvia, and Estonia to accept the presence of Soviet troops on their territory. Then he presented an ultimatum to Finland demanding the cession of strategic positions along the Soviet-Finnish frontier. When Finland rejected his demands at the end of November 1939, the Soviet army attacked. Shachtman said later, "Every possibility was foreseen except the one that actually came about."[11]

Shachtman was "thinking on the run" himself. But he was clear from the start that the Soviet invasion of Poland was wrong and that Trotskyists had to put forward an alternative policy to Stalin's. His alternative to Stalin's deal was the "revolutionary defense of Poland." Trotskyists should call on Poles to "rise in revolutionary struggle and, with their own armed forces, drive out the oppressors of the people—Hitler in one-half of the country and the Stalin Bureaucracy in the other."[12] They should tell Polish and Ukrainian workers to fight against the Soviet army in order to create an independent socialist Poland and an independent socialist Ukraine.

Shachtman rejected any support to the Polish government. But his strategy meant resisting Stalinism in eastern Poland before it was firmly established, before the existing Polish army and state were completely destroyed. His stand could not be squared with the "unconditional defense of the USSR." Trotskyists had never interpreted "defense" to mean that they would fight for the Soviet Union only if another country attacked first. They had said that they supported Soviet victory in any Soviet war against a capitalist state. Now that the Soviet army was acting just as a tool for German imperialism and Stalin's own ambitions, Shachtman said, Trotskyists should make clear that they would *not* fight for the Soviet Union in this war. Instead they should call on Soviet soldiers to mutiny in support of Polish revolutionary forces.

"Our slogan of unconditional defense of the Soviet Union has been proved by events, by reality, to be false and misleading, to be harmful," Shachtman argued. "It must be abandoned." It had rested on an assumption that whenever the Soviet army fought against a capitalist army it was fighting a progressive war. Shachtman now denied this assumption. The nationalized economy had little to do with war in the Soviet Union, "where the political superstructure (the Stalinist state apparatus) has acquired a degree and type of independence from its social basis without parallel, at least in modern times," he said.

> It is not the nationalized economy that goes to war; it is not the economy that decides when the war should be declared or started, or against whom it should be directed, or how it should be conducted. Nor does the working class make these decisions—either directly or indirectly—for it is gagged and fettered and straightjacketed. The decisions and directions of the war are *entirely* in the hands of the bureaucracy, which . . . [has] its own social, economic and political interests.[13]

Since the aims of Stalin's war were the expansion of the bureaucracy's power, and its consequences were to demoralize and disorganize the working class, the war was reactionary.

Shachtman was ready to call the Soviet invasion "imperialist." Lenin had defined imperialism as a consequence of a specific phase of capitalist development—monopoly capitalism—that had begun in the 1870s or 1880s. But Marxists had kept on using the word in a looser way to refer to many other ruling classes that had tried to expand their power at the expense of other states, from the ancient Egyptians to the modern Ottomans. Shachtman felt that it applied now to the Soviet bureaucracy. Right after the invasion he said that the bureaucracy was "playing with grandiose ideas of imitating the 'successes' of Hitler." He quoted Trotsky's own insistence that the Soviet economy's contradictions could not be solved within its borders. To resolve these contradictions in its own way, Shachtman and others said, the bureaucracy was now seeking "new territories, new wealth, new privileges, new power, new sources of raw material, new trade facilities, new sources of labor power."[14]

Cannon refused to accept Shachtman's innovations. "We always said the moment of danger will find the Fourth Internationalists at their posts defending the conquests of the great revolution," he said. "Now that the hour of danger is at hand—now that the long-awaited war is actually knocking at the door—it would be strange if the Fourth International should renege on its oft-repeated pledge." He urged people to "see the Soviet Union for what it really is, a gigantic labor organization which has conquered one-sixth of the earth's surface." His battle cry was, "Our program . . . shall not be changed!" When the Soviet Union invaded Finland, the Socialist Workers Party under Cannon's leadership urged Soviet Trotskyists to be "the best soldiers in the Red Army," even as the party condemned the invasion and called for Soviet withdrawal.[15]

Trotsky was first disturbed, then suspicious, then incensed by Shachtman's arguments. He never said in so many words whether Trotskyists should fight for the Soviet army against the Polish army in an intervention that they thought was wrong. But he could not accept an attitude of indifference to Soviet victory or defeat. He always considered the bureaucracy's expansionist tendency to be a minor factor, far less important than the basic antagonism between the workers' state and the surrounding capitalist states.

Shachtman and his allies felt that this emphasis led Trotsky astray in his predictions about the Finnish war. Trotsky predicted that Stalin would compromise with Finland rather than go to war; he was wrong. He predicted that as Soviet troops advanced they would begin expropriating Finnish capitalists; he was wrong. He had believed so firmly that civil war would begin in Finland that he had spoken of the imaginary civil war as fact. In short, he had argued that Stalin would stay on the defensive whenever possible, but if Stalin went on the offensive the socialist cause would benefit. In fact, Stalin went on the offensive against both Poland and Finland, and the socialist cause was set back.[16]

Trotsky disputed Shachtman's idea that Trotskyists had a practical alternative to offer. Obviously the best outcome would be if the working class had its own army to fight both Hitler and Stalin, Trotsky said. But it did not. It therefore had a choice of two evils, and Stalin's army was a lesser evil than Hitler's. Goldman defended Trotsky's argument in its crudest form when he said, "Between the slavery of a degenerated workers' state and the slavery of capitalism, we prefer the slavery of a degenerated workers' state." He said that the nationalized property in the Soviet Union was the only concrete thing the international working class had left, and he would not trade it in for "some abstraction of the world revolution."

Shachtman's followers, horrified, hissed Goldman loudly.[17]

Shachtman knew that the revolutionary movement was weak. At the same time that he was suggesting slogans for Polish revolutionaries, he was appealing for aid to Polish Trotskyists who had fled to Lithuania and were begging to be gotten out while there was still time. But Shachtman and his allies refused to dismiss the hope for revolution as "some abstraction."

> The forces of the *third camp* are already at hand—scattered, demoralized, without program or perspective. The problem is to bring them together, to infuse them with morale, to supply them with a program and perspective. . . . The third camp, however embryonic or weak, must orient itself at the very outset towards a decisive struggle not only against world imperialism but also against the Stalinist reaction.[18]

Even when he acknowledged the danger of Allied intervention against the Soviet Union in the Finnish war, Shachtman would not promise to support the Soviet Union against such an attack. The fact that the Soviet Union was fighting for territorial aggrandizement and not in defense of nationalized property would not be changed simply by Anglo-French intervention, he said. Only if the war were transformed into a war "whose aim is to restore capitalism in Russia" should Trotskyists support the USSR.[19]

One of the most important questions raised in the debate was how to assess Soviet economic policy in the western Ukrainian and Belorussian territories the Soviet Union had annexed. Stalin extended to these territories the same policies he had been carrying out in the rest of the Soviet Union: He collectivized agriculture and nationalized industry. Shachtman felt driven to deny that anything progressive had resulted from the invasion. The collectivizations and nationalizations were progressive, he argued—but the Soviet intervention had nothing to do with them! Working people had already been rising up and taking over factories and farms before the Soviet Union intervened, so the intervention had only contained the economic transformation within a bureaucratic straitjacket. As evidence that the Soviet bureaucracy did not want to abolish capitalism outside the Soviet Union, Shachtman pointed to the Baltic republics that the Soviet army had occupied without changing their societies.

Shachtman later admitted that he had been wrong. In fact the Soviet army did annex the Baltic states and restructure their economies on the Soviet model starting in June 1940, only a few months after Shachtman made his argument. During the Soviet-Finnish war he changed his position, promising to support any nationalizations the Soviet army carried out.[20]

But bound up with Shachtman's 1939 mistake was an important insight, an insight that flatly contradicted what Trotsky was saying about the Polish nationalizations. Trotsky could not imagine that the nationalizations were taking place without any popular initiative. He insisted that Stalin's invasion had only given a "bureaucratic impulse" to a revolutionary mass movement, even if Stalin was able to make sure that the movement was "semi-stifled." The expropriations were impossible without some kind of appeal to independent working-class action, he argued.[21] As long as there was any popular movement, Trotsky believed that his followers could and should find a way to take part in it.

Shachtman agreed with Trotsky that there had been factory occupations and land occupations in eastern Poland before Soviet troops arrived. But he understood something that Trotsky did not: Once Soviet troops were there, the only movement that was permitted was the official one. Any activity that Stalin's government allowed was so controlled and orchestrated that in the last analysis it was no more than a propaganda exercise. The nationalizations had been carried out by military force and administrative fiat. In this kind of nationalization, Shachtman argued, there was no significant advance toward socialism. What counted was not nationalization but working people's ability to run their own society. "The bureaucratic *proletarian* revolution—that I do not know of and I do not believe in it," he said. No force but the working class can free the working class—"not even for a day."[22]

This insight gave Shachtman his answer to Cannon's most popular argument: the analogy between the Soviet Union under Stalin and a gangster-controlled union. The Socialist Workers Party's rank-and-file members in unions responded to the argument that however bad the union leadership, they still had to defend the union. But Shachtman and his group pointed out that the whole analogy was flawed. Trotskyists had always urged even corrupt union leaders to expand their unions by "organizing the unorganized." They did not urge Stalin to expand the Soviet Union by "revolutionizing the unrevolutionized," because they did not equate revolution with conquest by a foreign bureaucracy. Bureaucracy in a trade union was an obstacle to expansion but did not negate the value of expansion. Bureaucracy in the Soviet Union made the aggrandizement of the state a defeat rather than a victory.[23]

The 1939–40 controversy in the Socialist Workers Party did not hinge only on Poland, Finland, and the Soviet Union. Nobody in the Socialist Workers Party argued in 1939–40 that a split could be justified merely by Shachtman's and Cannon's differences over the Soviet Union. But their different conceptions of Marxism convinced their followers that they could not live together in the same organization. Different approaches to Marxist theory and Marxist method found immediate expression in sharp disagreements about how socialists should discuss and decide disputed issues and what it meant for a socialist organization to function democratically. This "organizational question" directly precipitated Shachtman's break from the Socialist Workers Party.

Shachtman blamed Cannon for the stagnation of the SWP, which had lost at least 300 members between the beginning of 1938 and the end of 1939. Shachtman had already attacked Cannon during the July 1939 convention for resisting Shachtman's efforts to galvanize the group. There were objective reasons for Trotskyist losses that were probably more important than anything Cannon did: Leftists were demoralized by their defeat in the Spanish war; the Depression had deepened after Roosevelt's reelection; the CIO was faltering. But Shachtman also said that Cannon cared too much about remaining doctrinally safe and preserving his little apparatus to reach out boldly to people in the United States.[24] Right or wrong, Shachtman was able to capitalize on widespread discontent in the SWP at the group's stagnation in order to win sympathy for his criticisms of Cannon's "regime."*

From the beginning of the 1939–40 controversy on the Soviet intervention in Poland, Shachtman said that the whole Socialist Workers Party would have to discuss the issues he was raising. Trotsky agreed. "When these deviations are bearing their first fruits." Trotsky told Cannon, one should not be "very intransigent and impatient." Cannon agreed to have an open discussion bulletin and membership meetings to thrash out the dispute. But he took part in the discussion with distaste. "In debating with Shachtman I crawl on my belly through the mud for the sake of the Fourth International," he told Trotsky.[26]

In hindsight the 1939–40 debate looks like a high point for internal democracy in the Socialist Workers Party. In New York, the home of the party's national office and many of its branches, the debate took place in citywide membership meetings that were like gladiatorial contests in a coliseum. A hundred or more people might attend. Sometimes Cannon and Shachtman would each speak for an hour, the assembled members would speak for a couple of hours, and then Shachtman and Cannon would each have an hour for rebuttal. Even young Shachtman supporter Leo Seidlitz was impressed by the other side's speeches as well as his own side's: "Cannon was no slouch," he remembered. Al Glotzer remembered, "There

---

*Cannon discounted the discontent in the SWP by raising the old charge that malcontents were middle-class lightweights opposed by the real Trotskyist workers. Shachtman eventually counted 132 trade unionists among his 329 solid supporters, but as in 1931–33 most of them were New Yorkers and/or youth, and most of the longtime trade unionists supported Cannon. The question was whether trade unionist support necessarily made Cannon right. Shachtman denied that there was a direct correspondence in the short run between internal factional divides and class struggle in the outside world. He argued that Cannon's "demagoguery" about the working class, like Stalin's in the 1920s, said "to the rank and file . . . 'No thinking! Those at the top have more brains than you.'"[25]

was only one person who could handle Jim, that was Max." Irving Kristol said years later that he had never again heard the equal of those speeches. The audience would not head home until the early hours of the morning.[27]

Although the Trotskyists' 1939–40 debate among themselves was relatively democratic, Shachtman and Cannon disagreed on what was the democratic way for the Trotskyists to face the public. The most important organizational issue raised in the controversy was whether a major internal discussion like this one could or should be confined inside the organization.

On this issue the Leninist tradition was ambiguous. In Lenin's *What Is to Be Done?* of 1902 he had argued that socialist consciousness had to be brought to the working class "from the outside." In part he meant that workers needed more information and ideas than they could get from union organizing or strikes. But he also meant that workers could not develop correct socialist ideas on their own and needed to get socialism from intellectuals who understood social science.[28] Stalin used this argument as proof that the party was the repository of truth and the masses were destined to be instructed and led by it.

Lenin had usually *not* followed this logic. He had used the argument in 1902 only as a "polemical exaggeration," Shachtman said. In the midst of the big working-class radicalizations of 1905 and 1917, Lenin insisted that socialist ideas had meaning only as expressions of mass struggles and had to be shaped, refined, and corrected by living movements. He described the working class as "instinctively, spontaneously" revolutionary and called for Bolshevik groups to "let the fresh spirit of young revolutionary Russia pour in through them" and become "less rigid, more 'free,' more 'loose.'"[29] Only when the Russian working class was decimated and made apathetic by the bloody civil war of 1918–21 did Lenin speak again as if the party could lead and think without intimate contact with those living movements.

In 1939–40 Cannon felt profoundly distrustful of U.S. public opinion. The country was disappointed by the New Deal's failures, disillusioned by the German-Soviet pact; it was giving up its earlier sympathy for the Soviet Union and swinging to the right. The working class too was affected by this trend. Cannon's instinctive response was to fight back against the pressure of public opinion. He wanted the Socialist Workers Party to handle its business "without the intervention of the general public." He clung to Trotsky's theories, saying that preserving them intact was one of the Trotskyists' most important tasks.[30]

Shachtman reacted differently. After hard years of trying to get workers and radicals to hear what was wrong with the Soviet Union, he was glad that the party could at last get a wider hearing for its criticisms. He was also confident that the more open the party was to the outside world, the less likely it would be to uphold Cannon and "unconditional defense of the

USSR." Shachtman became a champion of the democratic, open Leninism of 1905 and 1917, when the Bolsheviks had "a richer and more democratic internal life than do most parties today." Accusing Cannon of a "spirit of Stalinist monolithism (palmed off as Bolshevik centralism)," he and his allies called for public debate.[31] Cannon fought for a Leninist tradition more like the one shaped in the experience of the Communist International.

In principle, Trotsky had some sympathy for Shachtman on this issue. "A developing and alive party must represent—to a certain extent—the different tendencies, disquietudes and, I repeat, even the confusion in the vanguard of the working-class," he told Cannon before the Socialist Workers Party was formed. "I believe that for the next period the emphasis must be on the *democracy*, not on the *centralism*." But as the fight went on he became convinced that Shachtman cared less about openness to the working class than openness to middle-class intellectuals. Trotsky decided that the minority had to be told, "You must wait for the verdict of the party and not appeal before the verdict is pronounced to the democratic patriotic judges."[32]

The concrete issue the two factions fought about was whether the internal party discussion should spill over into the party press. Cannon was willing to have the strictly theoretical issues discussed in the *New International*, which was meant for a sophisticated audience. Even there, however, he imposed conditions so restrictive that the opposition chafed bitterly under them. He was determined that the debate stay out of the *Socialist Appeal*, which was meant to reach the broadest possible audience. In his mind the party, in keeping with its established positions, had decided to defend the Soviet army in Poland and Finland. The *Appeal* should carry out that decision, not debate it.

Shachtman disagreed. The working class should not be the "passive recipient of programs 'finished' inside of locked party laboratories," he said later. The party should allow workers outside its ranks to hear and judge the arguments. Joe Carter pointed out that Lenin had taken his famous "April Theses," calling for socialist revolution in Russia, to the public in 1917 when most Bolshevik leaders disagreed with him. The pressure of working-class opinion helped Lenin win the Bolsheviks to his position. Without openness between the working class and the Bolshevik Party there might never have been a Russian Revolution.[33]

By early December 1939 the minority was pressing the Political Committee to allow discussion articles in the *Socialist Appeal*. In January and February 1940 the debate shifted to the contents of the *New International*, whose February issue turned out to be one long attack on Shachtman without a word in his defense. Together with the *Appeal*'s barely veiled attacks on "middle-class democrats" who "howl about 'Stalinist imperialism,'" the February *New International* convinced Shachtman that the Socialist Workers

Party press would never do his side of the debate justice. At a national conference in Cleveland at the end of February 1940, his faction announced that regardless of who won at the convention, it would issue its own independent publication to reach people outside the party. Shachtman had taken a big step toward breaking with Trotsky and Cannon. The strain showed. A majority observer in Cleveland said that Shachtman looked "thin, worried, wizened and bitter."[34]

The minority spent a frenetic weekend during the party convention on 5–8 April. During the day minority delegates argued with the majority; at night they attended their own conference. They were rallied—and cut off from the majority—by Shachtman's slashing polemics. He appealed to the majority: "You are wrong, horribly wrong, tragically wrong—but not irretrievably wrong. Do not force the split and tomorrow our paths may converge again." As Goldman moved to cut off Shachtman's report, Shachtman pleaded, "You would not expel me before letting me conclude the speech." He repeated the minority's pledge to publish its own paper whatever the convention decided.[35]

With neither side having backed down, the split was a foregone conclusion. On 16 April Cannon presented the new Political Committee with a motion pledging each member to abide by the convention decisions. When Shachtman and his allies refused to vote on it, they were suspended from membership on the spot. Shachtman said later, "Cannon took a look at his watch, turned to his friends . . . and said, 'Three minutes.' He was proud of the fact that the whole split had taken only three minutes to carry through."[36]

Shachtman had criticized the Socialist Workers Party's democracy as inadequate and its Marxism as petrified. Now he would have to show in practice the kind of democracy and Marxism he believed in.

Shachtman took his faction almost intact into his new Workers Party. He also worked to keep the political rethinking that he had unleashed within bounds. He was determined that his new organization should be Marxist. "Our movement is based precisely on Marxian theory—the nature of capitalist society, the role of the working class, the proletarian revolution, and so forth," he said. Marxism founded the prospects for socialism not merely on the belief that a socialist society would be a better society, but on the understanding that capitalism was the result of historical forces and was thrown into depressions and wars for historical reasons. Marxism also offered a way out of these crises: reliance on labor's conflict with capital, which was an inevitable, endlessly resurgent feature of capitalism. Marxism gave an understanding of politics as the only arena where class conflicts could be resolved, through the overthrow of capitalist political power and its replacement by working-class political power. Without Marxism,

Shachtman said, "we would have no reason to exist as a Party."[37]

Many people who had turned to Marxism in the early 1930s were rejecting it by the decade's end. The rejection was voiced most articulately by radical intellectuals, particularly some of the intellectuals who had worked with Shachtman to expose the Moscow purge trials. Shachtman had always been at ease with intellectuals and had worked well with the few (particularly around the *Partisan Review*) who joined in the campaign against the trials. But his disgust at the many radical intellectuals around the *Nation* and the *New Republic* who had defended the Soviet regime had outlasted the purges. Now it colored his relations with independent intellectuals he had worked with, as many of them turned against Trotskyism in the last months before the Second World War.

The years 1939 and 1940 were ones of hopelessness and renunciation for many leftists, years that provided a foretaste of postwar McCarthyism. The mood of the country was turning against radicals. By 1940 the Smith Act would criminalize advocacy of revolution and the Voorhis Act would outlaw any ties to the Communist International or Fourth International. Under this pressure, many intellectuals who had used Trotsky's help to cast off their Communist sympathies moved on toward social democratic, liberal, or right-wing politics. Many would join in the anti-communist crusade of the 1950s.

Shachtman imagined that he could hear these intellectuals' teeth "chattering with fright in the growing totalitarian darkness" as they fell back on "preserving a rotted capitalist order by 'democratic' means." Their failure to take part in the day-to-day work of building the socialist movement, he said, was depriving their thinking of "richness and reality and fruitfulness and purpose."[38]

Shachtman faced intellectual challenges to his brand of Marxism in 1939–41 from socialists such as Max Eastman, Sidney Hook, and Dwight Macdonald; young followers such as Philip Selznick, Irving Kristol, and Seymour Martin Lipset; and, most shockingly, his ally and fellow editor James Burnham. He responded to these challenges by reaffirming his Marxist identity and writing it into the Workers Party's basic documents.

In these debates he rejected his adversaries' portrayal of Marxism as a closed, undemocratic system. He believed that Marxists had to be independent, critical-minded thinkers. He pledged the Workers Party to complete freedom of discussion in the "undogmatic spirit that animated the great revolutionary thinkers after Marx—Lenin, Trotsky, Luxemburg, Mehring, and their like"—a spirit that welcomed vigorous disagreements.[39] He kept the Workers Party's discussion bulletins and even the *New International* open to dissenters.

Acknowledging the "terrible discreditment of the very name of socialism" by Stalinism, he wanted the Workers Party to approach with sympathy working people who were questioning the Marxist tradition.[40] But he showed neither sympathy nor restraint toward Eastman, Hook, Macdonald, or Burnham, whom he saw as simple renegades. Instead he devoted his energies to defending his core beliefs: the original, grassroots democracy of the Russian soviets and the Bolshevik Party; fascism as a manifestation of capitalism's deep crisis and inherent violence; and the need for an activist, disciplined revolutionary party and international.

Eastman, who had defended Trotsky in the U.S. press years before Shachtman became a Trotskyist, and Hook, a philosopher and one-time Musteite, began in 1938 to argue that Trotsky himself was responsible for the beginnings of Stalinism, particularly through his willingness to ban opposition parties. At about the same time, Socialist Workers Party member Dwight Macdonald began criticizing Trotsky's role in suppressing the March 1921 Kronstadt rebellion. Shachtman and James Burnham responded with a strong defense of bolshevism and Trotskyism in the January 1939 issue of the *New International*.

Shachtman defended the Bolshevik tradition in large part by interpreting it in his own way, emphasizing the democratic strain within it. He had never understood Marx's "dictatorship of the proletariat" to be a rejection of democracy. As early as 1934 he said that a revolutionary state in the United States would "suppress only those who take up arms against it." If at any time the revolutionary party lost its majority in democratically elected soviets, he said, "the party would submit and seek to convince the Soviets."[41] Now in 1939 he and Burnham amplified this commitment.

They still argued that in conditions of civil war the contending forces would be likely to divide into one legal party leading the revolution and counterrevolutionary parties fighting and being fought with force. In Catalonia in 1937, for example, a successful revolution might have required unification of POUM, anarchists, and Trotskyists into a single party. But once the civil war was won, the revolutionary party could develop into "a *coalition* of many parties, a federated party; and full democratic expression might be given, publicly and freely, through it." The federated party might in turn divide into several different parties as new issues arose. Shachtman said flatly in April 1939 that a workers' state "has no right to suppress other working class organizations for their political views."[42]

He soon drew the corollary that Lenin and Trotsky would have done better to relegalize opposition parties after the civil war even in Russia. "It was disastrous to outlaw them in perpetuity," he said. "The right of free speech, press and assembly, the right to organize and the right to strike are not less necessary under the dictatorship of the proletariat but more necessary and more possible." The Bolsheviks' decision to deny these rights permanently to their opponents helped make Stalin's bureaucratic dictatorship possible. "Proletarian democracy cannot exist for long if it is confined to one faction or one party," Shachtman concluded. He reiterated that in the United States the revolutionary state would guarantee the "widest, genuine democracy to all working class parties and organizations, and even (given . . . no attempt at counter-revolution) to bourgeois parties."[43]

Similarly, Shachtman and Burnham did not deny that there was a kernel of truth to Dwight Macdonald's assertion that the 1921 Kronstadt rebels— sailors in a naval base near Petrograd led largely by anarchists and Populists—had made a legitimate call for the restoration of democratic freedoms revoked by the Bolsheviks: elections by secret ballot, freedom of speech, free trade unions. Shachtman was willing to see the rebels as "unwitting victims" of unscrupulous anti-Bolsheviks and the Bolshevik assault on them as "one of the saddest necessities of the Russian Revolution."[44] He even admitted the possibility that different policies could have warded off the revolt. "We do not believe in the immaculate conception and evolution of Bolshevism, or in its flawlessness or infallibility," Burnham and he said.

But Shachtman could not stomach Macdonald's insistence that the Kronstadt tragedy resulted from "the very nature of Bolshevik political organization," with its "well insulated . . . hierarchic, bureaucratic party apparatus." He and Burnham ridiculed the notion that the Bolsheviks who led the assault on Kronstadt, almost all of whom Stalin would later kill to consolidate his power, were in any way akin to the Stalinist bureaucracy. On the contrary, they said, it was the restless peasantry, the social force behind the Kronstadt rebels, that later "found a far more finished and triumphant expression in the victory of Stalinism!"[45] To have overthrown the Bolsheviks in 1921 could only have contributed to destroying the last remnants of soviet democracy rather than expanding it. In a fight between Bolsheviks and rebels who sought to overthrow them, Shachtman believed that any clear-sighted socialist had to side with the Bolsheviks.

Whatever mistakes the Bolsheviks may have made, Shachtman defended them throughout the 1940s as the real representatives of the working class in 1917 and the real defenders of democracy. Bolsheviks were for giving non-Russian peoples their democratic right to self-determination, peasants their democratic right to the land they farmed, and peace to Europeans sick of war; Mensheviks were against. The Bolsheviks, together with revolutionary peasant allies, had won a majority in the soviets, the most democratic institutions then existing in Russia. Shachtman defended even the Bolsheviks' decision in January 1918 to dissolve the elected Constituent Assembly, "*a counterrevolutionary and unrepresentative parliament.*" Either the Constituent Assembly or the soviets had to go, and the Bolsheviks had rightly chosen the soviets as the more profoundly democratic institutions.[46]

"*To carry out the program of the democratic revolution*" in 1917 meant break-ing with capitalism, Shachtman concluded. The Bolsheviks proved it by carrying out "the most democratic revolution in history."[47]

Intellectuals' rejection of the choice the Bolsheviks had made and their insistence that that choice ultimately led to Stalinism with all its horrors could only reinforce the message that capitalism was constantly shouting at working people: Don't take power! There were two possible explanations for what went wrong in Russia, Shachtman said. One was the intellectuals' explanation, at bottom the capitalist explanation, that the attempt by the working class to hold exclusive power resulted in power only for bureaucratic tyrants: "*The Russian workers lost power because they took power.*" The other was Shachtman's explanation, the socialist explanation: "*The Russian workers lost power because the workers of other countries failed to take power.*" The socialist explanation was proved by the actual experience of those few years after 1917 when workers really did rule Russia, a trium-phant memory all the more precious since it had not yet been repeated in any other country.[48]

In this sense, Shachtman declared, "the defense of the Russian Revolution is the defense of Marxism." "Lenin and the Bolsheviks," as he had said earlier—"and nobody else—gave us a picture of the truly breath-taking prospects for human advancement and human dignity which are open to us as soon as capitalism is sent to the rubbish-heap."

> *It was our revolution.* It remains our revolution, our victory and vindication—even now. Even now when it has been killed, strangled by its imperialist encirclers, deserted by those who should have been its socialist comrades-in-arms, speared in the back by its Stalinist assassins, dragged in the mud by every backslider and faint-heart, it is our revolu-tion. How easy and contemptible it is to draw near the slain Achilles and kick his head now and spit on him.[49]

In Macdonald's writings, as well as in Hook's and Eastman's, Shachtman saw a dangerous tendency to let anti-Stalinism swell until it overwhelmed opposition to capitalism. Burnham and he called this inflated, distorted anti-Stalinism "Stalinophobia." They complained that most accounts of Stalinism were "moral rather than scientific or political" and "less a product of cold social analysis than of mental shock."[50] Stalinophobia ended by undermining anti-Stalinism, they added: Stalinophobes could not fight Stalinism effectively because they avoided seeing that it was capitalism, the failure of liberals and reformists to overthrow capitalism, and the encircle-ment of the Soviet Union by capitalism that gave rise to Stalinism.

Shachtman responded with particular sensitivity to complaints about the polemical tone of Trotskyists' replies to their critics. He was not only personally attached to his polemical style but believed that the nature of the criticisms justified it. Burnham and he complained that often

> amiable critics of the "Trotskyists" will say in the most sophisticated and nonchalant manner: "You people are just like the Stalinists, fundamentally." Or "Didn't you people massacre the Kronstadters?" . . . When we reply to such irresponsible or monstrous remarks with only half the sharpness they deserve, our critics become inexpressibly shocked, and exclaim, "How can you discuss with these Trotskyists? Their tone is insufferable, their manners deplorable!"[51]

Such complaints showed only the shallowness of people who had no conception of the life-and-death issues at stake.*

Despite Shachtman's polemics against them, Macdonald and other freethinkers around the Socialist Workers Party sided with him in the 1939–40 faction fight, only to face his renewed polemics against them as soon as the Workers Party was founded. In the fall of 1940, Shachtman attacked Macdonald for adhering to the newly fashionable theory that Nazism and Stalinism were two different forms of the same "totalitarian" historical force. In Shachtman's eyes this conflating of fascism and Stalinism denied the centrality of class at the heart of Marxism, because it treated the fact that there had been a workers' revolution and nationalization of industry in the Soviet Union—but neither in Germany—as a matter of no fundamental importance.

Trotsky and Shachtman had made a thorough Marxist analysis of fascism on the rise in the early 1930s—an analysis that treated class as central. Relying on the widespread knowledge of how Trotsky's predictions had been vindicated, Shachtman did not bother to lay out the whole analysis again in order to refute Macdonald. He valued Macdonald as his last tie to

---

*Shachtman had to make one compromise in order to write this article with Burnham. He had to forgo answering Hook's and Eastman's attacks on Marxist dialectics, since Burnham also rejected dialectics. The article argued that these philosophical issues had no immediate bearing on the political issues at stake. To Shachtman's surprise, Trotsky seemed more upset with this brief passage than he was pleased with the article's main thrust. "The section on the dialectic is the greatest blow that you, personally . . . could have delivered to Marxist theory," Trotsky told him. Shachtman pointed out in response that the famous German Communist leader Karl Liebknecht had opposed dialectics too, but that had not stopped Rosa Luxemburg from allying with him to oppose the First World War. He quoted Lenin's comment from another major philosophical dispute: "We must be at loggerheads over philosophy in such a way that . . . the Bolsheviks, as a faction of the party, *are not affected by it.*" Trotsky said soothingly, "I did not deny in the least the usefulness of the article you and Burnham wrote."[52]

Shachtman was upset when Trotsky revived this philosophical issue as a factional weapon later in 1939–40. He later spoke with resentment about Trotsky's readiness with opponents "to go back into their political biography." Yet he understood that Trotsky could not forgive him for disrupting the Fourth International's most solid group.[53]

the *Partisan Review* circle and kept the *New International* open to his heterodox articles. But the Workers Party dropped Macdonald from the *New
International* editorial board and refused to reinstate him even at the cost of
losing him as a contributor and party member.

The most unnerving of the intellectual challenges to Shachtman came
from James Burnham as the Workers Party was being founded. By April
1940, Burnham decided that the most important elements of Marxism were
"either false or obsolete or meaningless" and urged Shachtman to leave out
the references to Marxism in the new party's founding documents. More
forthrightly than any of Shachtman's other antagonists, Burnham blamed
Marxism itself for the rise of Stalinism. Shachtman tried to win Burnham
back, feeling that he was "torn" and "assailed by doubts." But he would
not give way on the issues. Even as the split took place, he had Burnham's
resignation letter in his pocket. Burnham "spoke and spoke very well at our
first public meeting" in early May 1940, Shachtman remembered, but on
21 May Burnham made his resignation public.*

By 1941 Burnham would see not only Stalinism and fascism but even the
New Deal as part of a single bureaucratic menace that required anyone who
valued freedom to support capitalism. Shachtman turned his back on his
former associate and turned to the task of building his Marxist organization.

Shachtman did not want his followers just to affirm their Marxism on
paper but to show Marxism's value in practice. The biggest issue behind the
Socialist Workers Party's split had been whether a group could have the
open, public discussions Shachtman called for and still function effectively.
Behind Cannon's charges against the minority was the insinuation that
Shachtman and his followers were people who only wanted to argue, while
Cannon's followers were the activists. Shachtman caricatured this version
of "Leninism": "We are hard people. We spit bullets. Shut up. Stop thinking." Once the Workers Party was founded he was eager to prove the
worth of his kind of Leninism, to show that his followers too could be
working-class leaders. The Workers Party was "a democratic organization,
but not a loose collection of talkers who do nothing," he said.

Our program today equips us better than any other labor organization in
the past to meet the crucial tasks we face. But . . . no program in the

---

*Burnham's basic challenge to Shachtman's Marxism was echoed in the spring of 1941 by a
group of Workers Party members gathered around Philip Selznick, a twenty-two-year-old
City College graduate. Selznick's group, which included the future sociologist Seymour
Martin Lipset and prominent neoconservative-to-be Irving Kristol, soon left the Workers
Party to join the Socialist Party. Kristol would later credit the *New International* with teaching
him how to "write . . . an intellectual discourse."[54]

world can transform a group of people into unflinching revolutionaries overnight. For that, a hundred tests are required, tests of experience, tests of struggle.[55]

Organizing Shachtmanites for political activity was even harder than getting them to agree on their political identity. Many of them were students or unemployed ex-students: Shachtman had won over not only almost half the members of the Socialist Workers Party but the great majority of the young Trotskyists in the Young People's Socialist League (Fourth International). These young rebels, "the vanguard of the 'locked-out generation,'" were drawn to Shachtman by restlessness born of unemployment, fascination with political debate, the feeling that great events were rushing to meet them, and an urge to fight against the rottenness they saw everywhere.[56] But once they graduated from college to joblessness they had nowhere to put their radical ideas into practice. Even the Workers Party's trade unionists had been cut off by the split from the central direction they had been used to in the Socialist Workers Party.

Shachtman set out to send inactive members into unions and movements and make all members' activity part of a collective project. The Workers Party's founding convention said that every branch should assign each member a specific task each week, so that in each city the group could have an impact in the unions and in politics.[57]

The abstract discussions about how to organize died down as Workers Party members actually started organizing. Through their activity they shaped a conception of Leninism different from the one they remembered from the Socialist Workers Party. They began to understand the words "professional revolutionary" more broadly than in Cannon's group, where "a professional revolutionary was somebody paid by the party as a functionary," remembered Leo Seidlitz, who left school to become a union activist in the early 1940s. Workers Party members who took factory jobs in order to put their politics into practice came to be seen as revolutionaries as much as anyone on the Political Committee. "You have to do this or that to make a living," Herman Benson said, "but the basic thing you are in life is a social revolutionary."[58]

As Shachtman worked to make his followers into working-class activists, he also worked to give them the leadership they needed. He had a somewhat heterogeneous collection of people from which to create a new leadership. Leaders of the SWP minority had included a circle of freethinkers such as James Burnham, Joe Carter, Hal Draper, and Manny Geltman, who were discarding or questioning many Trotskyist ideas. Other leaders of the minority were old allies of Marty Abern's who had opposed Cannon's leadership for so long that they were oppositionists almost by reflex. C. L. R. James came into the Workers Party with a set of his own ideas and people.

Shachtman formed an organizational core for his new group largely by relying on Ernest McKinney's trade union connections and organizing skills and Al Glotzer's loyalty. Glotzer moved back to New York to help build the organization, first as a volunteer and later as a full-time staff member. Glotzer and McKinney worked hard for the Workers Party and usually let Shachtman set its political direction. Others who disagreed with Shachtman on one issue or another also played important roles. For example, the Workers Party newspaper, *Labor Action*, was edited in the early 1940s by more heterodox members such as Geltman and Irving Howe.[59]

With no hard-and-fast factional lines in the group, Shachtman enjoyed uncontested predominance. It was no accident that others on the left called Workers Party members "Shachtmanites," though Shachtman "never threw his weight around except intellectually." Herman Benson remembered the proprietary pride with which Shachtman would say, "The WP, that's *mine*."[60]

Most of Shachtman's relationships revolved around his organization. Breaking with Cannon was not terribly hard for him, though he said years later that it was "a harsh hour that tore and kept us apart." Shachtman gradually became friendly again with Glotzer in the early 1940s, though he would tease his friend even about the most sensitive subjects. Geltman remembered Shachtman's bringing some pies Edith Harvey had made to the Workers Party office and saying to Glotzer, "'How could you leave a woman who could bake like this!' Most of us were embarrassed," Geltman said. Geltman too was fairly close to Shachtman despite their disagreements. Shachtman had warm ties to other young followers, including Benson and Julie Jacobson.[61]

The real blow to Shachtman in the split was his loss of Trotsky's friendship. Trotsky's affection and respect for his disciple were strong, but when the issue between them was the defense of the Soviet Union, affection and respect were strained and then broken. Shachtman's courage in standing up to Trotsky, a man he "loved, respected and feared," reflected his sense that he had come of age. Shachtman was thirty-five years old in 1939–40, a man approaching middle age, a father: His and Edith Harvey's son Michael was born in July 1939. (Shachtman was "crazy about his son." He was "very fond of children," Glotzer remembered; "he'd just grab 'em and squeeze their cheeks and kiss 'em and terrorize 'em with his enthusiasm.") Shachtman's parents were getting old; his mother died in February 1941. His age was also suggested by his increasing baldness.[62] He would no longer sit at Trotsky's feet or accept Trotsky's corrections as he had earlier in the 1930s. He would not even wait to hear Trotsky's opinion before making up his own mind. Shachtman's self-confidence, nurtured by the times he had been right in the past, now reinforced his tenacity.

Trotsky mourned the distance that grew up between him and Shacht-man. Even as Shachtman's opinions began to diverge from his, he praised Shachtman for "excellent ideas and formulations which seemed to me in full accordance with our common position." In late December 1939 he wrote to Shachtman, "I believe that you are on the wrong side of the barricades, dear friend." But he added, "If I could do so I would immediately take an aeroplane to New York City in order to discuss with you for forty-eight or seventy-two hours uninterruptedly. I regret very much that you do not feel . . . the need to come here to discuss the questions with me. Or do you? I should be happy." Shachtman answered Trotsky's appeals with public manifestos.[63]

He would neither ask for forgiveness nor give up hopes of receiving it. When Al Goldman ridiculed Shachtman's criticisms of Trotsky at the April 1940 Socialist Workers Party convention by sarcastically introducing the party's greetings to Trotsky, "the defender of the GPU" (Stalin's secret police), Shachtman shouted, "You sent your greetings; we will send ours." His followers sent greetings to the "teacher and champion of revolutionary Marxian internationalism" and expressed the hope that "the events of tomorrow will once more bring us into complete and unshakable union." When Trotsky was nearly killed in an attack on his house by Stalin's agents late in May, Shachtman sent a message of solidarity "and great relief" at Trotsky's and his wife's escape. When the next attack succeeded in August 1940, Shachtman mourned his mentor: "unbending, intransigent, incor-ruptible and tireless, true to himself and to the unflickering ideal of socialist freedom."[64]

"Our hearts are torn with grief," Shachtman wrote to Trotsky's widow, Natalia Sedova. Now, when Trotsky's forgiveness could no longer be had, Shachtman went down to Mexico to see if he could help or console her. Sedova and he got along well, renewing a relationship that would continue through the 1940s and 1950s. But she could not help asking why he had not come months before when Trotsky had asked him to. Shachtman often became emotional, even years later, when he tried to reconstruct his answer to her. He "couldn't face the Old Man," he would say. He was afraid that "we would have hollered at one another to no purpose."[65] Trotsky's friendship was still important to him, and its loss was painful. But making up his own mind had come to matter more.

Reaffirming his Marxist identity included for Shachtman reaffirming that his Workers Party belonged in Trotsky's Fourth International. The issues he had raised in the Socialist Workers Party were international issues, and he wanted the International to discuss them. He had reason to be optimistic about his chances in the International: Danish, Norwegian, Swiss, Indian, and Sri Lankan Trotskyists and a majority of the International Executive

Committee elected at the 1938 congress came out against Trotsky's position on the Soviet-Finnish war.[66] But war interfered with the discussion by bringing repression, censorship, and secrecy to many countries. By the end of 1939 the fate of those German, Czech, Polish, Lithuanian, and Latvian Trotskyists who had not escaped was unknown. By the summer of 1940, French, Belgian, Dutch, Danish, and Norwegian Trotskyists were cut off from the rest of the movement by German occupation. Contacts even between the United States and Britain or South America became difficult.

In these circumstances the Trotskyist movement could not have the full discussion Shachtman wanted.* But he continued to declare his loyalty to it. Oppressed people "*must* plant the flag of the Fourth International all over the world," he said in 1941. "There is no other way out—none, absolutely none." He maintained that despite his disagreement with Trotsky over the Soviet Union, he and his group were keeping alive the essence of Trotskyism: the theory of permanent revolution, the "defense of the great and fundamental principles of the Russian Bolshevik revolution . . . the struggle for democracy and socialism."[69]

Shachtman's intransigent defense of Marxism as he understood it, combined with his spirit of tolerance, made the Workers Party a place for lively, even iconoclastic debate, which made it stand out among U.S. Marxist groups. "The kind of party we have built up is our richest possession," he said proudly in 1945. He wanted thousands of working people to make it their possession as well. He acknowledged that many were confused by the disunity and conflict between Socialists, Communists, and two different groups of Trotskyists. But "when a worker learns that a tool is useful and necessary, he does not throw up his hands in despair merely because there are many varieties of that tool," he said. "He judges from experience which

---

*Trotsky and Cannon punished Shachtman for his split by excluding him from even a preliminary international discussion. In May 1940, U.S., Mexican, and Canadian Trotskyists called an "emergency conference" that purged the "petty-bourgeois" Workers Party from the International. The conference's claim to represent the world's Trotskyists was dubious. Its lists of the ten countries it claimed to represent varied: One list included the Soviet Union (where all the Trotskyists were dead), another Chile. Two more of the ten—Germany and Spain—had no real Trotskyist groups at all. A third—Belgium—was cut off from discussion by the war. Trotskyists in Argentina protested that someone had voted for them at the conference even though they had not authorized anyone to represent them. Brazilian Trotskyists, who supported Shachtman, protested their exclusion from it. Indian and Sri Lankan Trotskyists, who opposed Trotsky's position on Finland, were apparently never told about it. International Executive Committee members who supported Shachtman protested that they knew nothing about it.[67] The Workers Party responded by setting up its own American Committee for the Fourth International and keeping in touch with other Trotskyists as best it could. The disappearance or invisibility of so many groups made its purging from the official Fourth International seem meaningless. "The Fourth International—as an organized, unified movement with a united political program—does not exist," it concluded. Shachtman saw his group in the early 1940s as an integral part of a movement to rebuild the Fourth International.[68]

one really serves the purpose best."[70]

Shachtman may have been sure in 1939–40 that his position was right and Trotsky's wrong. But as long as he had neither reshaped nor rejected Trotsky's basic analysis of the USSR as a "degenerated workers' state," he could hardly claim to have a clear position of his own. There were strong pressures on him throughout 1940 from within his own Workers Party to take a distinctive theoretical stand.

He shrank from distinguishing his own analysis too sharply from Trotsky's, however, because he linked his efforts to keep the Workers Party Marxist to a defense of the heritage of the Russian Revolution. Remnants of that revolution's victories still survived in the Soviet Union, he argued in 1940–41, and still deserved support from socialists. Even after his campaign in the Socialist Workers Party against *unconditional* defense of the Soviet Union, he used defense of the Soviet Union as a rallying cry for his loyalists in the Workers Party.

It was also a practical issue for him. In September 1939 and again in April 1940, he predicted that Stalin's hope of avoiding full-scale participation in the war would be disappointed: An attack on the USSR was coming despite all Stalin's maneuvers. Shachtman did not say in so many words whether the tactics that Trotskyists had committed themselves to in 1934—calling for aid to the Soviet Union and opposing any interference with its production or shipment—would be appropriate in response to a German attack. But he stressed the danger of an attack on the USSR and the need to prepare for it. In September 1939 he said that if there were a 'direct imperialist attack upon the Soviet Union . . . the defense of the Soviet Union, even under the rule of the bureaucracy, will again become an immediate and paramount task." He restated the same position in April 1940 and again in December. A capitalist victory over the USSR would "give capitalism and reaction a new lease on life, retard enormously the revolutionary movement, and postpone for we don't know how long the introduction of the world socialist society," he said.[71]

At first Shachtman based his call to defend the Soviet Union on the old Trotskyist definition of it as a workers' state. Because he defined the Workers Party as the inheritor of the entire Trotskyist legacy, the inherited Socialist Workers Party position stood. Besides, Shachtman was reluctant to discard Trotsky's theory when he had nothing to put in its place. To the question of what kind of Marxist leader could not say what the Soviet Union was, he answered half defiantly, half ruefully: "Well, that's the kind of leader you've got." But by November 1940 Shachtman had to admit that all but a handful of Workers Party leaders either rejected Trotsky's analysis or were "in grave doubt" about it. The issue was declared open for debate.[72] People like Carter, Draper, Geltman, and James demanded that the idea of defending the USSR be rejected. Shachtman refused to give in. He continued to keep the question of defending the USSR open.

Shachtman's conclusions, laid out in the December 1940 *New International,* were that the Soviet Union was not a workers' state—there could be no workers' state without workers' political power. It was not capitalist. It had a new bureaucratic ruling class that had to be overthrown in order to create workers' democracy or move toward socialism. Even though every vestige of working-class political power had disappeared in the USSR, the collectivized property created by the revolution survived. Shachtman therefore called the USSR "bureaucratic collectivist": the economy and state were the collective property of the bureaucracy. Though bureaucratic mismanagement undermined this new form of property, it was showing its superiority for economic and human progress over the anarchy of capitalism. It enabled Shachtman to characterize the USSR as a transitional society, a peculiar product of the epoch in which the world was moving from capitalism to socialism. Marxists therefore had to defend it against any attempt to restore private property.

Shachtman's theory was an ambitious attempt to preserve the best of Trotsky's analysis and avoid its limitations. He built into it his own fundamental understanding of both the dangers of Stalinist expansion and the enduring achievements of the Russian Revolution. The theory remains today one of his chief contributions to socialist thought. But like his insistence on the Workers Party's Marxist identity, it antagonized many of those who had left the Socialist Workers Party with him. People like Carter, Draper, and Geltman, who also defined the Soviet Union as "bureaucratic collectivist," and James, who argued that the Soviet Union was "of the same inner essence as capitalism," opposed Shachtman's ideas about the superiority of Soviet collectivism to capitalism.[73] After fierce debate the Workers Party's 1941 convention endorsed Shachtman's theory—though he had already begun to slide away from it.

The orthodox Trotskyist analysis suffered from two fatal defects in Shachtman's eyes. One was the foolishness of speaking of a "workers' state" where the workers actually controlled nothing. The USSR was "a workers' prison . . . not a workers' state," Shachtman said. "There is not the slightest vestige of working class control left in it." Its motive force was not workers' interests but bureaucratic hunger for power and privilege.[74] For socialists who believed that socialism had to be consciously built by the working class and that democracy was essential to it, to call this a workers' state was at best misleading.

Shachtman insisted that democracy was central to any transition toward socialism. He said unequivocally that without real workers' power there could be no workers' state.

> The proletariat differs from all the classes that preceded it in history. It . . . does not own property in the sense that the capitalists own theirs, or the feudal lords owned theirs, or the slaveholders theirs. It "owns" social property *only* by virtue of the fact that the state, which is the repository of the means of production and exchange, is in its hands, is *its* state . . . the proletariat organized politically as the ruling class. That is the only way the proletariat *can* own the means of production and exchange.[75]

For this reason Shachtman was suspicious of any analogy between socialist revolutions and the earlier revolutions that had ensured the triumph of capitalism. There was an essential difference. Bourgeois revolutions had not required conscious leadership by capitalists, because the capitalist economy had already been developing within feudal societies. Removal of the "fetters, blocks and clamps" that feudal rulers had put on capitalist development "was all that was *essentially* required for the triumph of the bourgeois revolution." It could therefore be carried out by a Protestant general like Oliver Cromwell in England, Jacobins in France, or even a landowner like Otto von Bismarck in Germany. But only conscious, organized workers could make socialist revolutions. The socialist economy would function automatically only decades after the revolution, Shachtman said, "after civilized socialist thinking and behavior have become normal habit of all the members of the community."[76] Until then there could be no substitute for working-class leadership at the head of a workers' state.

Shachtman was not dogmatic about how a workers' state looked. He had an ideal: a state founded on democratically elected workers' councils with full democratic freedoms for all. But he thought that working-class power could be expressed through many institutions—"its Soviets, its army, its courts and institutions like the party, the unions, the factory committees"—some of which could atrophy without fatal results. The Soviet Union in the mid-1920s, when all parties but the Bolsheviks were banned, was still a workers' state for him. So was the Soviet Union even in the early 1930s, when soviets were rubber stamps and the workers ruled only "through a sick and bureaucratized party." But when even the Bolshevik Party became a bureaucratic instrument *against* the workers, as it had by the mid-1930s, Shachtman said that the workers' state had been crushed. "To recognize— that the bureaucracy *cannot* be submitted to the proletariat, that the Communist Party *cannot* be revived, that the régime *cannot* be reformed, that a new revolution *must* be organized—is to recognize that Russia is no longer a workers' state."[77]

Important as the argument from democracy was for Shachtman, he gave even more attention to a second argument. Trotsky's analysis had underestimated the Soviet bureaucracy's staying power, dynamism, and significance, he said. Trotskyists had predicted that the bureaucracy would weaken the monopoly of foreign trade and allow more and more space for private investment and profit. It did not. Instead, Shachtman said, the bureaucracy "enormously increased the importance of the state-property and state-production sector" in the 1930s.[78] Yet there were no higher living standards and no equality or greater freedom for workers. Instead the bureaucracy's power and wealth had grown, and the gap between bureaucrats and workers widened.

Soviet democracy was the main *obstacle* to Stalin's program, which required the "systematic hacking away of every finger of control the working class had over its state" as well as the bureaucracy's self-purgation and self-transformation, Shachtman explained. The interpretation made sense of the horrors of the Moscow trials, the killings, the concentration camps: They were "the one-sided but bloody civil war by which the new bureaucracy definitely smashed the last remnant of workers' power." Shachtman pointed out that old Bolsheviks who had been in the party since 1917 made up only 1.3 percent of Stalin's party after the purges. "It is a *new party*; it speaks for a *new class*; it is the political organization of the new bureaucracy that overthrew the workers' state."[79] Given the bureaucracy's strength and rootedness in society, only a deep-going social revolution could overthrow it.

Shachtman's disagreements with Trotsky ended with these two: that Trotsky had neglected the decisive importance of workers' democracy and the independent dynamic of bureaucratic power. "Most of what we learned about Russia," he said, "we learned from Trotsky." He agreed with Trotsky that the Russian Revolution had created forms of collective property that were superior to capitalism and had proved their superiority even under bureaucratic rule. "Compare 25 years of Russia with 25 years of Poland," he argued. The Soviet Union's growth had been dramatically higher—higher than in any contemporary capitalist country—despite the fact that the between-war Polish republic had included the most industrialized regions of the old Russian Empire.

> Starting at a low level, lowered still further by years of war, civil war, famine and their devastations . . . the Soviet Union nevertheless attained a rhythm of economic development, an expansion of the productive forces which exceeded the expectations of the boldest revolutionary thinkers. . . . Economic progress in the Soviet Union was accomplished on the basis of planning and of new, collectivist forms of property established by the proletarian revolution.[80]

On this basis Shachtman continued to believe that the new Soviet society was on a "higher historic plane" than capitalism. It was a "part—an unforeseen, mongrelized, reactionary part, but a part nonetheless—of the collectivist epoch of human history." He also agreed with Trotsky that the bureaucracy did not fit in harmoniously with collectivist property forms but had grown up despite them. Like Trotsky he blamed Stalinism not only for lack of democracy but for mismanagement, disorganization, and inefficiency as well. He repeated again and again Trotsky's point that democracy had become an economic necessity for the Soviet Union. By the late 1980s, even Soviet rulers belatedly and halfheartedly acknowledged this point. But Mikhail Gorbachev neither gave Trotsky credit nor drew Shachtman's conclusion: that overthrowing the bureaucracy would remove "a reactionary obstacle to the development of a collectivist society toward socialism."[81]

Shachtman considered his distinction between the Soviet Union's collectivist property forms, which were progressive, and its bureaucratic property relations, which were not, to be his own major contribution to the discussion. He told Workers Party leaders in the summer of 1941 that the party had added only two important contributions to the analysis made by Trotsky. This distinction, for which he took credit, was one. The fundamental difference Carter had pointed out between capitalist and workers' states—that workers, unlike capitalists, could not have economic power without political power—was the second.[82] These two contributions, together with what he had salvaged from Trotsky's analysis, made up the core of Shachtman's theory.

Even if the Soviet bureaucracy in Shachtman's theory was a new ruling class, it was "a unique class in a unique social order," a "national product of an unforeseen combination of conjunctural historical circumstances." Like other Trotskyists, he argued that only a delay in the working-class rise to world power made bureaucratic collectivism possible even in Russia. "The bureaucracy in Russia became the ruling class because capitalism in the rest of the world remained in power," he said. "The socialist revolution would reduce this new despotism to ashes, and [the bureaucracy] is keenly aware of this fact." He did not expect it to play a major role in world history. It was part of a "transitional order; hence, a transitional class."[83]

Shachtman did not adopt in 1939–41 or afterwards the position that Cannon raised as a specter against him: that Stalinism in the USSR would mean the end of all hope for socialism. This was a caricature of anything Shachtman ever thought. Even in his last years, Shachtman spoke of Stalinism as only a "historical *side*-motion ('a zigzag turn')," a by-product of capitalism's decline and temporary working-class unreadiness. "History is not an obsequious engine whose wheels are so set that it can only move forward along a route firmly prescribed by Marxism, without pauses, without ever running backward and without ever leaving the main rails," he said. "Society has wandered off on side excursions and even blind alleys before." "The view that Marxism presents an absolute scheme of an iron succession of social orders . . . does Marx 'too much honor and too much shame at the same time.'" He had "no greater confidence in the longevity of Stalinism than of capitalism, less if anything."[84]

But though Shachtman's analysis was not the heresy of Cannon's nightmares, Burnham had arrived at something like it. Shachtman was afraid that Carter, Burnham's old ally, was following in Burnham's footsteps by refusing to support the Soviet Union against capitalism. Capitalism and Stalinism were *not* "equally reactionary," Shachtman said; capitalism was *"the main enemy."* He warned that Carter's position could have "tragic" consequences.[85]

Germany attacked the Soviet Union in the midst of this debate in June 1941. Many of Shachtman's supporters assumed that he would now swing to supporting the Soviet Union in its war with Germany. The party's Los Angeles members, led by Shachtman supporter Jack Widick, took this position right away. They were surprised to discover that Shachtman opposed it. Instead he supported the party's first statement, which dismissed "Stalin's defense of Russia" as "a defense of the bureaucracy's dictatorial domination." Carter said that Shachtman had no consistent theoretical basis for rejecting defense of the USSR—and Shachtman supporters like Ernie Erber agreed. "Stalin can save his own neck only by resisting German imperialism," Erber said. "His interests coincide with those of the world proletariat." Another member who favored defense of the USSR said, "Comrade Shachtman, some explanation is in order." Carter supporters were heartened by the disorder in Shachtman's ranks.[86]

Shachtman conceded that the nationalized Soviet economy was jeopardized by the German invasion, and still said that its destruction would be a loss. Later he would welcome the news that Ukrainian guerrillas were fighting the German invaders independently of Stalin's government. But he argued now that there was no way to give any support to the Soviet army without supporting Germany's main enemies in the war, Britain and the United States. U.S. aid to the Soviet Union would intensify U.S. involvement in the war against Germany: "shipments to Russia mean convoys and . . . convoys, as our good president says, mean a shooting war." Soviet troops would soon be fighting in defense of British interests in Iran. Worst of all, the Communist International was suddenly portraying Hitler as the one important enemy of progressive people everywhere. Communists were urging everyone to join in a grand world alliance for Allied victory. The workers' movement in all the Allied countries was being put in a straitjacket for the duration of the war.[87] In the face of these blows to socialism, the fate of the Soviet economy was a secondary concern.

Shachtman could still imagine circumstances in which he *would* defend the USSR. If there was a civil war in the USSR that threatened a restoration of capitalism, he would support Stalin against the capitalist danger. If the right-wingers in Britain who favored peace with Hitler in order to crush the Soviet Union won out, so that Stalin no longer had Britain (and behind Britain the United States) as an ally, then he would want to defend the Soviet Union. But in 1941, he said, the working class had "more to gain by defeatism with regard to both imperialist camps than it has to gain by defensism in Russia."[88]

This argument seemed to save Shachtman's underlying commitment to Soviet collectivism. But Shachtman resorted to other arguments at the same time that would have meant not supporting the Soviet Union even if it stood alone against German attack. His American Committee for the Fourth International saw Hitler's victory as a force that would sweep Stalinism aside. "Hitler, like the sorcerer's apprentice of the fable, will have set loose the forces of history, bringing forth the torrents of revolution," it said—a prediction disturbingly reminiscent of German Communists' prediction in 1933. Shachtman also saw the Soviet army as an instrument of Stalin's imperial ambitions. Even in resisting Hitler's armies in their march on Leningrad and Moscow, Shachtman said, the Soviet Union was fighting to regain its conquests of 1939. "We were against the Stalin bureaucracy's acquiring those conquests. Why should we defend it when it seeks to retain those conquests?"[89]

The reasoning behind Shachtman's position in June 1941 assumed consequences of supporting the Soviet war that were not, in fact, inevitable. There was no need to support Soviet troops in Iran in order to support them in the suburbs of Moscow. There was no need to support Soviet advances into Eastern Europe once German defeat was assured. There was no need to call off all strikes in the United States in order to speed U.S. aid to the Soviet Union. The danger of deepening U.S. involvement in the war against Germany through U.S. aid to the USSR was small, since U.S. convoys were already risking German attack by delivering aid to Britain. U.S. involvement in the war would be total by the end of 1941 anyway—much as Shachtman had foreseen.

The dangers involved in a Soviet defeat, on the other hand, were greater than Shachtman admitted. Hitler meant to turn all the Slav lands to Germany's east into a new German colonial empire. If the German army had occupied Leningrad, Moscow, and Stalingrad, a German administration like the ones imposed on the Ukraine and Belorussia could have ruled there for years or decades. Millions of people could have been reduced to virtual serfdom. The resources of the destroyed Soviet Union might have ensured that the Nazis' New Order would survive for a generation. The third camp along with the rest of the human race would have been losers, since anti-Nazi resistance movements would have faced a stronger enemy. Shachtman had pointed out many of these dangers on the basis of his own analysis.

Shachtman's position had no dire consequences in the Soviet Union, since he had no followers there and no impact on U.S. policy. His position did have consequences for his own political evolution, however. The arguments he began making against defense of the USSR in 1941 would contribute to his step-by-step abandonment of his own theory of bureaucratic collectivism in favor of Carter's until, by about 1948, his differences with Carter had disappeared.[90] He would gradually embrace the implication of Carter's theory that Stalinism could be an even greater danger to socialism than capitalism was, including inside mass movements for social change. Although he would never follow Burnham in giving up on socialism completely, he would gradually come to see socialism as a distant objective and anti-Stalinism as a more compelling short-term imperative.

But in the early 1940s Shachtman pushed aside such qualms. He saw the Soviet regime as a relatively minor factor in the war, and Germany, Britain, and the United States as the major players. He was confident that popular movements born during the war would become another major player and a threat to all the warring governments. He welcomed these movements optimistically, seeing in them hope for democratic socialism in his time.

Notes

1. TA 4491, cited in Joseph Nedava, *Trotsky and the Jews*, 224–25.
2. Shachtman, "Fascism and the world war," LA v 4 n 33 (23 Nov. 1940), 2.
3. "The Second World War," NI v 5 n 10 (Oct. 1939), 292–93; "Liberty, equality, fraternity," NI v 6 n 7 (Aug. 1940), 131.
4. "Founding principles of the Workers Party," NI v 12 n 4 (Apr. 1946), 126 (also WP bul n 1 [26 Apr. 1940], ISM v 2).
5. Shachtman, *The Fight for Socialism*, 134; Shachtman, "The party that won the victory," NI v 10 n 11 (Nov. 1944), 363.
6. Harvey Klehr, *The Heyday of American Communism*, 387–90, 401, 482 n 31; Shachtman, "The Stalinist convention," NI v 4 n 7 (July 1938), 202–3.
7. SWP PC (22 Aug. 1939), MSC b 8 f 10 (r 3358); "Overflow meeting hears party leaders" (27 Aug. 1939), SA v 3 n 64 (1 Sept. 1939), 2; "The editor's comment," NI v 5 n 9 (Sept. 1939), 259.
8. SWP PC (18 and 26 Sept. 1939), MSC b 8 f 10 (r 3358); Shachtman, "Resolution on the Soviet Union in the present war" (late Sept. 1939—misdated 28 Aug. 1939), MSC b 8 f 21 (r 3359).
9. Shachtman, "Defense of the Soviet Union" (1941), MSC b 32 f 1 (r 3384);

Shachtman, "How not to hold a fruitful discussion" (25 June 1943), WP bul "On the National Question" (Summer 1943), ISM v 3, 276.

10. "Trotsky statement to press" (4 Sept. 1939), SA v 3 n 66 (9 Sept. 1939), 4.

11. "For the third camp!" NI v 6 n 3 (Apr. 1940), 67.

12. RMS 313; "Resolution on the Soviet Union," MSC b 8 f 21 (r 3359); Shachtman, "Report on the Russian question" (15 Oct. 1939), TA 17247.

13. "Report on the Russian question," TA 17247; Shachtman, "The crisis in the American party" (1 Jan. 1940), NI v 6 n 2 (Mar. 1940), 45 (also MSC b 9 f 1 [r 3359]).

14. Shachtman, "In this corner," SA v 3 n 73 (26 Sept. 1939), 4; Abern, Bernick, Burnham, and Shachtman, "What is at issue in the dispute on the Russian question?" (26 Dec. 1939), MSC b 8 f 21 (r 3359).

15. Cannon, "Speech on the Russian question" (15 Oct. 1939), NI v 6 n 1 (Feb. 1940), 9–10, 13; SWP PC, "The Soviet invasion of Finland" (5 Dec. 1939), SA v 3 n 92 (9 Dec. 1939), 1–2 (also MSC b 8 f 17 [r 3358]).

16. Abern, Bernick, Burnham, and Shachtman, "The judgment of events" (22 Mar. 1940), PMA b 16 f 20.

17. SWP convention (Apr. 1940—minority minutes), MSC b 8 f 2A (r 3357).

18. Shachtman, "In this corner," SA v 4 n 6 (10 Feb. 1940), 3; "What is at issue?" MSC b 8 f 21 (r 3359).

19. SWP opposition conference (24–25 Feb. 1940), MSC b 9 f 24 (r 3360); SWP opposition, "The second world war and the Soviet Union" (26 Feb. 1940), NI v 6 n 2 (Mar. 1940), 64 (also MSC b 9 f 1 [r 3359]).

20. RMS 313; Shachtman, "The Soviet Union and the world war," NI v 6 n 3 (Apr. 1940), 72.

21. Trotsky, "From a scratch—to the danger of gangrene" (24 Jan. 1940), in *In Defense of Marxism*, 130; Trotsky to Hansen (5 Jan. 1940), in *In Defense of Marxism*, 71; Trotsky, "The USSR in war" (25 Sept. 1939), in *In Defense of Marxism*, 18, 20.

22. "The crisis in the American party," NI v 6 n 2, 47.

23. Shachtman, "Is Russia a workers' state?" (3 Dec. 1940), BR 60 (also NI v 6 n 10 [Dec. 1940]). Trotsky ("Again and once again on the nature of the USSR" [18 Oct. 1939], in *In Defense of Marxism*, 30) pointed out himself that socialists should oppose some strikes, e.g., racist strikes, a point that Shachtman and his allies picked up ("What is at issue?" MSC b 8 f 21 [r 3359]).

24. James, "The roots of the party crisis" (late 1939), PMA b 16 f 19; Breitman to Wald (17 July 1985), cited in Alan Wald, *The New York Intellectuals*, 165; Shachtman, "Report on the Russian question" (15 Oct. 1939), TA 17247.

25. SWP opposition conference (24–25 Feb. 1940), MSC b 9 f 24 (r 3360); Shachtman, "The struggle for the new course" (14 May 1943), in Leon Trotsky, *The New Course*, 174, 246.

26. Trotsky to Cannon (19 Mar. 1940), TA 7566; Cannon to Trotsky (18 Jan. 1940), TA 532.

27. Interview with Seidlitz (16 Jan. 1989), s 2; interview with Glotzer (28 Mar. 1989), s 5; Irving Kristol, *Reflections of a Neoconservative*, 12–13.

28. V. I. Lenin, *What Is to Be Done?* 78–80, 39–40.

29. Shachtman, "Lenin and Rosa Luxemburg," NI v 4 n 5 (May 1938), 143; Lenin, "The reorganisation of the party," *Collected Works* v 10, 32, 34.

30. Cannon to Trotsky (21 Dec. 1939), TA 527; Cannon to Trotsky (7 June 1939), TA 509.

31. Shachtman, "Introduction" (1 May 1937), in Leon Trotsky, *The Stalin School of Falsification*, viii; Abern, Bernick, Burnham, and Shachtman, "Cannon organizes the split" (9 Mar. 1940), MSC b 8 f 23 (r 3359).
32. Trotsky to Cannon (11 Sept. 1937), TA 7505; Trotsky to Cannon (27 Dec. 1939), in *In Defense of Marxism*, 66–67 (also TA 7555).
33. Shachtman, "Introduction" (4 Dec. 1946), in Al Goldman, *The Question of Unity*, 8; Carter, "Socialist democracy or Bolshevik mythology?" (12 Mar. 1940), MSC b 8 f 23 (r 3359).
34. SWP PC (12 Dec. 1939), MSC b 8 f 10 (r 3357); "Motions in branch minutes" (1939–40), MSC b 8 f 23 (r 3359); SWP PC (30 Jan. and 6, 13 Feb. 1940), MSC b 8 f 11 (r 3357); NI v 6 n 1 (Feb. 1940); Goldman, "Stalin in Finland," SA v 6 n 12 (23 Mar. 1940), 3; SWP opposition conference (24–25 Feb. 1940), MSC b 9 f 24 (r 3360); Reid to Cannon (26 Feb. 1940), MSC b 9 f 8 (r 3360).
35. "Organizational report," MSC b 8 f 2 (r 3357); SWP convention (Apr. 1940—minority minutes), MSC b 8 f 2A (r 3357).
36. Shachtman to WP members (16 Apr. 1940), MSC b 9 f 34–35 (r 3361); RMS 316–19.
37. "Statement of the Political Committee in reply to Dwight Macdonald" (9 May 1941), WP bul n 9 (May 1941), ISM v 2, 143–44.
38. "The Marxists reply to Corey," *Nation* v 150 n 10 (9 Mar. 1940), 331–32; Burnham and Shachtman, "Intellectuals in retreat," NI v 5 n 1 (Jan. 1939), 21.
39. "Reply to Macdonald," ISM v 2, 145–46; "Bolshevism and democracy," WP bul n 8 (Apr. 1941), ISM v 2, 108–10, 114.
40. "Bolshevism and democracy," ISM v 2, 114, 109.
41. Shachtman, "Dictatorship of party or proletariat?" NI v 1 n 1 (July 1934), 11.
42. "Intellectuals in retreat," NI v 5 n 1, 12; Shachtman, "In this corner," SA v 3 n 23 (11 Apr. 1939), 4.
43. Shachtman, "The 'mistakes' of the Bolsheviks," NI v 9 n 10 (Nov. 1943), 304–6; Shachtman, "Under the banner of Marxism" (misdated 19 Mar. 1949), WP bul v 4 n 1 (Jan. 1949), ISM v 10, 2192, 2191.
44. Shachtman, "Explanatory notes," in Trotsky, *Stalin School of Falsification*, 313.
45. "Once more: Kronstadt," NI v 4 n 7, 213–14.
46. "Under the banner of Marxism," ISM v 10, 2160 (excerpted in "Soviets and the Constituent Assembly," NI v 15 n 7, 221).
47. "Under the banner of Marxism," ISM v 10, 2178; Shachtman, "Reflections on a decade past," NI v 16 n 3 (May–June 1950), 137 (omitted from BR).
48. "Under the banner of Marxism," ISM v 10, 2147.
49. "Under the banner of Marxism," ISM v 10, 2149; "The convention of the new party," NI v 4 n 1 (Jan. 1938), 13.
50. "Intellectuals in retreat," NI v 5 n 1, 19–20.
51. "Once more: Kronstadt," NI v 4 n 7, 214.
52. Trotsky to Shachtman (20 Jan. 1939), TA 10337; Shachtman to Trotsky (5 Mar. 1939), TA 5107; "Intellectuals in retreat," NI v 5 n 1, 7; Trotsky to Shachtman (9 Mar. 1939), TA 10339.
53. RMS 386.
54. Burnham, "Letter of resignation" (21 May 1940), ISM v 19, C2–C3 (also MSC b 9 f 31 [r 3361]); RMS 339, 342; Kristol, *Reflections of a Neoconservative*, 12.
55. Shachtman, "The party that won the victory," NI v 10 n 11 (Nov. 1944), 364; Shachtman, *The Fight for Socialism*, 148; "Bolshevism and democracy," WP bul n 8 (Apr. 1941), ISM v 2, 107.

56. Abern, Bernick, Burnham, and Shachtman, "Where is the petty bourgeois opposition?" (9 Mar. 1940), NI v 6 n 5 (June 1940), 111.

57. "Founding principles of the Workers Party," NI v 12 n 4 (Apr. 1946), 126 (also WP bul n 1 [26 Apr. 1940], ISM v 2).

58. Interview with Seidlitz (16 Jan. 1989), s 2; interview with Benson (6 Apr. 1989), s 2.

59. Glotzer to Drucker (6 Jan. 1990), 5–6.

60. Interview with Haskell (8 July 1989), s 1; interview with Benson, s 1.

61. Shachtman to Dobbs (9 Mar. 1968), MSC b 28 f 31A (r 3378); Glotzer to Drucker (6 Jan. 1990), 4; interview with Geltman (22 Mar. 1989), s 2.

62. Jacobson, "The two deaths of Max Shachtman," *New Politics* v 10 n 2 (Winter 1973), 98; New York City Department of Health, Bureau of Vital Records, Births (1939) and Deaths (1941); interview with Geltman, s 2; interview with Glotzer (28 Mar. 1989), s 4.

63. Trotsky to Shachtman (6 Nov. 1939), in *In Defense of Marxism*, 37; Trotsky to Shachtman (20 Dec. 1939), in *In Defense of Marxism*, 64.

64. SWP convention (Apr. 1940—minority minutes), MSC b 8 f 2A (r 3357); WP convention (5–7 Apr. 1940), MSC b 9 f 25 (r 3360); Shachtman to Trotsky (15 Apr. 1940), TA 5112; Shachtman to Trotsky (27 May 1940), TA 5113; Shachtman, "The struggle for the new course" (14 May 1943), in Trotsky, *The New Course*, 200.

65. Shachtman to Sedova, LA v 4 n 20 (26 Aug. 1940), 1; interview with Glotzer (4 Apr. 1989), s 10; interview with Kahn (7 Apr. 1989), s 2.

66. Gordon, "The Fourth International and the Russian question" (1940), MSC b 8 f 21 (r 3359); Plastrik, "Report on Ceylon" and "Political situation in India today," WP bul n 1 (1940), ISM v 15, 71, 74.

67. FI emergency conference, "Resolution on the internal struggle in the Socialist Workers Party" (19–26 May 1940), *Documents of the Fourth International*, 360, 306; Gordon to WP (May 1940), *Documents of the Fourth International*, 362 (also MSC b 9 f 26 [r 3360]); Milesi to Shachtman (26 Nov. 1940), MSC b 9 f 26 (r 3360); Brazilian Socialist Revolutionary Party to Trotsky (1940), MSC b 9 f 26 (r 3360); Gould, James, Pedrosa, and Shachtman, "Letter of members of the International Executive Committee" (25 Apr. 1940), WP international bul n 2 (28 May 1940), ISM v 2, A18–A21.

68. WP bul n 27 (29 Oct. 1940), MSC b 9 f 34–35 (r 3361); "Report of American Committee for the Fourth International," WP bul n 8 (Apr. 1941), ISM v 2, 92.

69. Shachtman, "The revolutionary optimist," NI v 7 n 7 (Aug. 1941), 170; Shachtman, "The struggle for the new course" (14 May 1943), in Trotsky, *The New Course*, 245–46.

70. Shachtman, "Five years of the Workers Party," NI v 11 n 3 (Apr. 1945), 81; Shachtman, *The Fight for Socialism*, 137–38. Marty Glaberman, who spent several years in both the WP and the SWP, said later that though the WP was more democratic the difference was "not qualitative" (Interview with Glaberman [Sept. 1984], in Wald, *NY Intellectuals*, 185). The fact that the SWP expelled minorities several times in the 1940s and 1950s (1946, 1953, 1957), whereas the WP never really expelled any (Selznick's group was expelled only retroactively in 1941, and Wohlforth's group was expelled only as the ISL was dissolving in 1958), seems to me to be a qualitative difference.

71. Shachtman, "Behind the Hitler-Stalin pact," SA v 3 n 67 (9 Sept. 1939), 2; Shachtman, "The Soviet Union and the world war," NI v 6 n 3 (Apr. 1940), 72;

Shachtman, "Resolution on the Soviet Union in the present war" (late Sept. 1939—misdated 28 Aug. 1939), MSC b 8 f 23 (r 3359); Shachtman, "Is Russia a workers' state?" NI v 6 n 10 (Dec. 1940), 204 (omitted from BR).

72. Interview with Benson (6 Apr. 1989), s 2; Shachtman, "Notes on the Russian question" (1940), MSC b 40 f 5 (r 3388); WP PC (11 Nov. 1940), MSC b 9 f 28 (r 3360); interview with Glotzer (28 Mar. 1989), s 6.

73. Carter, Geltman, Draper, et al., "The class nature of the Soviet Union" (1941), ISM v 15; James, "Resolution on the Russian question" (19 Sept. 1941), ISM v 15, 173. Shachtman actually called the Soviet Union "bureaucratic state socialist" in his Dec. 1940 NI article in order to distinguish his theory of Soviet society from Carter's. He accepted Carter's term "bureaucratic collectivism" a few weeks later in order to avoid calling the Soviet Union socialist. But he insisted at the time that his agreement with Carter was only "terminological."

74. Shachtman, "The struggle for the new course" (14 May 1943), in Trotsky, *The New Course*, 137; "Notes on the Russian question," MSC b 40 f 5 (r 3388).

75. Trotsky, *The New Course*, 232–33.

76. Shachtman, "Isaac Deutscher's 'Stalin,'" BR 229, 233 (also NI v 16 n 5 [Sept.– Oct. 1950]).

77. "Is Russia a workers' state?" BR 43–44 (also NI v 6 n 10 [Dec. 1940]); Trotsky, *The New Course*, 234; Shachtman, "Trotsky's letter to Borodin," BR 94 (also NI v 9 n 4 [Apr. 1943]).

78. Trotsky, *The New Course*, 212.

79. Ibid., 223, 225–26; "Is Russia a workers' state?" BR 45; WP 2nd convention, "The Russian question" (19 Sept. 1941), NI v 7 n 9 (Oct. 1941), 236 (also Basic Documents 1 [1946], ISM v 17).

80. "Is Russia a workers' state?" BR 37, NI v 6 n 10, 203 (omitted from BR); Shachtman, "The Soviet Union" (1940), MSC b 40 f 6 (r 3388).

81. Shachtman, "Class character of the Soviet Union" (1941), MSC b 11 f 12 (r 3363); Shachtman, "Central branch meeting" (1941), MSC b 11 f 12 (r 3363); "Is Russia a workers' state?" BR 56.

82. Carter, "Bureaucratic collectivism," NI v 7 n 8 (Sept. 1941), 219. Although Karl Marx was the first to say that "the emancipation of the working classes must be conquered by the working classes themselves" (Marx, "General rules of the International Working Men's Association" [Oct. 1864], *Political Writings Volume III*, 13), Shachtman gave credit for the discovery in this context to Carter.

83. Shachtman, "Character of the Soviet state" (1940), MSC b 40 f 6 (r 3388); Shachtman, "Debate on Russian question" (1941), MSC b 40 f 6 (r 3388); Trotsky, *The New Course*, 243; Shachtman, "Report on the Russian question" (15 Oct. 1939), TA 17247.

84. Cannon to Trotsky (8 Nov. 1939), TA 523; Shachtman to Weinrib (21 Dec. 1960), MSC b 31 f 43 (r 3383); Shachtman, "The end of socialism," BR 290–91, 294 (also NI v 20 n 4 [July–Aug. 1954]); Shachtman, "Stalinism and Marxist tradition," BR 76 (also NI [Apr. 1947]).

85. "The Russian question," NI v 7 n 9, 234, 240, 239; "Central branch meeting," MSC b 11 f 12 (r 3363).

86. Interview with Glotzer, s 6; Widick, LA v 5 n 27 (7 July 1941), 3; WP PC, "Motions on policy on the Russian German war" (24 June 1941), WP bul n 10 (Aug. 1941), ISM v 2, 154; Carter, "Bureaucratic collectivism," NI v 7 n 8 (Sept. 1941), 221; Erber, "The basis for defensism in Russia," NI v 7 n 7 (Aug. 1941),

189 (also WP bul n 10 [Aug. 1941], ISM v 2); Genecin, "The Soviet Union and its defense" (18 July 1941), WP bul n 10 (Aug. 1941), ISM v 2, 159; interview with Draper (13 Feb. 1989), s 4.

87. Shachtman, "The war today is what it was yesterday—imperialist!" LA v 5 n 27, 3; Shachtman, "Party policy towards Russia in the war" (8 Aug. 1941), WP bul n 10 (Aug. 1941), ISM v 2, 175.

88. "Debate on Russian question," MSC b 40 f 6 (r 3388).

89. American Committee for the FI, "The war in Russia," NI v 7 n 8 (Sept. 1941), 206; "Party policy towards Russia," ISM v 2, 176.

90. Interview with Draper (13 Feb. 1989), s 3; Draper to Drucker (11 Jan. 1990), 2.

5

The Third Camp

On 7 December 1941, the Japanese attacked the U.S. naval base at Pearl Harbor in Hawaii. Within hours the United States was at war not only with Japan but with Germany and Italy. The country's months of waiting and preparation were over. So was the Workers Party's initial breathing spell. Now Shachtman's idea of a third camp that would be a protagonist and possible victor in the war would be tested in his own country.

Looking back, most people would find Shachtman's decision to support a "third camp" instead of his country's war effort unbelievable. Shachtman did not equate Nazi Germany or imperial Japan with the democratic United States. He knew how much worse a fascist or dictatorial government was to live under than a capitalist democracy. He had made the distinction at length in the early 1930s, when he urged German Communists to join with Social Democrats to oppose the Nazis. He and his followers hoped fervently for the Axis's defeat. But he believed that the best hope for democracy and lasting peace after the Second World War would be movements independent of the Allied governments.

Nothing about the U.S. entry into the war raised any hesitations in the Workers Party about opposing it. Shachtman had convinced his followers that U.S. rulers were fighting for world supremacy: for example, by taking advantage of Britain's fight for survival to push it aside as a world power. U.S. corporations were grabbing British markets in Latin America. They had virtually transferred Canada and Australia from one empire to the other already, a power shift Shachtman had seen coming as early as 1926. "England is more at America's mercy than it is at Germany's," he said—which showed "the fraudulence of all claims that this is a war for democracy."[1]

Despite widespread indignation about the Japanese attack and Japanese atrocities, the U.S. war in the Pacific reinforced Shachtman's conviction that the Second World War had little to do with fighting fascism. The government ground out propaganda against the "yellow peril" and interned tens of thousands of U.S. citizens of Japanese descent in the name of defending democracy. The first U.S. battles against Japan were fought to

144

defend U.S. rule in the Philippines, while the British fought to defend their rule in Malaya, Burma, and India. The war against Japan, far from being democratic, was "racially chauvinistic in the authentic Nazi style," Shachtman said. From India to the Philippines, Asia was the scene of "an orgy of the imperialist swine."[2]

In the United States, the war was an orgy of arms profiteers, who were resisted by working people in North America as the colonial powers were being resisted in Asia. Even in the months before Pearl Harbor, when the country was in a fever of fear and "preparedness," Shachtman predicted radicalization ahead. In 1942–43 the radicalization began. Despite rising wages and high employment, workers grew more and more restive under the CIO's wartime no-strike pledge, which held them back while military contractors reaped record profits.

The Workers Party, prepared by a determined drive to put its members in industrial unions, began to win influence and recruits among militant unionists. At the height of war production it had 80 percent of its members in industry. It had strong presences—not thousands, but dozens—in International Harvester in Chicago, Lackawanna Steel in Buffalo, Ford Instrument in New York, and the Los Angeles and Philadelphia shipyards. The group began its life with about 400 members, half the size of the pre-split Socialist Workers Party; it grew during the war to about 500.[3]

Shachtman's followers found a more receptive audience in the unions they joined than they had initially expected. The war was by no means universally popular among working people in the United States. Most saw it as unavoidable, but they were not necessarily enthusiastic about it or ready to make all the sacrifices that were demanded of them. Battles by which unionists and radicals had secured basic freedoms of speech and assembly from a hostile government were still fresh in many people's memories. Whatever the U.S. government was fighting for, some suspected, it was probably not democracy—not when it banned publications like *Labor Action* from the mails. Yet the government could not stop Workers Party members from passing *Labor Action* and its anti-war message from one sympathizer to the next—even in army camps.[4]

The Workers Party's greatest success in the unions during the Second World War came in the United Auto Workers. Two factions had been fighting for control of this union, one of the CIO's most democratic, since its foundation in the 1930s. Each faction had staked out a position at the heights of the union hierarchy. In the face of rank-and-file opposition to the no-strike pledge, both of the rival factions defended it. The Workers Party helped catalyze the formation of a third faction, the Rank and File Caucus, based on Shachtman's analysis that the interests of union officials as a group tend inevitably to conflict with the interests of union members as a group.

At the auto workers' September 1944 convention in Grand Rapids, Michigan, Shachtman, "his skills at their sharpest and his energies at their peak,"[5] helped convince the Rank and File Caucus to reject any compromise with either of the two dominant factions. The Caucus succeeded in convincing 36 percent of the convention to vote for repudiating the no-strike pledge outright. It won a majority for a unionwide referendum on the issue.

Shachtman, remembering what he now considered to be wasted opportunities in the mid-1930s, began in 1944 to look for ways to help the rank-and-file upsurge in the unions find independent political expression. He used the Workers Party's influence to fight against Amalgamated Clothing Workers President Sidney Hillman's use of the powerful CIO Political Action Committee as an instrument in Roosevelt's 1944 reelection bid. The Workers Party called instead for turning the Political Action Committee into an independent labor party. Shachtman fought against Hillman's effort to tie the American Labor Party of New York even more tightly to the Democratic Party. After failing to repeat his United Auto Workers success and build an independent rank-and-file faction in the ALP, Shachtman backed David Dubinsky of the International Ladies Garment Workers against Hillman in order to keep a modicum of autonomy for the ALP.

Shachtman's maneuvers within the U.S. labor movement fit into an international vision, a vision of the warring empires' common defeat by popular resistance movements independent of the U.S., British, and Soviet governments. Looking back on Trotsky's 1940 prediction that Shachtman would surrender to the democracies' war drive, Shachtman said in 1942, "we can afford, even in these unpleasant days, to smile." Far from giving in to patriotism, he and his organization turned out to be the war's staunchest opponents on the left. The *New International* said from the start that it would side with neither Britain nor Germany.

> We say there is in this war a *third* camp . . . the camp of the world working class, cut off from all political control, inarticulate, brutally repressed when it raises its head, but ceaselessly in ferment, breaking through the surface to assert its human rights and needs. This is *our* camp. . . .
>
> It means Czech students fighting the Gestapo in the streets of Prague. . . .
>
> It means African natives going on strike in the Rhodesian copper mines. . . .
>
> It means the Irish Revolutionary Army keeping green the traditions of the Easter Rebellion. . . .
>
> It means Indian steel and textile and jute workers forcing concessions from the British Raj in militant strikes. . . .
>
> It means the anti-conscription rioters in Australia, the millions of AFL

and CIO rank-and-filers . . . the Polish peasants who seized the land when the landowners fled . . . before the coming of the Red Army.[6]

Shachtman's commitment to an independent working-class stance at home was bound up with his conviction that the war would create new revolutionary openings in Europe and Asia. Even before Pearl Harbor he foresaw a "revolutionary uprising" that would be born from the war in Europe. "The growing restlessness and even guerrilla warfare in the occupied territories, particularly in Poland, Serbia, Norway and France, contain the promise of mass popular and even revolutionary movements in the visible future," he said.[7] He believed that these movements could bring peace and democracy to Europe. As Lenin welcomed the 1916 Irish rebellion against Britain during the First World War, Shachtman looked for independent popular forces to emerge from the Second World War, forces that socialists could support and push in a revolutionary direction.

He identified the most promising independent European forces in 1943 as the Yugoslav partisans under Josip Broz Tito and the Italians who rose up after Benito Mussolini's fall. In contrast to the French Gaullists, the Polish Home Army, and most of the Communist-led resistance groups, who fought as guerrilla auxiliaries of the Allied high commands, the Yugoslavs and Italians initially struck Shachtman as genuinely independent forces. As 1943 gave way to 1944 and Allied troops advanced on every front, however, he lost hope that an independent force would actually manage to take power anywhere in Europe before the war ended.

He foresaw instead a "democratic interlude" in most of Europe, in which grassroots democratic forces emerging from resistance movements would fight for democratic constitutions and reforms without contending immediately for power. He urged European Marxists to join in postwar democratic movements: for abolition of the Belgian and Italian monarchies; overthrow of Spanish and Greek dictatorships; a united, independent, democratic Germany; expropriation of companies that had collaborated with the Nazis; and colonial independence. He urged Trotskyists in France to support a Socialist-Communist coalition government there, the better to defeat U.S.-backed right-wingers, expose Socialist and Communist timidity, and build a strong revolutionary socialist movement.

In Eastern Europe he predicted by 1943 that wartime anti-fascist movements would have to fight after the war for democracy against Stalinism. Before others on the left were ready to admit it, he saw that capitalism was being overthrown in Eastern Europe and Communists were coming to power. He predicted that the regimes and economies being established there would be just as repressive and give as little power to working people as Stalin's regime in the Soviet Union. He did more: He developed a general theory of the Stalinist movement that would explain both why Communists could overthrow capitalism in Poland—where the Soviet army could be relied on to install a pro-Soviet dictatorship—and why they would not overthrow capitalism in France—where a workers' revolution might ultimately threaten Soviet as well as U.S. power. He could feel with justice that his theory of bureaucratic collectivism had passed its biggest test yet with flying colors. In this discussion he "reached the peak of his intellectual powers."[8]

Revolutionary movements in Asia led Shachtman to hope for breakthroughs there even after he had moderated his hopes for Europe. He did not hope for much from the Indian Congress Party or the Chinese Guomindang. He criticized sharply and perceptively Chiang Kai-shek's subservience to the United States and Mohandas Gandhi's and Jawaharlal Nehru's failure to confront British rule decisively in India. But he admired the Vietminh that Ho Chi Minh led against both Japan and France in Vietnam. He saw the Vietminh as an independent force despite its Communist leadership. As late as 1947, the Workers Party picketed French consulates in solidarity with the Vietminh's fight for Vietnamese independence. Shachtman was also enthusiastic about the Indonesians who fought a war for independence from the Dutch in 1945–49, although he was alive to the danger that independent Indonesia could come under U.S. hegemony.

Although Shachtman was proud of the role his Workers Party played in the unions, U.S. politics, and solidarity movements, he developed a more clear-sighted modesty about his organization as the war ended. It was not a "party" in the full sense, he admitted, not an organization capable of leading U.S. workers in a revolution. It was a group educating working people about socialism, developing as an activist group putting socialist ideas into practice, and hoping to play an important role in forming a true revolutionary party. Shachtman wrote more about the kind of party he was working toward. He said that it had to be an "all-inclusive revolutionary party," with room for diverse tendencies. At the same time it needed a solid "cadre" of member-leaders who fully understood and agreed with the program it had decided on and who could defend, implement, and develop its program in the outside world.

The Workers Party's own cadre developed during the war only by fits and starts. It told its members to obey the draft laws so that they would go where other working people went and not be isolated and ineffective in jails or conscientious objector camps. Given the group's low average age, it paid a high price for this policy. "Among those who went off were some of our ablest and most experienced men, our indispensables; and we know that not all of them will be returned to us," Shachtman said in 1945. "It was an oppressive blow."[9]

The blow left Shachtman, Al Glotzer, and Ernest McKinney as the mainstays of the Workers Party office, despite Shachtman's efforts to keep younger leaders around. When *Labor Action* editor Manny Geltman got his draft notice in 1943, Shachtman urged him to make sure that the draft board knew what a dangerous subversive he was, so that the army (which surely didn't "want any goddamn reds") would keep him stationed on Governor's Island in New York Harbor. Somehow Shachtman expected Geltman to sneak away from Governor's Island to edit the newspaper at night. Geltman did his best, but an unmoved official told him, "If the attorney general wants you, he'll find you in the army."[10]

Glotzer had to take over Geltman's job. Shachtman, chagrined, urged the same tactics on Glotzer when his draft call came. While Glotzer told the draft board what a subversive he was, "Max and McKinney were sitting in the office waiting for me," he remembered. "They're down to me already, only those two old codgers were not going to be called up." Glotzer escaped the draft not because of his politics but because of his ulcers, a common complaint among Workers Party leaders.[11]

Much of the burden of keeping the party going was taken on by women. Women played a disproportionate role throughout the left during the war years, but especially in the Workers Party. Glotzer remembered that *Labor Action* would "have an editorial meeting of ten to fifteen and every one of them was a woman." The group's male leaders took pride in the commitment and intelligence of their "magnificent female comrades."[12]*

The cadre of newly confident women and the men returning from the army faced a formidable challenge once the war was over. The evidence of heightened U.S. power was plainly visible. As the Workers Party had predicted in 1943, the United States had given up isolationism for good. It had "acquired a power in world economics and politics that *exceeds* anything England ever possessed," Shachtman said. It was keeping "far flung bases on the seven seas and the five continents."[14] It was creating world banks and trade agreements under its direction. Shachtman's few hundred followers were committed to continuing the fight against this colossus. Shachtman continued to pin his hopes on the third camp that had formed during the war: the opposition to U.S. predominance in Western Europe; anti-Stalinist movements in Eastern Europe; Vietnamese and Indonesian fighters for independence; and inside the United States, the newly militant union rank and file, poised for the biggest strike wave in U.S. history.

---

*Women were not encouraged to organize around their own issues, however. Shachtman had argued earlier for "a socialist women's movement . . . distinct and separate from the feminist and other bourgeois movements";[13] but organizing a women's movement of any kind was low on his group's list of priorities.

In 1942–43, as the United States settled in for a long war, resistance grew in the unions to the sacrifices imposed on working people in the name of patriotism. Most of the left urged working people to resist less and sacrifice more. The Workers Party stepped into the vacuum created by the default of virtually every other leftist organization to encourage and organize working people's assertive spirit. It played a role that parties with thousands of members could have envied.

Shachtman believed that in the United States as in Europe, the third camp's fight was crucial not only to the future of socialism but also to the future of democracy. Although most progressives in the United States were enthusiastic about the "war for democracy," Shachtman saw anti-democratic tendencies at work that would fuel postwar McCarthyism. To protect war industry, wages were being kept down. To keep wages down, the right to strike was curtailed. To insulate these decisions from political pressure, they were taken out of the political arena. The powers of the presidency were increased. More decisions were made by executive decree, fewer by debate and legislation. The decision to intern virtually all Japanese Americans was made with a stroke of the presidential pen. One man decided to drop the first two atomic bombs. The war ended without a peace treaty, so the postwar settlements were taken out of congressional hands. The "national security state" was being born.

The Workers Party, together with some pacifists and civil libertarians and a few other socialists, resisted these attacks on democratic freedoms. Shachtman called on the government to give substance to its propaganda by giving democratic rights to African Americans: "American 'democracy' stinks with the odor of the slave market," he said. The party put forward democratic slogans with special relevance to the war: the right to vote at eighteen (over forty years before the right was won); the people's right to vote on any declaration of war; open diplomacy; a people's army; guaranteed jobs for ex-soldiers; unions, grievance committees, and civil rights for soldiers.[15]

It focused its organizing efforts among working people in the unions, where it saw the one force powerful enough to stop the erosion of democracy. It credited the United States' "vigorous, undefeated and undemoralized labor movement" for preventing the kind of all-out crackdown on radicals that there had been during the First World War.[16] It tried to turn the unions into the adversary of the national security state.

This effort brought Shachtman's organization into direct opposition to almost all union officials it encountered as well as to the U.S. government. He was not disturbed by this antagonism, which only confirmed the suspicious attitude he had had toward union officials since he began his radical career. "*Taken as a whole*—not this or that individual labor official"—the union bureaucracy was "closer to the middle class than to the working class. . . . It enjoys special privileges and powers in society," which it could keep "only in so far as it keeps the labor movement tied to capitalism." Shachtman and his followers in the unions urged workers to organize independently of these "*capitalistic* labor leaders . . . oppose their ideas at all times and seek to replace them with leaders who understand what capitalism is and who know how to fight it."[17]

Against overwhelming odds, Shachtman and his followers helped build a strong tendency in the unions in 1943–45 to oppose the union bureaucracy, the government, the Republicans and Democrats, and the way the war was being fought. He said later, "The labor movement was bent to its knees by the union leaders, but they could not prostrate it; they could not even prevent it from rising to its feet and fighting for its interests." The wartime boom helped by making workers more restive. "Every new announcement of growing company profits is worth ten union organizers' speeches," he said in 1941. Wartime patriotism was not having the dampening effect he had expected. "The workers' patriotism is a reluctant one, cold to the beating of the war drums. . . . If fascism is to be smashed because it means super-intensified exploitation and oppression of labor, then the workers want none of it introduced here in the name of opposition to it."[18]

The Workers Party began to work urgently in 1941 to muster its troops for the "war at home." Even before the split from the Socialist Workers Party, Shachtman's faction demanded that young Trotskyists be sent into industry. After the split the party was determined to push its members into industrial jobs. It ordered every eligible member to join a trade union and began moving members out of New York and Chicago into industrial areas in Pennsylvania, Ohio, and California. Every member who was not in a factory was interviewed to find out why not, and some members who could not or would not go in forfeited their membership. Enormous pressure was put even on members who were unprepared to make "the sudden, disorienting leap from the lecture hall to the assembly line."[19]

Leo Seidlitz was typical of the students turned revolutionaries who enlisted in Shachtman's industrial army. He dropped out of Brooklyn College only months before his graduation. He received rudimentary training from his Young People's Socialist League friend Herman Benson on how to use a lathe. Then he started applying for jobs as a skilled machinist. The first jobs he was hired for he was fired from before he had finished his first day. But he kept coming back, kept learning, and eventually he *was* a machinist. He remained a machinist for two years, until he was drafted.[20]

The Workers Party was too weak to do much in the first show of wartime labor militancy: the 1941 strike wave, in which the CIO organized Ford Motors and Bethlehem Steel and more workers went out on strike than in any year since 1919. A temporary fall in the level of labor activism in 1941–42 gave the party more time to prepare. In April 1941, United Auto Workers leaders insisted on mediation to avoid a strike at General Motors. In June, UAW leaders and the government crushed a Communist-led strike at North American Aviation in California, as *Labor Action* mocked "the army in action—against strikers!"[21] When Germany invaded the Soviet Union a few days later, Communists called off every strike they could in order to spur war production. The government restrained the Socialist Workers Party's resistance by sending eighteen of its leaders to jail in 1943 for advocating revolution. The AFL, which stuck to an attitude of trade unionism as usual longer than the CIO, finally knuckled under after Pearl Harbor and made its own no-strike pledge. The day after Pearl Harbor, strikes were called off around the country.

At first the Workers Party's efforts to put down roots and make trouble in industry were set back by the war, since many of the 150 party members drafted into the military were its best-placed industrial workers. But in the end its determination paid off. By the last two years of the war it had replaced its drafted members with women and younger men and pushed even more members into industry.[22]

More members with jobs meant more money for the party. "When the war started most of us had been unemployed for a long time. We'd learned to live with no money at all," San Francisco railroad worker and Workers Party leader Gordon Haskell explained later. "Now we all had industrial jobs and we felt as rich as Croesus. We had guys giving a week's pay out of a month without feeling it." This flow of riches helped the Workers Party turn *Labor Action* into a popular newspaper for and sometimes by workers. From a circulation of only 4,000 to 4,500 in 1941, the paper's press run grew to 40,000 by 1943. Five thousand copies of each issue were distributed in Detroit alone.[23]

The new factory activists were finally able to ride the tide as the interrupted 1941 strike wave came flowing back in 1943. The Workers Party played an outstanding leadership role in the United Auto Workers. Strangely enough, the party had not mentioned the auto industry as a focus in 1940; it decided to move people to Detroit only in March 1941 and assembled half a dozen activists there only in the summer of 1942. But by 1943, Workers Party members were entrenched in several locals. Besides a central concentration of about fifty in Detroit, the party had strong influence over the Brewster Aeronautical Corporation local in Long Island City, New York, whose June 1944 sit-down strike set a radical example and whose *Aero Notes* spread a radical message across the union.[24] The Workers Party established a network of sympathizers who shared its socialism and even its opposition to the war.

The Workers Party recruited some Black as well as white unionists, in keeping with the insistence of its founding convention. Although most African-American recruits stayed in the party only a few months before drifting away, the few that stayed sufficed to make the Workers Party a bridge between white and Black workers. Ernest McKinney worked with African-American steelworkers and autoworkers in Buffalo, for example, urging them to take part and fight for equality in their unions. Shachtman's speeches in Detroit would draw forty or fifty African-American trade unionists.[25]

The spirit of interracial solidarity in the auto plants, which radicals had benefited from and encouraged, showed its strength during the race riots that swept Detroit during 1943, as whites attacked African Americans who had moved north to work in the factories. Although "there was race against race *in the streets*," Leo Seidlitz remembered, and entire blocks were being surrounded by whites or African Americans, there was "not a *single* racial incident inside a factory plant."[26] Shachtman's insistence on seeing Blacks as workers rather rather as a distinct people showed its most positive side here.

Workers were being drawn together by discontent with the wartime no-strike pledge. Once workers got over their initial bliss at wartime full employment, the squeeze on their stagnant wages by skyrocketing prices frustrated them. The cruelest expression of the price workers paid for the war was the government's so-called Little Steel formula. This formula, imposed in July 1942, limited wages to 15 percent above their levels of 1 January 1941 — thus backdating the war by a year to erase the gains of the 1941 strike wave.

The AFL and CIO acquiesced in this formula in return for a maintenance-of-membership agreement that increased their ranks (and dues) without putting them to the trouble of organizing anyone. "They sold labor's most powerful weapon, the right to strike, and didn't even get a mess of potage for it," Shachtman said. Inflation, higher taxes, forced war loans, and elimination of premium pay all ate away at frozen wages. Despite the fact that by November 1943 the Little Steel formula was virtually a dead letter — thanks to a United Mine Workers victory after a twelve-month strike battle — real wages rose only 5 percent during the wartime boom. Net profits of major corporations, on the other hand, rose 107 percent in 1939–42 alone.[27]

Through 1943, United Auto Workers members went out on wildcat strikes more and more often, despite union officials' resistance and the government's willingness to draft strikers into the army as punishment. Entire locals began to call for repudiation of the no-strike pledge. But neither of the two factions fighting to control the UAW backed the demand. One, led by George Addes, the union's secretary-treasurer, was supported by Communists. It usually controlled the union. The other faction, led by Walter Reuther, head of the union's General Motors department, was supported by Socialists. It was often a strong opposition.

Reuther would be the polestar around which Shachtman's perspective on labor would revolve for years to come. The son of a German immigrant socialist brewery worker and labor organizer, Reuther went to college in Detroit but returned to the auto plants as an organizer in the mid-1930s. He acquired a certain radical aura when he joined the Socialist Party in 1932, although he left it in 1938. He made a name for himself in the war's early months by his patriotism—coming up with a plan to turn out 500 planes a day and calling on workers for "equality of sacrifice"—and later in the war by his attempts to turn workers' grievances into support for his fight against Addes. In 1943, for instance, he helped beat back a plan by Addes and the Communists for "incentive pay" (piecework).

In October 1943, the United Auto Workers convention reaffirmed the no-strike pledge despite its members' unrest. Shachtman blamed the Communists—a "fifth column, *the most conscious, best-organized and most dangerous right wing in the labor movement today*"—for the convention defeat. But he also blamed the "fence-sitting and double-talk" of people like Reuther. He complained that the real militants were not organized separately from Reuther's faction and urged "organization now!"[28] The Workers Party stood at the center of a growing opposition network. In July 1944, the party's contacts came together to form a Rank and File Caucus united around a three-plank platform: rescind the no-strike pledge, form an independent labor party, and elect a new union leadership.

The challenge from the Rank and File Caucus came to a head at the union's convention in Grand Rapids in September 1944—a convention remembered afterwards as the high point of the Workers Party's wartime prestige in the unions. Reuther tried to square the circle at this convention: win support from radicals opposed to the no-strike pledge without challenging the government. He put forward a compromise proposal: rescind the no-strike pledge only for those plants completely unrelated to war production, and only after Germany was defeated.

The overwhelming defeat of his middle position gave Reuther the greatest humiliation of his union career. One delegate said that the Reuther position was "full of the splinters you get from sitting on top of a fence." Perhaps a hundred delegates out of 2,300 voted for it while hooting resounded in the hall. The Rank and File Caucus's straightforward repudiation of the pledge got over 36 percent of the vote. Rank-and-filers rounded up wounded veterans of their own to counter wounded veterans that the leadership threatened to bring in; they waved tiny U.S. flags whenever a leadership speaker indulged in rhetorical flag-waving.[29]

Shachtman proposed that the Rank and File Caucus refuse any compromise with Reuther's halfhearted position. Other caucus members followed Shachtman's lead. This independent stance paid off. The caucus succeeded in defeating the Addes leadership's proposal to reaffirm the no-strike pledge on the convention floor and won the right to a membership referendum on the issue. "The militants were *organized*, openly and consciously, for the first time," Shachtman crowed in the *New International*. They had "a *program* of their own for the first time. . . . They no longer trailed along, exasperated but helpless, behind the Reuther group." They overcame Communists' appeals to "the Great New Deal on which our union was founded (lie), on which it was built (lie), to which we owe our advances (lie), on which we depend for our future (lie)."[30]

The Rank and File Caucus went all out to win the referendum, putting out three issues of a special paper, the *Rank and Filer*, in the winter of 1944–45. The results were paradoxical. In a referendum in which only a fraction of union members voted, two-thirds of those voting upheld the no-strike pledge in February 1945. Yet the pledge barely passed in the union's Michigan strongholds—Detroit, Flint, Lansing—despite wording on the ballot that argued for voting yes and procedures that may have allowed many company executives to vote.[31]

Furthermore, many more union members than voted for the pledge in the referendum violated it in practice by going out on strike in 1944 and 1945. Around the country there were more strikes in 1944 than in any other year in this century. There were far more strikes overall during the less than four years of the war (December 1941 through August 1945) than during the fabled first years of the CIO (1936–39). Union members may not have had the political self-confidence or trust in elections to vote against the pledge, but neither did they let patriotism interfere with their going out on strike.

The fights to build and defend this militancy hardened Shachtman's hostility to the Communist Party. In 1940 Jim Cannon defended Trotskyists' practice of allying with "even the conservative labor fakers against the Stalinists," because Communists were willing to disrupt a union at Stalin's orders while ordinary union officials tended "from self-interest" to be "a little more loyal to the unions." Cannon even argued for "purging the labor movement of the curse of Stalinism . . . by the conscious democratic action of the ranks." Shachtman and his party held this same attitude in the early 1940s, but in a remarkably balanced way. The Workers Party wanted to eliminate Communist influence in the unions, but it rejected any alliance with "reactionary and red-baiting elements" to do it. Shachtman warned in July 1940 that the government was persecuting the Communists, "the most unpopular group, the better later to smash the whole working class movement." The Workers Party was willing to work openly hand in hand "with the Communist Party as a party."[32]

Wartime battles with the Communists pushed Shachtman and his party toward a stance of more rigid hostility. Communists would do anything to keep war production going, including trying to ban *Labor Action* from plants, informing to the boss on troublemakers, and getting them fired from their jobs. The idea of working "hand in hand" with Communists was obviously impossible, and Shachtman stopped mentioning the possibility. Communists wanted *"the same strangled, blinded, gagged and fettered labor movement here that their Moscow overlords have established in the Soviet Union,"* he charged in June 1942. The *New International* said in 1945, "The time is fast approaching when whoever seriously aspires to leadership in the American working class and refuses to align himself in merciless struggle against the Communist Party will thereby prove himself either a traitor or a blind fool."[33]

His group's record in the unions also made Shachtman somewhat condescending toward the Socialist Workers Party. Cannon's followers, intimidated by the government's imprisonment of their leaders, followed a policy of "caution" in the unions. "And by 'caution,'" Shachtman said, "they meant abstention from any notable activity in the unions." He contrasted Cannon's followers in the unions with his own, who "did not retire to a storm cellar for the duration 'until it blows over.'"[34]

As the Workers Party gained members and influence in the unions and helped lead rebellions against the no-strike pledge, Shachtman paid more attention to labor's political potential. He renewed his interest in the idea, which the Workers Party had inherited from the Socialist Workers Party, of an independent labor party. Unless the labor movement defended its prewar victories through independent politics, the Workers Party warned, everything it had gained could be lost.[35]

Although the labor party movement was dormant in the early 1940s, the Workers Party used the labor party slogan as a weapon against Republicans and Democrats while giving electoral support almost exclusively to its own candidates. Shachtman himself ran for Congress in the Bronx on the Workers Party ticket, twice for city council, and twice for mayor of New York. Each time he got a couple of thousand votes at most, drawn largely from the South Bronx, Harlem, the Lower East Side, and Brownsville. The party kept clear even of electoral cooperation with other leftist groups (though it endorsed Socialist Workers Party candidates).[36]

By late 1943, the Workers Party said that with thirteen million workers in unions, U.S. labor was as militant and organized as any labor movement in the world. It was bound to become a crucial political force. The party saw

"unmistakable signs" of interest among U.S. workers in independent politics. It resolved to encourage this interest.[37]

Shachtman thought more about labor party politics in the last years of the
war than he ever had before. Although third parties existed in only a few
parts of the country and were only in their first stage, he wanted his
organization to play a part in them. Leaders of existing third parties were
firmly committed to the Roosevelt administration, but Shachtman began
arguing that there were ways to oppose these leaders, use them, and
maneuver among them in order to bring a real labor party and working-
class power closer.

He knew that creating a labor party would mean defeating Communists
and the same officials he was battling in the unions. He also faced the
probability that any labor party that arose anytime soon would be controlled at first by many of those same officials. They "would try to head the
movement in order to head it off," he warned, "take the steel out of the
organization and replace it with putty." He set about designing tactics for
fighting inside it against them. The Workers Party would fight for "an
independent labor party based on the trade unions and democratically
controlled by them," it said in January 1944; but it would fight inside the
labor party for a militant program of struggle against capitalism, with the
aim of making labor the "ruler of the country."[38]

At first Shachtman put forward a program to urge on a hypothetical labor
party that amounted to a program for socialist revolution, including forming workers' councils. But in December 1944, the Workers Party proposed
a new program, this time focusing less on workers' councils and more on
demands that could get an immediate echo among working people after the
war. It called for the right to a job; a guaranteed annual wage; two years'
pay for returning veterans; a shorter workweek; a $250 billion housing
program; nationalization of banks, monopolies, and transport; and a big
war profits tax. It made clear that these measures presupposed an independent labor government. They were "*the first important steps toward the achievement of socialism!*" Shachtman said. Organizing working people to win and
administer the reforms was the most important step toward socialism, since
"*by its very nature* [socialism] demands . . . constant control and direction
by the people."[39]

Although a real labor party with a working-class program was bound to
lead toward socialism, Shachtman thought, alleged labor parties that supported Democrats or were not based on unions, like the Minnesota Farmer-
Labor Party and the American Labor Party of New York, would only help
prop up capitalism. At first the Workers Party paid little attention to these
parties. It said that they would be swept away in the depression that would
hit the United States after the war. The party also foresaw the rise of

McCarthyism and its "subtle totalitarian measures," which it detected in embryo in wartime restrictions on workers' rights to organize. In the face of dramatic crisis and repression, the party anticipated a relatively fast radicalization that would create a radical labor party.[40] There would be no opportunity for the kind of diversion LaFollette had created in 1924.

In November 1942, Shachtman argued that socialists should look critically even at supposedly independent American Labor Party campaigns. Even when these campaigns were ostensibly directed against both Republicans and Democrats, he said, they were often maneuvers by pro-Roosevelt Democrats against other Democrats. The ALP had simply been "assigned by the New Deal machine the task of . . . doing its dirty work." Its candidates would deserve support only when they encouraged working people to oppose the whole Democratic Party, not just one or another of its factions.[41]

But by 1944 Shachtman decided that even halfhearted third parties could have an impact on the rise of a radical labor party, and he made a first attempt to push the American Labor Party in the right direction. The stage was set when the CIO created a Political Action Committee to fight for Franklin Roosevelt's reelection and made Sidney Hillman of the Amalgamated Clothing Workers, Roosevelt's closest labor ally, its chairman. Hillman worked energetically to organize labor for Roosevelt and unite all pro-Roosevelt unionists under his sway. Shachtman said that Hillman's successes showed labor's potential to transform the country's political climate. He put forward a slogan that would loom larger in his thinking after the war, "Transform the PAC into a Labor Party."[42] But at the moment, Shachtman saw Hillman's work as setting back independent labor politics. Hillman succeeded in merging the Minnesota Farmer-Labor Party into the Democratic Party, which, until then, had been a minor force in Minnesota politics. Then Hillman allied with Communists to win control of the American Labor Party.

There Hillman ran into opposition from David Dubinsky of the International Ladies Garment Workers. Dubinsky supported Roosevelt just as enthusiastically as Hillman, but he had come to view the American Labor Party as his personal fiefdom. By delivering its endorsement to an occasional Republican, Dubinsky had forced Democrats to court him. He had gone so far as to run an independent candidate for governor in 1942. He opposed letting the Democrats reduce the ALP to a dependable appendage. Besides, Dubinsky had been at odds with Hillman since the Ladies Garment Workers had gone back to the AFL fold in 1940, and he was a bitter anti-Communist.

Shachtman agreed with Dubinsky that Communists were a menace and that the American Labor Party should be something more than an extra ballot line for Democrats. He had little use for the ALP as it was but cherished hopes that it might be transformed someday into something worthwhile. "Although the ALP was not *our party*—the party of the working class," he said, it was "*our problem*—the problem of the working class." Besides, he hated to stay out of a fight. At first he said that Dubinsky's faction, like Hillman's, deserved no support. To expect Dubinsky to form a real labor party was "to expect a reed to stand up like a pillar"; Dubinsky only wanted to salvage the ALP as "a middle class party with labor pretensions." Shachtman tried to organize a third faction around a proposal to put the ALP under the democratic control of unions committed to political independence. But Shachtman's third faction never got off the ground. Instead, he urged his followers to back Dubinsky's candidates in the March 1944 primaries, as the lesser evil. Dubinsky was at least making "halting, tentative, but unmistakable moves" toward expanding the third-party movement, he said, while Hillman was "Roosevelt's direct political ward heeler." Besides, the Communists had to be stopped.[43]

Hillman won the primaries, and Dubinsky split from the American Labor Party in June to form his own New York Liberal Party. No one in the Workers Party whispered the thought yet of supporting the Liberals. "Neither the ALP nor the Liberal Party is an independent Labor Party," Shachtman's independent New York mayoral campaign said in 1945. "They trail along after one or another of the capitalist machines, pleading with shabby politicians to select 'good' candidates . . . capitalist candidates of capitalist parties." Such a party was nothing but "a miserable bargaining agency," Shachtman said.[44] But he was thinking more and more about how these bargaining agencies could be saved for genuine labor politics.

With the turn in the war's tide at the end of 1942, Shachtman's attention was drawn more and more to the battle against fascism being fought in Europe. With Germany and Italy on the defensive, he began to put forward ideas about how European revolutionaries should fight against German and Italian occupation. His ideas fit in with his underlying attitude toward the war: that socialists should be hostile to either side's victory. But he watched resistance movements in Europe with growing enthusiasm, seeing in them the main hope for his politics. If Marxists could become leaders in these movements, there might at last be hope for socialism in Europe.

In Shachtman's eyes the core of the anti–fascist resistance was a revolutionary third camp being born, which had to separate itself from the Allied camp that was alien to it. The resistance to German occupation was at the heart of the European strategy he advocated. It became his model for wars of national liberation, a model he would also adapt to anti-colonial revolutions in Asia. National revolutions, he decided, were the key to socialism in his time.

By 1942 the German Reich stretched from the Atlantic coast of France to central Russia. Shachtman saw the "slavery" the Germans imposed on the peoples they occupied as a regression to the open violence of capitalism's earliest years. It was the crudest form of capitalist "wage slavery"—though like the French who extracted forced labor from colonized Africans, the Germans supplemented paid labor with forced labor, especially in the occupied Soviet territories. What Britain and France had done to millions of Africans and Asians, Germany was doing to millions of Europeans. For "the 'white man's superiority'" it had substituted "the still more aristocratic and more preposterous 'Nordic superiority.'" Its labor camps, mass deportations, and mass murders were signs, Shachtman said, that Europe had been "hurled back . . . to neo-barbarism."[45]

In the summer of 1941, even before German expansion had been checked, he heard rumors of underground resistance to German occupation in France, Norway, Yugoslavia, and Poland. He urged European Trotskyists to join the resistance wherever and however it arose, taking as his model Lenin's support for the German-backed Irish army that launched the 1916 Easter Rebellion against the British. The Irish rebellion was a "national liberation war" in which the German role was unimportant, Lenin had said. The rebels' demand for democracy implicitly threatened all the imperial powers. Most important, the Irish rebels, not the Germans, began the rebellion, controlled it, and were waging it in a revolutionary way. The Irish rebellion alone was "capable of going all the way to insurrection and street fighting, capable of breaking down the iron discipline of the army."[46] Therefore it was less a tragedy and a problem than an opportunity for socialists.

Shachtman saw the anti-fascist movement being born in the underground as potentially the Easter Rebellion of the Second World War. He saw all other anti-fascist forces as unreliable by comparison. The Soviet Union and Communists had changed sides twice already, in 1939 and 1941. As for capitalist politicians in occupied Europe, many of them could live almost as easily with a Nazi victory as an Allied victory and wanted mainly to be on the winning side. Almost any capitalist would cooperate with Germany to achieve "his main aim—*the protection of his capital*," Shachtman said. Rightists' allegiance was as easily lost as won. Many supporters of the pro-German Vichy government in France "announced themselves as great French patriots" as soon as the Allies began winning victories in 1942 and 1943, but they could easily become German patriots again.[47] With individual exceptions, only those in the resistance who had no commitment to capitalism could be counted on to fight the Nazis until the end.

Even those who could be counted on to fight Germany could not necessarily be counted on to create a truly democratic Europe after the war.

Shachtman believed that the Allied governments and the governments in exile they patronized would be halfhearted democrats at best. Charles de Gaulle, the British-backed candidate to lead the French resistance, was not much of a democrat: He had chosen the royalist Cross of Lorraine over the republican tricolor as his Free French emblem. Shachtman foresaw that the Allies would seize even more German territory after the Second World War than after the First and trample on the rights of minorities (such as Germans in Czechoslovakia and Poland and Hungarians in Yugoslavia and Romania). He foresaw that they would suppress democratic movements in French, Belgian, and Dutch colonies and would keep the European economy in the hands of people who had funded or collaborated with fascism.

Above all, he foresaw that a Europe freed by U.S. and Soviet troops and their guerrilla "auxiliaries" would be ruled from Washington and Moscow. The fundamental decisions about Europe's future would be made by U.S. and Soviet rulers, not by Europeans.

This kind of Europe—a Europe of restored colonial empires and national antagonisms, ruled by foreign powers—was not the Europe Shachtman hoped to see after the war. For the resistance to take aid from the Allies was acceptable and sensible, he said, but it should fight against Allied governments' attempts to control it and to impose their postwar plans. He believed that another kind of postwar Europe was possible, in which democratic freedoms were fully established, no people ruled over any other, and the working class was well positioned to fight for power. This Europe could be created only by an independent resistance with its own democratically controlled leadership.

Shachtman said later that national resistance movements, more than U.S. or British troops, were crucial to the Nazis' defeat. "Hitlerism could unite the continent only by converting it into a prison," he said. When the prisoners rebelled, they "prevented that thorough utilization of the continent's resources by which alone Germany could hope to win the war." Nazism "broke its neck" in the fight with the resistance.[48]

The movement for national liberation was not unified or classless, the Workers Party said. It included "every political current, from native, anti-Hitler fascist to revolutionary-socialist." The strongest forces were Gaullists and similar nationalists, Communists, and social-minded Catholics. Marxists had to take part and had to gain strength: The rebirth of their movement would be through the underground if it was to happen at all.[49]

Shachtman argued that socialist revolution in Europe would have to be ushered in by basic struggles for democracy that had already been won decades before and then lost with the rise of fascism. Socialists had to push the rock up the hill from a point even lower than where they had first found it in the late nineteenth century, refighting battles that had already been historically outlived. The strongest levers to lift the rock were democratic and national slogans. Although European peoples had little desire for the return of their own native capitalists to power, "the overwhelming majority of them want *first of all* the destruction of *foreign* fascist domination, that is, of Hitler's rule." By joining in the movement and influencing it, Marxists could achieve "*the linking of the aims of the national movement to the aims of socialism.*"[50]

By 1943, Shachtman saw the brightest, most immediate promise for linking national liberation to socialism in Yugoslavia and Italy. He was impressed by the way Tito's Yugoslav partisans had organized their fight against German and Italian occupation: redistributing land to the peasants, burning archives and land registries, setting up "liberation committees" to replace discredited puppet governments, and swelling the partisans' ranks and authority in each stretch of territory they captured. Though "Stalinist-inspired and largely Stalinist-led," the Workers Party said, the Yugoslav movement was "popular, democratic and organizationally and programmatically fluid." An article in the *New International* said that Yugoslav revolutionaries should join the partisans. Shachtman said that Yugoslav Communists were appealing to Yugoslavs' desire for democracy, waging an "uncompromising and uncorrupted" fight against the Germans, and "organizing an armed force of all the peoples of Yugoslavia, in which neither national origin nor religious belief was made the basis of discrimination." One Workers Party member speculated that "Trotskyists" rumored to be among the Yugoslav partisans were "just old communist revolutionaries who refused to follow Stalin's counter-revolutionary line."[51]

Tito's strategy pitted him not only against Hitler and Mussolini but also against Draza Mihailovic and his troops, who were loyal to the Yugoslav royal government in exile in London, and even against Stalin. In November 1943, Tito proclaimed a provisional government and renounced all loyalty to the monarchy. Stalin responded to Tito's policy by hailing Mihailovic as the leader of free Yugoslavia, offering Britain a 50 percent share of influence in postwar Yugoslavia, refusing for months to send Tito's partisans arms or ammunition, censoring Radio Free Yugoslavia, and urging Tito to accept the monarchy.

While Yugoslav partisans were still fighting in the hills, a more decisive test of Shachtman's analysis came in Italy in August 1943. The approach of Allied armies to Rome provoked Benito Mussolini's fall from power and anti-fascist uprisings. Shachtman greeted the Italian events with excitement and optimism. Italians were fed up with the war and indifferent to its outcome, he said, and "once that mood sets in . . . the stage is all set for a revolutionary upheaval." After twenty-two years of fascism, during which it had apparently crushed all opposition, it crumbled under the impact of popular anger. "The upheaval in Italy will undoubtedly be written into history as the event that ushered in the second big wave of revolutions in the twentieth century," he said. "Once more, the [proletarian revolution], even though scarred and wounded in many battles, can raise its head proudly and cry out, in the ringing words of our Rosa [Luxemburg] . . . I was, I am, and I shall be!"[52]

But the events in Italy were not a socialist revolution, only "a harbinger." Italian capitalists had acted shrewdly to prevent one. Faced with a choice of a revolution from below or a "revolution-from-above, quiet, orderly, mildly sacrificial," the bourgeoisie grabbed at revolution-from-above in the person of new premier Badoglio. The Italian working class could not "simply pick up, over night, where it left off when Mussolini took power," Shachtman said. Much of the pre-Mussolini revolutionary leadership had been corrupted by Stalinism, the rest decimated by fascism. "The great tragedy of world politics is the tragedy of the revolutionary party . . . its absence at every crucial moment . . . except in the Russian crisis of November, 1917."[53]

"The direct struggle for socialist power is a distance off" in Italy, Shachtman concluded. By the spring of 1944, the leftist groups that had sworn to overthrow Badoglio's government joined it. "When the pressure grew, these fake democrats collapsed like a jack-knife," Shachtman said. Italian Communists were willing to settle for control of the ministry of interior: "police and prisons." The Allies, for their part, were glad to ornament their government of "Mussolini's general, Mussolini's King and a mob of discredited fascist gunmen" with republicans and leftists who could more easily win popular support for the Allied war effort. Marxists had to expose this farce by fighting for democratic rights, such as elections, that Badoglio's government still denied. Only by waging this struggle wisely and well could Marxists "slide over" in the future to the fight for workers' power.[54]

The outcome of the Italian uprising made Shachtman more cautious about the prospects for revolution in Germany. He was as eager to see a German revolution as anyone, but he felt that its prospects would depend on events outside Germany. "*At the given moment, the key to Germany lies . . . in the Nazi-occupied countries of Europe,*" the Workers Party said. Supporting the resistance outside Germany was a "means of stimulating, preparing and supporting the coming revolution in Germany." As time passed, Shachtman doubted whether the German revolution was coming at all, particularly after the failure of a generals' plot to kill Hitler in July 1944. If the United States had offered the German military peace on the terms Woodrow Wilson had offered it in 1918, "the war would long ago have been over, and the Nazi régime with it," he said. But Hitler was too barbaric to ask for an armistice as Germany had in 1918, and Roosevelt was too barbaric to offer one. The standards of capitalist civilization had declined in twenty-five years.[55]

Shachtman concluded that Marxists would probably not be able to lead revolutions in Europe immediately after the war. But he doubted that the Allies would be able to impose Latin American–style puppets. The Workers Party predicted a "'democratic' interval" after Hitler's defeat, a period of "bourgeois democracy with a strong 'social' tinge." Marxists would have more time to organize themselves and fight for socialist democracy, European independence, and unity. Meanwhile Allied governments would be organizing their forces to carve Europe up into spheres of influence.[56]

This prediction contradicted Trotsky's 1934 prophecy that socialist revolutions would arise from the Second World War "much faster, more decisively and relentlessly" than after the First World War. But Shachtman's thinking was compatible with Trotsky's more cautious suggestion in 1940 that Europe would face "long years, if not decades, of war, uprisings, brief interludes of truce, new wars, and new uprisings."[57] Shachtman now foresaw one of the "interludes of truce" Trotsky had talked about.

"Interlude" was a key word. The Workers Party did not expect new capitalist democracies to last longer than the fifteen years the prewar German Weimar Republic lasted. Nor did it see these regimes as anything to support. But Marxists should fight to protect democratic freedoms during this intermission so that they could organize the "crushed and atomized" working class. Under the occupation, most Europeans had little contact with any anti-fascist groups, Workers Party leaders pointed out. Before Europeans could accept anyone's leadership, they had to have a chance to get to know the different groups. This made democratic rights a crucial goal.[58]

The struggle would be all the easier since the armed forces of the resistance would survive after the war. The old owners would demand their factories back, but if the owners had collaborated with fascism, workers would call for nationalization of the factories; if the workers suspected collaboration, they would demand to see the books; and if the workers had suffered under a vicious management, they would demand a say in postwar management. Thus "dual power in the factories will exist from the very first day of the 'national' revolution," the Workers Party said. The experience of power in the factories and in the anti-fascist militia would give people a sense of what real democracy was like. Revolutionaries would have every opportunity to win people to the culminating demand of true democracy—the demand for "the most democratic and representative of institutions, the councils of workers and peasants."[59]

Even when he couched his analysis in this relatively optimistic way, Shachtman had to wage an uphill fight to convince his revolutionary-minded followers that revolution was not around the corner. He had no way of reaching all his followers in Allied uniforms, so he had no chance to warn them that the European revolution might be delayed. As Leo Seidlitz marched into Germany he looked everywhere for signs of the expected German revolution. "I was convinced, the only way the war could end would be revolution. . . . I saw *nothing* like that. . . . And I thought: This could go on forever," he remembered. "I got personally very depressed, I mean *black* depression."[60]

The "Johnsonites" led by C. L. R. James ("Johnson") and Raya Dunayevskaya in Shachtman's own organization rejected his whole analysis. Dunayevskaya and James had brought together a circle of followers when they fought for their "state capitalist" theory of the Soviet Union in 1940–41. They grew more hostile to Shachtman in the next few years. James "held court" at the house of a New York architect who supported him politically and financially. Johnsonites were set off from the rest of the Workers Party by their conviction that working people showed in everyday life their readiness for revolution. This conviction led them to take an interest in comics, jazz, and popular culture. James, Dunayevskaya, and other Johnsonites studied Hegel together. The group had a "cliquish quality," Johnsonite supporter Steve Zeluck said later: "there was one person and he laid down the law." James became convinced that even without big revolutionary parties the revolutionary tide would be irresistible. In October 1943 he predicted that the European revolution would come in "a year" or "a few months."[61]

The Socialist Workers Party said that big revolutionary parties were necessary but could be formed and take power in Europe "in a very short time." "Another long period of bourgeois democracy" was ruled out. By mid-1943, a group critical of Cannon's approach and sympathetic to Shachtman's formed in the Socialist Workers Party, led by Al Goldman and Felix Morrow, a New Yorker about Shachtman's age who had joined the Trotskyists in 1934.[62] Similar debates took place throughout the Fourth International. In fact, thousands of miles from the fighting, Shachtman had arrived at a strategy similar to the one improvised by Europeans such as Belgian Trotskyist Ernest Mandel. His main divergence from most European Trotskyists was his insistence that Marxists were unlikely to be in a position to fight for power immediately after the war.

The last months of the war showed that even Shachtman had been too optimistic about postwar revolutionary prospects in Europe. As Allied armies marched south into France and north into Italy in 1944–45, working-class resistance fighters turned their guns over to the victors and their factories over to the old owners at Communists' and social democrats' urging, far more docilely than Shachtman had imagined.

Kept quiet by their leaders' urgings and by caution in the face of U.S. and

British troops, European workers were also kept in line by gratitude—and hunger. France "must come crawling to Washington for food," Shachtman realized. The United States had "the bludgeons of food and capital for 'reconstruction' in each hand and a stockpile of atomic weapons at its back." The *New International* denounced the "cold-blooded use of the most generous sentiments of the American people, the expenditure of their strength and the blood of their sons, the ballyhoo about liberating Europe for freedom and democracy and now, this."[63]

"The wreckage and prostration of Europe are almost beyond our imagination," Shachtman reported on his return from a visit there. "You see things that turn you weak with horror." He spoke of London's East End dock area, "razed to [the ground], seared, twisted, ghostly," and the French town of Caen in Normandy, consisting of "scattered piles of rubble—stone, brick, timber, grotesque bits of furniture—as if the city had been struck repeatedly by some colossal white hot sledgehammer." The sight of the wreckage reinforced his conviction that capitalism had to be destroyed before it could spawn another war. He saw the atomic bomb as the "symbol of capitalism in its death-throes" and of what capitalism's survival would do to humanity.[64]

But he saw no immediate prospect of socialist revolution, because there was no leadership in place to lead one. He returned more convinced than ever that Marxists had to do more than criticize parliamentary democracy in the name of an ideal democracy of workers' councils, as they had done after the First World War when workers' councils actually existed in many European countries. Instead Marxists had to find more modest goals to rally popular support, goals that would highlight the inadequacy of the new European regimes even by ordinary democratic standards. They had to identify themselves with the democratic aspirations that people were expressing.

Europeans would resist U.S. support for right-wing, undemocratic forces, "because resistance is the condition for life," Shachtman said in September 1945. The Fourth International had to focus on demands such as adoption of democratic constitutions, nationalizations under workers' control, and immediate independence for colonies. For Greece, Italy, Belgium, and Holland, abolishing the monarchy and setting up a democratic republic headed Shachtman's agenda. "For a unified and independent Germany!" and unilateral U.S. withdrawal to bring it about were other key slogans.[65] By rallying people behind these democratic demands, Marxists could gather the forces to create a more thoroughgoing, socialist democracy.

The forces mobilized in Western Europe to resist fascism in fact helped create a relatively democratic and progressive postwar Europe. Thanks to them, Italy became a republic; at least some of the industrialists who had collaborated had their companies nationalized; strong welfare states were established. But the anti-democratic tendencies Shachtman had feared from an Allied victory were also real. They appeared most nakedly in Greece, where Britain and the United States imposed a repressive, right-wing regime by violently suppressing resistance forces, and in the Spanish and Portuguese dictatorships that the United States tolerated and aided. U.S. and British occupation authorities never finished "denazifying" West Germany or Austria, because anti-Communism became a higher priority. Even the most democratic Western European countries largely gave up control of their armies to a U.S.-dominated joint command and control of their economies to U.S. aid administrators. Several of them waged long, atrocity-ridden wars against colonial peoples in Indonesia, Malaya, Vietnam, and Algeria.

Shachtman recognized in the mid-1940s that many workers were supporting social democrats, who were aiding U.S. efforts to control Europe and supporting the colonial wars. Despite their none too democratic actions, social democrats were capitalizing on Europeans' enthusiasm at regaining "their own" democratic institutions. Communists were winning support with democratic and anti-capitalist slogans that were equally hollow. Shachtman said that revolutionary Marxists had to find ways to expose and outflank these inconsistent, even hypocritical, democrats: in the first instance, by pushing them toward action, unity, and the fight for power.

Shachtman's attitude toward Communist parties in Western Europe in 1946 and 1947 was founded on his conviction that the Soviet rulers who gave them their orders were afraid of confrontation with the United States and of uncontrolled social revolution. In Western Europe, therefore, he saw Communists as reformists of a kind, not as "totalitarian parties in the traditional sense." He did not expect them to fight for power. In late 1946, the Workers Party dismissed the idea of a Stalinist Spain, for example, as a "political impossibility."* Shachtman also continued to say—in 1946 as in 1941, over objections from Joe Carter, Hal Draper, and Manny Geltman—that if there was an attempt to restore capitalism by force from within the Soviet Union, Marxists should side with Stalinists against capitalist forces. "The differences that we had I have to this day," Shachtman said.[67]

He was so confident that Stalinist regimes were not a threat in Western Europe that he was willing to try to push Communists into government. In January 1946, the Workers Party called for a government in France that

---

*Herman Benson and Jack Widick tried to get the party to say in so many words that Communists outside the USSR did not "represent any new class in society" and could never come to power without direct Soviet backing.[66] Though not formally endorsed, Benson's and Widick's assumptions were reflected in 1946–47 Workers Party decisions.

would unite the Socialist Party, Communist Party, and Communist-led trade unions. In this call the party subordinated its anti-Stalinism to the need it saw to have the French working class stop playing the game of "national unity" that was keeping capitalism going in France. Shachtman believed that it was crucial to encourage radicalizing workers, even under social democratic and Communist leaders, to break with Charles de Gaulle, the Christian Democrats, and the U.S. power behind them.[68]

In May 1947, when the Communist Party was thrown out of the French coalition government, Shachtman commented that the move clearly showed the U.S. government's hand. "Our slogan of CP-SP government is confirmed all over in my opinion," he said. Even as Communists sent their supporters out on strike and into the streets against the French government, he remained calm. The Communists were only trying to get back into the coalition by showing that they could "guarantee disorder" as well as "guarantee order," he said. Since Communists would not actually win power, the constant disorder they were creating would only lose them support. As late as December 1947, *Labor Action* urged support for Communist-led strikes in order to push aside Communist leadership and pose a real challenge to the French regime.[69]

Shachtman had no confidence in Socialist or Communist leaders. Although nobody could stop them from creating a socialist France if they mobilized their supporters, he said, they would mobilize no one without a "tidal wave of working class pressure." The Workers Party said that a call for a Socialist-Communist government had to be combined with demands for nationalization of basic industry, a democratic constitution, replacement of Allied occupation forces with a popular militia, and independence for French colonies. It also warned against the Communists' threat to democratic freedoms. It opposed raising the Communists to power or any share of it if there was "a clear threat of its use of the state police power for the extermination of the independent working-class and revolutionary movements." But it saw no such threat. The only possible means of seizing power—"soviets, factory committees, workers' militias—would constitute a mortal danger not only to the Stalinist party but to the Russian empire."[70]

Although Shachtman downplayed the danger of Stalinism in Western Europe after the Second World War, he was very much alive to the danger in Eastern Europe. As U.S. and British troops moved eastward into Germany and northward into Italy and Greece in 1944–45, the Soviet army moved westward. Stalin had kept a firm grip on power through the defeats of 1941 and 1942; he consolidated his power through victory. By the summer of 1944, the Soviet army defeated the Germans at Minsk in Belorussia, reached the prewar frontiers of Poland, and moved southward into the Balkans. Shachtman and almost everyone else had underestimated the

Soviet Union's military staying power. "The world-wide total casualties of the United States since it entered the war hardly compare with what Russia loses in a few weeks," he said.[71] In the last months of the war, Stalin's regime began to collect the dividends on Soviet peoples' sacrifices. It imposed Soviet domination on Eastern Europe.

The events in Eastern Europe posed a challenge to existing theories of Stalinism. Before the war, Shachtman and other Trotskyists had seen Stalinism as a distortion arising from the overthrow of capitalism in one isolated, backward country. They had upheld Trotsky's theory that Stalinism could only oppose and undermine revolutions, not lead them. They interpreted the theory to mean that Stalin's regime could not continue to rule a noncapitalist Soviet Union for much longer, much less overthrow capitalism anywhere else. The theory was the basis for the foundation of the Fourth International, the force that would have to overthrow capitalism on an international scale because of the default of social democrats and Stalinists.

The first crack in this theory came with the Soviet occupation in 1939–40 of eastern Poland, the Baltic states, and eastern Finland. Trotskyists saw that Stalinism was capable after all of eliminating capitalism outside the Soviet Union. They propped up the theory of Stalinism's counterrevolutionary nature by saying that Stalinism's international policy as a whole in 1939–40 was as counterrevolutionary as ever, because the international working class lost more through the strengthening of fascism than it gained through the loss to capitalism of a small part of Eastern Europe. Shachtman was distinguished by his insistence that even the destruction of capitalism in newly acquired Soviet territories was no advance for socialism. Overturning capitalism by bureaucratic fiat to consolidate bureaucratic power, he said, did nothing to help working people win power for themselves and create a system that would serve their interests. Therefore it did nothing for socialism.

Shachtman was as well equipped as any other theorist to understand Soviet expansion in Eastern Europe. But to consolidate his mature understanding of Stalinist expansion, Shachtman had to abandon the notion that the Soviet bureaucracy was merely an untrustworthy guardian of collectivist property. He had toyed in 1939 with the idea that the Soviet rulers had not wanted to nationalize industry in eastern Poland. As late as May 1943, he suggested that far from shrinking the capitalist-dominated area of Europe, the Soviet alliance with the United States and Britain could lead to a restoration of capitalism in the USSR. But by July 1943 he laid that suggestion to rest. Far from undermining collectivist property, the Soviet bureaucracy "draws its sustenance and power from it," he said.[72]

He inched closer to the position Joe Carter had argued against him in 1940–41: that there was nothing worth defending in the Soviet Union, including the nationalized industry. *"Every trace of the great revolutionary promise of 1917 has literally been wiped out,"* Shachtman said. "If the rule of Stalin continues, it will make no difference to the masses whether Russia is victorious in the war or is defeated." He renounced the idea he had put forward in 1941 of defending the Soviet state if its British and U.S. allies were defeated and it faced Nazi Germany alone.[73]

Shachtman's analysis enabled him in late 1943 to make an accurate prediction about the future of Eastern Europe and to account for the policies of most of the world's Communist parties, across national variations and sudden shifts of line. He predicted that Communists would not take power by leading revolutions; they would take power where Soviet troops could give it to them and the Soviet bureaucracy could control them. He foresaw that Communist parties in Eastern Europe would become instruments for the imposition of Stalinist societies there, while Western European Communists would help capitalism survive.

As early as March 1942, Shachtman said that Soviet victory in the war would spread a *"new slavery"* westward into Europe, to the limits of Stalin's 1939–40 annexations and beyond. In February 1943, immediately after the Soviet victory at Stalingrad, the Workers Party predicted that after the war the USSR would try to make Eastern Europe its "imperialist stamping ground."[74] The party warned that wherever Communists took power they would kill the real Marxists and destroy independent working-class organizations, as they had in the USSR and Catalonia. But it did not try to predict what kind of societies Communists might install in Eastern Europe. It did not rule out Stalinism's evolution into some kind of capitalist dictatorship.

In October and November 1943, Shachtman amplified: "Stalin aims to place all of the countries east of Germany under the domination of the Kremlin." For the first time he predicted that capitalist property would be expropriated in Poland, Finland, Bulgaria, Romania, much if not all of Yugoslavia, and northwestern China. (He suggested that Stalin might settle for "vassal states" instead in some places, depending on deals that the USSR might make with the United States and Britain.) Shachtman predicted that the Soviet Union would loot Germany, especially the sophisticated German machine-tool industry, to make up for Soviet wartime losses.[75]

These predictions might be explained as a simple extrapolation from the position of armies in Europe—though they contradicted not only the repeated declarations of the world's Communist parties but also the contemporary wisdom of Western observers, all of whom knew the military position. In any event, no one duplicated the sweeping generalization Shachtman made, going beyond the specifics of Eastern Europe:

> Where the Stalinist bureaucracy does not dominate the working class and the labor movement, be it by persuasion or by violence; and where an

attempt to overturn capitalism . . . would promptly bring reprisals against Russia by strong capitalist powers in a position to execute them; and especially where geographical remoteness makes the physical control of the country by Moscow extremely difficult—in such countries the Russian bureaucracy works to prop up capitalist rule, [above all] if a genuinely socialist revolution threatens. [Otherwise] the bureaucracy tolerates neither the rule nor the existence of the capitalist class, democrats and fascists included. Such countries . . . it seeks to annex and subjugate.[76]

Shachtman's theory made possible two different lines of attack on Communist policy: that Communists were obstructing social revolution in the West, and carrying out social revolution—the wrong revolution—in the East. For Marxists in the United States, Britain, and France, it legitimized an aggressive revolutionary policy by showing why the danger of creating new Stalinisms there was minimal. For Marxists in countries close to Soviet borders and Soviet troops, it legitimized all-out resistance to Communist rule by showing that to the extent Communists were overthrowing capitalism, they were replacing it with an equally unjust order.

In December 1944, with the Soviet army approaching Warsaw, Warsaw tried to free itself by revolting against the Germans. The Soviet army stayed put on the other side of the Vistula and allowed the Germans to suppress the uprising. Stalin thus threw "his main enemy, the organized Warsaw proletariat . . . into the jaws of the German army," Shachtman said, and ensured that "no vote, free or unfree, will alter the fate of Poland." In March 1945 he pointed out that the Soviet Union had taken Germany's place as the dominant European power. Soon Eastern European peoples were living under Soviet occupation. They had been "disenfranchised in the interests of Stalinist slavery," the Workers Party said. "The revolutionist loses title to his name who does not protest and fight against this enslavement."[77]

By 1946 Shachtman saw the destruction of capitalism that he had predicted in Eastern Europe already in progress. The Workers Party did not oppose the nationalizations in Eastern Europe; it called for "the preservation of nationalized economy under democratic control." But Shachtman expected the Soviet Union to install a collectivized economy in Eastern Europe without giving any aid to the working class or socialism, just as it had in 1939–40. He called for resistance to this collectivism from above in the name of collectivism from below. The Polish working class was the "only worthy and reliable banner-bearer" of resistance to Stalinism in Poland, he said. The nominal leaders of independent Poland who had spent the war in London were "a gang of landowners, feudal barons, capitalists and militaristic thugs."[78]

Shachtman hoped that Eastern European opposition to Soviet conquest would grow into full-scale, successful revolution. Hitler had broken his neck in a struggle with national liberation movements; why not Stalin? "What Stalin looks upon as a garland of oak-leaves around his Caesarian brow," said Shachtman, making the wish father to the thought, "will prove to be a noose around his criminal's throat."[79]

Soviet expansion finally settled for Shachtman the issue of defending the Soviet Union in war, even with the whole capitalist world arrayed against it. Foreseeing a war in which the Soviet Union would fight alone against the United States, both to resist U.S. expansion and to safeguard Soviet expansion, he decided that he could defend neither one against the other. He ruled out defending the USSR in any international war he could foresee. In April 1946, the Workers Party said flatly, "We are against the defense of the Stalinist state"—though it would not "lay claim to a position which applies forever and under all conceivable circumstances." Seeing the "'peace-loving' nations . . . sharpening their claws to get at each other's throats," Shachtman decided that fighting for peace meant opposing them all.[80]

In the first months after Pearl Harbor, any sign of an Asian third camp was overwhelmed by the rapid Japanese advance and U.S. attempts to stop it. In order to make a third camp's emergence possible, Shachtman was convinced that Marxists had to safeguard their independence from the U.S. government. No movement of resistance against Japan that took orders from the United States or Britain could be considered a genuine national liberation movement, he said. Middle-class Asian nationalists would side with U.S. or British or Japanese armies a hundred times before they would resort to the desperate expedient of supporting a peasant or popular army, which would pose a threat to their own interests. Only where Allied forces were absent and an independent leadership present was a real liberation movement against Japan possible.

Shachtman applied this logic in his analyses of popular movements in China, India, Vietnam, and Indonesia. By 1945 he saw that the war had shaken European colonial empires to their foundations. Asians would never accept European domination tamely again. He used the spread of revolution in Asia to extend the theory of national liberation that he had developed for Europe. He saw Asian liberation movements as challenges to U.S. world power, which he believed was the main force behind the dying empires.

He saw forces such as the Chinese Guomindang, by contrast, as accomplices of European and U.S. power in Asia. Trotskyists had supported Chiang Kai-shek's army since 1937 in its defensive war against the Japanese, and the Workers Party had continued supporting China in 1940–41. But Shachtman was mindful of the statement by the Fourth International congress in 1938 that Trotskyists would *not* support U.S. or British intervention on China's side. The congress had warned that Japan's defeat by the

United States and Britain, as opposed to an indigenous Chinese force, would mean the "enslavement of China by Anglo-American capital." Like most Chinese Trotskyists, the Workers Party ended its support for Chiang's war as soon as the United States declared war on Japan in December 1941.[81]

After Pearl Harbor, Chinese airfields were directly controlled by the United States. Chinese troops were shanghaied into the British battle for control of Burma. "The American General Stilwell, as head of the Chinese general staff, symbolizes the decisive subordination of China's struggle to the interests and exigencies of the imperialist war between Washington and Tokyo," Shachtman said. Chiang's subservience to the United States and his retreat or passivity in the face of Japanese attacks were of a piece. In the context of U.S.-Japanese war, Shachtman said, "*a genuine struggle for national independence demands such an arousing and mobilizing of the masses*" that Chiang's government would itself be threatened. Shachtman advised Chinese people who wanted to throw out foreign occupiers to "remove the main obstacle in the road of that fight, Chiang."[82]

There was one Chinese leader who followed Shachtman's advice, though Shachtman never acknowledged the fact. Mao Zedong, though he paid lip service to Stalin's calls for unity against Japan and nominally accepted Chiang's authority during the war, preserved an independent Communist base in Yenan and an independent Communist army. He disobeyed orders from both Chiang and Stalin to commit his army to full-scale battles against the Japanese, where it would have been destroyed. Instead it fought a war of position with the Japanese that made possible the consolidation and expansion of its revolutionary base. The Chinese Communist army even clashed with Chiang's U.S.- and Soviet-backed forces. Soon after the war ended, Mao's army put an end to Chiang's rule and U.S. power in China.

The tactics Shachtman urged on Indian Marxists were more complicated, because the popular movement against British rule that flared up sporadically during the war, particularly during the time of greatest Japanese threat in 1942, accepted the leadership of the Indian Congress Party. The Congress controlled the movement with considerable skill. It flirted with the Japanese in order to improve its bargaining position with the British. It used the popular movement as a bargaining chip with its colonial masters. It rushed to claim leadership of the movement, which it had done little to organize, in order to make sure that the protests did not become too radical. But what no major Congress leader did, Shachtman said, was make "the categorical demand: Withdraw the military forces and military rule of Britain."[83]

He would have supported any movement that did fight for British withdrawal, particularly if Mohandas Gandhi had fought the British "with a little money and some rifles" from Japan. But instead, just as Shachtman would have expected, the arrest of the Congress leaders saved them from responsibility for "the millions who promptly responded to the mealy-mouthed and half-hearted Congress call for 'non-cooperation.'"[84]

While Indian leaders were trying to avoid head-on confrontation with Britain and hoping to make a deal that would free their country, Allied troops in North Africa were showing the real Allied attitude toward colonialism. Backed by a U.S. and British invading force, French troops in Morocco suppressed a revolt in the mountainous Rif. The revolt bolstered Shachtman's case against the U.S. "war for freedom." "Just who is it that is to be freed in Morocco, Algiers and Tunisia?" he asked. "The Moroccans, the Algerians, the Tunisians? Not on your life!"[85] Far from giving independence to North Africa, Allied victory would make necessary another decade of colonial warfare in the 1950s and early 1960s before the French would be expelled.

As the Second World War neared its end, Shachtman looked with growing interest toward Indonesia, where nationalists had been granted independence by the defeated Japanese in 1945 and were unwilling to return to Dutch rule, and Vietnam, where the Vietminh had fought the Japanese and were ready to fight the returning French. Both countries had long histories of resistance to colonialism. Indonesian Communists had led an uprising against the Dutch in 1926. Vietnamese Communists had led their first uprising against the French in 1930–31. After the uprisings, the two countries' histories had diverged: Nationalists under Sukarno had replaced Communists as the main anti-Dutch force in Indonesia, while Communists and Trotskyists had kept the leadership of the Vietnamese movement. Sukarno had cooperated with the Japanese throughout the war, even helping to recruit "voluntary" Indonesian labor for Japanese military projects; Ho Chi Minh and his followers had formed the Vietminh to fight the Japanese in 1941.

In 1945, the two histories seemed to converge again. Sukarno joined with the anti-Japanese underground and the rebelling Japanese-armed guerrillas to proclaim the Republic of Indonesia. General strikes in Hanoi, Hue, and Saigon led to the creation of the Democratic Republic of Vietnam under a Communist-nationalist government, despite Stalin's refusal for several years to recognize it. Communists in both countries tried to arrive at a negotiated settlement with their former colonial masters. The Allies used peace talks to gain time as Chinese and British troops occupied Vietnam and British and Australian troops occupied Indonesia. Soon these surrogates had played out their roles and turned the territories they had occupied over to the Dutch and the French, who began military offensives against the new republics.

Shachtman was enthusiastic about the Indonesian and Vietnamese revolutions. He called them "the first struggles of the Third Camp to emerge during the war free from compromising entanglements in one or the other imperialist camp." Now the United States had become their main enemy. "It is with planes built in Los Angeles and tanks built in Detroit that the Anglo-Dutch reconquer Java and the Anglo-French reconquer Indo-China," he said. "The 'arsenal of democracy' emerges in its real role—the arsenal of world reaction." Even though the Vietminh killed Vietnamese Trotskyists when they briefly held Saigon in 1945, the Workers Party picketed French consulates in January 1947 to show solidarity with Vietnam's "heroic struggle."[86]

Shachtman saw that the new U.S. empire would try to keep Asians from attaining true independence, just as the old European empires had. Even if the United States cut its support for Dutch and French colonialism and the old colonial systems crumbled, Asia was threatened with a new kind of subjugation. He foresaw that formal independence for Asia might mean only the kind of sham independence that Latin American countries had, with governments manipulated from Washington instead of appointed from Amsterdam or Paris. "The United States counts on its stupendous economic power to take all these countries in tow," he warned.[87]

Shachtman emphasized the need for Marxists to become part of Asian liberation movements before they could think about leading them, an attitude that the early Communist International had also taken. Lenin had supported Turkish nationalists under Kemal Atatürk who were fighting against an alliance of Britain, France, Italy, and Greece that wanted to carve up their country, even though Turkish nationalists persecuted and killed Communists. Communist leader Karl Radek had told Turkish Communists, "Protest against the persecution, but understand . . . you still have a long road to travel in the company of the bourgeois revolutionaries."[88] In the same spirit, Shachtman supported the existing leaderships of the Indonesian and Vietnamese revolutions, despite the repression these leaderships used against democratic socialists.

Indonesian nationalists led by Sukarno persisted in relying on U.S. pressure to reach a settlement with the Dutch, despite U.S. aid to Dutch forces that were occupying more and more of the country, setting up puppet regional governments, and unleashing terror against civilians. Sukarno's prime minister, Sjahrir, said that it was crucial not to "earn the enmity of capitalism." The Indonesian government conciliated capitalist opinion in March 1946 by suppressing independent communists led by Tan Malaka, who were demanding confiscation of Dutch property and complete Dutch withdrawal before negotiations, and in January 1948 by dropping Moscow-line Communists from the government. But the Workers Party justified Indonesians' "seeking to play off American imperialism against its rivals."[89]

Shachtman was similarly generous in evaluating the Vietnamese independence movement. He knew that Vietminh leader Ho Chi Minh was a Communist. But he would not say that Ho's prominence meant "Stalinist leadership of the movement." Shachtman and his followers remained sympathetic to the Vietminh even as Communists consolidated their hold over it, with the murder of Trotskyist leaders in the south in 1945 and the departure of middle-class nationalists from the rebel government soon afterwards. In March 1947, *Labor Action* said that in the absence of Soviet troops, Ho "can maintain his leadership only as long as he represents, in some way at least, the strivings of the people for independence."[90]

The allowances Shachtman made for Asian nationalists in the mid-1940s did not imply abandonment of socialist revolution as his goal for Asia. Experience with the Chinese Guomindang had shown that the strategy of supporting revolutionary nationalists could be disastrous unless communists kept to an independent policy and were prepared to organize on their own to defend revolutionary gains and their own lives. Shachtman kept the Chinese experience in mind. He was convinced that the vast majority of people in Asia, who then as now were living in rural poverty, could be freed to live better lives only by socialism.

> Only the socialist road can liberate the peasant from the centuries-old curse of what Marx harshly called "rural idiocy." It liberates him by completely abolishing his status as peasant. . . . It converts him into a free producer on the land, which has been reorganized on a modern, mechanized, large-scale, cooperative basis. This is possible only when large-scale industry has developed to the point where it not only dominates overwhelmingly the entire country, but where the productivity of labor is higher than it has ever been in any capitalist country and is therefore in a position to produce the comforts as well as the needs of life in abundance, for all to enjoy. This, in turn, is conceivable only after the victory of the proletariat in several advanced capitalist countries.[91]

Asian liberation movements were therefore bound up in Shachtman's mind with socialist movements in Western Europe and North America. In the mid-1940s, when he still believed that socialist breakthroughs were possible in Europe, he saw revolutions in Asia as jolts that could start events in Europe moving. Colonial independence was an invariable item of the democratic program that he counted on to raise socialists to power in Europe. He saw revolution in Europe, in turn, as the Asian revolutions' best hope for victory.

The emergence of a transformed postwar world prompted Shachtman to take another look at issues of socialist organization, particularly at his own Workers Party. Instead of seeing his group as the party destined to lead the revolution, he began in 1945–46 to take a longer view. With no socialist revolution on the U.S. horizon, he saw the need for a long process in which a real revolutionary party would be built by stages.

The party that Shachtman saw as the outcome of this process would be more diverse than any existing group on the left; it would be an "all-inclusive revolutionary party." Shachtman wrestled with this heterogeneous party's need for a hard inner core, a "cadre," that could make it strong and effective in action as well as pluralist in composition. His model was, if not a departure from the Bolshevik tradition, a development of it, even an innovation within it.

"Is the Workers Party really a party? . . . The answer . . . is an emphatic 'No!'" Shachtman said in 1945. "In calling ourselves the Workers *Party*, we did no more than proclaim *our intention to become a party*."[92] A party has to be able to mobilize thousands of people for action when it needs to, he explained. The Workers Party had nowhere near enough members or influence yet to act as the leader of thousands. If it tried, it would either attempt initiatives beyond its strength, which no one would follow, or end up discarding its revolutionary ideas in order to give itself the illusion of leading thousands.

New mass parties arise very rarely, and never in the space of a single decade, Shachtman pointed out. "In *our* time mass parties generally speaking came out of mass parties." No new mass parties had been built from scratch in the advanced capitalist countries since before the First World War. The Communist parties became mass parties only through splits within big social democratic parties. In the United States, the mass Socialist Party that was emerging before the First World War was derailed by wartime and postwar repression and splits.

"We are handicapped primarily by the fact that we do not operate within a *politically-organized working class*. That is point A, B, C, and all the other letters down to Z," Shachtman said. Building an independent labor party and building a revolutionary party were closely intertwined projects. A mass revolutionary party would come only "at the end of a road of fusions and splits and regroupments into a big movement."[93] Shachtman still hoped that his followers would play a decisive role in the bigger movement. But his newfound modesty about his group contrasted strikingly with the Socialist Workers Party, which proclaimed in 1946: "The revolutionary vanguard party . . . already exists, and its name is the SOCIALIST WORKERS PARTY."[94]

The Workers Party instead began to see itself not as *the* party but as one effort to help build a broader party. Shachtman began referring to his goal as the "all-inclusive revolutionary party." This heretical-sounding phrase borrowed the term "all-inclusive" from Norman Thomas's Socialist Party of the mid-1930s, a party whose "all-inclusiveness" had been part and parcel of its reformist shapelessness. But Shachtman made the paradox seem workable. He wanted an all-inclusive party in the "revolutionary Marxist sense," not in Thomas's sense, he said: a multitendency party all of whose tendencies would be revolutionary and Marxist. Looking back, he saw the Bolshevik Party of 1917 as just this kind of party.[95]

In the process of building a broad revolutionary party, the Workers Party had to go through the stages of "propaganda group"—a group gathering an initial core of members around its complete program—and "agitational group"—a group translating its ideas into short-term slogans for existing movements. The Workers Party had moved beyond being a mere propaganda group during the war, Shachtman said, because it came out of the Socialist Workers Party already "trained and educated," foresaw that workers would be open to radical action and ideas during the war, and followed up its analysis with hard work.

It was held back from consolidating itself as an activist group for two reasons: first, the existence of the Socialist Workers Party. To "even the average *radical* worker the two parties look and sound and feel pretty much alike, at least at first blush," Shachtman admitted. The Workers Party was forced into endless explanations to justify its existence, which got in the way of a more activist approach. Shachtman continued to advocate reunification of the two groups as the solution to this problem. Second, the Workers Party had not integrated its newer recruits. Instead of spending enormous amounts of time " 'straightening out the last hair' in our position," older members needed to train recruits in basic Marxism. Shachtman complained about "smarter" old-timers who continually dropped remarks like, "You know, of course, about the laws which drove to the dissolution of the slave economy in the days of the Roman Empire."[96]

The result of the thorough training of the best recruits and the retraining and recommitment of older members would be the creation of a strong, unified "cadre" for the Workers Party. In its usual meaning, the group's "cadre" was just its most experienced and active members who worked hardest to build it. Shachtman called the group's cadre its "spinal column."

> The cadre is not a faction and certainly not a clique. . . . Being part of the cadre does not bring anyone immunity from failure to discharge party responsibilities, or special rewards for discharging them. . . . It does mean being part and parcel of the leadership of the party. . . . The local leadership does not allow any center to say, "Leading the party is exclusively our business." The center, in turn, allows no local leader to speak and act as if to say, "Leading the party is not my responsibility, let 'them' take that load."[97]

Shachtman argued that *not* every experienced and active member necessarily qualified as cadre. His definition limited the cadre to those who, without trying "to deprive critics and opponents . . . of their right to criticize and oppose," understood and basically agreed with the group's program. The cadre was "the propagandist and defender of the party program within the ranks of the party itself." Shachtman said that his narrow conception was unavoidable precisely because the Workers Party was so broad. "It is precisely the *inclusive* revolutionary party that cannot have an *inclusive* cadre," he said. C. L. R. James, for example, had moved closer to Cannon's politics on one issue after another since the war, until he disagreed with most of Shachtman's followers more often than he agreed with them. Shachtman insisted that there was still a place for James in the Workers Party. But if James chose to spend more time arguing about the group's program than putting it into practice, then he was not part of its cadre.[98]

Shachtman worried that some of his older followers showed signs of "losing their nerve" due to the strain they had been under during the war, which was "trivial compared with what we must yet endure in the future." "They are not standing up as well as they should under our enforced isolation," he said, "an isolation to which we are condemned for the next period even if we had twice and four times our membership and a tenfold improvement in our activity." Too many of these older members were neglecting their responsibilities. Too many were searching "for some magic formula that will save us all."[99]

In an essay on Trotsky's unfinished biography of Stalin, Shachtman implicitly suggested that a would-be revolutionary cadre could even learn some things from Stalin. There were admirable things about Stalin, Shachtman said, qualities than won him respect in the Bolsheviks' hardest years from 1907 to 1912. "Stalin was one of the not-too-many who did not flinch and did not quit," who "continued without perturbation to risk his life and freedom." He "discharged well the task of tasks—imbuing others with tenacity, with contempt for the deserters." "*With all things properly arranged,*" Shachtman concluded, "the Zinovievs and Stalins and all other first-class second-raters also find their place in the leadership and enrich its capacities." The Workers Party was suffering from a shortage of selfless secondary leaders. In this respect, Cannon's organization seemed to have an edge over Shachtman's.[100]

Shachtman's modesty about his organization had its limits. Even if the Workers Party was not *the* revolutionary party, it did represent a "clear-cut political tendency in the working class . . . recognized and known as such in *all* informed political circles," he said. It was a "centralized Marxist organization in which the widest and freest discussion is not only 'tolerated' but encouraged." He still said that it was "the truest link with the great past of Marxism."[101]

Notes

1. Shachtman, "Weekly international review," DW v 3 n 256 (11 Nov. 1926), 3; Shachtman, "The U.S. and the war," WP educational bul n 2 (20 Dec. 1940), ISM v 21, 497–99; WP PC, "Political resolution" (5 Sept. 1941), ISM v 15, 145–46.
2. Shachtman, "Balance sheet of the war," NI v 11 n 6 (Sept. 1945), 164–65.
3. Milton Fisk, *Socialism from Below in the United States*, 16; WP PC (1 Nov. 1940), MSC b 9 f 28 (r 3360); Shachtman, "National report to New York City party convention" (Nov. or Dec. 1940), MSC b 9 f 32 (r 3360); "Membership figures November 23, 1946 and October 1, 1947," MSC b 11 f 11 (r 3363).
4. LA v 6 n 48 (30 Nov. 1942); interview with Glotzer by Bloom (13–21 Dec. 1983), OHAL, 35; interview with Zeluck by Buhle (15 Dec. 1982), OHAL, s 1.
5. Weir, "Requiem for Max Shachtman," *Radical America* v 7 n 1 (1973), 71.
6. Shachtman, "Two years of the Workers Party," LA v 6 n 18 (4 May 1942), 3; "For the third camp!" NI v 6 n 3 (Apr. 1940), 68.
7. "The editor's comment," NI v 7 n 7 (Aug. 1941), 164; Shachtman, "The future of the war," NI v 8 n 2 (Mar. 1942), 35.
8. Jacobson, "The two deaths of Max Shachtman," *New Politics* v 10 n 2 (Winter 1973), 98.
9. Shachtman, "Five years of the Workers Party," NI v 11 n 3 (Apr. 1945), 80.
10. Interview with Geltman (22 Mar. 1989), s 3–4; LA v 7 n 25 (21 June 1943), 4.
11. Interview with Glotzer (28 Mar. 1989), s 6.
12. "The legacy of the Workers Party" (6–7 May 1983), ed. Paul Buhle, OHAL, 12; "Five years," NI v 11 n 3, 80.
13. Shachtman, "The death of com. Klara Zetkin," M v 6 n 36 (22 July 1933), 3.
14. WP NC, "The coming crisis in the U.S.," NI v 9 n 11 (Dec. 1943), 328 (also "Resolution on the political situation," WP bul [Nov. 1943], ISM v 3); Shachtman, "The role of the U.S. in Europe," NI v 10 n 7 (July 1944), 198; Shachtman, "Six years of the Workers Party," LA v 10 n 13 (1 Apr. 1946), 1-M.
15. WP PC, "Political resolution" (5 Sept. 1941), ISM v 15, 147–50.
16. Shachtman, "Labor and strikes in wartime," NI v 7 n 3 (Apr. 1941), 39.
17. Shachtman, *The Fight for Socialism*, 98, 94.
18. Shachtman, "Five years of the Workers Party," NI v 11 n 3 (Apr. 1945), 77; "Labor and strikes," NI v 7 n 3, 39.
19. SWP opposition, "Resolution on organization" (Apr. 1940), NI v 12 n 3 (Mar. 1946), 93; "Founding principles of the Workers Party," NI v 12 n 4 (Apr. 1946), 125 (also WP bul n 1 [26 Apr. 1940], ISM v 2); "Program of action" (10, 11 Aug. 1940), WP bul n 3 (29 Aug. 1940), ISM v 2, 5; WP PC, "Supplementary resolution to the political resolution" (9 Sept. 1941), WP bul n 11 (Sept. 1941), ISM v 3, 182; Jacobson to Drucker (10 Sept. 1992), 3.
20. Interview with Seidlitz (16 Jan. 1989), s 3.
21. LA v 5 n 24 (16 June 1941), 1.
22. WP NC, "Trade union resolution" (May 1946), MSC b 12 f 2 (r 3365).
23. Interview with Haskell (15 July 1983), in Maurice Isserman, *If I Had a Hammer*, 46, 227; WP bul n 8 (April 1941), ISM v 2, 81; Martin Glaberman, *Wartime Strikes*, 79; WP NC, "Draft on the tasks of the party," WP bul (Nov. 1943), ISM v 3, 402A.

24. "Program of action" (26 Apr. 1940), ISM v 2, A8; WP bul n 8 (Apr. 1941), ISM v 2, 81; Glaberman, *Wartime Strikes*, 79–80; interview with Benson (6 Apr. 1989), s 2.

25. "Program of action," WP bul n 1 (26 Apr. 1940), ISM v 2, A9; WP PC, "Resolution on the Negro question" (30 Sept. 1941), ISM v 15, 133; Feeley, "Fighter for the unemployed," *Socialist Action* (Feb. 1984), 10; interview with Benson (6 Apr. 1989), s 2.

26. Interview with Seidlitz (16 Jan. 1989), s 3.

27. Shachtman, *For a Cost-Plus Wage*, 6 (originally in LA v 7 n 33 and 34 [16, 23 Aug. 1943]); "Big business lies about its profits," LA v 7 n 46 (15 Nov. 1943), 1.

28. Shachtman, "The auto workers' convention," NI v 9 n 9 (Oct. 1943), 263, 260–61, 265; Shachtman, "The progressives at the UAW convention," LA v 7 n 43 (25 Oct. 1943), 1, 4.

29. Art Preis, *Labor's Giant Step*, 232–34; Glaberman, *Wartime Strikes*, 108, 111; Nelson Lichtenstein, *Labor's War at Home*, 195–96; Irving Howe and B. J. Widick, *The UAW and Walter Reuther*, 123; Shachtman, "Referendum on no-strike pledge!" LA v 5 n 39 (25 Sept. 1944), 3.

30. Glaberman, *Wartime Strikes*, 111–12; Shachtman, "Politics among the auto workers," NI v 10 n 10 (Oct. 1944), 310–11.

31. Glaberman, *Wartime Strikes*, 114–16; Lichtenstein, *Labor's War*, 196; Preis, *Labor's Giant Step*, 236; "Irregular balloting in UAW no-strike voting," LA v 9 n 10 (5 Mar. 1945), 1.

32. Cannon, "The Stalinists and the united front," SA v 4 n 42 (27–29 Sept. 1940), 2; SWP PC (17 Oct. 1939), MSC b 8 f 10 (r 3358); "Political resolution," ISM v 15, 150; WP 2nd convention, "The Russian question" (19 Sept. 1941), NI v 7 n 9 (Oct. 1941), 237 (also WP Basic Documents n 1 [1946], ISM v 17); Shachtman, "Shachtman sees workers victory," LA v 4 n 16 (29 July 1940), 2.

33. Shachtman, "Who is behind the conspiracy to suppress Labor Action," LA v 6 n 43, 1, 3; interview with Benson (6 Apr. 1989), s 3, "A national service act," NI v 11 n 1 (Jan. 1945), 5–6.

34. "Five years of the Workers Party," NI v 11 n 3, 79, 77.

35. WP PC, "Political resolution" (5 Sept. 1941), ISM v 15, 152.

36. Fisk, *Socialism from Below*, 16; LA v 5 n 46 (17 Nov. 1941); WP PC (8, 26 Oct. 1940), MSC b 9 f 28 (r 3360).

37. WP NC, "The fight for a labor party," NI v 9 n 11 (Dec. 1943), 329–30 (also "Resolution on the political situation," WP bul [Nov. 1943], ISM v 3); WP NC, "The coming crisis in the U.S.," NI v 9 n 11, 327 (also "Resolution on the political situation," WP bul [Nov. 1943], ISM v 3).

38. Shachtman, *The Fight for Socialism*, 133; WP 3rd convention, "The struggle for an independent labor party" (Jan. 1944), ISM v 17, 693.

39. Shachtman, "Tasks of the party" (15 Oct. 1943), MSC b 10 f 1 (r 3361); WP NC, "The ten-point plan of the Workers Party for the reconversion and post-war period," Information bul (Dec. 1944), ISM v 16, 297; Shachtman, *The Fight for Socialism*, 117, 116.

40. "The fight for a labor party," NI v 9 n 11, 331; "The coming crisis in the U.S.," NI v 9 n 11, 327; WP NC, "American capitalism in the war," NI v 9 n 11, 326 (also "Resolution on the political situation," WP bul [Nov. 1943], ISM v 3).

41. Shachtman, "Should labor have supported Dean Alfange?" LA v 6 n 45 (9 Nov. 1942), 3.

42. "The P.A.C., the elections and the future," NI v 10 n 10 (Oct. 1944), 309; "The PAC and the elections," NI v 10 n 11 (Nov. 1944), 356–57.

43. "Ups and downs of the labor party movement," NI v 10 n 4 (Apr. 1944), 100–101; "The ALP fight," NI v 10 n 2 (Feb. 1944), 38–40.

44. WP Campaign Committee, *How to Get Jobs for All*; Shachtman, *The Fight for Socialism*, 106.

45. WP NC, "The national question in Europe," NI v 9 n 2 (Feb. 1943), 38–39; WP NC, "The national and colonial struggles," NI v 9 n 1 (Jan. 1943), 9; Shachtman, "Notes for national question discussion" (1943), MSC b 10 f 10 (r 3362).

46. Lenin, "The Junius pamphlet" (October 1916), *Collected Works* v 22, 310–11; Lenin, "The socialist revolution and the right of nations to self-determination" (October 1916), *Collected Works* v 22, 145; Lenin, "The discussion on self-determination summed up" (October 1916), *Collected Works* v 22, 355–56.

47. Shachtman, "Nine lessons of North African invasion," LA v 6 n 48 (30 Nov. 1942), 3.

48. "Balance sheet of the war," NI v 11 n 6 (Sept. 1945), 164.

49. "The national question in Europe," NI v 9 n 2, 39–40; "The national question in Europe," NI v 9 n 2, 38–39.

50. "Notes for national question discussion," MSC b 10 f 10 (r 3362); "The national question in Europe," NI v 9 n 2, 38–39; "Discussion guide on the national and colonial question" (1943), ISM v 21, 549 (also MSC b 10 f 11 [r 3362]).

51. "The national question in Europe," NI v 9 n 2, 45; Young, "The struggle in Yugoslavia," NI v 9 n 11 (Dec. 1943), 333–34; Shachtman, "The meaning of the new Yugoslavian provisional government," LA v 8 n 1 (3 Jan. 1944), 4; R. Gould," Preview of revolution," WP bul (Sept. 1943), ISM v 3, 300.

52. Shachtman, "The revolution in Italy" (8 Aug. 1943), MSC b 39 f 22 (not microfilmed).

53. Shachtman, "Problems of the Italian revolt," NI v 9 n 8 (Sept. 1943), 238, 233, 235.

54. "Problems of the Italian revolt," NI v 9 n 8, 237; Shachtman, "The second stage opens in Italy," NI v 10 n 4 (Apr. 1944), 107; Shachtman, "The present stage of the Italian revolution," LA v 8 n 18 (1 May 1944), 6.

55. WP NC, "Supplement to the resolution on the national and colonial question," WP bul (Nov. 1943), ISM v 3, 432–33; "The Allies versus Europe," NI v 10 n 8 (Aug. 1944), 245–46.

56. "The national question in Europe," NI v 9 n 2, 43.

57. IS, *War and the Fourth International*, 35; FI emergency conference, "Imperialist war and the proletarian world revolution" (19–26 May 1940), *Documents of the Fourth International*, 345–46.

58. "The national question in Europe," NI v 9 n 2, 43–44.

59. "Discussion guide on the national question," ISM v 21, 550–51.

60. Interview with Seidlitz (16 Jan. 1989), s 3.

61. Paul Buhle, *C. L. R. James*, 83; interview with Zeluck by Buhle (15 Dec. 1982), s 1–2; James, "Socialism and the national question," NI v 9 n 9 (Oct. 1943), 285.

62. SWP NC, "Perspectives and tasks of the coming European revolution" (2 Nov. 1943), FI bul (Aug. 1945), MSC b 44 f 9 (r 3399); SWP 11th convention, "The European revolution," *Fourth International* v 5 n 12 (Dec. 1944), 369;

Alan Wald, *The New York Intellectuals*, 47–48, 102.

63. WP 4th convention, "Resolution on the international scene" (June 1946), NI v 13 n 4 (Apr. 1947), 115 (also WP bul v 1 n 11 [27 Apr. 1946], ISM v 6); "The Yalta conference," NI v 11 n 2 (Mar. 1945), 37.

64. Shachtman, "Europe today" (1948), MSC b 40 f 8 (r 3389); Shachtman, *The Fight for Socialism*, 180.

65. "Balance sheet of the war," NI v 11 n 6, 168, 166, 169; "Resolution on the international scene," NI v 13 n 4, 120.

66. Benson and Widick, "Amendment to international resolution" (May 1946), ISM v 17, 745–46 (also MSC b 12 f 1 [r 3364]); WP NC (25–26 May 1946), MSC b 12 f 2 (r 3365).

67. WP 4th convention, "Declaration on the resolution on the United States" (27–31 May 1946), ISM v 17, 752 (also MSC b 12 f 1 [r 3364]); WP PC (20 Dec. 1946), MSC b 9 f 29–30 (r 3360); WP NC (25–26 May 1946), MSC b 12 f 2 (r 3365); WP 4th convention (27–31 May 1946), MSC b 12 f 1 (r 3364).

68. WP NC, "Statement on the slogan of the 'Socialist Party-Communist Party-C. G. T. government in France'" (Jan. 1946), WP bul v 1 n 8 (22 Mar. 46), ISM v 5, 968.

69. WP PC (8 May 1947), MSC b 12 f 5 (r 3365); WP PC (21 Nov. 1947), MSC b 13 f 1 (r 3367); "French strikes," LA v 11 n 49 (8 Dec. 1947), 1, 3.

70. "The crisis in France," NI v 12 n 2 (Feb. 1946), 37, 38; "Statement on the 'Socialist Party-Communist Party government,'" ISM v 5, 969–70.

71. Shachtman, "The program of Stalinist imperialism," BR 119 (also NI v 9 n 9 [Oct. 1943]).

72. Shachtman, "The struggle for the new course" (14 May 1943), in Leon Trotsky, *The New Course*, 221; Shachtman, "The counter-revolutionary revolution," BR 112 (also NI v 9 n 7 [July 1943]).

73. Shachtman, "On the twenty-fourth anniversary of the great Russian revolution," LA v 5 n 46 (17 Nov. 1941), 3; "The counter-revolutionary revolution," NI v 9 n 7, 209 (Shachtman omitted these words when his article was republished in BR); Shachtman, "Russia in the war: the dissolution of the Comintern" (July 1943), MSC b 11 f 12 (r 3363).

74. Shachtman, "The victories of the 'Red Army,'" LA v 7 n 11 (15 Mar. 1942), 3; WP NC, "The national question in Europe," NI v 9 n 2 (Feb. 1943), 46, 41.

75. Shachtman, "Germany and the control of Europe," BR 136, 139 (also NI v 9 n 10 [Nov. 1943]); "The program of Stalinist imperialism," BR 128.

76. "The program of Stalinist imperialism," BR 127.

77. "The Yalta conference," NI v 11 n 2 (Mar. 1945), 38–39; WP NC, "Resolution on the international situation," WP bul v 1 n 11 (27 Apr. 1946), ISM v 6, 1081.

78. "Resolution on the international scene," NI v 13 n 4, 120–21; Shachtman, "Seeds of a third world war," BR 147 (also NI v 10 n 1 [Jan. 1944]); Shachtman, "The reasons behind the Russo-Polish break," LA v 7 n 18 (3 May 1942), 3.

79. "Balance sheet of the war," NI v 11 n 6 (Sept. 1945), 166.

80. WP NC to SWP NC (30 Apr. 1946), MSC b 11 f 15 (r 3363); "Six years," LA v 10 n 13, 1-M.

81. FI 1st congress, "The war in the Far East" (3 Sept. 1938), *Documents of the Fourth International*, 232–33, 241.

82. Shachtman, "China in the world war," NI v 8 n 5 (June 1942), 169, 171, 172; Shachtman, "China in the war, "NI v 8 n 9 (Oct. 1942), 274; NI v 13 n 8 (Oct. 1947), 253.

83. Shachtman, "National and colonial problems," NI v 9 n 3 (Mar. 1943), 78.
84. "China in the war," NI v 8 n 9, 277; WP NC, "The national and colonial struggles," NI v 9 n 1 (Jan. 1943), 12.
85. Shachtman, "Nine lessons of North African invasion," LA v 6 n 48 (30 Nov. 1942), 3.
86. "Colonial world in ferment," NI v 11 n 8 (Nov. 1945), 229–30; Organization Directive n 10 (11 Jan. 1947), WP documents b 1 f 11, Tamiment Library, New York University.
87. Shachtman, "The role of the U.S. in Europe," NI v 10 n 7 (July 1944).
88. Branko Lazitch and Milorad Drachkovitch, Lenin and the Comintern, 391, 562.
89. Anthony Reid, The Indonesian National Revolution, 69; WP 4th convention, "Resolution on the international scene" (June 1946), NI v 13 n 4 (Apr. 1947), 123 (also WP bul v 1 n 11 [27 Apr. 1946], ISM v 6).
90. "Colonial world in ferment," NI v 11 n 8, 229; Stein, "Indo-Chinese leader seeks deal," LA v 11 n 9 (10 Mar. 1947), 7.
91. Shachtman, "The struggle for the new course" (14 May 1943), in Trotsky, The New Course, 164–65.
92. Shachtman, "The character and perspectives of the party today," WP Active Workers Conference bul n 6 (1945), ISM v 16, 418 (also WP NC, "Resolution on the party" [Jan. 1946], WP bul v 1 n 7 [15 Mar. 1946], ISM v 5); "Resolution on the party," ISM v 5, 937.
93. "Character and perspectives," ISM v 16, 425, 424.
94. SWP 12th convention, "Theses on the American revolution" (15–18 Nov. 1946), Fourth International v 8 n 1 (Jan. 1947), 13.
95. Shachtman, "Balance sheet of the negotiations," WP bul v 1 n 6 (8 Mar. 1946), ISM v 5, 895.
96. "Character and perspectives," ISM v 16, 419–23.
97. "Resolution on the party," ISM v 5, 954; Shachtman, "The task before the party," Active Workers Conference bul n 2 (1945), 361, 359.
98. "The task before the party," ISM v 16, 361; Shachtman, "Answers to questions on the cadre," WP bul v 1 n 13 (8 May 1946), ISM v 6, 1226.
99. Shachtman to Erber (17 Apr. 1945), MSC b 11 f 6 (r 3363); "The task before the party," ISM v 16, 356.
100. Shachtman, "Trotsky's 'Stalin,'" BR 157–58, 160 (also NI v 12 n 8 [Oct. 1946]).
101. Shachtman, "'Party' or "propaganda group'?" WP bul v 3 n 4 (11 Aug. 1948), ISM v 9, 1847.

PART II
"The American Working Class as It Really Is"

The Second World War and its aftermath first eroded, then virtually obliterated, the working-class world in which Shachtman had grown up. Mobilizing the U.S. labor force into the armed forces and war industry did more to assimilate immigrants and their children into the U.S. mainstream than all the schooling and propaganda about "Americanism" had in the previous half century. Millions of people were uprooted from their neighborhoods and ways of life. Though most returned to the old neighborhoods in 1945–46, their world had begun to be altered out of recognition.

Once the big waves of European immigration had been halted by Congress in 1924, time was working against immigrant working-class culture. Even the labor organizing drives in the 1930s helped in some ways to "Americanize" immigrants' children, though enough of them were shaken up by the Depression and the threat of fascism to form a sizable pool for the left's renewal.

More important than the cutoff of immigration was the end of the prolonged capitalist downturn of the 1920s and 1930s. Throughout the years 1918 to 1939, despite periods of relative prosperity, frequent and prolonged hardship kept working people from being entirely and securely wedded to the economic system they lived under. During the 1940s, 1950s, and 1960s, despite recurring recessions, rising living standards kept working people from being widely and consistently antagonistic to the economic system they lived under.

Large-scale migrations, poverty, racism, and alienation from the dominant culture continued to exist throughout the postwar boom. African Americans moving north, displaced farmers from the prairies moving west, Appalachians moving to the industrial Midwest, Puerto Ricans moving to big eastern cities, and Mexicans moving north across the border made up a lower stratum of ill-paid and widely despised workers. But whereas in the late nineteenth and early twentieth centuries native-born Protestant workers had been virtually drowned in a flood of southern and Eastern European immigrants, the established white working class held its own after the Second World War.

After 1955, the reunified AFL-CIO ensured the predominance of a gradually conservatized upper stratum in the labor movement. Although unions expanded to include over a third of the work force and workers of color came to make up a higher proportion of their ranks, a large, mostly white, politically moderate official-dom consolidated the unions under its control. The union bureaucracy kept its unions a tame fiefdom of Franklin Roosevelt's, Harry Truman's, Adlai Stevenson's, and Hubert Humphrey's Democratic Party.

Rank-and-file acquiescence was cemented by a large-scale transformation of workers' ways of life that was systematically though informally orchestrated by corporations and the federal government. Steadily rising wages made ownership of a house and a car—the mark of a privileged working-class minority in the 1920s—possible for the working-class majority (though many people entering the work force in the 1980s and 1990s would again find home ownership out of reach). Metropolitan areas were redesigned around the automobile, through highways, dismantling of urban transit systems, government-subsidized real estate speculation, and underfunding of inner-city schools and services.

The disappearance in the 1920s of the Jewish Harlem Shachtman had grown up in foreshadowed far more drastic changes in the 1950s and 1960s. New York's Jewish working-class neighborhoods vanished one after another: the South Bronx, where Shachtman's family and parents lived; the Lower East Side; Brownsville. His parents did not outlive their world: His mother had died in 1941; his father in 1948. Shachtman, however, did outlive the world he had grown up in. He moved to a house in the Long Island suburb of Floral Park in 1954.

The people who made up Shachtman's Workers Party did not all escape to the suburbs, but many did escape from the working class. Compared to the Socialist Workers Party, fewer Workers Party members had been trade unionists with roots and seniority before the Second World War. A high proportion of Shachtman's male followers who had gone to work in factories in the 1940s were drafted. Female comrades who replaced them in the plants were fired when the war ended. Although returning veterans could usually get their jobs back, many of them chose instead to use the GI Bill to go to school and get professional jobs. Others took union staff jobs in the 1950s.

Shachtman's politics in the 1920s, 1930s, and 1940s had been founded on a conviction that the working class could transform the United States. Not that he idealized workers' existing values, politics, or culture—far from it. But he felt instinctively that to the extent their values, politics, and culture alienated them from their rulers and bosses, they had a great if usually dormant potential for resistance and rebellion. The weakening of cohesive working-class communities by the 1950s left him without a lever with which to change the world.

Unable to change the United States, he joined the working class he came from in adapting to it. He insisted in the 1950s that any viable left had to be based "upon American social conditions as they really are, upon the American working class as it really is."[*] This sane insistence on recognizing the reality of working-class life instead of clinging to a rosy, obsolete picture gradually turned into a resigned conviction that the working class would remain as it was—conservative and quiescent—indefinitely. By the mid-1960s, the working class gradually gave way in his thinking to a stand-in for it: the top officials of the AFL-CIO. He remade himself in their image as a Cold War Democrat.

---

[*]Shachtman, "American Communism," NI v 23 n 4 (Fall 1957), 241–43.

In the late 1940s, he found in Walter Reuther a bridge from the working class he had dreamed of leading to the union bureaucracy he would later be content to follow. Reuther won Shachtman over by acting as the outstanding militant leader of the last great old-style strike wave in 1945–46. Shachtman thought in the late 1940s that Reuther would help create the United States' first independent, mass working-class party, conceived as a national Liberal Party modeled on the New York Liberal Party. Reuther also helped lead the fight in the CIO against the Communists, whom Shachtman and his followers had come to hate and fear, with a program that at least initially seemed more militant than the Communists'.

A defining moment for Shachtman came when the CIO banned Communists from its leadership, provoking a split between Communist-aligned "progressive" and Cold War "liberal" unions in November 1949. Shachtman and his followers opposed persecuting unionists on the basis of their politics, in principle. They nonetheless said, "without hesitation: we stand with the CIO!"*

At almost the same moment, Shachtman gave up long-standing commitments to working-class revolution and complete independence from the Democratic Party. He had already broken with the Fourth International in 1947–48, in keeping with his new conviction that Marxists' place was in mass social democratic parties. In October 1949, he announced that the British Labour government raised the possibility of a new way forward to socialism in the capitalist democracies: not through his old scenario of revolution from below, but through peaceful, legal, electoral victories. That same month he began arguing that socialists should support union activists' running in Democratic primaries, as a way to increase working-class influence within the Democratic Party.

In the early 1950s, Shachtman's politics, though no longer founded on a revolutionary strategy for reaching socialism, nonetheless remained the politics of a left-wing socialist. He and his followers believed that even if they were following a road to socialism different from the one Lenin and Trotsky had mapped out, they were still pushing forward toward the same destination with the same intransigent spirit. As the worst of the Cold War eased and new opportunities for radical organizing in the United States arose, many of them hoped to challenge U.S. capitalism and its international policy with new vigor.

To many of his followers' dismay, the 1955 AFL–CIO merger, the rise of the civil rights movement, and the crisis of the Communist movement after the 1956 Khrushchev revelations set Shachtman moving further to the right, into the mainstream of social democracy. In 1958 he took his followers into the Socialist Party. In the early 1960s he developed close ties to AFL–CIO officials around George Meany. He developed a strategy of "realignment," by which labor and liberals would harness the energy of the Black civil rights movement in order to drive southern reactionaries and big-city machine politicians out of the Democratic Party and transform it into a social democratic party. By 1964 this kind of realignment was too radical for him: He moved toward keeping the Democratic Party united and working for its victory.

Shachtman's clear-sighted, democratic opposition to Stalinism was a constant even through the changes of his later years, enabling him to expose the consolidation of bureaucratic rule in Eastern Europe and the limits of Nikita Khrushchev's reforms in the Soviet Union. Giving up his old dream of workers' revolution in the West, he found the imagery of workers' uprisings in East Germany in 1953 and

---

*ISL PC, "The split in the CIO" (12 Nov. 1949), MSC b 14 f 6 (r 3369).

Hungary in 1956 all the more compelling. But his anti-Stalinism was gradually reshaped in the image of the AFL-CIO and the Democratic Party, coming to resemble the Stalinophobia Burnham and he had analyzed in 1939. He grew increasingly hostile to third-world revolutionary movements, seeing them as fated either to accept the limits of capitalism or to create new Stalinist dictatorships. By contrast, he grew more sympathetic to middle-class third-world nationalist movements such as Jawaharlal Nehru's Congress Party in India, which he saw as the democratic alternative to Stalinism.

Opposition to U.S. global power was the element of his old revolutionary outlook that Shachtman gave up most slowly, grudgingly and covertly. But he gave it up all the same, under the guise of anti-Stalinism. He began in 1951 by saying that he would support the U.S. war in Korea if it were conducted by a labor government with a democratic foreign policy, and in the meantime he opposed any anti-war tactic that would contribute to U.S. defeat. In 1961 he publicly refused to condemn the U.S.-backed Bay of Pigs invasion of revolutionary Cuba. In the late 1960s and early 1970s he went much further—beyond hesitating to oppose U.S. intervention unreservedly or condemn it outright to supporting it openly. He split apart what was left of his own socialist following by swinging to support of the U.S. war in Vietnam.

He first put forward his rationale for supporting the Vietnam War in 1965. He and his allies developed it at length in 1970. "Under capitalism as it exists in the most advanced countries there are extensive possibilities for expanding the wide degree of political democracy that already exists," they said. Communism "smashes all . . . democratic rights and movements." Therefore socialists should back "the countries of political democracy over the countries of totalitarian communism."* With this statement Shachtman abandoned the idea that he had held to during his pre–Cold War years: that the working class can create a democracy more profound than anything offered by U.S. democracy so far, and that it can defend democratic freedoms without supporting the nominally democratic government that is its main enemy.

Shachtman changed his beliefs during the last twenty-five years of his life "under the banner of Marxism." He never carried his self-"Americanization" to the point that he was able to give up this most "un-American" of conceptual frameworks. The worldview he ended up with had little in common with the Marxism of Lenin or Trotsky or even Debs, but he managed to continue seeing himself as a Marxist by identifying with a different set of Marxists: the U.S. Socialist Party Old Guard around Morris Hillquit, who also had clung to a Marxist phraseology as they allied with AFL officials and supported Roosevelt's New Deal. In identifying with these dead or aging social democrats, Shachtman took back almost every word he had spoken in their 1930s heyday. But in identifying with these former adversaries who, like him, spoke Marxism, he preserved one last, twisted link to the working-class radical world of his youth.

---

*Shachtman et al., "Statement on Vietnam" (1970), MSC b 18 f 14 (r 3375).

6

Between Reformism
and Barbarism

In the years after the Second World War—1946, 1947, 1948—Shachtman realized that many of his wartime hopes had been disappointed. The Fourth International had not taken the leadership of any European resistance movement. In the third world, movements for independence were led by either Communists or middle-class nationalists. The capitalist order, far from being in crisis at the war's end, seemed in some ways reinvigorated. Shachtman had expected the United States to dominate the world after the war, but he had not expected its people to prosper. Its workers were not about to support revolutionary projects while their lives were tangibly improving.

Shachtman recognized these postwar realities faster and more thoroughly than almost any other Marxist. He was still determined to fight against ascendant U.S. power and build a working-class opposition in the belly of the beast. "If there is a gram of Marxist blood left in me, it will take a hundred miracles to get me to support the U.S.," he said. He told a Trotskyist heckler who predicted that the Workers Party would back the United States in the next war, "'When you have long hairs growing on the palm of your hand, my dear swine, we'll support American imperialism.' For my part," Shachtman added in a letter to Manny Geltman, "it will take this gentleman a long time to grow hair of any length on his palm."[1]

The power of U.S. capital after the war seemed to be seriously challenged at home by the U.S. working class. The wartime militancy that Shachtman's followers had encouraged and helped organize exploded after Japan surrendered in August 1945. At the height of the 1945–46 strike wave, almost two million U.S. workers were out on strike. Most prominent among the strikes was the United Auto Workers' strike led by Walter Reuther against General Motors. Rebounding from his September 1944 humiliation at the Grand Rapids convention, Reuther regained prestige among leftists through his strike

189

leadership. His "GM Program" challenged corporate prerogatives to set wages, set prices, and keep management secrets.

Shachtman urged his followers to use Reuther's GM Program as a tool to radicalize workers and expose Reuther's halfhearted commitment to his own radical demands. But the organized Rank and File Caucus no longer existed in the United Auto Workers to push Reuther from the left, and the Workers Party was not well positioned to help reorganize it. Many of the group's activists in the auto industry were taking advantage of postwar opportunities to leave the plants, over Shachtman's vehement objections. At first reluctantly, Shachtman and his followers came to support Reuther as the most progressive leader available in the CIO. Their enthusiasm for Reuther grew as he inflicted a crushing defeat on the Communists in the UAW in 1946–47. In February 1947, Shachtman announced that he and his followers were "100% Reutherites."[2] He stayed firmly behind Reuther even after Reuther announced in November that the UAW would comply with the anti-labor, anti-Communist Taft-Hartley Act.

Reuther reinforced Shachtman's enthusiasm in April 1946 by joining David Dubinsky of the International Ladies Garment Workers Union to form a National Educational Committee for a New Party. Reuther and Dubinsky seemed ready to unite with the Communists and virtually the whole left to back former vice president Henry Wallace for president in 1948, as the standard-bearer of an independent labor-based party against both Democrat Harry Truman and Republican Thomas Dewey. Shachtman was eager to have his followers join the new party. But once he realized in 1947 that Reuther and Dubinsky would not support Wallace's Progressive Party and that Communists would control it, he backed away from supporting it. Instead he clung to the hope that Reuther and Dubinsky would form a national Liberal Party modeled on Dubinsky's New York Liberal Party, sometime after the 1948 election.

With revolution off the immediate agenda in the United States and Western Europe, Shachtman saw that Trotskyists had to break out of their isolation by reaching out to working people who had more limited goals. As he prepared his own followers for a future inside a U.S. Liberal Party, he decided that Western European Trotskyists also needed to disband their small groups in order to root themselves in a broader movement. In January 1947, the Workers Party began urging West European sections of the Fourth International to join social democratic parties.

Encouraged by the Labour Party's 1945 election victory in Britain, Shachtman began building ties to non-Trotskyist left-wingers among British Labourites and other European social democrats. He seized on the idea of an independent Western European union as a means by which European social democrats could counter both U.S. and Soviet power. He saw

European union as a project that could rally a "broad socialist left wing" to fight for a "democratic foreign policy."

Shachtman was all the more committed to having revolutionary socialists find a place in broader, usually social democratic movements, because the war's aftermath exacerbated his sense of the danger of Stalinism. He began in August 1945 to say that Stalinism was not simply a regional danger in the Soviet Union and Eastern Europe but a regime that Communists everywhere would like to install in their own countries. He used the argument in 1946–47 to justify unconditional support for Reuther against the Communists in the United Auto Workers.

In September 1946 he began to argue that anti-Stalinist socialists in Eastern Europe should support middle-class-led anti-Stalinist movements like Mikolajczyk's Polish peasant movement. In February 1948 he suggested for the first time that Stalinists could come to power without a prior workers' revolution and without any aid from Soviet troops, simply by abusing their control of trade unions. This suggestion repudiated his 1943 analysis, applied successfully to France and Italy in 1946–47, that Soviet-controlled Communists beyond the reach of Soviet troops would "prop up capitalist rule" in their own countries.

Shachtman's new orientation toward international social democracy and broad anti-Communist unity doomed his last hope of reintegrating his followers into the Fourth International. His idea of reunifying the Workers Party and Socialist Workers Party, put forward with new emphasis in 1945–46, actually seemed plausible for a few bewildering months from February to July 1947. European Trotskyist leaders like the Greek Michel Raptis and the Belgian Ernest Mandel seemed energetic in their encouragement of reunification. But reunification failed, due in part to Jim Cannon's renewed hostility and C. L. R. James's decision to take his followers out of the Workers Party. In April 1948 Shachtman, without a vote or allies, found himself completely isolated at the Fourth International's congress in Paris. In July he broke off his ties to the world Trotskyist movement.

Although Shachtman still called himself a Trotskyist for a few more years, he eventually concluded that "Trotskyism died with Trotsky."[3] He headed into the political storms of the Cold War cut loose from his Trotskyist moorings.

His last innovations within his old Trotskyist worldview in 1946–48 recognized realities and opportunities that other Trotskyists missed: the radical promise of Reuther's GM Program; the potential for organizing an anti–Cold War left wing inside European social democracy; and the rise of a democratic opposition in Eastern Europe. His attachment to revolutionary Marxism was manifested in 1948–49 as he fought against several Workers Party leaders who said that the Communist threat to Western Europe required democratic socialists to support the Marshall Plan.

But in some ways Shachtman's thinking in the late 1940s began to undermine what had been key aspects of his revolutionary perspective. His growing enthusiasm for Reuther began to undermine his commitment to independent rank-and-file organizing in the unions. His loyalty to the "democratic labor movement" began to undermine his commitment to organizing not just a "broad socialist left wing" but a distinctive revolutionary current within the labor movement. Starting from Trotsky's description of Stalinism as a "neo-barbarism,"[4] Shachtman came to see Stalinism apocalyptically as a potential tyranny on a global scale and began to see social democratic currents that backed or accepted U.S. hegemony as lesser evils. By 1949 he was poised to redefine his socialist worldview in fundamental ways.

The war's end transformed the climate in the CIO. Workers scoffed at the idea of extending the no-strike pledge into peacetime. They were starved for ordinary consumer goods that had been scarce or unavailable during the war and feverish to make up for lost time—especially because their real incomes fell 15 percent from August to November 1945 as the workweek fell from fifty-two hours to forty. "The standard of living was not handed down at Mount Sinai nor written into the Constitution," the *New International* pointed out; it was the result of endless battles. Now the battles began again with a "clean slate," since either the workers' hourly wage would go up or their weekly paycheck would go down.[5] Most workers were determined to keep their paycheck the same and increase their wage. All leaders and groupings tried to ride the new wave of militancy.

In this strong tide, the third force that the Workers Party had helped build in the United Auto Workers was swept away. Walter Reuther turned leftward and swam with the tide. Even before the war ended he refused to serve on the union committee to enforce the no-strike pledge he had fought to uphold. In November 1945 he launched a strike against General Motors, that lasted 113 days and spread to industry after industry. By late January 1946, the biggest strike wave in U.S. history was on, with almost two million out on strike. Reuther advanced a "GM Program" for his strike that demanded not only a 30 percent wage increase but also a freeze on car prices and opening of the company's books so everyone could see its inflated profits. One flustered GM vice president blurted out, "We don't even open our books to our stockholders."[6]

Shachtman seized on Reuther's GM Program as an opening for the left. His exposition of the program's radical promise was a model of a transitional approach to labor politics. At the same time, critically at first, he swung his followers not only behind Reuther's program but behind Reuther's faction in the United Auto Workers. His followers, for their part, were often ready to take advantage of the respect they had gained from their fellow unionists to climb into UAW leadership jobs. Support for Reuther, justified at first by politics, became difficult to give up.

The fact that Communists were prominent among Reuther's adversaries reinforced Shachtman's support for Reuther. In 1945–48 Shachtman magnified the danger of Stalinism in the United States and made opposition to the Communist Party an unbreakable rule of his politics. Only when the Communists were crushed in the UAW did he again raise the call to organize a rank-and-file opposition. By that time his followers were reluctant to follow his lead.

Reuther had handed the Workers Party a program that "gripped the imagination of tens and probably hundreds of thousands of workers, perhaps even of millions," Shachtman said in 1946. Now the group could fight for transitional demands that auto workers themselves were enthusiastic about. He suggested using the GM Program, "not in the literal way in which it was presented by Reuther but in the most radical interpretation that we can give it." The Workers Party should bring out the revolutionary implications of workers' demanding that they should decide wages, prices, and profits. The next step was to demand a government that would control wages, prices, and profits in working people's interests.[7]

At first Shachtman's admiration for Reuther's tactics was grudging. He admitted that Reuther was "more daring and skillful" than other UAW leaders. But he complained that Reuther and his allies were "scared by their own boldness" and "jack-knifed under the capitalist press barrage." Shachtman told his followers to point out Reuther's shortcomings.[8]

The record of the negotiations confirms Shachtman's critical assessment. Reuther even offered to cut back his wage demands if they interfered with GM's making "a nice profit." Walter Reuther's brother Victor gave away the thinking behind the GM strike: "to take the ball out of the hands of the stewards and committeemen and put it back in the hands of the national leadership."[9]

Shachtman would have liked his followers to help take the ball from Reuther and give it back to the rank and file. But Reuther's initiative came at a moment of weakness for the Workers Party's union activists. Many of its wartime gains in getting industrial jobs were lost when the war ended, as prewar workers returned from the army and pushed Workers Party members out of their jobs. In Detroit many members whose jobs were secure drifted off to go back to school or take professional jobs, giving in to temptations they had never faced before. By May 1946, the party's trade union work was "all but disestablished." Disturbed and frustrated by the setback, Shachtman insisted,

Our "new" industrial workers must learn to share the fate of the class to which they belong, with which their fate is tied. The idea of being in that class in "prosperity" times and "leaving" it in time of economic adversity must be relentlessly combatted in our party as a true-blue petty-bourgeois manifestation. A revolutionist does not go slumming in the working class.

"No backsliding! No de-industrialization!" Shachtman insisted. "We are and we remain flesh of the American working class—or we shall be unworthy of our good name."[10]

Leo Seidlitz remembered years later Shachtman's anger when Seidlitz announced his own "tortured" decision not to go back into the factories after his release from the army. Seidlitz did not feel useful as a shop activist. Shachtman disagreed. He "called me in and said, 'Leo, you can't do this. If you do this, people will look to you and *others* will do it! . . . No *question* you've got to go back in the shop.' . . . He was *heavy* on me." Seidlitz ended up working in the party office for a year instead. Joe Carter, as a party leader, was more vulnerable to pressure, "If there was anybody totally inappropriate to work in a factory . . . *totally* inappropriate and useless" it was Carter, Seidlitz said. Carter "couldn't hold a hammer." Yet, "he came."[11]

The Workers Party kept an industrial base that accounted for almost half its members and recruits. It consolidated a group of almost fifty members in the United Auto Workers. It stopped and reversed the slide in the group's size.[12] But while its union activity was at an ebb, sticking to an independent position was difficult even in the UAW bastion, especially as most of the old rank-and-file constituency rallied to Reuther.

While Reuther was turning left, Communists and their allies remained enmeshed in their wartime attitudes and tried to hold back the tide. While the General Motors strike was still on, George Addes settled with Ford and Chrysler for wage increases that were half what Reuther was asking. Worse still, the Communist-led United Electrical Workers signed a contract with GM in February 1946 while the auto workers were still fighting, again for half Reuther's demands. When Reuther accepted roughly the same terms in March, most GM workers felt that they had been stabbed in the back by Reuther's enemies and had no choice but to accept the settlement. They took their revenge at the union's convention. The popularity Reuther earned from his strike leadership—and the unpopularity Addes earned— helped Reuther win the United Auto Workers presidency, though the Addes group kept control of the union's executive board.

Ernest McKinney, the Workers Party's trade union expert, estimated that it would have to have 100 delegates out of the almost 2,000 at the United Auto Workers' 1946 convention in order to play a significant role there. It had three. It simply supported Reuther. Its support was strengthened by the friendliness that many Reutherite leaders, often socialist-leaning anti-Stalinists, showed toward the Workers Party. There was increasing sympathy for the Workers Party among "local union officials who are, of course, not tied to the labor bureaucracy," Shachtman said in 1945 (without explaining what distinguished these officials from the "bureaucracy"). He valued these local officials' friendly attitude. By April 1946, as Reuther gathered strength for the fight against Addes, Shachtman concluded that he should not preach a plague on both their houses as he had in 1944. He told his followers to work for Reuther "on the basis of . . . *our* interpretation of the GM program, of *our* critical attitude towards Reuther himself."[13]

The Workers Party's May 1946 convention turned the pro-Reuther position into a virtual article of faith by substantially revising Shachtman's theory of the Communist Party. In August 1945, Shachtman had begun to argue that U.S. Communists were not merely agents of the Soviet bureaucracy but a U.S. bureaucratic class in embryo. He said that the Communist leadership "dreams of one day . . . establishing itself as ruler of substantially the same bureaucratic despotism that its Russian colleagues enjoy." In April 1946 the Workers Party tentatively endorsed Shachtman's idea. It drew the corollary that in the unions social democrats were always preferable to Communists because Communists wanted to "exterminate" unions as independent organizations.[14]

This characterization of the U.S. Communist Party was a departure from the theory of Stalinism Shachtman had put forward in 1943. Then he had said that the Soviet bureaucracy would tell Communists to overthrow capitalism only where the Soviet state could guarantee its direct military control. Shachtman would continue to use this theory to explain the relative restraint of Communist parties in France and Italy in 1946–47. Yet in the United States, where Communists had far less of a social base and far less prospect of power, he raised the danger of Communists exterminating the unions as a consideration relevant to day-to-day union tactics. He argued as if U.S. Communists, like Soviet Communists, had a secret police force behind them. He moved away from the willingness to work in the unions "with the Communist Party as a party" that the Workers Party had expressed in 1940–41.

At this same time he was willing to applaud third-world nationalists for playing one imperialist power against another. Yet he denied this privilege to U.S. workers, who, in allying with Communists, were arguably playing a more remote imperialism against the one they faced at home. Hatred for Stalinism, or eagerness to conciliate pro-Reuther officials, or both seem to have made him adopt an approach in the United States that was different from his approach in Europe and Asia.

The May 1946 Workers Party convention converted the old Trotskyist rule of thumb of supporting social democrats over Communists into an almost ironclad principle. It said that the Workers Party would side with "all genuine working-class elements" against Communists (though it might support Communists against "reactionary, Fascist, anti-Semitic or racketeering elements"). The Workers Party would still work together with rank-and-file Communists in hopes of winning them away from the Communist Party. It would even join in broad coalitions that might include Communists. But the group now said for the first time—in the same convention where it urged pushing French Communists into a coalition government—that it would never make proposals for united action to the Communist Party.[15]

The Workers Party's new hard line toward the Communist Party came just as Communists, embarrassed about their role in the 1945–46 strike wave, began moving leftward. The San Francisco Workers Party branch, led by railroad worker Gordon Haskell, felt that this was the wrong moment to limit the party's freedom to maneuver, the wrong moment to rule out appeals for united action with Communists.

Haskell was a maverick within the party, a man who had never quite fit in. He had grown up as one of ten children of Congregationalist ministers in Bulgaria and moved to California when he was fifteen. Although Haskell joined the Young People's Socialist League in Berkeley and went along with the majority into the Workers Party, he had never felt entirely at home among Trotskyists. Together with Ernie Erber, he was one of "the two notorious goyim in the party."[16] Not much of a theorist himself, he was immune to the appeal of Shachtman's theorizing and inclined to resist it.

Haskell was friendly with Communists, who made him an exception to their rule of never talking politics with Trotskyists. He could not accept that the Communists he knew were "hirelings" of a movement that would make the United States Stalinist. Shachtman responded that Communists posed the most "deadly trap" when they appeared in a more "'radical' guise." He steadily escalated his rhetoric, saying that unless the "cancer of totalitarian Stalinism" was "burned out of the labor movement . . . slavery will ensue."[17]

Communists' turn to the left had not softened their hostility toward Trotskyists, which seemed to make any idea of united action a fantasy. For the time being, all Trotskyists agreed on opposing Communists in the labor movement, as shown in January 1947 over events in the maritime unions. The two Communist-led CIO seafarers' unions had organized a Committee for Maritime Unity to urge unity on the two AFL maritime unions. In general, the Workers Party favored unity over disunity and the CIO over the AFL. But Communists formed their Committee for Maritime Unity just as National Maritime Union President Joseph Curran, who had already gone against Communist policy by supporting the fight against the no-strike pledge in the United Auto Workers, was breaking with them. The Workers Party saw the Committee for Maritime Unity as a tool for reasserting the endangered Communist stranglehold on the CIO maritime unions. The Committee's attacks on rival AFL unions also looked more like preparations for raids than overtures for unity. So the Workers Party decided not to support it. Instead the group began its own campaign for genuine maritime unity. The Socialist Workers Party took the same position. Shortly afterwards, in February 1947, Shachtman threw nuance aside and called his followers "100% Reutherites."[18]

Shachtman's pledge of allegiance to Reuther came just before a new attack on Communists in the unions. In April 1947, right-wing Republicans backed by a majority of Democrats in both houses of Congress passed the Taft-Hartley Act. No union supporter could fail to see the act as a harsh attack and historic challenge to the labor movement. Besides the provision encouraging unions to require officers to sign affidavits that they were not Communists, it contained a host of anti-union provisions. It allowed states to ban the union shop with so-called right-to-work laws (an invitation most southern states took up, with disastrous consequences for organizing in the South). It banned sympathy strikes, supportive boycotts, wildcat strikes, common-site picketing, and union campaign contributions. It allowed the president to bring a strike to a halt just by declaring it dangerous to national security.

Shachtman called Taft-Hartley *"probably the stiffest legislative blow struck against the labor movement in a century or more."* "Labor's offensive has come to an end," he said. But he argued that the law could be beaten if only the unions would take the offensive, mobilize their members, act politically and together. With wage increases won in hard-fought strikes being canceled out by inflation, the events of the previous two years showed the need for the unions to act politically anyway. A full front-page spread in *Labor Action* called for a nationwide fight against the law capped by a demonstration in Washington, D.C.[19]

Behind this call to battle lurked a question: Who would mobilize to defeat Taft-Hartley? The AFL would not, leading John L. Lewis of the United Mine Workers to lament that U.S. workers were "lions led by asses." Most CIO leaders took advantage of the law to purge their unions of Communist opposition. Communists, however docile they had been during the war, now had no choice: They had to fight the law with all their resources in order to survive in the unions.

Faced with this situation, the Workers Party decided that union officials should vote against signing Taft-Hartley non-Communist affidavits, but if outvoted they should sign. Although Shachtman did not want to put a "damper upon those left wing workers whose natural tendency is to fight this thing," he was willing to say, "once the front has been broken, those who didn't want to sign are, so to speak, driven to it." Above all he wanted to avoid seeing the issue of non-Communist affidavits as "the real litmus test." He wanted to avoid antagonizing sympathetic union officials who would sign or allying with Communist officials who would not.[20]

The Taft-Harley affidavits became the central issue in the United Auto Workers, which was already convulsed by a virtual civil war in 1946 and 1947 between Reuther, its new president, and its Addes-controlled executive board. The decisive battle would be the November 1947 UAW convention. Although Addes saw which way the wind was blowing, distanced himself from Communists, and even agreed to purge Communist officers from the union, he could not let the Communists go down to total defeat without destroying his own faction. The Addesites made all-out resistance to Taft-Hartley their factional banner. Reuther's slogan was "Against Outside Interference"—but he meant Communist interference, not the government's. Barely a week before the convention opened, he announced that the UAW would comply with Taft-Hartley.[21]

The Socialist Workers Party backed Addes, but Workers Party activists were bound to Reuther. Even if Reuther himself had not been consistently militant, Shachtman argued, those who had been consistently militant during the war were now supporting Reuther. Shachtman excused Reuther's decision not to resist the Taft-Hartley affidavits. It was impossible to expect auto workers "to strike on behalf of the rights of 'Reds,'" he said. Preaching militancy now, at a time of disorientation, would be fruitless. The Addesites were doomed anyway. The best the Workers Party could do at the moment was hold onto its ties with the "'retreating' and 'passive' troops" of the labor left, the once and future militants among the Reutherites.[22]

Hostility to the Communists, who had fought Workers Party activists and even gotten them fired during the war, was another of Shachtman's arguments for Reuther. To ally with Stalinism or help it out of its difficulties was "giving aid and comfort to reactionary totalitarianism," Shachtman said—though the same issue of *Labor Action* urged support for Communist-led strikes in France. Workers Party activists were also attached to the positions they had acquired in Reuther's faction. Herman Benson represented the Reutherites in debates as an open WP member, which he could never have done as an Addesite.[23]

The Workers Party therefore stayed loyal and shared in the Reutherite triumph, which was overwhelming. Reutherites won even in Communist-led locals. The result was a quiet convention, an almost chilling contrast to the liveliness of earlier union gatherings. Reuther not only won reelection as president but won eighteen out of the twenty-two executive board seats for his faction.

Shachtman quickly became uneasy about Reuther's overwhelming power in the United Auto Workers and the Workers Party's vulnerability. Even before the convention, *Labor Action* made a feeble effort to rally Reuther's left-leaning supporters to a show of independence around the demand for a labor party. The paper looked to one-time Rank and File Caucus leader Emily Mazey as a standard-bearer. But Mazey, taking over Addes's old job as union secretary-treasurer with Reuther's backing, was unwilling to bite the hand that fed him. After the convention, Shachtman decided that his followers should strike out on their own. He attacked Reuther for "vacillation" on the labor party issue and "shelving" the GM Program. From now on in the UAW, Shachtman said, "'progressive' groups in which we participate must be 'our' groups . . . under the leadership of the WP fraction."[24]

Workers Party activists in the United Auto Workers were divided over Shachtman's attempt to change direction. Their discontent with Reuther was growing. Haskell was upset that the group "could not find its tongue to criticize Reuther" for his stand on the Taft-Hartley affidavits. The activists wanted to resist Reuther's drift back toward moderation. But having given up on Taft-Hartley almost without a fight, they were left without a rallying cry. The labor party slogan was not immediately compelling for the UAW ranks.[25] Even if Shachtman's followers wanted to push Reuther now, they were left without any solid ground to push from.

Led by Benson, Workers Party activists protested that the tasks Shachtman proposed for them were impossible. By July 1948, the party softened its tone. Auto workers could gain the necessary courage to challenge Reuther only "on the basis of *their own* experience," it said. For the moment the party would only help form groups of progressive Reutherites that would fight to keep "our Administration" from moving rightward. Later, it suggested, the groups might draw in anti-Reuther progressives.[26]

The postwar strike wave intensified Shachtman's interest in a labor party and encouraged him to develop more intricate tactics. He began to see that prosperity, not depression, would follow the war. He concluded that the emergence of a labor party would be more tortuous than he had thought. At first he saw the prosperity as "temporary and tenuous" and predicted, "The millions at work will enjoy not a higher living standard than during the war but a lower one." But the May 1946 party convention stressed that in the near future the boom would continue.[27]

Only Johnsonites failed to see the truth. Johnsonite Marty Glaberman said that the majority position was "just like an empty barrel. What happens to an empty barrel when you hit it? You hear, 'Boom! Boom! Boom!'" The Workers Party majority laughed but was not convinced.[28]

High consumer demand, bank and private cash reserves, high farm incomes, heavy equipment exports, military spending, and the accumulated mass of wartime corporate profits could prolong the boom for some time to come, the majority said. Full production had become possible under capitalism only when the economy was organized to "provide the means of killing and destroying" during the war, Shachtman said. After the war, arms production was continuing to be the motor force of economic growth. The wartime expansion was now being sustained by a continuing drive for world domination.

> American capitalism may achieve a surface stability, certainly in comparison with the rest of the world over which it stands as master. . . . Alone among the capitalist nations, the United States is today capable of continuing the wartime economic revival into a period of peacetime boom. But the economic energies that were released by the war's termination are paralleled by the class energy of the American proletariat. Vigorous economic actions, as characteristic of the American working class as its political backwardness, will be particularly characteristic of the period ahead.[29]

The task of Marxists was to translate those economic actions into politics. Shachtman believed that rank-and-file militancy was pushing the unions into conflict with the government and Democratic Party and creating the basis for independent labor politics. The Democratic Party's role as a coalition between liberal capitalists and labor was played out, he argued. Its defeat in the 1946 elections was evidence. Corrupt urban machines in the North and racist Dixiecrats in the South dominated it more and more. "The old political moorings are no longer holding labor so firmly rooted to its ineffectual place," he said. At least some union leaders were thinking about acquiring "political bargaining power which is directly under their control."[30]

Looking back, Shachtman said that in the mid-1930s the Trotskyist movement had "missed an unparalleled opportunity to root itself . . . in the most important new mass movement of the twentieth century in the United States," the CIO. But the new labor party would be even more important. He believed that it could save the Workers Party from its isolation, which had worsened with the loss of many of its union activists after the war. Even if the weakened Workers Party could not expect to win leadership of a labor party overnight, it would find the labor party's ranks receptive to socialist ideas. "The fact that the labor party is already on the political horizon but not yet actually established affords us invaluable time in which to prepare and orient our own movement," he said.[31] Just as the Workers Party had been the best organized force fighting the no-strike pledge during the war, it could become the best organized force fighting for a labor party now.

Shachtman set out to develop new tactics for independent labor politics, building on the ideas he had put forward to oppose Sidney Hillman's attempt to subjugate labor to the Democrats in 1944. The CIO had won the 1944 election for Roosevelt and elected many congresspeople in 1946. This was not real working-class politics in Shachtman's eyes. But it raised a new possibility for creating a labor party by defeating the CIO's pro-Democratic leaders and winning over the CIO Political Action Committee to the idea. The Workers Party endorsed and emphasized the slogan Shachtman had put forward in 1944: "Turn the PAC into a Labor Party."[32]

Given the postwar boom, Shachtman began to see the likelihood of a LaFollette-type "third party" as the first form of a CIO-based party. But he edged away from his earlier insistence that such a third party would only be an obstacle to a real labor party. Instead he focused on the possibility of a real labor party's taking shape at first as an ambiguous third party. In April 1946, David Dubinsky and Walter Reuther took a step in this direction by forming a National Educational Committee for a New Party. There was also a potential standard-bearer for a third party: Henry Wallace, a former New Dealer and vice president who was criticizing President Harry Truman's Cold War policies. Communists were pushing Wallace forward as a candidate against Truman.

Shachtman had many problems with Wallace's politics. Wallace called for economic planning, a guaranteed annual income, and new social programs in the same spirit that Roosevelt had advocated New Deal reforms: in order to save capitalism, not to bury it. Wallace wanted the government to create jobs but only *"to see to it that private enterprise is assisted until it can absorb this slack."* In foreign policy Wallace resisted the Cold War on the grounds that there were no vital conflicts between the United States and the Soviet Union. Shachtman thought that this attitude was naive from a capitalist point of view and useless from a socialist point of view: He wanted socialists to resist both U.S. and Soviet power, not try to reconcile them. But Shachtman cared less about Wallace's own politics than about Wallace's usefulness in winning labor away from the Democrats. In the summer of 1946, the Workers Party looked toward the movement with cautious optimism. "No labor party will spring into existence pure and undefiled," it said. The Workers Party would fight against Wallace, but it would not condemn a labor-controlled party just because Wallace led it.[33]

Shachtman's big problem with the Wallace movement was the dominant role Communists played in it. The problem became more urgent when the Independent Progressive Party of California was formed in August 1947 by 500 delegates from AFL, CIO, and railroad locals. Hal Draper wrote from Los Angeles that the Communists would inevitably dominate the party; it had no affiliated unions; it would not oppose liberal Democrats. But he also said that it was firmly based on the labor movement. The Los Angeles and San Francisco Workers Party branches both decided by October to use the new party to argue inside their unions for a labor party and to send members into its neighborhood clubs once it set them up. Despite its Communist leadership (and unlike the New York Liberals), the Progressive Party was not "top-down" but an activist party with "spontaneous, independent things going on."[34]

About this same time, Shachtman was looking for ways to promote independent political action among African Americans. He believed that African-American emancipation would require "the maximum of independent organization and measures of self-defense against the Jim-Crow bourgeoisie." He defended the idea of supporting an African-American candidate, even a middle-class candidate with an inadequate program, who was "the candidate of the authentic Negro community, running more or less independently of . . . the Democrats and the Republicans."[35]

Shachtman's innovations in 1946—the idea of putting pressure on the CIO Political Action Committee, openness toward the Wallace movement and independent African-American candidates—moved him toward a fully developed set of tactics for creating a labor party. But over the course of 1947 he began to inch away from the whole labor party strategy. Reuther and Dubinsky were refusing to support Wallace and postponing any break with the Democratic Party. Shachtman decided that he would not support any third party, particularly a Communist-led one, that was not backed by major CIO leaders. Instead he gambled on the prospect that leaders like Reuther and Dubinsky would eventually form a national third party of their own.

Since Reuther's and Dubinsky's party, unlike Wallace's, was still somewhere over the rainbow, looking to them for a third party began to soften Shachtman's antipathy toward the Democrats. Since 1944 the CIO had had a Dollar Fund meant to channel workers' contributions toward candidates backed by its Political Action Committee. The fund won little interest from CIO members—fewer than 5 percent of them contributed—and less from the Workers Party. But by May 1947 Shachtman said wistfully, "If we could see the beginnings, actually organized beginnings of an independent labor party in it, I would say, let's take a chance tomorrow, let's back all out PAC." Even without such beginnings Shachtman wanted to defend the Dollar Fund whenever it was "attacked from the right from the standpoint of the legitimacy of labor being in politics with its own political arm." When there was not an attack from the right, he thought that it would be "a mistake to fight about the dollar." He wanted to "duck it."[36]

In September 1947 Shachtman raised the possibility that one wing of the CIO leadership would both support Truman and form a third party that would run candidates for local office. He foresaw a national Liberal Party modeled on the New York Liberal Party, an organization for which he had had little use. But now he argued that Marxists should be inside this halfhearted third party, "perhaps even to support it critically." He wanted his followers "to become the outstanding participants in the unions of today and their political party of tomorrow."[37]

The first roadblock Shachtman pushed out of the way of his Liberal Party project was the Workers Party's cautious interest in the Henry Wallace–led Progressive movement. By late 1947 he realized that Reuther would not support Wallace and that Communists would control the Progressive Party, which meant that Wallace's project and Shachtman's were incompatible. Shachtman applauded the Wallace movement for its broad support and its advocacy of African-American civil rights. But he dismissed Wallace as "the creation and the tool of Stalinism" and Wallace's anti–Cold War foreign policy as "reactionary through and through." Shachtman convinced his followers to have nothing to do with the Progressive movement.

The only solution he saw was to split Wallace's party, free it from "the cancer of Stalinism" as Dubinsky had freed the American Labor Party in 1944, and join it with Reuther's forces. Once this happened—presumably sometime after 1948—Shachtman said that the Progressive Party might be transformed into an independent labor party. He rubbed his followers' faces in the fact that the third party he wanted might start out with an even more moderate domestic program than the Progressives'.[38]

Meanwhile Shachtman lost any chance to have an impact on the third-party movement that actually existed, Wallace's Progressive Party. The Workers Party and Socialist Workers Party stayed aloof from the movement. They gave little encouragement or direction to the working-class forces that had joined it, even though non-Communists inside it could and did challenge Communist control of it. They helped ensure that the Communists would control what was left of it after 1948.

Not much survived of the Progressive Party after the election. Its presidential vote total was disappointing, barely one million, compared with LaFollette's nearly five million in 1924. It attracted no support from top AFL or CIO officials, only from "progressive" officials close to the Communists. Wallace broke with it when he decided to support the Korean War in 1950. After being reduced to an ineffectual Communist front group, it fell apart in the early 1950s.

Yet Wallace's movement had more potential in some ways than the LaFollette movement in 1924. It had a proportionately greater working-class composition than LaFollette's campaign. It followed the 1945–46 labor upsurge more closely than LaFollette's campaign had followed the 1919 upsurge. Unlike LaFollette, who dragged the existing Farmer-Labor parties in tow behind a campaign over which he kept personal control, Wallace was the candidate of a national, grassroots activist party.

In the increasingly right-wing climate of the early Cold War, the Progressive Party influenced far more people toward independent, progressive political action than the Socialist Party, Socialist Workers Party, or Socialist Labor Party, whose candidates the Workers Party told its members to choose among to cast a socialist protest vote. It pulled thousands of people at least temporarily away from the Democratic Party—which Reuther and Dubinsky did not. Shachtman's decision to look toward Reuther and Dubinsky in 1948 instead of the Progressives appears in hindsight to be a warning sign about his political evolution.

At the same time that Shachtman was planning to join the "loyal left wing" of a reformist labor party in the United States, he projected the same strategy onto Europe. He looked increasingly to social democratic parties as the proper home of Western Europe's left. Three trends in his thinking propelled him toward social democracy. He lost hope that the Fourth International's sections would achieve wide influence. He came to have more hope in existing left wings in the British Labour Party and European Socialist parties. He came to see Communism, including in the United States and Western Europe, as an overwhelming threat that required uniting with social democrats against it.

Shachtman's shift toward the "democratic labor movement" was simpler to carry out in Western Europe than in the United States, because the European labor movement already had its own parties. With the war's end and the return to ordinary parliamentary and trade union existence, Socialist parties, which had been relatively unimportant in the resistance and dormant under the occupation, won back their prewar strength and more. Shachtman was excited by the British Labour Party's election victory in July 1945, which he called "the most spectacular parliamentary victory of labor in modern history." He decided that it was hopeless to ask workers to leave flourishing social democratic parties for tiny Trotskyist groups. In January 1947 the Workers Party began urging Trotskyists to join Socialist parties, particularly in Britain, Holland, Belgium, Scandinavia, Germany, Italy, and Spain.[39]

Shachtman argued that Trotskyists were too weak to have any impact, too weak to mobilize workers around an anti-capitalist program. Capitalism was widely discredited in many Europeans' eyes; there were crises and revolutionary opportunities "almost every six months," yet never had the revolutionary Marxist movement been "so small, so isolated and uninfluential."[40] Only the Socialist parties had the potential, if a strong anti-capitalist left wing grew up inside them, to be an effective anti-capitalist force.

At first Shachtman did not imagine Trotskyists spending a long time inside social democratic parties. He did not expect long-term economic growth in capitalist Europe or long-term stabilization of the social democratic movement there. He said that Socialist parties would be polarized between their leaderships, which were committed to alliance with the United States and cross-class coalitions, and a rank and file that would grow more and more restive. In a short time, he predicted, each Socialist party would "decay into an outright bourgeois party," be derailed by Communist infiltration (the Communist movement "lives on S.P. crimes like [a] parasite," he said), or shift to the left.[41] Marxists should throw their weight onto the scales to save these parties for working-class politics.

Other people in the Fourth International suggested that European Trotskyists join social democratic parties even before Shachtman took up the idea. Felix Morrow began advocating the policy in the Socialist Workers Party in July 1945. British Trotskyists began debating the idea of going into the Labour Party in 1946 and carried it out under the Fourth International leadership's goading in 1947–48. In the late 1940s and early 1950s, Belgian, Austrian, and West German Trotskyists would follow the British example.[42] But Shachtman distinguished himself by the urgency with which he advocated the policy, the way he generalized it, and, above all, the specific tactics he called for in carrying it out. He opposed any attempt to maintain a revolutionary faction inside social democratic parties. Now was not the time to stress Trotskyist doctrines, he argued. Marxists should help build a "broad left wing" united around working-class political independence, opposition to U.S. and Soviet power, and the fight for democratic reforms.

The tactics Shachtman advocated for left-wing social democrats were often those that many social democrats had already adopted. In the fall of 1948, for example, he backed the call for an "Independent Western Union," which had become popular in the British Labour Party. Although there was no inherent contradiction between Western European unity and alliance with the United States, Shachtman saw it as a way to create a pole of counterattraction to the United States as well as the Soviet Union. He argued that a European union could "use all its strength and influence to resist the drive of the two world powers to plunge us into a war." In a country like France, the call for an independent Europe could be linked to calls to stop colluding with the United States in occupying Germany, drop claims on colonies that could be retained only with U.S. power, and nationalize companies that had bought into the U.S.-dominated world economy.

At first Shachtman said that the European union could be born only "under the banner of revolutionary socialism."[43] But he quickly adapted to the attitudes of social democratic advocates of European union who had no intention of raising a revolutionary banner. Like some European left-wing social democrats, he hoped to win the whole British Labour Party and the West German Social Democrats to the idea. His proposals were therefore modified to fit in with more mainstream social democratic politics. In December 1948, Shachtman said that he would not expect the Labour Party to adopt a revolutionary foreign policy. He suggested that a European union could fit in with a more modest goal: a "democratic foreign policy."[44]

This idea of a "democratic foreign policy" became a crucial slogan for Shachtman. He began to focus his attention on measures he thought could be won from a labor-controlled government even in a capitalist society. He counterposed his ideas for a broad left wing—whose defining slogans at any particular time would depend on circumstances, such as the state of the economy, the possibility of paying for social programs without cutting into profits, and the severity of international conflicts—against any attempt to build an explicitly revolutionary current.

Along with finding roots in the social democratic movement, Shachtman emphasized uncompromising hostility to Stalinism. With the Soviet occupation of Eastern Europe and especially the imposition of Communist-dominated governments in the summer of 1947, Shachtman saw fighting Stalinism in Europe as an overriding priority. By 1948 he stopped minimizing the danger of Communist takeovers in Western Europe and the United States, seeing Communists as serious threats in the West as well as the East. He argued aggressively for the theory that he had arrived at in 1945–46: that even in countries immune to direct Soviet control, Stalinism was a qualitatively greater danger than any other force.

When Shachtman had begun saying that Western Communists aspired to set up dictatorships in their own countries, he had not said how or whether such a takeover could take place. In early 1948 he began to sketch out a scenario for a Stalinist takeover in the West, one that would proceed neither through corruption of a workers' revolution, as in the Soviet Union, nor through imposition by armed Soviet force as in Eastern Europe. He suggested that a Western Communist Party might use organized labor as "*a ladder on whose rungs it can rise . . . to collectivist power organized along totalitarian social lines.*" The real class base of such a Communist Party would not be labor, however, but the increasingly declassed middle classes. Communists could mobilize middle-class elements that were turning against capitalism, while preserving the ideology that "command is the privilege of superiors, obedience the lot of inferiors."[45] From the debris of capitalist society, on the backs of deluded workers, Communists could create new bureaucratic regimes.

There were holes in this theory that Shachtman saw and tried to fill. "Collectivist power cannot grow organically out of capitalism," he admitted. The diverse mix of Communist leaders and alienated intellectuals he saw as a potential new class could become a ruling class only "*after* it gets power." He failed to explain, though, how a class that did not yet exist could fight for power. He also admitted that this embryonic bureaucracy was hamstrung under capitalism by its inability to "control firmly those masses it must set into motion in order to seize and establish power."[46] In fact, although Communists have controlled trade unions in several countries, no Communist party has ever risen to power by mobilizing organized labor in the way Shachtman described. But hypothetical as it was, the theory was crucial to his thinking.

Shachtman saw a Stalinist threat to Western Europe partly because he did not foresee the prolonged economic growth of the 1950s and 1960s. He had predicted the "bourgeois democracy with a strong 'social' tinge" that predominated in Western Europe after the war, but he failed to see that it would outlast the fifteen-year limit he had set for it and that the social democracy he was orienting toward would, in the long run, be a more formidable adversary for the revolutionary left than the Communists he feared.

He still saw European social democracy as a bulwark against U.S. capitalism, not as U.S. capitalism's ally in the Cold War. Some of his followers thought differently and decided in the spring of 1948 that U.S. capitalism was in fact a lesser evil than Soviet Communism. Shachtman fought against these dissidents in 1948–49, in defense of what he saw as his own intransigent revolutionary Marxism. In some ways the 1948–49 battle recalled his 1940–41 clashes with Burnham, Macdonald, Selznick, and Carter during an earlier, briefer time of demoralization on the left.

The battle was fought at first over the Marshall Plan, which Harry Truman had announced in June 1947. During Shachtman's absence in Europe from March to June 1948, Ernie Erber, shaken by the February 1948 Communist coup in Czechoslovakia, decided that the Workers Party would have to support the Marshall Plan in order to prevent the Soviet Union from overwhelming Europe. On his return from Europe, Shachtman denounced Erber, saying that Erber was supporting U.S. plans to control Europe. He also denounced Manny Geltman, who had put forward a compromise position. Along with Hal Draper, who had left his Los Angeles shipyard job at the end of 1947 to edit the *New International* in New York, and Al Glotzer, who had reluctantly taken Draper's place as organizer in Los Angeles, Shachtman blocked any support by the Workers Party for the Marshall Plan.[47]

Erber had been a loyal ally of Shachtman's through many earlier disputes.

He was one of the most vehement denouncers of pro-U.S. social democrats as late as 1946. But he joined their ranks in 1948 on his way out of Shachtman's organization, with a long letter of resignation calling for support for the United States in any war with the USSR, retrospectively supporting the New Deal, and renouncing the Bolshevik tradition. Shachtman's response was his longest polemic ever: 119 single-spaced pages of argument and vituperation.[48]

Al Goldman, who had been expelled from the Socialist Workers Party and joined the Workers Party in June 1946, fought alongside Erber, whom he had won to Trotskyism in the 1930s. He also left the Workers Party in 1948. Shachtman commented that Goldman's and Erber's resignations were "saddening examples of demoralization" that made him "feel pretty sad and pretty sick." He insisted that the group, weakened and wounded by desertions, would go on. "In this life, so many Erbers have come and gone that we remember their names only because obloquy saved them from oblivion."[49]

But unlike earlier polemics that had rallied his followers, Shachtman's attack on Erber was received by many of his followers with indifference, disquiet, or even distaste. The doubts Erber was articulating flowed from the politics Shachtman was developing. Although Erber left, others whose thoughts differed little from Erber's stayed. The doubts he raised could not be laid to rest.

At the same time that Shachtman argued for unity with social democrats against both capitalism and Stalinism in Western Europe, he called for a liberation movement against Soviet domination in Eastern Europe. Beginning in September 1946, he argued that Marxists should join the resistance in Soviet-occupied Eastern Europe as they had a few years before in German-occupied Western Europe. But whereas he had foreseen in 1943 that the anti-fascist resistance would be divided along lines of class and politics, he foresaw in 1946 that the anti-Stalinist resistance would be more diverse politically.

In resisting the Germans, workers had often simultaneously resisted employers who were collaborating with the Germans. The Soviets, by contrast, were moving to expropriate Eastern European capitalists rather than collaborate with them. Anti-capitalist consciousness among Eastern European workers was correspondingly weakened. In Eastern Europe, Shachtman said, there was an "infinitely *greater degree of levelling* of all classes or former classes than under [the] Nazis." Rebellions would be "confused, vague, a mélange of elements from all classes" united by the yearning for democracy.[50]

He said nonetheless that Marxists should join these rebellions. A consistent fight for democracy would be the best way to mobilize people against Stalinism, he said, and identical with the fight for socialism. He did not see capitalist restoration as a danger in Eastern Europe. "There is a powerful yearning for freedom from the new bureaucratic yoke," he said, "but no one longs for the return of the old regime."[51] Only foreign intervention, which he assumed at the time would mean a U.S.-Soviet world war, could really restore capitalism where it had been overthrown.

He was neither surprised nor disoriented to see a middle-class democratic opposition rise up in Eastern Europe, most prominently the Polish national-ist peasant movement led by Mikolajczyk. He called for support for the "*camp, for [the] masses,* with which [Mikolajczyk's] name was associated." Within this camp Marxists should fight for independent working-class organizations in order to win the leadership from Mikolajczyk, while accepting that political differentiation among anti-Stalinists would develop slowly.[52]

Shachtman believed that only his theory of bureaucratic collectivism would enable socialists to lead the anti-bureaucratic resistance in Eastern Europe, so that it could grow into a movement for democratic socialism. He was contemptuous of any notion that Soviet conquest and dictatorship were helping to create socialism or workers' states there—that socialism could be brought about bureaucratically instead of democratically, "from above" instead of "from below." He believed the opposite: Socialism would be created either democratically from below or not at all.

> The difference between the revolution "from below" and the revolution "from above" . . . might be compared to the difference between crop-ping a dog "from the front" and "from behind." By one "method," the tail is cut off, and the dog, according to some fanciers, is healthier and handsomer; but if the other "method" were employed and his head were cut off, we would not have a "bureaucratically-degenerated dog" but a dead one.[53]

One possibility that Shachtman did not foresee in his strategy for Eastern European democratic socialism was that an internal Soviet crisis might allow the anti-Stalinist opposition to take over Eastern European govern-ments and that pro-capitalist elements in the opposition would win out thanks to both Western economic and ideological pressure and support from a wing of the Eastern European bureaucracy. This is what would eventually happen in 1989–90.

European Trotskyists like Ernest Mandel did suspect that people like Mikolajczyk would work for a capitalist victory in Eastern Europe. But at the same time Mandel told the Workers Party that Eastern European capitalists were being expropriated "only in your imagination!" He scoffed at the idea of mobilizing Poles against Soviet rule. As late as April 1946, the Fourth International urged Eastern Europeans to accept the presence of the Soviet army "only to the extent that it is a friendly proletarian armed force." This mistaken short-run perspective discredited in Shachtman's eyes anything that European Trotskyists said about Eastern Europe. As they moved slowly toward embracing British Trotskyist Jock Haston's theory that the new Eastern European regimes were "deformed workers' states," Shachtman said that they there were ceasing to be Marxists and becoming the "shapeless tail of Stalinism."[54]

Although Stalinist expansion was as real and as unpopular with Eastern European peoples as Shachtman said, it did turn out to have built-in limits. Far from being military assets, the Eastern European satellites required a big military commitment from the Soviet Union to guard against rebellion. The spectacle of Eastern Europe was also a political liability for Communists in Western Europe and North America.[55] The Stalinist threat that Shachtman saw in Eastern Europe actually helped undermine the Stalinist threat that he imagined in the West.

Shachtman's turn toward Walter Reuther in the United States, social democracy in Western Europe, and mainstream anti-Communists in Eastern Europe brought him into conflict with his fellow Trotskyists in the Fourth International. He thought that they were insufficiently flexible and insufficiently alert to the dangers of Stalinism. Gradually his hope to find a place in the International faded. His hope of reunifying the Workers Party with the Socialist Workers Party had one last fleeting lease on life in early 1947, thanks to overtures by European Trotskyists Michel Raptis and Ernest Mandel. But by the summer of 1947 a new flare-up of tensions between the two groups doomed the attempt at unity. The Fourth International's April 1948 congress revealed Shachtman's complete political isolation within its ranks. He gave up on the whole International.

His July 1948 decision to break with the Fourth International ended a three-year effort on his part to reclaim a place for the Workers Party in its ranks. Since the Fourth International had functioned only in fragments during the war—one makeshift leadership in Continental Europe, one in South Asia, two rival ones based in New York—he had thought that his group could reasonably expect to take part in reorganizing it on a world scale. He described the Workers Party early in 1946 as "only the link, in the United States, of a world chain of similar parties" working to reestablish the International.[56]

There was strong sentiment among Trotskyists abroad for healing the split in the United States, since both U.S. groups seemed to have stayed faithful to Marxism. The willingness among European Trotskyists to greet

Shachtman's followers as comrades reinforced the belief of many Workers Party members that they could feel at home in the European groups, where "the benevolent despotism exercised by Cannon does not find its counterpart." Al Glotzer found the new generation of European Trotskyists appealing: "They were young, they were intellectuals."[57]

During 1945 and 1946, Shachtman saw new potential allies in the International. The Irish group, a majority of the Greek organization, and Trotsky's widow in Mexico City, Natalia Sedova (who often stayed with Shachtman when she visited New York), all gave up Trotsky's analysis of the Soviet Union. Jock Haston, a British Trotskyist leader who would become Shachtman's friend, and Yvan Craipeau, who led a faction in France, seemed sympathetic. The *New International* even said in May 1946 that it "identified" with Belgian Trotskyist leader Ernest Mandel, who, like Shachtman, said that the International should be in the forefront of fights in Europe for elected constituent assemblies, abolition of monarchies, colonial independence, and other democratic demands.[58]

But for Shachtman the acid test of international leaders became their willingness to give him and his Workers Party a full hearing and support its reunification with the Socialist Workers Party. The WP founding convention had pledged in 1940 to work for reunification. After the SWP said in March 1945 that defending the USSR was "off the agenda" and Al Goldman and Felix Morrow raised the issue of reunification in the SWP, the WP responded by suggesting reunification then. All Shachtman asked was the right to defend his position and publish a discussion bulletin inside a united party. But in November 1946 an SWP convention rejected unity as "a shabby maneuver." When the Fourth International's European Secretariat, which included Mandel, Raptis, and French Trotskyist Pierre Frank, seemed in late 1945 to back the SWP's position, the Workers Party responded by calling for a new international leadership.[59]

In September 1946 the international leadership's adversaries won their first victory. Because Pierre Frank and other French Trotskyist leaders had rejected any possibility of a "democratic interlude," Trotskyists had failed to grab headquarters and printing presses in Paris when everyone else on the left was doing so in 1944. The French group was now operating in precarious semilegality. In the summer of 1946, Frank still insisted that Europe was in a revolutionary crisis "of a depth and extension far superior to that of the years 1917–23" and called on the left to seize power by force. Yvan Craipeau took advantage of many French Trotskyists' frustration at their leaders' poor judgment to organize an opposition bloc that won control of the group.[60]

The climax in this battle would come at the world congress of the International, the first to be called since 1938. On Saturday, 1 February

1947, Shachtman met the International's representative, Michel Raptis, in New York to discuss conditions for the Workers Party's participation in the congress. To Shachtman's surprise, Raptis told him that if the Workers Party would attend the congress and accept its decisions, Raptis could promise unity with the Socialist Workers Party right after the congress at the latest. Raptis repeated his offer in WP meetings on 3 and 5 February, saying that Cannon had already agreed to its terms. He promised the Workers Party that its rights would be protected in the International, which would never let any tendency be "suffocated."[61]

Shachtman decided to make the best of Raptis's offer. "I don't relish being under Cannonite leadership for one hour," he admitted. But, he said, "there is going to be a marriage." He expected the International to ensure a minimum of democracy in a united party. "I don't think it will be so easy for the Cannonites to impose the regime they like on us," he said. And in return for putting up with Cannon, Shachtman expected "a tremendous increase of support and friendship" in the International. On 24 March the Socialist Workers Party's *Militant* and the Workers Party's *Labor Action* printed a joint statement outlining their agreement to reunify.[62]

But the more clearly Shachtman articulated his perspective on orienting toward social democrats in Western Europe and anti-Stalinist unity in Eastern Europe, the less support he got for it in the Fourth International's ranks. The hopes he had for alliances in the summer of 1946 melted away in the following year and a half, and his differences with the rest of the International deepened. Besides the Workers Party, none of the third-camp socialists in the International—the Greek majority, the Mexico City group around Sedova, the Irish—shared Shachtman's commitment to uniting with a broad socialist left wing. Craipeau in France and Haston in Britain shared little of Shachtman's outlook on Stalinism. Shachtman became convinced that the problem with the International went deeper than Cannon's machinations or a mistaken theory about the USSR. Trotskyists' efforts to keep their separate little groups alive were keeping them in complete marginality, he said. Unless they gave up their isolation to join a broader socialist left wing, "they are sunk."[63]

Cannon's abandonment of the "absolutely cordial" attitude he had shown in February 1947 increased Shachtman's alienation from the Fourth International. Cannon later attributed his change of attitude to two letters hostile to the Socialist Workers Party that were printed in *Labor Action*. Whatever the reason, the SWP began giving signals in late March that it was pulling back from unity. It decided against joint May Day meetings, with the result being "two meetings on May Day in the same hall [in New York], with a policeman standing in the lobby shouting, 'Socialist Workers, this way; Workers, that way!'" SWP leader Morris Lewit denounced Shachtman's

"Menshevik concept of an all-inclusive party" and called for a "homogeneous party . . . based on one—and only one—program." Cannon said that Shachtman wanted to "break up the party as we have built it" and create "a windbag's paradise, with permanent discussion, driving out the workers." There would be no unification before the Fourth International's congress, Cannon said.[64]

As late as the end of May, Shachtman still hoped that the Fourth International's "moral pressure" would make unity possible. But in July, C. L. R. James took his followers out of the Workers Party, despite Shachtman's appeals to them to stay, leaving it with under 400 members. For Shachtman, the Johnsonite split reduced the idea of unity to "a bad joke." In September the Workers Party took back its promise to abide by the world congress decisions.[65]

The Fourth International punished Shachtman by taking away his vote at its congress, which met for almost a month in April 1948 in Paris. But he could and did attend and speak, and he gave lengthy presentations on the Soviet Union and the Workers Party. His "consultive vote" was duly recorded on each resolution—a procedure that highlighted his isolation, since he recorded his vote as against or an abstention for almost every resolution. Nonetheless he appealed to the congress one last time to recognize the Workers Party as an affiliate. "Don't you see [the] tremendous importance of our *desire* to be a section?" he asked the congress. "We get a new arena for our views. You dissolve a rival [and] discipline it." He came within an inch of winning over a majority: The resolution failed by only fourteen votes to fifteen.[66]

Shachtman called the congress "a tragedy [and] disaster." In July 1948, at Shachtman's motion, the Workers Party declared that the Fourth International had "forfeited any right to be considered the revolutionary international of the Marxist vanguard and lost all opportunity to achieve that position in the future." In later years, as he moved toward the mainstream of international social democracy, he would say that Trotsky's International had never amounted to much and never would. Its foundation in 1938 had been a "stillbirth," he said, "which was never to be resuscitated by the breath of life."[67]*

---

*Although the Fourth International has never led any revolutions or become a major political force in the world, many of Shachtman's dismal predictions about it were wrong. It did not become cut off from the European labor movement: Most of its European affiliates joined large reformist parties in the 1950s and stayed in them well into the 1960s. It has allowed a genuine pluralism in its ranks, including participation by tendencies that rejected its theory of "workers' states." Although it did adopt Haston's theory that the Eastern European regimes were "deformed workers' states," it supported anti-Stalinist upsurges in Hungary in 1956, Czechoslovakia in 1968, and Poland in 1980–81. Although it has remained relatively small, it has grown to become many times the size of the organization Shachtman broke with in 1948.

Notes

1. Shachtman to Geltman (4 May 1948), MSC b 11 f 2 (r 3362).
2. WP PC (28 Feb. 1947), MSC b 9 f 29–30 (r 3360).
3. Shachtman to Alexander (7 Dec. 1970), MSC b 28 f 4 (r 3376).
4. Trotsky was the first to use the term "neo-barbarism" to refer to Stalinism (and fascism). "Again and once more again on the nature of the USSR" (18 Oct. 1939), *In Defense of Marxism*, 31.
5. Art Preis, *Labor's Giant Step*, 267; "The strike wave," NI v 12 n 1 (Jan. 1946), 4.
6. Preis, *Labor's Giant Step*, 265; Irving Howe and B. J. Widick, *The UAW and Walter Reuther*, 139.
7. Shachtman to WP members (13 Apr. 1946), ISM v 17, 619–20; WP NC, "Resolution on the United States," WP bul v 1 n 5 (28 Feb. 1946), ISM v 5, 853.
8. Shachtman to WP members (13 Apr. 1946), ISM v 17, 619, 621–22; Shachtman, "The road to victory," LA v 9 n 51 (17 Dec. 1945), 1; Shachtman, "The struggle for the GM strike program," LA v 10 n 13 (1 Apr. 1946), 3-M.
9. Howe and Widick, *The UAW and Reuther*, 132–36; Nelson Lichtenstein, *Labor's War at Home*, 226; "The strike wave," NI v 12 n 1, 5.
10. Interview with Benson (6 Apr. 1989), s 2; "Trade union resolution," MSC b 12 f 2 (r 3365); WP to members (3 Apr. 1946), MSC b 9 f 34–35 (r 3361); Shachtman, "The task before the party," Active Workers Conference bul n 2 (1945), ISM v 16, 364–65.
11. Interview with Seidlitz (7 Feb. 1989), s 3; interview with Seidlitz (16 Jan. 1989), s 4; interview with Glotzer (28 Mar. 1989), s 6.
12. WP NC, "Resolution on the party" (1946), ISM v 5, 960–62; "Membership figures," MSC b 11 f 11 (r 3363).
13. McKinney, "Report on UAW convention" (22 Apr. 1946), ISM v 18, 866–68; Shachtman, "The task before the party," Active Workers Conference bul n 2 (1945), ISM v 16, 365; Shachtman to WP members (13 Apr. 1946), ISM v 17, 622.
14. "The upheaval in the Communist Party," NI v 11 n 5 (Aug. 1945), 136; WP NC to SWP NC (30 Apr. 1946), MSC b 11 f 15 (r 3363); WP PC, "Tasks of the party in the present situation," WP bul v 2 n 9 (25 Sept. 1947), ISM v 8, 1736. Trotsky had already suggested in 1940 that Communists dreamed of winning power in their own countries "with the aid of this same Soviet bureaucracy and its GPU." Trotsky, "The Comintern and the GPU," *Fourth International* v 1 n 6 (Nov. 1940), 149. The novelty in Shachtman's argument was the idea that Communists' dream was a practical danger in a country like the United States. Joe Carter said that he was unanimously denounced in the summer of 1945 when he made this suggestion at a Workers Party meeting that Shachtman missed. Carter, "For unconditional opposition to Stalinism!" WP bul v 1 n 14 (15 May 1946), ISM v 6, 1211.
15. WP 4th convention, "Declaration on the resolution on the United States" (27–31 May 1946), ISM v 17, 753 (also MSC b 12 f 1 [r 3364]); WP 4th convention, "Trade union resolution" (27–31 May 1946), MSC b 12 f 1 (r 3364).
16. Interview with Haskell (8 July 1989), s 1.
17. Interview with Haskell (8 July 1989), s 1; "The upheaval in the Communist Party," NI v 11 n 5, 136; Shachtman, *The Fight for Socialism*, 165–66.
18. WP PC, "The situation in the maritime unions" (10 Jan. 1947), ISM v 18,

940–43 (also MSC b 12 f 3 [r 3365]); WP PC (28 Feb. 1947), MSC b 9 f 29–30 (r 3360).

19. Shachtman, "Two policies in the auto workers union," LA v 11 n 52 (29 Dec. 1947), 4; WP PC (10 Apr. 1947), MSC b 9 f 30 (r 3360); "MARCH ON WASHING-TON!" LA v 11 n 15 (21 Apr. 1947), 1.

20. WP PC (17 July 1947), MSC b 12 f 6 (r 3366); WP PC (26 Nov. and 4 Dec. 1947), MSC b 13 f 1 (r 3367).

21. Preis, *Labor's Giant Step*, 320.

22. "The fight inside the auto union," M v 11 n 41 (13 Oct. 1947), 1, 2; WP PC (17 Oct. 1947), MSC b 9 f 30 (r 3360); "Two policies," LA v 11 n 52, 4; "Two policies," LA v 11 n 50 (15 Dec. 1947), 4.

23. "Two policies," LA v 11 n 49 (8 Dec. 1947), 3; "French strikes," LA v 11 n 49, 1, 3; interview with Benson (6 Apr. 1989), s 3.

24. LA v 11 n 36 (8 Sept. 1947); WP NC, "Statement of policy for the UAW fraction" (Dec. 1947), MSC b 12 f 8 (r 3366).

25. WP PC (26 Dec. 1947), MSC b 13 f 1 (r 3367); Haskell, "The Workers Party and the UAW," WP bul v 3 n 2 (24 Apr. 1948), ISM v 8, 1791–92; WP PC (Feb. 1948), MSC b 13 f 3 (r 3367); interview with Benson (6 Apr. 1989), s 3.

26. Benson, "Discussion of statement on UAW policy" (Mar. 1948), MSC b 13 f 3 (r 3367); WP NC (3–5 July 1948), MSC b 13 f 3 (r 3367).

27. WP NC, "Resolution on the United States," WP bul v 1 n 5 (28 Feb. 1946), ISM v 5, 852, 849; "Balance sheet of the war," NI v 11 n 6 (Sept. 1945), 167; WP 4th convention, "Declaration on the resolution on the United States" (27–31 May 1946), ISM v 17, 747 (also MSC b 12 f 1 [r 3364]).

28. Interview with Seidlitz (7 Feb. 1989), s 3.

29. WP NC, "Resolution on the United States" (post-convention 1946), ISM v 17, 786; Shachtman, *Socialism: The Hope of Humanity*, 8 (originally Shachtman, "Workers Party platform," LA v 8 n 16 [17 Apr. 1944]); "Resolution on the United States," ISM v 5, 845.

30. Gould and Shachtman, "Resolution—The situation in the United States" (14 Sept. 1948), WP bul v 3 n 5 (21 Sept. 1948), ISM v 9, 1873–74, 1878–79; Shachtman, "Six years of the Workers Party," LA v 10 n 13 (1 Apr. 1946), 1-M.

31. "Resolution—The situation in the United States," ISM v 9, 1881.

32. "Resolution on the United States," ISM v 5, 855.

33. Shachtman, "Behind the Jones-Wallace fight," LA v 9 n 7 (12 Feb. 1945), 4; "Resolution on the United States" (post-convention 1946), cited in ISM v 8, 1732.

34. Draper to WP PC (6 Oct. 1947), Haskell to Draper (13 Oct. 1947) and WP PC (17 Oct. 1947), MSC b 9 f 30 (r 3360); interview with Seidlitz (7 Feb. 1989), s 3.

35. Shachtman, "On the Supreme Court decision on the Texas primaries" (1944), ISM v 15, 208; Shachtman to Draper (18 July 1947), MSC b 28 f 32 (r 3378).

36. WP PC (26 May 1947), MSC b 12 f 5 (r 3365).

37. WP PC, "Tasks of the party in the present situation," WP bul v 2 n 9 (25 Sept. 1947), ISM v 8, 1732; "Resolution—The situation in the United States," ISM v 9, 1879, 1884; WP PC (22 Sept. 1947), MSC b 12 f 7 (r 3366).

38. "Resolution—The situation in the United States," ISM v 9, 1874–77; WP NC (5–6 Nov. 1947), MSC b 12 f 8 (r 3366).

39. Shachtman, "British labor goes left!" LA v 9 n 32 (6 Aug. 1945), 1; WP PC, "The Fourth International and the European social democracy" (17 Jan. 1947), WP bul v 2 n 1 (Feb. 1947), ISM v 7, 1487.

40. Shachtman, "Europe today" (25 June 1948), MSC b 40 f 8 (r 3389); Shachtman

to Rousset (30 Sept. 1948), MSC b 32 f 12 (r 3384) (also in Shachtman, "Letters to comrades in Europe," WP bul v 3 n 6 [10 Nov. 1948], ISM v 9); Shachtman, "Speech on political report" (Apr. 1948), MSC b 11 f 13 (r 3363).

41. WP PC (17 Jan. 1947), MSC b 12 f 3 (r 3365); "Europe today," MSC b 40 f 8 (r 3389).

42. Morrow to European Secretariat (10 July 1945), *Fourth International* v 6 n 3 (Mar. 1946), 83; Mandel to Drucker (9 May 1989); IS, "It is now urgent to orient toward the Labor Party masses" (Jan. 1947), MSC b 44 f 12 (r 3399).

43. Shachtman to Rousset (30 Sept. 1948), ISM v 9, 1920, 1913–16.

44. WP PC (7 Dec. 1948), MSC b 13 f 5 (r 3368).

45. Shachtman, "Stalinism: anti-labor in theory and practice," LA v 12 n 7 (16 Feb. 1948), 4; Shachtman, "Reflections on a decade past," BR 29–30 (also NI v 16 n 3 [May–June 1950]).

46. "Stalinism," LA v 12 n 7, 4.

47. WP PC (4 Mar. 1948), MSC b 13 f 3 (r 3367); Erber to Shachtman (6 Apr. 1948), MSC b 11 f 3 (r 3362); Draper to Shachtman (21, 25 May 1948), MSC b 11 f 3 (r 3362); Glotzer to WP NC and PC (18 May 1948), MSC b 15 f 5 (r 3369); interview with Draper (17 Feb. 1989), s 5; interview with Glotzer (24 Mar. 1989), s 3; Geltman to Shachtman (10 May 1948), MSC b 11 f 3 (r 3362); "Socialist policy on the Marshall Plan," LA v 12 n 20 (17 May 1948), 3; WP NC (3–5 July 1948), MSC b 13 f 3 (r 3367); WP NC, LA v 12 n 29 (19 July 1948), 3–4.

48. Erber, "Statement of resignation" (28 Sept. 1948), WP bul v 4 n 1 (Jan. 1949), ISM v 10, 2056; Shachtman, "Under the banner of Marxism" (misdated 19 Mar. 1949), WP bul v 4 n 1 (Jan. 1949), ISM v 10. The Marshall Plan debate, in which Geltman's middle position prevailed in the PC in May only to be defeated in the NC in July, continued through the spring and summer in LA.

49. Shachtman to Burbank (4 Aug. 1948), WP bul v 3 n 4 (11 Aug. 1948), ISM v 9, 1865; "Under the banner of Marxism," ISM v 10, 2100–101, 2205.

50. Shachtman, "Speech on political report" (Apr. 1948), MSC b 11 f 13 (r 3363).

51. Shachtman, "Europe today" (1948), MSC b 40 f 8 (r 3389).

52. "Speech on political report," MSC b 11 f 13 (r 3363); "Poland's political pattern," NI v 12 n 7 (Sept. 1946), 197–98.

53. Shachtman, "Isaac Deutscher's 'Stalin,'" BR 235–36 (also NI v 16 n 5 [Sept.– Oct. 1950]).

54. Mandel, "Open letter to the National Committee" (10 Oct. 1947), WP bul v 3 n 1 (5 Mar. 1948), ISM v 8, 1754; Mandel, "The conflict in Poland" (15 Nov. 1946), *Fourth International* v 8 n 2 (Feb. 1947), 50; FI conference, "The new imperialist peace" (Apr. 1946), *Fourth International* v 7 n 6 (June 1946), 182; Shachtman, "The nature of the Stalinist parties," BR 312 (also NI v 13 n 3 [Mar. 1947]).

55. Finkel to Drucker (8 May 1989).

56. Shachtman, *The Fight for Socialism*, 155.

57. Gordon, "A brief report on the French, Belgian, and German sections," WP bul v 1 n 4 (14 Feb. 1946), ISM v 5, 823; interview with Glotzer (4 Apr. 1989), s 9.

58. Interview with Glotzer (24 Mar. 1989), s 2; Shachtman-Haston correspondence (1947–64), MSC b 29 f 18 (r 3379); Parti Ouvrier Internationaliste, "The situation in France" (Sept. 1941), NI v 8 n 4 (May 1942), 120; introduction to Mandel, "Sectarianism and the democratic demands," NI v 12 n 5 (May 1946), 150.

59. Shachtman to Trotsky (15 Apr. 1940), TA 5112; "Review of the month," *Fourth International* v 6 n 3 (Mar. 1945), 68–69; "The question of unity," NI v 11 n 6 (Sept. 1945), 186; Shachtman to Cannon (29 Oct. 1945), NI v 11 n 8 (Nov. 1945), 255 (also WP bul v 1 n 1 [30 Oct. 1945], ISM v 5), SWP 12th convention, "Motion on unity with the Shachtmanites" (15–18 Nov. 1946), *Fourth International* v 8 n 1 (Jan. 1947), 31; "Resolution of the European Secretariat," WP bul v 1 n 6 (8 Mar. 1946), ISM v 5, 904; WP 4th convention, "Resolution on the international scene" (June 1946), NI v 13 n 4 (Apr. 1947), 124 (also WP bul v 1 n 11 [27 Apr. 1946], ISM v 6).
60. Richard, "Report on the French party convention" (Sept. 1946), WP bul v 1 n 20 (23 Oct. 1946), ISM v 7, 1435–37.
61. WP PC (3 Feb. 1947), MSC b 9 f 29–30 (r 3360); WP NC (5 Feb. 1947), MSC b 9 f 27 (r 3360).
62. WP PC (8 Feb. 1947), MSC b 12 f 3 (r 3365); WP PC (28 Feb. 1947), MSC b 9 f 29–30 (r 3360); SWP NC and WP NC, " Joint statement" (11 Mar. 1947), LA v 11 n 11 (24 Mar. 1947), 1 (also M v 11 n 12 [22 Mar. 1947], 1; MSC b 11 f 16 [r 3363]).
63. WP PC (10 July 1947), MSC b 12 f 6 (r 3363); WP PC (10, 17 Jan. 1947), MSC b 12 f 3 (r 3365).
64. James P. Cannon, "The SWP and internationalism," in *Speeches to the Party*, 77; Shachtman to WP members (24 Mar. 1947), MSC b 11 f 18 (r 3364); Howe to Shachtman (May 1947), MSC b 11 f 3 (r 3362); "Speech by M. Stein" and "Speech by J. P. Cannon," NI v 13 n 6 (Aug. 1947), 186–88 (also WP bul v 2 n 4 [27 May 1947], ISM v 8).
65. WP PC (29 May 1947), MSC b 12 f 6 (r 3366); WP PC (17 July 1947), MSC b 12 b 6 (r 3366); Shachtman to Tobin (28 May 1947), MSC b 11 f 3 (r 3362); "Membership figures November 23, 1946 and October 1, 1947" (1947), MSC b 11 f 11 (r 3363); Shachtman to Péret (22 July 1947), MSC b 30 f 37 (r 3381); WP PC (11 Sept. 1947), MSC b 12 f 7 (r 3366); WP NC, "Why SWP blocked unity" (5 Nov. 1947), NI v 13 n 9 (Dec. 1947), 286–87 (also WP bul v 2 n 8 [19 Sept. 1947], ISM v 8).
66. IEC 5th plenum (Feb. 1948), MSC b 4 f 29 (microfilm incomplete); Shachtman to Geltman (4 May 1948), MSC b 11 f 3 (r 3362); "Procès verbal sommaire des séances du II° congrès mondial" (2–21 Apr. 1948), IS bul (Nov. 1948), MSC b 4 f 26 (microfilm incomplete); "Speech on political report," MSC b 11 f 13 (r 3363).
67. "Europe today," MSC b 40 f 8 (r 3389); WP NC (3–5 July 1948), MSC b 13 f 3 (r 3367); Shachtman, "Speech to Stanford University Conference" (5 Oct. 1964), MSC b 39 f 27 (r 3388).

7

Beyond Lenin and Trotsky

By the end of the 1940s, Shachtman saw that U.S. capitalism was not merely undergoing a brief postwar prosperity but was entering a whole new stage. Major changes that he saw in capitalism convinced him that he had to rethink the kind of Marxism he had inherited from Lenin and Trotsky.

He adopted the theory, pioneered by an economist and Joe Carter supporter named Ed Sard, that postwar capitalism depended on a "permanent arms economy." "Production of the means of destruction" was becoming a third major kind of production in the U.S. postwar economy, alongside the traditional categories of capital goods production and consumer goods production.[1] Shachtman also saw that U.S. capital benefited considerably from the devastation of every other major industrial economy by the war. Profit rates in the United States had been rising since 1940, while European capital contended with low profit rates through most of the 1940s.

The United States was buying prosperity at a high cost: a distorted economy, McCarthyist witch-hunts, and the risk of a third world war. Looming over the other consequences of the arms economy was the prospect that the weapons would be used. The system's endemic crisis had been "transformed into the most comprehensive, profound, convulsing and agonizing crisis the human race has ever known—modern total war," Shachtman's group said. "The age of atomic warfare only emphasizes the one way out for all humanity: death (capitalism and Stalinism) or socialist freedom."[2] While mainstream politicians gloried in the U.S. monopoly of atomic weapons from 1945 to 1949, Shachtman already saw atomic bombs as compelling evidence of capitalism's threat to civilization.

At first his apocalyptic vision of "socialism or death," which brought Rosa Luxemburg's old slogan of "socialism or barbarism" up-to-date for the later twentieth century, increased his loyalty to followers who were "unshaken and unshakeable, who do not flinch and weaken."[3] But in the years 1949–51, although he continued to identify with Lenin's and Trotsky's tradition, he abandoned much of their strategy for socialist revolution

218

as inapplicable to the postwar capitalist democracies. In the early 1950s, his politics—though still the politics of a left-wing socialist—would no longer be founded on a revolutionary strategy as he had defined it during the previous quarter century.

By August 1949 he gave up on the idea of building a rank-and-file opposition in the United Auto Workers. He no longer spoke about an inherent conflict of interests between union officials and the rank and file. He also spoke less about an independent labor party arising in opposition to the Democratic Party. Beginning in October 1949, he took more interest in labor's role inside the Democratic Party. That same month, analyzing the record of the British Labour government, he began to say that capitalist democracy could be an instrument of peaceful transition to socialism. At first an intransigent enemy of U.S. world power, he began in the midst of the Korean War to become a more cautious and qualified opponent, avoiding any tactic that might give aid to Communism. By 1951 he abandoned the idea of permanent revolution and stopped calling himself a Trotskyist.

By the early 1950s, his allegiance to an international "third camp" took on a fundamentally new meaning. During the Second World War and even afterwards, his idea of the third camp had fit into a basically bipolar worldview: capitalism on one side, the working class and liberation movements on the other. The third camp was a *third* camp only because capitalism was divided against itself, as different capitalist powers (such as the United States and Germany) fought with one another to dominate the world. But the division between two different capitalist camps was unstable and secondary in his mind compared to the fundamental divide between capitalism and its adversaries.

As for the Soviet Union, he saw it until 1943 as a tertiary factor, an auxiliary in one capitalist camp or the other. In 1943 he foresaw that the Soviet Union would be one of the two great postwar powers, but he still did not see it as posing a global alternative to capitalism. The Soviet bureaucracy would expand its own power at capitalism's expense where it could, he said, but in most of the world it would work to prop up capitalism rather than threaten it.

By 1948 Shachtman's bipolar model of the world gave way to a triangular one. He now saw the United States and the USSR not only as two superpowers but as exemplars of two rival social systems contending for complete global supremacy. A fresh look at the Yugoslav and Chinese revolutions made him see that new Communist dictatorships could come to power anywhere, with or without armed Soviet backing, even through national liberation movements or other popular mobilizations. He saw divisions within the capitalist or Communist camps (such as the Yugoslav-Soviet split) as secondary. Convinced that capitalism could not destroy

Stalinism, he was afraid that "the Stalinist barbarism . . . can triumph over capitalism."[4]

"Where in this conflict is the proletariat?" he asked, and answered, "Program, goal, army and leadership of its own, it has none today." It was the weakest force in "a three-cornered fight for power" against "a degenerating capitalism which is anti-Stalinist and a totalitarian Stalinism which is anti-capitalist." As long as Communism was strong it would bring "demoralization and disorientation and paralysis into the working-class movement all over the world."[5] Previously he had seen Stalinism as a tyranny in power in the Soviet Union, a tyranny consolidating its power in Eastern Europe, and a major obstacle to revolutionaries' efforts to abolish capitalism in the rest of the world. Now he saw Stalinism as a potential tyranny in every corner of the globe and as the decisive question for socialists in our time.

Shachtman's organization said that the global Communist threat required "the adaptation of Marxism to the problems of our day in at least as sweeping a fashion as the adaptation accomplished by Leninism in its time."[6] He had seen himself for almost thirty years as a disciple of Lenin and Trotsky. Now, while reaffirming his continuity with them, he decided that he had to move beyond them. He looked for a new, post-Trotskyist kind of Marxism.

His new brand of third-camp Marxism presupposed an asymmetry among the three contending camps. Within the Stalinist camp he could see conflicts between rival bureaucracies but no social movement organizing openly against bureaucratic power. Within the capitalist camp, by contrast, he saw labor leaders like Walter Reuther, whose movement fought to raise wages more than U.S. corporations wanted, politicians like Clement Attlee, whose Labour Party was nationalizing industry in Britain, and third-world nationalist leaders like Jawaharlal Nehru, who adopted foreign and domestic policies at odds with the U.S. government's. All of them expressed a commitment to democratic freedoms and a desire for peace. They gave Shachtman hope that McCarthyism and third-world dictatorships could be defeated and a third world war averted.

He came to see Reuther's, Attlee's and Nehru's movements as forces for democracy and social progress. They became the core of his newly conceived third camp, which thus differed in another crucial way from his old conception. Before, he had seen the union officialdom, social democracy, and middle-class nationalism in the third world as enemies, as auxiliaries in the camp of democratic capitalism. Now he saw them as members of his own camp. Although he still considered himself a left-wing socialist rather than a social democrat, he came to define the side he was on not as the insurgent rank and file and the socialist left wing but as the "democratic labor movement."

His new worldview focused on the U.S. trade unions, which he saw as a powerful movement with socialist potential in which he wanted to root himself. He saw the unions challenged from within by Communists he feared and hated and challenged from without by the power of the Soviet Union. He decided to defend them unconditionally.

In the fall of 1949, while opposing in principle the CIO's decision to purge Communists because of their politics, his organization chose publicly to side with CIO leaders against the expelled, Communist-aligned unions. At the same time, losing confidence in Reuther's and Dubinsky's commitment to founding a national Liberal Party, he began looking for ways to increase labor's influence inside the Democratic Party. Over opposition from some of his followers, he advocated supporting labor-based campaigns in Democratic primaries. He cautiously moved toward a strategy— which he still called a less desirable, "discreditable and foul" strategy—for creating a labor party through maneuvers and realignments within the Democratic Party rather than a decisive break with it.

The tortuous route toward a U.S. labor party loomed larger in his mind, as it became for him less a tactic toward the creation of a broad revolutionary party and more the key instrument for creating a socialist society. His enthusiasm for the British Labour Party solidified in October 1949 into an openly expressed conviction that a party like the Labour Party could overthrow capitalism and create socialism by legal, parliamentary, relatively peaceful means. His new strategic vision helped him, at first without condemning his past revolutionary strategy of the 1920s and 1930s, to see his U.S. followers and West European co-thinkers as loyal participants in union leaderships and social democratic parties in the 1950s. Now no one could legitimately accuse them of biding their time until they had their chance to split the labor movement and resort to violence.

His new vision of a labor party that could bring about socialism peacefully in the United States put the identity of his own Workers Party in question. By 1945 he had said that the Workers Party was called a "party" only in hopes that it would become a real party someday. Now that he saw an eventual labor party as *the* party, his group's name and self-conception made no sense at all. In 1949 he convinced it to change its name to the Independent Socialist League. A heart attack in 1951 cut back his day-to-day involvement in running it; Hal Draper and Gordon Haskell took on most of its organizational tasks. Shachtman's move out to the Long Island suburb of Floral Park in 1954 reinforced a sense of distance that grew up between him and the people running the League.

As he redefined his third camp in the United States and Western Europe as the "democratic labor movement," he virtually wrote off the third camp that he had seen crystallizing in the rest of the world in 1943–46. He did keep his faith in Eastern European resistance to Stalinism, and Eastern Europeans would justify his faith by revolting against their rulers later in the 1950s. He kept his faith as well in the Indonesian republican revolution, but only by accepting as inevitable its confinement within the limits of U.S.-dominated world capitalism. On the other hand, he gave up on the third-camp forces he had seen earlier in Yugoslavia and Vietnam, which he thought had been manipulated and twisted until they were purely Stalinist.

He treated the third-world insurgent movements born during the Second World War as stories whose endings—capitalism in Indonesia; Stalinism in Yugoslavia, China, and Vietnam—were known. He no longer paid as much attention to unresolved tensions and possibilities within these movements, even though a one-sided civil war in Indonesia, conflicts over self-management in Yugoslavia, and the Chinese Cultural Revolution were all still to come. After 1951 he rejected breaking with capitalism as a short-term goal for the third world and looked to movements like the Indian Congress Party as its best hope for democracy and independence.

He saw a movement like the Indian Congress Party not only as a force for democracy, independence, and social reform but also as a bulwark against Stalinism in Asia. By the early 1950s, he and his followers agreed that democratic capitalism was a lesser evil than Communism, not only in terms of democratic freedoms but overall, not only in the United States and Europe but in the third world as well. They refused to support a democratic capitalist power like the United States in its battles against Communism, however. They said that declining capitalism was doomed to lose, and they had faith in the rise of a third camp that could win.

In 1951, however, in the midst of the Korean War, Shachtman began making statements that suggest in hindsight that his faith in the third camp was weakening and that he was beginning to count on U.S. power to halt the Communist advance. To many of his followers' disquiet, he began suggesting that even if he would not support the current U.S. government's war in Korea, he might support a U.S. labor government's war in Korea; he might support the British Labour government's war in Korea. In any event, he would avoid opposing the U.S. war in ways that might facilitate a Communist victory.

As yet, Shachtman's caveats barely made a dent in the Independent Socialists' identity as a Marxist group on the extreme left of the U.S. political spectrum. Those who wanted to support the Korean War or the Democratic Party or break out of a Marxist conceptual framework invariably decided that they had to leave the group, as Manny Geltman, Irving Howe, and Stanley Plastrik did in 1952 on their way to found the magazine *Dissent*.

Stalin's death, the end of the Korean War, and the East German workers' uprising in 1953 gave democratic socialists new hope. Young people reject-ing the stifling Cold War consensus found the Independent Socialists appealing. A new youth group shaped by Julie Jacobson began linking radical clubs on several campuses. In 1954, young socialists, led by Mike Harrington, who had been forced out of the Socialist Party because of their opposition to the Korean War joined with Shachtman's young followers to form the Young Socialist League. As the Young Socialists grew in the mid-1950s, they took on some of the countercultural aura of the beat poets and the 1960s student radicals to come.

Radical as Shachtman's movement was in the early 1950s, it rested on an analysis of the world that was open to question in some ways. Shachtman was right in 1949–51 to stress the importance of temporarily eliminated competition and military spending for U.S. capitalism in the 1950s. But he underestimated both capitalism's strength and the integration of social democratic and third-world nationalist movements into capitalist society. The U.S. economy turned out not to be quite as dependent on war produc-tion and global stagnation as he thought. At its postwar peak in 1951–53, military spending was 13.5 percent of the U.S. gross national product—high, but far below the 1943–44 peak of 42.8 percent. Once the Eisenhower administration cut military spending after the Korean War, the economy kept growing through the 1950s and 1960s, fueled by a profound techno-logical revolution founded on new automation techniques and machine processing of raw materials.[7]

The argument that Shachtman made in 1948—that the United States was "the last of the truly capitalist countries," which prospered "despite the agony of capitalism all over the world," even "because of this world agony"—contributed to his underestimation of capitalism's strength.[8] European capitalism, though at first a junior partner to that in the United States, recovered rapidly and staked out a strong position. Indigenous capitalists prospered even in economically dependent countries such as India. The Soviet Union could not match capitalist economic or military power. As a result, U.S. union leaders, European social democrats, and third-world nationalists spouting socialist rhetoric could all exist comfort-ably within the reformist consensus of the 1950s and 1960s. Shachtman originally supported these forces because he saw them as sources of anti-capitalist resistance. He ended up allying with forces that were acquiescing in the Cold War.

Shachtman's writings on Eastern Europe in the later 1940s eliminated some of the nuances that his analyses earlier in the decade had had room for. Independent Socialists said in 1949 that the economic and political system in all of Eastern Europe was "identical with that of Russia itself in every important respect." The purity of their anti-Stalinism now made them give up their 1946 idea of preserving and democratizing Eastern European nationalized industries. They described the nationalizations as "an abortion," "in no sense progressive," creating a system that was a "deadly enemy of socialism."[9]

In 1950 Shachtman completely gave up his 1941 defense of the USSR's collectivist property forms by arguing that the economic growth made possible by collectivism in the USSR in the 1930s was not much faster than Japan's in the same period. "The *potential* for social progress" was implicit in a collectivized economy, he said, "but only the potential." He no longer saw preventing capitalism's return to the USSR as anything positive either.[10] The Communist system benefited only the Russian bureaucracy.

At first he maintained that Communist parties everywhere served only the Russian bureaucracy. Events in 1948 and 1949 in Yugoslavia and China made him modify his schema, however. He acknowledged that Communists in these countries had escaped control from Moscow. They had relied on popular mobilization rather than Soviet troops and administrative edicts to overthrow capitalism. They eventually broke with the Soviet Union. Shachtman now drew on the history of Yugoslav and Chinese Communism to argue that Stalinism's expansion created contradictions within it that could contribute to its downfall. At the same time he predicted that the Yugoslav and Chinese regimes would be as undemocratic as their Soviet adversary.

In fitting Yugoslav and Chinese Communism into his theory of bureaucratic collectivism, Shachtman rejected ideas that had been central to his worldview. For the previous twenty years he had upheld Trotsky's argument that only the working class could free backward, dominated countries from their backwardness and foreign domination. Yugoslavia and China now became counterexamples for him. The revolutionary movements that had overthrown capitalism and foreign domination there were in no sense working class, he said. They were Stalinist movements, so the states they installed were essentially the same as the states Stalin had created in the Soviet Union and Eastern Europe. Stalinism too was a force, a reactionary force, that could overthrow capitalism in the third world.

For Shachtman, the Yugoslav and Chinese revolutions were the first unqualified victories of the declassed middle classes. The new bureaucratic class was rising to power not on the backs of organized labor (as he had predicted early in 1948) but on the backs of peasants. By fitting Yugoslavia and China into this model he finished the shift from his old view of Stalinism as a local aberration, his firm position through the Second World War, to his new vision of Stalinism as a global danger.

He eventually added the corollary that *only* new repressive societies could come from attempts to overthrow capitalism in countries where the working class and economy were underdeveloped. He decided that Trotsky's theory of permanent revolution, which in the early 1940s he had called "the 'heart' of Trotskyism," had been flawed even as Trotsky applied it to Russia.[11] The attempt to preserve any kind of working-class rule in the Soviet Union had been futile, doomed by the failures of socialists in Western and Central Europe. In looking at contemporary third-world countries like India and Indonesia, he accepted that socialism and working-class rule were unattainable goals. Instead he supported middle-class movements fighting for political independence and democracy, whose cause he saw as the democratic alternative to Stalinism in the third world.

Shachtman renounced the willingness he had expressed during the Second World War to support Communist-led guerrillas. As early as October 1943 he ended his earlier support for the Yugoslav partisans, predicting Stalinism in postwar Yugoslavia as the consequence of Communists' wartime leadership. He dismissed Tito's provisional government as a "vassal regime of Russia." After the war the Workers Party briefly denied that Yugoslavia had been freed by Yugoslavs, attributing Tito's victory to "direct and decisive aid of the armed forces of Russian imperialism." The *New International* treated Yugoslavia as just another Russian colony. It demanded in December 1946 that the disputed city of Trieste be turned over to capitalist Italy instead of Communist Yugoslavia: It was "a choice between slow poison or the bullet through the head."[12]

Only after Tito split with Stalin did Shachtman acknowledge that Yugoslav Communists had come to power "without the direct aid of the Russian army . . . in the course of a great national struggle." He said that he could not overestimate the importance of the split, which signaled *"the beginning of the end of Stalinism."*[13]

The break between the Yugoslav and Soviet regimes resulted from Yugoslav Communists' stubborn independence. They rejected Soviet advice to industrialize slowly, resisted management of Soviet aid by Soviet-controlled "joint companies," resisted placement of Soviet agents in the Yugoslav army and police, pushed for a federation with Bulgaria that Stalin opposed, and aided Greek Communist guerrillas more than Stalin wanted them to. In late February 1948, the Soviet Union told Yugoslavia that it would not renew the Yugoslav-Soviet trade agreement. In mid-March, all Soviet military and technical advisers left. Stalin demanded that Tito dismiss several ministers.

When Yugoslav Communists rejected Stalin's ultimatum, Eastern European Communist parties joined in May in denouncing Tito as "anti-Soviet." The chief Yugoslav Communist newspaper responded by printing half a million copies of Stalin's denunciation, along with the Yugoslav reply. Yugoslav Communists upheld Tito's leadership in a special congress and reelected it in their first election held by secret ballot. Three pro-Stalin generals then tried to overthrow Tito in a coup. When the coup failed, Stalin resorted to a total cutoff of Eastern European trade with Yugoslavia and massed troops on its borders.

The Tito-Stalin split took the world by surprise. Even when Shachtman and his followers acknowledged the split, they rejected any kind of support for Tito against Stalin. Independent Socialists said that Tito's movement had been "not primarily a working-class movement but overwhelmingly a peasant force." Tito had used his easily manipulated peasant base to construct a new bureaucratic regime in Yugoslavia that was independent from the Soviet Union but socially identical to it. Shachtman dismissed any talk of support for Tito as "preposterous": "his fight against Stalin right now is confined to consolidating the domination of his own despotic bureaucracy over the people of Yugoslavia." The only circumstance in which he could envision supporting Tito (militarily, not politically) would be in a war with the USSR, in which Yugoslav Communists would be defending their country's independence.[14]

The Independent Socialist position on Yugoslavia, elaborated largely by Hal Draper, used Tito's break with Stalin as evidence that Tito's regime was *more* like Stalin's than any other Eastern European government's. Communist leaders in the rest of Eastern Europe, militarily dominated and politically dependent on Stalin, could not build up their industry on a collectivist basis and consolidate themselves as full-fledged ruling classes. Tito, independent of Stalin, could and did. With this argument, Independent Socialists explained why Stalin's break with Tito had given the signal for purges of independent-minded Communists throughout Eastern Europe, in particular Polish leader Wladyslaw Gomulka: Communists like Gomulka were yearning for independent Stalinisms of their own like Tito's. Tito and Gomulka needed industry as a foundation for their own power, and the Soviet bureaucrats preferred to drain away their resources to build the Soviet war machine. Gomulka's dissent, like Tito's split, showed an inherent "contradiction between totalitarian war planning and national independence."[15]

Shachtman arrived through a similar process of trial and error at the same basic attitude toward the Chinese revolution led by Mao Zedong. His first error was shared by the whole Fourth International, which said in 1938 that Mao's Communists had "formally liquidated 'Soviet China,'" surrendered to Chiang Kai-shek, dissolved their armies, and stopped supporting peasant struggles. In October 1943, Shachtman traded in his first error for a second one: that the Communist Eighth Route Army was merely an arm of the Soviet government. During the postwar fighting between Communists and

Guomindang, the Workers Party justified its indifference by referring, as in Yugoslavia, to the Communists' peasant base. It said that Chinese Communists were "dismembering China in order to annex its wealthiest section, the North, to the Russian Stalinist Empire."[16] In reality, just as Stalin had urged Tito to cave in to Mihailovic in 1942–44, he asked Mao to make peace with Chiang in 1945–46.

After the Tito-Stalin split, Shachtman took a fresh look at the civil war being fought in China and changed his analysis. He saw the parallel between China and Yugoslavia right away and no longer attributed Mao's aggressiveness to Soviet expansionism. On the contrary, he predicted that Communist victory in China meant eventual conflict with the Soviet Union. (Stalin was looking ahead fearfully, and the U.S. State Department hopefully, to this same development.) He commented in November 1948 on Mao's declarations of loyalty to Stalin, "I think the lady doth protest too much." He said, "A 'Titoist' development in China is absolutely inevitable." Before the outbreak of the Korean War, the *New International* predicted a U.S. rapprochement with China directed against the USSR.[17] In the 1960s and 1970s, both these predictions came true.

Even though Shachtman would not give any support to Chinese Communists, his prediction of their eventual break with Moscow made their victory easier for him to accept. Aid to Chiang Kai-shek was not only ruled out "right off the bat" by socialist principles; it would also be "absolutely throwing away money," he said in November 1948. Chiang would only hold out for "another month or six months, another year."[18] In fact, Mao entered Beijing in January 1949, and the Communists occupied the whole mainland by the year's end.

Shachtman saw the Communist victory as a blow to the old empires. But he said that it was also a setback for democracy and socialism. Although he no longer saw Mao's movement as a Soviet tool, he still used its peasant base as an argument against it. Pointing out that as early as the end of 1928 the Chinese Communist Party had been made up overwhelmingly of peasants, he said, "This alone voids the Maoist claim of fidelity to Marxism." Nor did it make the Chinese Communists a class-conscious peasants' party. In China, he said, "the peasantry proved for the hundredth time in modern history that it cannot organize and maintain its own national state and national economy."[19] Instead Chinese peasants provided the troops for the emerging bureaucratic class.

Looking back later on the Chinese revolution, Shachtman admitted that the Chinese Communists did lighten the peasantry's burden of tax, rent, and debt. He even admitted that during the civil war "the population in [the] 'sovietized' areas gained a greater feeling of participation in political and even economic life than ever before." But because real democratic soviets never existed in China, he saw no possibility that China would move toward democracy or socialism. On the contrary, just as in the Soviet Union, he saw in China "an extraordinary harsh exploitation of living indigenous labor in field and factory." He saw Chinese Communists as "the most chemically pure" Stalinists.[20]

As Shachtman predicted, the Yugoslav and Chinese revolutions did not create socialist democracy in either country. Those who, like the Maoists of the 1960s, acclaimed either of these revolutions uncritically ended only by discrediting the socialist vision, as Shachtman saw that they would. But unlike Shachtman's account of Stalin's triumph in the Soviet Union, which looked carefully at each stage of the long, drawn out process of bureaucratization, his account of the Yugoslav and Chinese revolutions obscured some of their contradictory features.

Once he acknowledged that the Yugoslav partisans had not in fact been Soviet surrogates, Shachtman never fully laid out a rationale for giving up his original inclusion of them in his concept of the "third camp." After all, the third camp as he defined it was not limited to the democratically organized working class. It included all popular movements that relied on mobilizing oppressed people and fought independently of the existing powers, capitalist or Stalinist. Yugoslav and Chinese Communists in the 1940s seem in retrospect to fit this definition. Since Shachtman supported Mikolajczyk's anti-Stalinist camp in Poland and Sukarno's anti-colonial camp in Indonesia in the late 1940s despite his opposition to their pro-capitalist politics, he could reasonably have supported Tito's and Mao's independent, anti-capitalist camps in Yugoslavia and China despite his opposition to their authoritarian politics.

He might also have acknowledged some contradictory facts about Yugoslav and Chinese Communists' social composition and dynamics. He might have noted that the core leaders of both parties had joined the parties in the 1920s, when they were mass parties with trade union roots, and were still the backbone of party leadership thirty years later, when 40 percent of the Yugoslav cadre came from working-class backgrounds. The Yugoslav guerrilla army began with a core of "proletarian brigades" deliberately recruited from factory and mine workers.[21] After they seized power, Yugoslav and Chinese Communists tried to increase the proportion of workers among their members and the weight of the working class in their societies.

Given the uncompleted Stalinization of these originally working-class-led parties, Shachtman might have analyzed Yugoslav and Chinese Communists in the 1940s as he had analyzed the Soviet Communist Party in the early 1930s: as "sick, bureaucratized workers' parties." Like the Soviet party of the early 1930s, the Yugoslav and Chinese parties had strong tendencies to rein in and repress the mobilizations they led. A new privileged elite of factory managers, planners, and other bureaucrats began to form once they took power, making full-fledged bureaucratic rule a likely eventual outcome—and the actual outcome—of the Yugoslav and Chinese revolutions. In China the repression and military predominance in which the Cultural Revolution culminated and the repression of the 1989 movement for democracy proved that the bureaucracy could rely on its state to crush working people's resistance. Yugoslavia's collapse after 1989 showed that rival nationalist bureaucracies had snuffed out any earlier possibilities for working-class participation.

But bureaucratic triumph was not necessarily the *only* possible outcome in Yugoslavia and China. The same economic policies that fostered a bureaucratic elite greatly expanded the working class in both countries. The momentum derived from mobilizing people to fight in the revolutions was held back, contained, and denied independent political expression by the new states, but not immediately crushed. The self-confidence working people gained through their activism sometimes fostered impulses toward democracy, which dissident Communists sometimes tried to harness. After Tito tried to counter the Soviet embargo in 1949–50 by creating workers' councils and experimenting with workers' self-management, Yugoslav Communists were divided about how far to move in this direction. At the height of Mao's Cultural Revolution, Communists in Shanghai took his references to the Paris Commune of 1871 more literally than he meant them to and clashed with Mao and the army in an attempt to create true workers' democracy.

Democratic socialists were never able to organize freely in Yugoslavia or China, of course. The Communist regimes there were implacably hostile to any stirrings of dissent (as were the Marxist-backed revolutionary nationalists in Turkey and Indonesia). Mao imprisoned and killed Chinese Trotskyists after he came to power. The threat of repression gave democratic socialists all the more incentive to try to take advantage of tensions and conflicts inside the Communist ranks. Shachtman foresaw that there would be tensions and conflicts, as when he predicted the Sino-Soviet split. What he failed to foresee was that democratic movements that arose to challenge the regimes, such as the Shanghai Commune, would see themselves as fulfilling rather than repudiating the Yugoslav and Chinese revolutions.

During the 1930s and most of the 1940s, Shachtman had rejected the idea that middle-class movements in the third world could win real independence or democracy. His followers began to question this position when India became independent in 1947–48. Independent Socialists said that "India's political independence is as real as the political independence of any state today other than the Big Two themselves."[22] Shachtman maintained at first that India was economically dependent on European and North American capitalism after independence, just as it had been before. But by 1951 he began to portray Indian and Indonesian nationalists as forces for economic as well as political independence and as obstacles to U.S. domination of Asia.

By late 1948, Shachtman's sympathy for the new Asian states was reinforced by Communist opposition to them. After their exclusion from the republican government in early 1948, Indonesian Communists veered leftward, supporting strikes, calling for land redistribution, and borrowing independent leftist Tan Malaka's demand for "100 percent independence." In September, Communists and their allies in the Indonesian army rebelled. Although some of Tan Malaka's followers wanted to support the new Communist militancy, Tan Malaka's organization (which Shachtman's followers had been cheering on) backed the republican government, called for "strong action" against the coup, and demanded a purge of Communists from the government, army, and popular organizations.[23]

No sooner was the Communist rebellion suppressed in December 1948 than the Dutch launched a new offensive, which quickly captured the republican capital of Yogyakarta and all the major cities of Java. This apparently decisive Dutch victory was the beginning of the end for Dutch power in Indonesia. Republican leaders now had no alternative but to launch all-out guerrilla warfare throughout the archipelago, which soon put an effective end to Dutch control in most of the Indonesian countryside and many towns. Tan Malaka, released from jail, formed an autonomous and effective guerrilla force.

The Independent Socialists' newspaper, *Labor Action*, called for "*utmost loyalty to the Republic*" and praised Tan Malaka for defending the republic against the Communists. The newspaper's chief authority on Indonesia, Jack Rader, rejected Trotsky's "underestimation" of the colonial bourgeoisie, which Rader saw as an ally. Indonesian socialists could "become the Republic in fact; but only by defending it now," he argued. *Labor Action* saw India's Jawaharlal Nehru and Indonesia's Sukarno as leaders of an Asian third force and called for an alliance of Southeast Asian socialist and nationalist parties. Independent Socialists in San Francisco protested the newspaper's abandonment of an independent working-class outlook. Gordon Haskell complained that permanent revolution had been "dumped . . . down the drain" without a discussion.[24]

As late as the fall of 1950, Shachtman defended the theory of permanent revolution and dismissed the "quarter-solutions provided by the caricatures recently achieved by the native bourgeoisie of some of the colonial lands of Asia." In the summer of 1951, however, he began arguing that middle-class nationalists in Asia deserved socialist support. An "open door" in Asia meant veiled domination by U.S. capital, he said. But whereas in the past he had portrayed the Indian and Indonesian nationalists as holding the door open to U.S. infiltration, he now said that they were holding the door shut. "Peaceful economic infiltration" by the United States required social calm, he said. Asian nationalists instead agitated their peoples and encouraged suspicion of foreigners. The United States could not dominate India and Indonesia economically without suppressing Indian and Indonesian nationalism. Chiang Kai-shek and similar reactionaries who were "despised by their own people" might be reliable U.S. allies, he said; real nationalists like Nehru and Sukarno were not.[25]

Shachtman's new perspective on Indian nationalism meant abandoning the theory of permanent revolution as he had understood it since his first writings on India twenty years earlier. He rejected the theory as a guide even to Russian history when he commented in 1954 that Russian history "did *not* confirm Trotsky's prognostications." Overthrowing capitalism in a country whose poverty ensured that "socialism could *not* be built" had not led to the spread of socialism as Trotsky had thought. Even the attempt to begin building socialism there had been hopeless while revolutions elsewhere were delayed.

The Soviet Union needed a high rate of industrial growth and a big surplus for investment, and that surplus could be extracted only from the working class, Shachtman said. Bureaucrats could extract that surplus from workers through coercion and repression; workers could not extract it from themselves. Therefore the working class in power could not industrialize fast enough. "Others can exploit the working class, but it cannot exploit itself," he said. "The workers' power had to be destroyed to allow free play to the development of productive forces in Russia." The inevitable result was Stalinism.[26]

Given his sense of the hopelessness of anti-capitalist revolution in any backward country, Shachtman and those who followed his lead would inevitably be suspicious at best of third-world revolutionary movements in the 1950s. By 1961 he said that Latin Americans *"can do nothing"* without "a middle-class *democratic* revolution." In the end, in the words of his latter-day follower Tom Kahn, he "rejected, from a Marxist standpoint, the notion that the Third World could serve as a launching pad for socialism."[27] Because the building of socialism could not be successfully achieved in a backward country, he concluded that the attempt to build socialism should not even be begun.

Shachtman did not repeat in later years his analysis that Asian nationalism checked foreign economic infiltration, perhaps because he could see that it did not. U.S. and European corporations kept on investing in India and earning high returns on their investments. In Indonesia, the suppression of the September 1948 rebellion helped convince the U.S. government that the republic would be a bulwark against Communism and a stable country to invest in. The United States cut off Marshall Plan aid to the Dutch in Indonesia and threatened to cut off all Marshall Plan aid to the Netherlands—an amount roughly equal to the whole cost of the Dutch war. The Dutch had to settle. Under the May 1949 Roem-Van Royen agreement, they left Indonesia in return for the republican government's ending guerrilla warfare, protecting Dutch property, incorporating Dutch troops into the Indonesian army, and repaying most of the Dutch war debt. Tan Malaka was a casualty of the settlement: The republican army executed him in June.

The settlement that gave Indonesia independence in 1949 did not eliminate capitalism or U.S. power there. But it did not entirely suppress anticapitalist forces that arose in the war either. The revolution broke the power of the old aristocracy in the villages and drastically reduced the peasants' burden of taxes and debt. It fostered an ongoing movement to eliminate the legacy of Dutch and foreign economic power, a movement largely led by Communists and accommodated by Sukarno. The movement succeeded in forcing the dissolution of the Netherlands-Indonesia Union in 1956 and the expropriation of Dutch companies in 1957, British companies in 1964, and U.S. companies in 1965. But it relied on the patriotism of the republican army, just as Tan Malaka had in 1948–49, with even more disastrous results. Hundreds of thousands, perhaps millions, died in the 1965–66 coup that suppressed the Communist Party, overthrew Sukarno, and put Indonesia firmly in the U.S. camp. Accommodation to Indonesian nationalism ultimately vitiated the anti-capitalist potential that did in fact exist within the Indonesian revolution.

By late 1949, Shachtman decided that revolution might not be necessary to turn capitalist societies toward socialism. Socialism could be brought about legally and peacefully by the normal procedures of capitalist democracy.

This conclusion broke with the revolutionary Marxist tradition as Shachtman had understood it throughout his political career. When he and his friends mentioned in 1932 that Marx once thought that workers might take power peacefully in Britain, Holland, and the United States, they hastened to add, "Today there are no grounds whatever for this belief." They believed that the strengthening of bureaucracies and armies in all capitalist countries since Marx's time made violent clashes inevitable. "A fine picture [the capitalist class] presents, whining piously about revolution and violence!" Shachtman said in 1946. It maintained its rule by the organized violence of governments, and it periodically plunged the world into war. Parliamentary democracy, supposedly "the best expression of the will of the people, is nicely suited to cover up the actual rule of the enormously wealthy minority," he said. "The workers cannot possibly rule by means of such a governmental machine."[28]

By the fall of 1949, Shachtman changed his mind. "We do not differ from the Social Democrats because they are for democracy as the road to socialism," he announced. "That we believe."[29] He decided that people could simply elect a government that would, perhaps with supplementary goading, create socialism.

In his own mind, at least at first, this new strategic outlook did not require him to repudiate the Communist and Trotskyist politics he had held to during the 1920s, 1930s, and almost all of the 1940s. He did not say that he had been wrong before; he simply said that the world had changed. During the early 1950s, he would continue to say that revolution had been the appropriate strategy for Russian socialists in 1917, even if it was not an appropriate strategy for Britain or the United States now. But he did begin to argue that the capitalist "governmental machine," which he had said in 1946 could not "possibly" be an instrument of working-class rule, could become an instrument of working-class rule.

The decisive factor in his turnaround was his changed evaluation of the Labour government that had taken office in Britain in 1945. Once he had decided in 1947 that British Marxists should join the Labour Party, a number of consequences followed. People who joined the Labour Party would presumably vote for it. They would work to help it win elections and take office. Since the Labour Party, unlike the U.S. Democratic Party, was organically linked to the labor unions and to some extent controlled by them, even British Marxists who chose not to work in the Labour Party saw calling for a Labour victory as a reasonable step. They saw the Labour Party in some sense as a working-class institution. But until 1949, Shachtman never said that Marxists could actually take the Labour Party over, much less use it to install socialism in Britain by parliamentary means. Before 1949, in fact, he did not even consider the Labour government a real "workers' government."

The idea of a "workers' government" had a long history in the communist movement. Lenin and Trotsky prevailed on the Communist International's 1922 congress to adopt it as a goal. The congress talked about several different kinds of workers' governments. One kind of workers' government was just a popular synonym for a democracy of workers' councils. A "bourgeois workers' government" was a social democratic government that stayed inside a capitalist framework. Between these two known possibilities, the 1922 congress suggested that there might be another kind of workers' government: a government formed by working-class and possibly peasant parties, coming to power in a legal way, taking such energetic steps toward complete workers' power that it might deserve Communist support.[30] In the late 1940s, Shachtman called this kind of government a "socialist labor government" to distinguish it from a labor government that did not seriously threaten capitalism.

He did not consider the British Labour government that took office in 1945 a socialist labor government. It did represent the labor movement's interests in some ways, however. It created a national health service, for example, and in 1946 it repealed a 1927 labor relations law similar to the Taft-Hartley Act. But although it came to office with a large parliamentary majority and a mandate for sweeping change, it did little before 1949 to frighten British capitalists. It cut income tax rates and repealed the wartime excess profits tax. The industries it nationalized—coal, railways, canals, long-distance trucking, electricity—were mostly unprofitable, in need of new infusions of capital, or of secondary economic importance. Almost all the board members and managing directors running the nationalized industries were drawn from the old corporate managements.

In foreign policy, British Labour mostly followed U.S. dictates: joining NATO; pioneering counterinsurgency warfare in Malaya; supporting a repressive, royalist government in Greece; and opening the British empire to U.S. economic penetration. Conservative foreign policy spokesperson Anthony Eden later said about Labour Foreign Secretary Ernest Bevin, "I would publicly have agreed with him more, if I had not been anxious to embarrass him less."[31]

Once Trotskyists began joining the Labour Party in 1947, they began to outline what would have to be done to replace the existing government with a genuine socialist government. The 1922 Communist congress had given its answer: a real workers' government could be "neither won nor maintained without a revolutionary struggle."[32] Shachtman arrived at a different answer. Without giving up the distinction between a capitalist labor government and a socialist labor government, he began to argue that changing the Labour government into a real socialist government could be a smooth, relatively painless process. He gave the existing Labour government increasingly enthusiastic support. He went from being an opponent of social democracy in Britain and elsewhere to being an only sometimes critical supporter.

He took the first step in this direction in February 1949 when he defined a workers' government not as one headed for a decisive break with capitalism but as one that "carries out a program for the achievement of the most basic and important interests of the workers regardless of the institutions of private property." The British Labour government did not meet this definition yet, he said, but it would be wrong "for the Marxist to tell his social-democratic comrades that their common party *cannot* achieve a workers' government."[33] This argument conjured up the possibility of the victory of a socialist left wing within the Labour Party, followed by the peaceful establishment of socialism.

Other clues to the changes in Shachtman's thinking came at about the same time, when he responded to Ernie Erber's months-old letter of resignation. His reply to Erber became a sorting through of ideological baggage. He dragged many of his old anti-reformist polemics out of their closets. He defended "the banner of Marxism." But "although he seemed to be the most adamant, ferocious defender of the ancient faith . . . it sort of changed as he went along."[34] His asides were as revealing as his main argument. They showed that he thought that there *could* be a road to socialism between Lenin's strategy of confrontation with the old state and the social democratic strategy of gradual reform. While he condemned Erber as a social democrat, he showed why he thought that his own place was in a broad labor party.

Even as he defended the Russian Revolution against Erber, he suggested that nothing like it would have to happen in the United States. A socialist party could win a majority in elections, he said. It could put through its socialist program without violence if capitalists decided "not to offer resistance to the democratically expressed will of the people." Congress might be "transformed into something radically different." Shachtman was even willing to swear, "We do not and will not call for armed insurrection to overthrow a 'democratic state,' a 'state that rests on political democracy.' It is an oath."[35]

To some extent, Shachtman was saying nothing new. In a country like the United States, where the working class made up a large majority of the population, Marxists had never foreseen taking power without a popular majority. Luxemburg, Lenin, and Trotsky all saw the winning of this majority as revolutionaries' key task. But Shachtman's willingness to accept existing institutions of capitalist democracy as a reliable measure of the majority's will was a departure.

Marxists had always seen elections as indicators of popular feeling to some extent. But they had stressed that elected officials were unreliable between elections and that elected bodies that did try to carry out the people's will could be neutralized by constitutional and unconstitutional "checks and balances." Even a sizable socialist majority could be frustrated in a country like the United States by a Supreme Court defending constitutional property rights, a Senate inevitably lagging behind public opinion, and an entrenched civil service and military command, Shachtman had pointed out earlier.

Revolutionary majorities arise out of mass movements in months or days rather than in the years that go by between elections: A revolutionary opportunity could be missed if revolutionaries simply waited it out in the hope that it would eventually be reflected in an electoral victory. For this reason communists always said that the people have the right to overthrow even a formally democratic state if that state flouts the people's democratic will. They saw even a democratic capitalist state as a repressive bureaucracy and army rather than as a reliable means to express the popular will.

In his reply to Erber, Shachtman turned his thoughts away from the idea of overthrowing the capitalist state to the possibility of winning power through it, however much he hedged his new direction. He still rejected alliances or coalitions between working-class and middle-class parties and any "sharing of control" or "identity of interests" with capitalists. He still said that the working class had to take power from the capitalists, take over the state's "body of armed men," and use it as a weapon against the capitalists, not share it with them. He said that socialists should be prepared for "*all* conceivable forms of resistance to the inevitable social change which the tenacious bourgeoisie may offer" and "not only have enough votes in their hands, but enough power to enforce their will."

"Nothing can be lost by instilling the revolutionary concept into the minds of the working class!" he said. "A lot can be lost, including seas of proletarian blood, by instilling the rosy reformist concept into the minds of the working class!"[36] In context, however, these afterthoughts meant that socialists should guard against violent counterrevolution *after* they had won normal elections. It did not imply that they should take power in any way *besides* normal elections.

Barely a year after his anti–Erber polemic, Shachtman converted his first thoughts about a legal road to socialism into a firmly held theory, from which he stripped away the caveats. He dropped most of the militant pronouncements he had made in his polemic against Erber. "The Russian revolution has been destroyed; it is no longer the polestar of the socialist proletariat," he said. Workers' "parliamentary illusions" were no longer a big danger.[37]

Shachtman began this final clarification with a flip-flop about the British Labour government. He had been increasingly impressed by Labour's nationalizations, saying, "Nobody expected it to go as far as it did." In 1949 the Labour government moved for the first time, after fierce debates inside the cabinet, toward nationalizing an industry that was both profitable and central to the British economy—the iron and steel industry. In October Shachtman concluded that the existing British Labour government was "a workers' government which permits a peaceful development toward socialism."

He dismissed the argument that four-fifths of British industry remained in private hands, saying that Labour had already nationalized the crucial parts of the economy. It commanded a much stronger public industrial base than the Bolsheviks had created by nationalizing all of Russian industry in 1918, he said. He saw a possibility that socialism could be achieved "(a) without violence, and (b) without soviets."[38]

He elaborated his new view in the *New International* a year later. The British working class had an "opportunity of reconstructing British society on socialist foundations by parliamentary means, by peaceful means, with a tiny minimum of social setbacks and losses," he said. Every socialist should work to realize this "golden" opportunity. Britain could become "the great independent rallying center that proletarian Russia was a generation ago . . . now, without violent convulsions, democratically, peacefully."[39]

Three qualifications tempered Shachtman's new perspective. First, he deplored the fact that workers did not share in the management of national-ized industries. This still prevented his calling the Labour government a "genuinely socialist government." He even warned that the Labour Party could create "the type of totalitarian collectivism which is the distinguishing mark of Stalinist society." But the working class was strong, committed to socialism, and impatient with the government, he said. A "broad socialist left wing" could mobilize British workers to change the Labour Party's course and "by entirely democratic means . . . transform the government into a genuinely socialist workers' regime."[40]

Second, he still would not rule out the possibility of capitalist revolt. Failing to prepare for violent resistance could lead to a "horrible trap," he said. But he minimized this danger on two grounds: that the army cast "the heaviest pro-Labour party vote" and that the U.S. government "could not give direct military aid" to a British anti-democratic revolt.

Third, he attacked Labour's foreign policy, particularly its war against rebels in Malaya, which he called "as outrageously imperialistic, rotten and barbarous as the French in Indo-China." He excused Labour's acquiescence in U.S. Cold War policies by saying that an independent British policy was "an economic impossibility." But he worried that "socialism will break its neck in England" by going it alone rather than creating an independent, democratic socialist Western European union.[41]

Before the 1950 British elections, *Labor Action* said that a Labour victory would keep "the line of fight open" toward socialism. As Labour held on with a shrunken parliamentary majority and headed toward another elec-tion, the Independent Socialist League declared at its 1951 convention that British workers had "an unparalleled opportunity for a relatively *peaceful* road to socialism"—although the 1951 Labour manifesto was the first since 1923 not to call for socialism. Independent Socialists urged British Marxists to be "the *most* energetic and enthusiastic supporters . . . of the maintenance of the Labor Party at the head of the government and the nation." They endorsed the idea that a "broad socialist left wing" could win the Labour Party through normal party procedures to a fully socialist course.[42]

Shachtman's statement that a British socialist government would not face U.S. intervention could be questioned today in light of subsequent history. In 1973, for example, U.S. covert action contributed to the removal from office of the elected Labour government in Australia. The initiative in ousting Labour was taken by the governor general, who, like the monarch in Britain, is charged with upholding the constitutional order. In his writings on Britain, Shachtman did not mention the monarchy or the House of Lords as possible obstacles to a constitutional transition to socialism. The U.S. government has taken part in or supported coups that overthrew several other elected governments: in Iran in 1953, Guatemala in 1954, Chile in 1973. Although Shachtman suggested that because soldiers voted Labour they would spontaneously mutiny in the event of a military coup, Chilean soldiers who voted in large numbers for the left did not in fact mutiny at the time of the 1973 coup.

The "broad socialist left wing" that he aligned himself with in 1949–51, the Labour Party left, nonetheless tended to see the United States as a friendly power. Except for a small minority, the Labour left supported the Marshall Plan. The left-wing *Tribune* defended British and U.S. policy in Greece and endorsed Truman in 1948. Labour Party leaders vigorously reined in those on the left who overstepped the permissible boundaries of dissent, mostly Trotskyists or Communist sympathizers, even threatening thirty-seven members of Parliament with expulsion in March 1948.

Capitalists' untouched reserves of economic and political power made them take a fairly tolerant attitude toward the Labour reforms of 1945–51, reforms that were only partially rolled back—notably through the speedy, almost unresisted denationalization of steel—in the following decade of Conservative rule. In retrospect, Shachtman seems to have overestimated Labour's socialist potential and underestimated its integration into the Cold War consensus.

The idea that Independent Socialists might help build an independent rank-and-file group in the United Auto Workers was put to rest by a statement of policy drafted by Herman Benson in August 1949. Benson had decided that socialists pitting themselves against union leaders was, in general, "an absurdity." He described Walter Reuther as the "unchallengeable single leader" who had made his union the "vanguard of the American labor movement." Independent Socialists would support "more progressive Reutherites" against conservative ones, but the idea of moving toward a challenge to Reuther was jettisoned.[43]

This statement marks in hindsight the incorporation of Shachtman's followers into the Reuther wing of the CIO. Shachtman accepted the end of rank-and-file independence in the labor movement for a generation. Since the days in 1944 when he had helped the Rank and File Caucus challenge and defeat Reuther, his union strategy had made an about-face. During the late 1940s and 1950s, a time when rank-and-file union activism was at a low ebb, Independent Socialists in unions were less often rank-and-filers, more often officials or staffers. The consequences for the Independent Socialist League were "isolation from a mass base, tapering off of our political propaganda, failure to recruit or even to establish a circle of worker sympathizers."[44]

Independent Socialists' loyalty to Reuther posed a dilemma for them. Having crushed the Communists in his own United Auto Workers, Reuther joined in CIO leaders' offensive against Communists' remaining positions in the unions. Shachtman feared that McCarthyism was the welling up of authoritarianism he had foreseen during the war. He saw the U.S. government's attack on Communists' rights as part of a general narrowing of democratic freedoms and a general offensive against the left. Independent Socialists said that there was less real democracy in the United States in 1950 than in Germany in 1914. They saw the United States preparing for war, socially and politically, through bureaucratic planning, limits on wages, a shift of power to the presidency, narrowing of political debate, and the witch-hunts that Shachtman called an "ideological reign of terror." Without the "intransigent opposition of the working class," Independent Socialists warned, McCarthyism could usher in a dictatorship.[45]

Shachtman called sending Communists to jail for their politics "a blow at democracy, a gift to the Kremlin." In response to Sidney Hook's argument that Communists, as members of a "conspiracy" rather than just advocates of a "heresy," should be banned from university teaching, Independent Socialists campaigned vigorously in the early 1950s in defense of Communists' right to teach. In the unions too, Shachtman called for "complete and democratic rights for the Stalinists . . . and not the aping of Stalinism in the fight against it." The March 1949 Independent Socialist convention rejected automatic support for non-Communist officials against Communists, especially when Communist defeat would replace "a weak Stalinist regime, which in order to maintain its power has been forced to conduct a militant policy and to operate in a relatively democratic manner, by a powerful, reactionary and totalitarian labor bureaucracy."[46]

But with a final showdown looming in the CIO between Reuther and the Communists, a vigorous defense of Communists' rights would risk sundering the ties with Reuther that had became central to Independent Socialists' strategy. Shachtman was determined to back Reuther to the end. In an article in the September *New International*, he prepared his followers for an unflinching last stand against the Communists. The article pronounced an anathema against Communists that seemed to put them beyond the pale of any alliance, no matter how tactical or temporary. Both the article's tone and its substance raised questions about whether Shachtman would choose under any circumstances to defend Communists in the unions. He said that they were

> no less the enemy of the working class than capitalism and the bourgeoisie. *Indeed, inside the working class and its movement, Stalinism is the greater and more dangerous of the two. . . . Stalinism is a reactionary, totalitarian, anti-bourgeois and anti-proletarian current IN the labor movement but not OF the labor movement.*

"Every increase in the strength of the Stalinists means another step toward that triumph which is a catastrophe for the movement," he said. "Stalinism is the most virulent poison that has ever coursed through the veins of the working class and its movement. The work of eliminating it makes the first claim on the attention of every militant."[47]

No matter how right-wing or undemocratic Communists' adversaries might be, Shachtman seemed to say, Communists were worse. This marked a change in his position. In 1946 he had described even liberal union officials as "closer to the middle class than to the working class." Officials' privileged way of life and their role in negotiating and enforcing contracts, he had said, made them to some extent alien to their own rank and file. Now, by saying that Communists were "*IN the labor movement but not OF the labor movement,*" he asserted that Communists were a qualitatively *more* alien force than anyone else in the unions. He asserted that any tactic that might even temporarily strengthen the Communists could lead to "catastrophe." He had passed the point where he would consider what Cold War forces might benefit if unionists made anti-communism their overriding priority.

By 1949, anti-communism was in fact CIO leaders' overriding priority. In May 1949, the CIO National Executive Board said that it would expel any board member who failed to support the Marshall Plan. The CIO convention in early November explicitly banned Communists from the board. When the United Electrical Workers, the only large union still led by Communists and their allies, responded by quietly walking out of the convention, the CIO expelled it and openly invited other unions to raid it. The other nine unions close to the Communists were all expelled in the spring of 1950. Although Shachtman and other Independent Socialist leaders said that they opposed expelling unions from the CIO for their politics, they said "without hesitation: we stand with the CIO!"

The Communists had chosen a split as a way to preserve a "pro-Kremlin faction" in the unions, they said. Democratic methods of struggle would have resulted in the same split, and "it would be folly to 'bemoan'" it. They justified the purge by arguing that Communists purged opponents just as relentlessly from unions they controlled. Independent Socialists stood "for the democratic struggle *against* Stalinism, not with it in defense of 'democracy.'" They wanted to eliminate Communist influence "so that over its corpse the labor movement can go forward."[48]

In fact, the initiative for the split came mostly from top CIO officials. The United Electrical Workers had allowed the opposition to win 40 percent of its convention delegates in 1949. It had not carried out its threats to expel members who were preparing to split it. The San Francisco Independent Socialists rejected Shachtman's stand, asking whether CIO officials should be allowed to expel unions "led by this political minority today, and others in the future." Gordon Haskell remembered "getting sick to my stomach" seeing Communists' old CIO allies turn on the Communists. He said that the purge put all radicals in danger. But Shachtman had most of his members behind him. Benson remembered, "I was delighted at the chance at last . . . to get these sons of bitches."[49]

By acquiescing in the purge, Shachtman helped make the fight for democracy in the unions more difficult. Independent Socialist leaders advised their own members who were attacked in the anti-radical hysteria to "withdraw into the ranks" and wait "for a more favorable period."[50] But there would be no favorable period in the purged unions for several years to come.

The symbol of the new epoch in labor came when Reuther signed the famous "treaty of Detroit" in 1950. This five-year contract with General Motors promised half a decade of labor peace in return for annual wage increases that would be tied to productivity increases. From now on, for five years at a stretch, there was little for union activists to organize or debate. They could assist management and the union in administering the contract, or they could grumble. Shachtman sugarcoated the pill as best he could. The five-year contract was "a high and bitter price" to pay for higher wages, he said: "To think of planning wages five years ahead without being able to plan anything else in society is like planning to keep warm with a box of matches in an uncertain wind." But he hailed the contract as "a real victory for the GM workers" and "*a good next goal to shoot at for all other workers.*"[51]

Since they were denied a more favorable period, Shachtman and other Independent Socialist leaders adapted to the period that faced them. Although they complained about the officialdom, although they pointed out that not one union had defended its members' democratic rights categorically against witch-hunts, they insisted in mid-1951 that union officials would still, in a "restricted, distorted, inconsistent, wavering" way, resist the employers and government. They said generously, "In its own way, [the bureaucracy] fought the Taft Hartley law." They said that militant unionists could take "the actions of the leadership as a point of departure." But Shachtman was losing interest in rank-and-filers. In 1952 he said, "By 'the labor movement,' we must perforce refer today [to] the politically active officialdom."[52]

Shachtman inched closer to the politics of the "politically active official-dom" as well as their union policies in the late 1940s and early 1950s. In his eagerness to jump on board the labor party he saw coming, he cast aside strictures he had upheld for over twenty years about defining a genuinely independent party. Shachtman wanted to push them out of his way, and he was ready to be blunt about it. He argued that any compromises made now were fully justified in order to take part in labor's political debut. Under the guise of joining the coming labor party, he was in fact ready to get involved in Democratic Party politics.

In the resolution on the United States he drafted with Nathan Gould in late 1948, he resisted for the first time the temptation to forecast a new depression and radicalization. True, consumers were using up their savings, and a "tendency toward overproduction" was appearing in some industries. But this tendency had not spread and would not spread to the steel, oil, rubber, and coal industries. Instead the economy had become centered on a never-ending drive toward military production, he said. He pointed out that U.S. military spending had "no parallel in the peace-time history of the country." He predicted still higher military spending to come.[53]

War economics brought prosperity to the United States, he acknowl-edged. In the United States, "the lowly Negro is better off than the most highly-skilled German workers," and conservatives could "sing whole lyrics to capitalism at a labor convention" and escape uninjured. But he was convinced that the unions had not permanently embraced capitalism. Even if they seemed quiescent now, they would surely push any labor-based party leftward as the war drive began to pinch. He came back from Europe in the summer of 1948 shaken by the contrast between socialists' weakness in the United States and their relative strength in Europe.[54] He was more determined than ever to become part of the actually existing labor movement.

He began to mute Independent Socialists' criticisms of labor's support for the Democratic Party. At their March 1949 convention, they described labor's mobilization for Truman in the 1948 election as a "leftward swing," a way of endorsing "the increasingly radical line which Truman was astute enough to present during his campaign." The "paradoxical" result was to delay any prospect of labor's actually breaking with the Democratic Party, they admitted. But they still foresaw a break sometime soon and the creation of Shachtman's national Liberal Party, which they looked forward to eagerly.[55]

Events after the convention showed the groundlessness of immediate hopes for a labor-based third party. As Shachtman saw that his favored union leaders were not leaving the Democratic Party after all, he looked for ways to aid their efforts inside the Democratic Party. In August 1949, his new Political Committee urged Independent Socialists to start working in Americans for Democratic Action, although the group was committed to NATO, the Marshall Plan, capitalism, and the "preposterous utopia" of resurrecting the New Deal Democratic Party. In September, Shachtman announced that Independent Socialists' attitude toward the Democratic Party was too "abstract" and the "road to [a] labor party" might run through the Democratic Party.[56]

In October, Independent Socialist leaders learned that their Detroit branch was divided over whether to support Willoughby Abner, the Reutherite who had led the fight for compliance with Taft-Hartley in 1947 and was now running for city council as a Democrat. Shachtman proposed that Independent Socialists *encourage* unions to run their own candidates in Democratic primaries. The League should promise to support union nominees who won primaries, he said, because these labor campaigns would "deepen and sharpen the conflict of interests between the bureaucracy of the official capitalist parties and the labor leadership." He said that union leaders were bringing "the irrepressible conflict of class interests . . . right inside the Democratic Party. It takes on a mutilated and twisted form, but it is there."[57]

Shachtman's proposal meant abandonment of his lifelong opposition to support for Democratic campaigns. Led by Benson and Draper, Independent Socialists rejected Shachtman's idea as "ludicrous and deceitful." But Shachtman kept on fighting. At the 1954 convention, backed by Al Glotzer and even Haskell, he finally won the organization over. It urged labor to run "its own—labor controlled—slate of candidates in primary and general elections": "By this means labor's *active* commitment to the Democratic Party can be turned into a progressive channel."[58]

In the summer of 1952, Shachtman took another step toward the Democrats. He hailed workers' unity in voting Democratic as a sign of "highly advanced political consciousness." Although he still argued for "forcing the labor leaders out of the Democratic Party," he said that another way was possible: forcing them to act inside the Democratic Party so as to "precipitate the muted conflict between the old machine and the new 'interlopers' and lead by another road—an indirect, tortuous, discreditable and foul one—to the same inevitable conclusion: the declaration of political independence of the American working class."[59] This "discreditable and foul" strategy was the one Shachtman himself would pursue.

The smoothness with which Shachtman moved from elaborating labor party tactics to supporting maneuvers in the Democratic Party suggests the complexity of a labor party strategy for Marxists. When labor was mobilized against capital, as it was during the strike waves of 1935–37, 1941, and 1943–46, the call for a labor party could give working people's economic radicalism a political channel. But when the union ranks were passive and the unions' main activity was maneuvering by their leaders, the call for a labor party could be used as a cloak for deals between union leaders and liberal politicians. Shachtman's ideas about a coming labor party in the late 1940s and early 1950s in practice facilitated his alignment behind labor Democrats.

In June 1950, North Korean troops crossed the thirty-eighth parallel and attacked South Korea. Before North Korea succeeded in uniting Korea under Communist rule, U.S. and allied troops under a United Nations flag arrived and turned the war into the biggest confrontation yet between the U.S. and Soviet blocs. The Korean War provided the impetus for massive rearmament in the United States and Western Europe, staved off a recession, and completed the division of most of the world into two armed camps. Many people thought that the third world war had begun. For a while, as U.S. troops pushed the North Koreans back to the Chinese border and U.S. commander Douglas MacArthur talked about dropping atomic bombs on Manchuria and pushing onward to Beijing, a world war did seem to be at hand. Only massive Chinese intervention ensured that the war would stay confined to the Korean peninsula and stop after three years and almost two million deaths.

Shachtman treated the war from the beginning as if it were the first act of the gathering third world war. In keeping with his past pronouncements, he condemned both sides. He rejected even "whispering the idea of support, however 'critical,' to American imperialism." When Chinese troops inflicted a humiliating defeat on the United States in North Korea in December 1950, he said that the United States should withdraw its troops.[60] But as the war dragged on, his outlook changed. He put new limits on the ways in which he was willing to oppose the war and discovered new circumstances under which he would be willing to support it.

By the time the Korean War broke out, everything in the climate of Shachtman's organization encouraged its members to see Communism as the world's greatest evil—an "obsession," he admitted later, "that sometimes warped our judgment."[61] The horrors of capitalism gradually paled in his oratory, while his speeches stirred his followers again and again by reminding them of comrades in other countries who had been murdered by

Stalinists. The roll call of martyrs became one of the standard set pieces of his speeches.

He used it to greatest effect in his famous debate in March 1950, a few weeks before the Korean War began, against Earl Browder. Browder had been demoted from Communist Party general secretary in 1945 and then expelled from the party, but he still defended Communism and the Soviet Union. An audience of 1,200 listened to Shachtman as he intoned the list of those whose blood Browder's movement had on its hands. Shachtman asked,

> Suppose Browder's Stalino-socialists were successful in establishing their socialism in this country . . . who would be the first to go? Who would be the first to get the GPU bullet in the base of his skull? Who would be the first to be denounced in the obituary articles as a counter-revolutionary mad dog, a viper, a restorationist, a wrecker? . . .
>
> Rajk was the general secretary of the Hungarian Communist Party, and was shot, or hanged, or garotted. Kostow was the general secretary of the Bulgarian Communist Party. And when I thought of what happened to them, I thought of the former secretary of the American Communist Party, and I said to myself: There—there but for an accident of geography sits a corpse![62]

Shachtman spun around and pointed at Browder as he shouted his last line. Browder's face turned ashen.[63]

In theory, the horror of Stalinism that Shachtman instilled in his followers was an argument for socialism. During the Second World War, he had explained that since Nazism was a product of capitalism in crisis, capitalist governments could not be counted on to destroy fascism. Now he taught his followers that capitalism could only feed the Stalinist evil, and only the working class could extirpate it. His anti-Stalinism no more implied support for the U.S. war effort in 1950 than his anti-fascism had implied support for the U.S. war effort in 1941.

But neither Shachtman nor his followers could help seeing that socialist forces were weak, and Stalinism was winning power in country after country. He began to whisper, then speak aloud a new thought: Although socialists should not support capitalist forces, socialists should stand out of the way while capitalist democracies held back Stalinism and allowed socialists to gather strength. This thought was foreshadowed in a resolution for the 1951 Independent Socialist convention. Soon afterwards, Shachtman expressed it in the *New International* so bluntly that his opposition to the war—in theory to the coming third world war, but also to the war in progress—became conditional and qualified.

The U.S. working class "identifies national defense essentially with its own class interests: with the preservation of its organizations, its relatively high standard of living, its hard-won democratic rights," he said. U.S. victory would probably preserve some degree of democracy and some rights for democratic socialists. Communist victory would not. "All the things that the working class identifies with national defense *are* actually threatened by Stalinism," he said. "The only greater disaster that humanity could suffer than the war itself . . . would be the victory of Stalinism as the outcome of the war." He added, "We socialists are at one with the working class in wishing to resist this threat and overcome it."

Shachtman therefore argued for *"transforming the imperialist war into a democratic war."* He called for breaking off alliances with dictators like South Korea's Syngman Rhee and promising to "abide rigidly by the democratic principle of the right of self-determination of all nations." (Shachtman apparently forgot that Woodrow Wilson had made this promise long before, to no effect.) He called for a program of aid to the third world like the $13 billion package proposed not long before by Walter Reuther. These measures alone would "virtually overnight alter the attitudes and political conduct of tens of millions," he said. They would either postpone the outbreak of a third world war or ensure that the United States and democracy would win it.

Given these policy changes—ending support for dictators, giving aid to the third world, and respecting the right of self-determination—Shachtman was willing to support the war. He did not expect these policies from *"this or any other capitalist regime."*[64] But he proposed that Independent Socialists support in war any labor government that adopted a democratic foreign policy, even if it was not a socialist government. Hal Draper pointed out that the British Labour government also had troops in Korea: The group could hardly oppose the U.S. war in Korea while supporting Britain's. He prevailed on other leaders to say that they would support a nonsocialist labor government in war only if it followed "a genuinely democratic course in foreign and domestic policy which is not in fact subordinated to the interests of capitalism and imperialism." Shachtman voted against even this qualification.[65]

Since Shachtman was isolated among Independent Socialists in his new position and hardly ventured to defend it, it is difficult to say exactly what he meant in 1951. But he probably did want the League to support the British Labour government in Korea in some way. Two factors would have pushed him in this direction. The Korean War was backed by Labour left-wingers to whom he felt close, people who had broken with the Trotskyist-led Socialist Fellowship over Korea. He also saw the Labour government as a force for peace in Korea, particularly since a visit to the United States by British Prime Minister Clement Attlee at the end of 1950 was widely credited (at least in Britain) with persuading Truman not to invade China. Shachtman did not know that in May 1951 the Labour government secretly pledged to support the United States in the event of war with China.

Shachtman still said that as long as there was no labor government in the United States he refused to give U.S. authorities his *"political confidence, to support their policies, to take responsibility"* for their war in Korea. He said that people would not fight for democracy under U.S. leadership. They knew too well that U.S. victory, especially in Asia, meant dictatorships, poverty, and subservience for their countries. Koreans in particular would never mobilize to support Rhee's regime. In South Korean elections, as in North Korean elections, the government won by having dissidents "beaten to a pulp, imprisoned, murdered on their own doorsteps or otherwise discouraged from running." As a result, the U.S. government had no feasible political strategy against Stalinism. Its purely military policy was futile: North Korea was safe from military destruction as long as Mao's China stood behind it, and no sane person would risk sending U.S. troops into China. The United States was "caught on the hook of the Korean adventure and does not know how to wiggle off it."[66]

Yet while Shachtman criticized U.S. rulers' policies in Korea, he began to set limits on the ways he would oppose U.S. wars. He stopped calling on the United States to get out of Korea. He rejected any peace with Stalinists that involved acceptance of their conquests. "Labor and socialism CANNOT 'coexist peacefully' with Stalinism in the same world," Independent Socialists said. They condemned any call for peace that accepted Stalinism's survival. Shachtman said in the *New International* that socialists should not take any action during a U.S. war against Stalinism, even a capitalist war, that "would clearly 'imperil the military position of the government.'"[67] He questioned the idea of going on strike in a vital war industry—a reservation he had strongly resisted when Reuther raised it in the United Auto Workers in 1944.

Other Independent Socialist leaders were upset by this passage from Shachtman's article. To some extent they refused to accept Shachtman's new ideas, as when Draper successfully resisted Shachtman's apparent intention to support British Labour's role in Korea. To some extent they tried to deny the implications of Shachtman's argument, as when Gordon Haskell wrote a letter to the *New International* in which he assured its readers that Shachtman was not proposing any degree of support to the U.S. government. Yet to some extent Independent Socialists seemed to go along with Shachtman's argument, as when they said officially in 1954 that they would not do anything before or during war with the Soviet Union "in any way or degree to facilitate [a Soviet] victory."[68]

Draper tried to clarify the issues at stake with a series of articles on "revolutionary defeatism," the old principle that communists should fight against war and capitalism even by means (e.g., strikes in vital industries) that might risk their own country's defeat. Draper suggested that the idea of "defeatism" had always been confused and confusing and that Shachtman was turning its ambiguities upside down in a way that undermined opposition to U.S. wars. The idea was controversial when Lenin first put it forward during the Russo-Japanese War of 1904–1905. Trotsky and Luxemburg opposed it during the First World War on the grounds that socialists should prefer the war to end without victory or defeat for any of the capitalist powers. Trotskyists reaffirmed Lenin's "defeatism" in the 1930s, using it alongside the call for peace and equating it with German Communist Karl Liebknecht's slogan, "The chief enemy of the people is in its own country."

Draper may have intended to clear up the confusion that Shachtman had sown, but he did not refute the specific tactical points that Shachtman had made. On the contrary: Everything Shachtman said about not helping the other side to victory was "absolutely correct," Draper said, and "*should have held good in 1914.*"[69]

The Korean War faced Shachtman with the hypothetical danger he had seen in Finland in 1940: a Stalinist war of expansion that provoked an imperialist response. He saw that a North Korean conquest of the South in 1950, like a Soviet conquest of Finland in 1940, would have been a setback for socialism, not an advance. Socialists' task was to organize working-class resistance to Stalinist rule, not to aid Stalinist victory. But when the United States responded to North Korea with military force, it threatened not only Communist expansion in Korea but the newly victorious Chinese revolution, just as British and French intervention on Finland's side in 1940 could have threatened the Soviet Union. In 1940, Shachtman's response was ambiguous. In 1950, he seemed to decide that opposing Western intervention could not be allowed to interfere with opposing Communist victory.

With his 1951 articles in the *New International*, Shachtman qualified his responsibility to resist U.S. power in Asia by conjuring up an even greater danger: not just a Stalinist victory in Korea but a Stalinist victory in the United States and the consequent destruction of working-class organizations, freedoms, and living standards. But he never explained concretely how Stalinism could win power in the United States. He had dismissed the danger of Stalinists coming to power in France in 1946 and 1947; he could have dismissed (with as much justification) the danger of Stalinism in the United States, whether through Soviet occupation of North America or any other means. To speculate about such "victories" in the age of nuclear weapons would have been mind-boggling.

The *New International* looked back on the Korean War in 1954 and said that it had been not only "barbaric" but "futile." "The war was fought, the land desolated, the economy destroyed, the mass graves and the unknown graves filled, the blood of the maimed and wounded drained, for nothing."[70] Yet Shachtman had begun to say, in veiled language, that preventing Communist victory did accomplish something. Although he did not trust the U.S. government to promote democracy in the third world, he had begun to rely on U.S. power as a shield behind which democracy—capitalist democracy, since he no longer saw socialism as a realistic goal for the third world—could be fought for.

Nothing that Shachtman said during the Korean War amounted to open reliance on U.S. power. Past radical impulses still held him and his movement back. But the same issue was bound to face them again. The victory of the Chinese revolution in 1949 gave new strength to the Vietnamese revolution, enabling the Vietminh to occupy the mountainous northern region near the Chinese border. The Soviet Union finally recognized Ho Chi Minh's government. These stronger ties to China and the USSR helped convince Independent Socialists to give up their earlier support for the Vietminh. In 1954 they resolved to oppose the Vietminh as a "power instrument of Stalinist imperialism."[71] A decade later in Vietnam Shachtman would have to face another U.S. intervention against another potential Communist victory—and make a clearer choice.

Stalin's death, the end of the Korean War, and the East German workers' rising in 1953 "pierced the gloom" of the Cold War. Shachtman greeted the East German rising as the broadest movement ever against Communism. He pointed out that workers' one demand on their rulers was, "Disappear!" He speculated, in an excess of optimism, that the revolt was led by a powerful underground revolutionary organization.[72]

World war was less likely in the mid-1950s, he said, because both the United States and the USSR were weaker. The drama of revolt and repression in East Germany, which confirmed that Soviet expansion in Europe had come to a halt, supported his hypothesis. So did the refusal of ex-colonial countries such as India and Indonesia to line up with either superpower. Prospects for building a left-wing, democratic socialist movement began to look brighter. A new generation of young radicals began gathering around the Independent Socialists.

Julie Jacobson had left his job as a machinist at General Electric in the late 1940s to take charge of organizing a new youth group to replace the group that had dissolved in 1941 when the Workers Party sent everybody it could into factories. Over Shachtman's objections, Jacobson decided to look to the campuses to find a new generation of young radicals. Though radical students were hard to find at first in the depths of McCarthyism, by the early 1950s his Socialist Youth League had members in about a dozen cities and universities. It inspired such groups as the New York Student Federation Against War and the Politics Club at the University of Chicago.[73] At the height of the Korean War, it organized campus demonstrations against U.S. support for Spanish dictator Francisco Franco.

The youthful radicalism of Jacobson's recruits helped make Shachtman's movement an inhospitable place for members like Ernest McKinney and Irving Howe, who welcomed Shachtman's reservations about opposing the Korean War and wanted to take them further. McKinney left the group in 1950. Howe, who had resigned from the *Labor Action* editorial board in 1947 and begun writing for *Commentary, Partisan Review,* and *Time,* left in October 1952 along with longtime leader Stanley Plastrik. Howe and Plastrik said that the Independent Socialist League was torn between its Trotskyist roots and "a new view of American socialism." They said that it was time to give up the idea of a third camp and join the "Western world" in its fight against Stalinism.[74]

Manny Geltman resigned soon after Howe and Plastrik, partly because he felt that Shachtman had failed to defend him when he suggested that the League reconsider its attitude toward the Democratic Party. When Howe, Plastrik, and Geltman founded a new socialist magazine called (at Lewis Coser's suggestion) *Dissent* in February 1954, Shachtman would have nothing to do with it. For people who had "deserted the movement and its ideas," he said, "I feel only contempt."[75]

His movement remained a pole of attraction for people who hated and opposed the Cold War, such as several dozen young people who broke with the Socialist Party in 1952 over its support for the Korean War. Mike Harrington was the outstanding member of this new generation of Shachtman disciples. Like many of his young cohorts, Harrington came from a background that was different from that of most of Shachtman's older followers. The son of middle-class Irish parents, he had come to radicalism by way of Bohemia (he left his native St. Louis to be a poet in Greenwich Village) and the Catholic Church, which even after he broke with it contributed a deeply felt pacifism and a certain spiritual anguish to his politics. But these differences in background did not stop Harrington from drawing steadily closer to Shachtman, whose oratory and socialist erudition captivated him. In 1954, Harrington's followers came together with the young people Jacobson had recruited to form the Young Socialist League.

The Young Socialists' activism and lively discussion leavened the atmosphere of retreat and discouragement that had taken hold of Shachtman's followers. Young Socialists had the freedom, and the spirit, to challenge ideas that had become shibboleths among adult Independent Socialists: Two

Young Socialists even argued in 1954 that democratic socialists should support the victory of the Communist-led Vietminh in Vietnam. Young Socialists' culture also contrasted strikingly with that of Shachtman's older followers. One student recruited at Antioch College recalled that Young Socialists wore

> jeans, long hair, sandals, berets. We believed in sex. We knew the Beat poets. We were interested in some other way of life, some other values, some other symbols besides those we had grown up with.[76]

The Young Socialists' growth and energy raised hopes that the left-wing socialist current that came together around Shachtman's new worldview in the early 1950s could survive and grow. But several factors combined to undermine these hopes. The group was struggling against a still powerful McCarthyism, which continued to isolate them. Shachtman and many of his older followers were suffering from the destruction of their old working-class communities and their old working-class left; their level of energy and commitment was often low. His own closest personal connection to the old world of the immigrant working class snapped when his father died of cancer in December 1948.[77] His strategy, which now emphasized holding on in the unions and working patiently for a labor party, did not necessarily make his older followers feel the compelling importance of building a marginal socialist group.

The Independent Socialist League was under siege in the 1950s by a hostile outside world. It spent the whole decade of its existence fighting inclusion on the attorney general's list of subversive organizations. The State Department refused to give Shachtman a passport until the Justice Department had taken his organization off the list; in a Kafkaesque twist, the Justice Department refused even to say when it would hold a hearing. As members of an organization on the list, Independent Socialists were liable to dishonorable discharges from the armed forces. The FBI went through the League's wastebaskets at night.[78]

Shachtman drifted toward a less active role in the embattled Independent Socialist leadership, particularly after the heart attack he had in 1951. His relationship with Edith Harvey, who had been his companion through many of his years as a Trotskyist, came apart. She parted from him in a spirit of bitterness, taking their twelve-year-old son, Michael, with her to California. Shachtman saw his son only once after the separation, when Michael came to hear his father speak in California a few years later. Although the two had a warm reunion in Shachtman's hotel room and planned another get-together, Michael never saw his father again. Shachtman's letters and gifts were sent back unopened. Several years later Glotzer, having heard that Michael had married and had children, greeted Shachtman, "'Hello grandpa.'"

Shachtman "went very grim for a minute, didn't say a word," Glotzer remembered.[79]

After separating from Harvey in 1951, Shachtman moved in with Yetta Barsh in Brooklyn. Unlike Harvey, Barsh was an active Independent Socialist, hardworking and loyal, a former member of Shachtman's youth group. She was married to Natie Gould, the youth group's leader, before the Second World War, but their marriage broke up soon after Gould came home from the army. She and Shachtman had grown closer during the time she spent in the Workers Party office after the war. When she and Shachtman married, Glotzer and his wife, Maggie, were the only witnesses.[80] Barsh would be Shachtman's companion for the rest of his life.

In 1954 the two of them left New York, the city where the office was and where he had lived most of his life, for the Long Island suburb of Floral Park. He built all the cabinets and bookshelves in his new house and started a garden of rare orchids, where young followers would come and garden with him. He began repairing radios and stereo systems, partly as a hobby, partly as a business. Then he and Barsh founded a Long Playing Record Society to market high-quality records. Pleased with his marriage, he told Herman Benson, "I was never happier in my life." But he no longer spoke for the organization or wrote for the *New International* as much as he had before. By the early 1950s, he "rarely showed up at the office before eleven in the morning—and often not before two, or just not at all."[81]

Shachtman had attacked Jim Cannon for a similar discouraged withdrawal twenty years earlier. Now the Independent Socialists running the office hung back from open criticism but felt a certain estrangement just the same. The ranks of Independent Socialist leaders thinned. Joe Carter "disappeared from the face of the earth," dropped out of the organization, and drifted as a clerk from one bookstore to the next. Natie Gould had a nervous breakdown. Marty Abern died from a heart attack he had on a bus in April 1949.[82] McKinney, Geltman, Plastrik, and Howe were gone.

Three people took on most of the work of running the Independent Socialist League in the 1950s: Draper, who took over *Labor Action* in 1949; Gordon Haskell, who moved from San Francisco to New York to run the office that same year; and Julius Jacobson, who took over the *New International* in 1952. When *Labor Action* was mailed out each week, there were often only half a dozen people sitting around the table stuffing the envelopes.[83]

All three people putting in the longest hours for the group felt a certain distance from Shachtman in the early 1950s. Draper resisted Shachtman's slide toward the Democratic Party. Haskell resisted Shachtman's support for anti-Communism in the unions. There were also personal tensions. Draper and Haskell were hard-working, dedicated people, constantly behind in their wages, but neither was comfortable with Shachtman's teasing and roughhousing. Haskell was "too prickly" and bridled at Shachtman's profanity. The one time Shachtman tried to pinch Haskell's cheeks in his usual rough gesture of affection, Haskell told him to "knock it off." "The old women in Bulgaria used to do that to me when I was a kid," Haskell said. "I didn't like it then, and I certainly won't stand for it now."[84]

Al Glotzer and Herman Benson moved back to New York from Los Angeles and Detroit in 1949 to help hold the group together. Benson, the group's New York organizer, supported himself by operating a machine shop along with Jacobson. Glotzer, the only survivor besides Shachtman of the old Communist Party and Communist League days, was finding more work as a court reporter. Though some Independent Socialists saw Glotzer as Shachtman's alter ego, the two men's friendship had soured again in the late 1940s. Even though the breach was healed once more after Glotzer came back to New York, he remembered that his relations with Shachtman were "not quite like they were in the earlier years of my growing up."[85]

Independent Socialist leaders' difficulties in the early 1950s reflected certain contradictions between Shachtman's new, non-revolutionary perspective and their lingering Leninist self-conception. Lenin once said, 'Anybody who accepts or rejects the Bolshevik party organization independently of whether or not we live at a time of proletarian revolution has completely misunderstood it." Shachtman too had always derived the kind of organization he wanted from what he wanted it for. Once he turned away from the idea of revolution in the United States, he stopped trying to create an "all-inclusive revolutionary party." The Workers Party could never have become a real party, Shachtman and Draper said in 1949.[86]

The organization that Independent Socialists needed in this isolating time, Shachtman said, was not an "all-inclusive" group but a tight, supportive one. Socialists who understood that their place was in the democratic labor movement and appreciated the dangers of Stalinism needed to stick together. Just as Bolsheviks until 1912 saw themselves as a faction in the larger social democratic movement and Trotskyists until 1933 saw themselves as a faction in the larger Communist movement, Shachtman's followers now had to see themselves as a faction in a larger labor movement, he said. Independent Socialists would hold together through firmer adherence to "*our* ideas, *our* conceptions, *our* program."[87]

But Shachtman no longer tried to hold Independent Socialists to a Bolshevik standard of activism. He limited himself to the wistful hope that the "best members" would "set the pace" for the rest.[88] In fact, the Independent Socialists who tried to set the pace for the rest in keeping a left-wing socialist group going would soon find that Shachtman no longer supported their efforts.

Notes

1. "The nightfall of capitalism," NI v 14 n 2 (Feb. 1948), 38; ISL 2nd convention, "Social forces, politics in the U.S." (July 1951), NI v 17 n 4 (July–Aug. 1951), 207 (also ISL bul [Apr. 1951], ISM v 11).
2. WP PC, "Tasks of the party in the present situation," WP bul v 2 n 9 (25 Sept. 1947), ISM v 8, 1727–28.
3. Shachtman, "Under the banner of Marxism" (misdated 19 Mar. 1949), WP bul v 4 n 2 (Jan. 1949), ISM v 10, 2086.
4. Shachtman, "Stalinism and the Marxist tradition," BR 87 (also NI v 13 n 4 [Apr. 1947]).
5. "Under the banner of Marxism," ISM v 10, 2087; ISL 1st convention, "Capitalism, Stalinism, and the war" (Mar. 1949) NI v 15 n 4 (Apr. 1949), 116 (also WP bul v 3 n 7 [23 Nov. 1948], ISM v 9; Shachtman, "The new exploitive system," LA v 18 n 19 (10 May 1954), 3.
6. WP PC, "Resolution—The struggle for the world today," WP bul v 3 n 7 (23 Nov. 1948), ISM v 9, 1951–52.
7. Ernest Mandel, *Late Capitalism*, 276, 191–92.
8. Shachtman, "Europe today" (1948), MSC b 40 f 8 (r 3389).
9. ISL 1st convention, "Capitalism, Stalinism, and the war" (Mar. 1949), NI v 15 n 4 (Apr. 1949), 122–23 (also WP bul v 3 n 7 [23 Nov. 1948], ISM v 9).
10. "Is Russia a socialist community?" NI v 16 n 3 (May–June 1950), 156; Shachtman, "Socialist policy and the war," NI v 17 n 4 (July–Aug. 1951), 200.
11. Shachtman, "An epigone of Trotsky," NI v 10 n 8 (Aug. 1944), 268; Shachtman, "The end of socialism," BR 248 (also NI v 20 n 2 [Mar.–Apr. 1954]).
12. Shachtman, "The meaning of the new Yugoslavian provisional government," LA v 8 n 1 (3 Jan. 1944), 4; WP 4th convention, "Resolution on the international scene" (June 1946), NI v 13 n 4 (Apr. 1947), 120 (also WP bul v 1 n 11 [27 Apr. 1946], ISM v 6); "Trieste—city between two worlds," NI v 12 n 10 (Dec. 1946).
13. Shachtman, "Tito versus Stalin" (9 July 1948), NI v 14 n 6 (Aug. 1948), 176, 172; Shachtman to M. Haston (5 Aug. 1948), MSC b 32 f 15 (r 3384) also "Letters to comrades in Europe," WP bul v 3 n 6 [10 Nov. 1948], ISM v 9).
14. "Capitalism, Stalinism, and the war," NI v 15 n 4, 123; Shachtman to M. Haston (5 Aug. 1948), MSC b 32 f 15 (r 3384).
15. Interview with Draper (13 Feb. 1989), s 4; "Capitalism, Stalinism, and the war," NI v 15 n 4, 123.
16. FI 1st congress, "The war in the Far East" (3 Sept. 1938), *Documents of the Fourth International*, 232; Shachtman, "The program of Stalinist imperialism," BR 131 (also NI v 9 n 9 [Oct. 1943]); WP PC, "Situation in China," WP bul v 1 n 3 (8 Jan. 1946), ISM v 5, 811; "Resolution on the international scene," NI v 13 n 4, 123.
17. WP PC (23 Nov. 1948), MSC b 13 f 3 (r 3367); Shachtman to Gilbert (29 Dec. 1949), MSC b 29 f 6 (r 3378); "China policy at work," NI v 16 n 1 (Jan–Feb. 1950), 8.
18. WP PC (23 Nov. 1948), MSC b 13 f 3 (r 3367).
19. "The power of the third camp," NI v 20 n 4, 198; Shachtman, "Foreword" (April 1967), in Leon Trotsky, *Problems of the Chinese Revolution*, vii, xiii.

20. Trotsky *Problems of the Chinese Revolution*, x, xv; Shachtman, "The new exploitive system," LA v 18 n 19 (10 May 1954), 3.
21. Michael Löwy, *The Politics of Combined and Uneven Development*, 112–13, 115.
22. ISL 1st convention, "Capitalism, Stalinism, and the war" (Mar. 1949), NI v 15 n 4 (Apr. 1949), 117–18 (also WP bul v 3 n 7 [23 Nov. 1948], ISM v 9).
23. *Murba (Proletariat)* (6 Sept. and 15 Oct. 1948), cited in George Kahin, *Nationalism and Revolution in Indonesia*, 267 n, 317.
24. Rader, "Tanmalaka," LA v 13 n 3 (17 Jan. 1949), 4; Rader to LA, LA v 13 n 7 (14 Feb. 1949), 2, 4; "On Southeast Asian Regional Union," LA v 13 n 6 (7 Feb. 1949), 3; Martinson, "Socialist policy in Indonesia," WP bul v 4 n 6 (17 Mar. 1949), ISM v 10, 2344–46; Haskell to ISL PC (17 June 1949), MSC b 14 f 3 (r 3369).
25. Shachtman, "Leon Trotsky, 1879–1940," NI v 16 n 5 (Sept.–Oct. 1950), 261; Shachtman, "Socialist policy and the war," NI v 17 n 4 (July–Aug. 1951), 197–98; ISL PC, "Independent socialism and the third world war," ISL bul (Apr. 1951), ISM v 11, 2486–88.
26. Shachtman, "The end of socialism," BR 248 (also NI v 20 n 2 [Mar.–Apr. 1954]); NI v 20 n 4 (July–Aug. 1954), 179 (line omitted in BR); BR 284–85 (also NI v 20 n 4).
27. Max Shachtman and Hal Draper, *Two Views of the Cuban Invasion*, 5; Kahn, "Max Shachtman," NA v 10 n 22 (15 Nov. 1972), 5.
28. Abern, Glotzer and Shachtman, "The situation in the American opposition: prospect and retrospect" (4 June 1932), TA 17238; Shachtman, *The Fight for Socialism*, 140–41, 145.
29. Shachtman, "Reflections on a decade past," NI v 16 n 3 (May–June 1950), 143 (wording changed in BR 33).
30. Communist International 4th congress, "Theses on Comintern tactics" (1922), *Theses, Resolutions and Manifestos of the First Four Congresses of the Third International*, 399.
31. Anthony Eden, *Memoirs: Full Circle*, 5, cited in Ralph Miliband, *Parliamentary Socialism*, 303.
32. "Theses on Comintern tactics," 399
33. WP PC to Socialist Youth League National Bureau (1 Feb. 1949), ISM v 10, 2252. Shachtman and Draper were assigned to draft this letter jointly.
34. Interview with Haskell (8 July 1949), s 3.
35. Shachtman, "Under the banner of Marxism" (misdated 19 Mar. 1949), WP bul v 4 n 1 (Jan. 1949), ISM v 10, 2144, 2168–69, 2186–87 (also Shachtman, "Soviets and the Constituent Assembly," NI v 15 n 7 [Sept. 1949], 221).
36. "Under the banner of Marxism," ISM v 10, 2144–45, 2130, 2188.
37. Shachtman, "Reflections on a decade past," BR 28 (also NI v 16 n 3 [May–June 1950]).
38. Shachtman, "Tug-of-war in Europe," LA v 12 n 29 (19 July 1948), 4; ISL PC (8, 15 Oct. 1949), MSC b 14 f 6 (r 3369).
39. Shachtman, "Aspects of the British Labour government," NI v 17 n 1 (Jan.–Feb. 1951), 12, 18.
40. "Aspects of the British Labour government," NI v 17 n 1, 13, 12, 16–18. Draper remembered that Shachtman resisted "in a grumbling fashion" and "dragged his feet" when Draper put forward in 1948 the idea that social democracy could make capitalism more like Stalinism and carry out a "'bureaucratic-collectivization' of capitalism." Shachtman would rarely use the

idea, although he allowed the ISL to adopt it in 1949. Interview with Draper (13 Feb. 1989), s 4; ISL 1st convention, "Capitalism, Stalinism, and the war" (Mar. 1949), NI v 15 n 4 (Apr. 1949), 119 (also WP bul v 3 n 7 [23 Nov. 1948], ISM v 9).

41. "Aspects of the British Labour government," NI v 17 n 1, 5, 12, 16; ISL PC (8, 15 Oct. 1949), MSC b 14 f 6 (r 3369).

42. "May Labor win!" LA v 14 n 7 (13 Feb. 1950), 3; ISL PC, "The meaning of the British Labor government," ISL bul (Apr. 1951), ISM v 11, 2492, 2493, 2499–2500 (also in LA v 15 n 30 [23 July 1950]).

43. Interview with Benson (6 Apr. 1989), s 3; Benson, "Situation in the UAW" (18 Aug. 1949) and ISL PC (15 Aug. and 6 Sept. 1949), MSC b 14 f 5 (r 3369).

44. WP PC, "Trade union resolution," WP bul v 4 n 4 (1 Mar. 1949), ISM v 10, 2299.

45. Shachtman, "The nightfall of capitalism," NI v 14 n 2 (Feb. 1948), 40; Shachtman, "Reflections on a decade past," BR 26 (also NI v 16 n 3 [May–June 1950]); ISL 1st convention, "Capitalism, Stalinism, and the war" (Mar. 1949), NI v 15 n 4 (Apr. 1949), 116, 126 (also WP bul v 3 n 7 [23 Nov. 1948], ISM v 9); "Resolution—The situation in the United States," ISM v 9, 1871–72.

46. "Reflections on a decade past," BR 33; Shachtman, "A blow at democracy," LA v 13 n 43 (24 Oct. 1949); ISL NC (31 Dec. 1949–1 Jan. 1950), MSC b 14 f 7 (r 3369); Haskell, "A third camp policy in the unions," WP bul v 3 n 8 (13 Dec. 1948), ISM v 9, 1983; WP 5th convention (24–27 Mar. 1949), MSC b 14 f 1 (r 3368).

47. Shachtman, "A left wing of the labor movement?," BR 305–6, 304, 309 (also NI v 15 n 7 [Sept. 1949]).

48. ISL PC, "The split in the CIO" (12 Nov. 1949), MSC b 14 f 6 (r 3369); "Basic issues in the CIO split," LA v 13 n 43 (24 Oct. 1949), 1.

49. ISL San Francisco branch, "Resolution on the CIO" (28 Oct. 1949), MSC b 14 f 6 (r 3369); interview with Haskell (8 July 1989), s 3; interview with Benson (6 Apr. 1989), s 3.

50. ISL NC (31 Dec. 1949–1 Jan. 1950), MSC b 14 f 7 (r 3369).

51. Shachtman, "It was a victory, but—," LA v 14 n 24 (12 June 1950), 6.

52. ISL PC, "The unions in a period of mobilization" (June 1951), ISM v 18, 1050, 1049, 1051–52, 1054–55; Shachtman, "Why labor supports Democrats," NI v 18 n 4 (July–Aug. 1952), 181.

53. Gould and Shachtman, "Resolution—The situation in the United States" (14 Sept. 1948), WP bul v 3 n 5 (21 Sept. 1948), ISM v 9, 1868–70; "Reflections on a decade past," BR 26.

54. Shachtman, "Under the banner of Marxism" (misdated 19 Mar. 1949), WP bul v 4 n 2 (Jan. 1949), ISM v 10, 2098; interview with Draper (17 Feb. 1989), s 7.

55. Draper, Shachtman, and Gould, "Resolution—The situation in the US," WP bul v 3 n 9 (14 Jan. 1949), ISM v 9, 2040–41, 2045–46.

56. ISL PC, "Labor party perspectives" (1 Aug. 1949), MSC b 14 f 5 (r 3369); ISL PC (6 Sept. 1949 [misdated 1959]), MSC b 14 f 5 (r 3369).

57. ISL PC (29 Oct., 17 Nov., and 2, 8, 12 Dec. 1949), MSC b 14 f 6 (microfilm incomplete).

58. Benson and Shachtman, "Motions on political action," ISL bul v 1 n 2 (Jan. 1950), ISM v 11, 2424; ISL 3rd convention, "Growth of American conservatism," NI v 20 n 4 (July–Aug. 1954), 220 (also ISL bul [May 1954], ISM v 12).

59. Shachtman, "Why labor supports Democrats," NI v 18 n 4 (July–Aug. 1952), 180, 186.

60. Shachtman to McKinney (5 May 1948), MSC b 30 f 7 (r 3380); Shachtman, "U.S. disaster in Korea," LA v 14 n 51 (18 Dec. 1950), 8.
61. Michael Harrington, *Fragments of the Century*, 206–7.
62. "Is Russia a socialist community?" NI v 16 n 3 (May–June 1950), 155, 167.
63. Irving Howe, *A Margin of Hope*, 107.
64. Shachtman, "Socialist policy and the war," NI v 17 n 4 (July–Aug. 1951), 204–6, 200; "Socialist policy and the war," NI v 17 n 3 (May–June 1951), 171–73. Shachtman claimed, on weak grounds, that Lenin supported the idea of "transforming the imperialist war into a democratic war" for a few months after March 1917.
65. Shachtman, "For a democratic foreign policy!" LA v 17 n 18 (4 May 1953), 6; ISL PC, "Independent socialism and the third world war," ISL bul (Apr. 1951), ISM v 11, 2486–88 (also in LA v 15 n 30 [23 July 1950]); interview with Draper (17 Feb. 1989), s 7; Draper to Drucker (10 July 1989).
66. "Socialist policy and the war," NI v 17 n 4, 204, 202; Shachtman, "An open letter to Dean Acheson" (May 1952), MSC b 39 f 18 (not microfilmed) (originally in LA v 15 n 11 [12 Mar. 1951]); "Aftermath of the Korean truce," NI v 19 n 4, 183–84.
67. Shachtman, "'Co-existence' as a catchphrase," NI v 21 n 1 (Spring 1955), 26–27; "Independent socialism and the third world war," ISM v 11, 2482, 2485; "Socialist policy and the war," NI v 17 n 4, 205.
68. Haskell to NI, NI v 17 n 5 (Sept.–Oct. 1951), 295; ISL 3rd convention, "The power of the third camp," NI v 20 n 3 (May–June 1954), 200 (also ISL bul [July 1954], ISM v 12).
69. IS, *War and the 4th International*, 26; Draper, "The myth of Lenin's defeatism," NI v 20 n 1 (Jan.–Feb. 1954), 55–56.
70. "Aftermath of the Korean truce," NI v 19 n 4, 176–78.
71. "The power of the third camp," NI v 20 n 4, 196–97.
72. Interview with Haskell (8 July 1989), s 5; Shachtman, "Who were the leaders of the East German uprising" (2 July 1953), LA v 17 n 28 (13 July 1953), 6–7.
73. Jacobson to Drucker (10 Sept. 1992), 2–4.
74. Howe, *A Margin of Hope*, 111; Glotzer to Drucker (6 Jan. 1990), 5; Howe and Plastrik, "Statement of resignation from the ISL" (12 Oct. 1952), ISL bul (Jan. 1953), ISM v 11, 2538–39 (also MSC b 15 f 8 [r 3369]).
75. Interview with Geltman (22 Mar. 1989), s 3; Shachtman to Coser (9 Mar. 1954), MSC b 28 f 30 (r 3377).
76. Barnes and Gale, "Socialist policy for the war in Indochina," YSL bul v 1 n 1 (15 May 1954), ISM v 23, 304; interview with Betty Denitch (6 Aug. 1984), in Maurice Isserman, *If I Had a Hammer*, 60.
77. New York Health Dept. Bureau of Vital Records, Deaths (1948).
78. Interview with Harrington by Friend and Hacker (19 Aug. 1988), s 1; interview with Glotzer (28 Mar. 1949), s 7.
79. Interview with Glotzer (4 Apr. 1989), s 7; Haskell, "Max Shachtman," 7 (unpublished ms).
80. Interview with Glotzer (4 Apr. 1989), s 7, 1. Shachtman's last encounter with his son probably took place during his 1955 tour to California, when Michael was sixteen (see LA v 19).
81. Interview with Harrington by Friend and Hacker (19 Aug. 1988), s 1; interview with Geltman (22 Mar. 1989), s 1, 4; Haskell, "Max Shachtman," 11–12; interview with Benson (6 Apr. 1989), s 5; interview with Glotzer (24 Mar. 1989), s 9; interview with Haskell (8 July 1989), s 2.

82. Interview with Glotzer (28 Mar. 1949), s 7; interview with Geltman (22 Mar. 1989), s 2; interview with Glotzer (24 Mar. 1989), s 3; Shachtman, "Martin Abern," LA v 13 n 19 (9 May 1949), 1; NI v 15 n 4 (Apr. 1949), 99.
83. Interview with Haskell (8 July 1989), s 2, 5; interview with Weir by Thompson (15 Aug. 1983), OHAL, tape 6, s 2.
84. Haskell, "Max Shachtman," 9.
85. Ibid., 12; Glotzer to Drucker (6 Jan. 1990), 4.
86. Georg Lukács, Lenin, 26; Draper, Shachtman, and Gould, "Resolution—The situation in the US," WP bul v 3 n 9 (14 Jan. 1949), ISM v 9, 2047.
87. Shachtman, "'Party' or 'propaganda group'?" WP bul v 3 n 4 (11 Aug. 1948), ISM v 9, 1852–55; Shachtman and Gould, "Resolution—The situation in the United States" (14 Sept. 1948), WP bul v 3 n 5 (21 Sept. 1948), ISM v 9, 1883.
88. "'Party' or 'propaganda group'?" ISM v 9, 1852–53.

8

To the Right

Major events of the mid-1950s, both international and domestic, lifted the spirits of Shachtman's beleaguered followers. Internationally, the danger of a third world war receded; ferment and uprisings in Eastern Europe gave new hope for anti-Stalinist revolutions; and Soviet leader Nikita Khrushchev's 1956 admissions about Stalin's crimes shook the world Communist movement. In the United States in 1955, the reunification of the Congress of Industrial Organizations with the American Federation of Labor cemented the strength of the union movement at its peak; and the civil rights movement cracked U.S. society's monolithic façade and made possible a new beginning for the left.

The Hungarian revolution of 1956 gave Shachtman hope that Stalinism had entered its decline and democratic socialism was beginning its resurgence. In the aftermath of the Hungarian revolt, Stalin's successor Nikita Khrushchev pushed forward with a program of "de-Stalinizing" the Soviet Union, restoring the rule of law, sharing the benefits of economic growth with workers, and trying to streamline and decentralize economic planning. Shachtman was convinced that Communist efforts at self-reform would fail. He said that no Communist leader could afford to ally with rank-and-file workers in a decisive confrontation with the bureaucracy; that decentralization without full democratization would destabilize the economy; and that trying to distribute political power more broadly would unleash conflicts that would force a reconcentration of power at the top.

Shachtman saw the democratization of U.S. society advancing more smoothly and swiftly. The union movement went from strength to strength: The mid-1950s were the high point for U.S. unionization levels. Independent Socialists hailed the 1955 reunification of the AFL and CIO, saying that it was based on acceptance of the CIO's principles. Although the AFL went into the merger with 64 percent of union members in its ranks to the CIO's 20 percent, AFL unions had adopted many of the CIO's structural innovations and organizing tactics.[1]

At the same time, U.S. democracy's most glaring failure, the segregation and disenfranchisement of African Americans in the South, was challenged directly and decisively. Shachtman was enthused about the civil rights movement from its beginning with the 1955 Montgomery bus boycott. He came to see civil rights activists as labor's key allies. He built his ties to the civil rights movement particularly through African-American socialist Bayard Rustin, who emerged by 1956 as a key northern organizer in support of Martin Luther King, Jr.'s southern movement.

De-Stalinization, the AFL-CIO merger, and the civil rights movement gave new prospects to the left. But they enabled Shachtman to glide further to the right. Though he would insist for the rest of his life that he had found the keys to Marxism in his era, he was recutting the keys as he went along. In the early 1950s he had spoken, written, and acted as a left-wing, though no longer revolutionary, socialist. By the late 1950s he said that he was looking for "an opening to the right." In the early 1960s he moved into the mainstream of U.S. social democracy.

Although the Independent Socialists announced in 1957 that the time of "triumphant Stalinist expansion" was over and "the resurgence of world socialism" had begun, Shachtman's new optimism had little in common with his old revolutionary dreams. Instead he felt that the working class now had leisure to regroup its forces and wend its way slowly, even circuitously, toward power. Socialists needed "*time*–time in which to persuade, to clarify, to mobilize, to assemble the largest and strongest possible host," he said. He wanted to build surely, guarding against the slightest compromise with the authoritarian wrong turns of the past. He said that Communism had "postponed the socialist agenda by perhaps a hundred years."[2]

He placed his hopes on a Fabian strategy, on preventing the spread of Stalinism and preserving democratic space in capitalist society until someday the working class would aspire again to power. He took heart from the fact that the disintegration of Stalinism seemed to be happening faster than the disintegration of capitalism. Marxism told Shachtman that "the fate of the world will not be decided in the Congo, in Egypt, in Brazil or even in India"—whose economies were too weak either to sustain capitalism or to create socialism—but in West Germany, Britain, and the United States. In these advanced capitalist countries Stalinism had been "utterly if not definitively crushed."[3] In West Germany, Britain, and several other countries, democratic socialist ideas had captured the imagination of masses of working people. In the United States, democratic socialists had survived McCarthyism and found an honorable if marginal niche in the unions.

Shachtman was confident that democratic socialism would reemerge as an alternative in the United States, thanks particularly to a spreading web of connections that his followers were weaving to trade union leaders. In the late 1940s and early 1950s, he had regretfully accepted that there was no longer an organized, left-leaning rank and file in the unions. He had accepted that the more progressive union officials would have to stand in for "the labor movement" until a new generation of activists grew up. By the late 1950s, he no longer talked regretfully about the old activists or hopefully about new ones. He treasured every follower who got a union staff job and every sign that he had influence on union leaders. He welcomed his followers' taking more staff jobs with the United Auto Workers.

Leaders of the old Workers Party Buffalo branch, such as Don Slaiman and Sammy Fishman, played a key role in Shachtmanites' rise first through the United Auto Workers, then in the national AFL-CIO. By the mid-1950s there was "a joke going around . . . that the best way to become a union bureaucrat was to join the Shachtmanites. . . . With a couple of articles to your credit in *Labor Action* you were a likely candidate to be appointed to UAW staff." Shachtman's followers took care that their politics were "carefully formulated" so that they would not "squander [their] first capital" in the unions. Herman Benson checked articles on the United Auto Workers that ran in *Labor Action* to make sure that nothing offensive to Walter Reuther appeared in the paper.[4]

In the 1940s, Shachtman had argued that if labor did not find an independent political voice, its gains of the Depression and war years could be lost. In fact, by the mid-1950s union strength was beginning to crumble behind the solid façade. Despite the apparent acceptance of the CIO's principles in the 1955 AFL-CIO merger, CIO "industrial" unions were adopting old AFL-style patterns of organization by craft in new guises, such as separate elections and seniority lists for different categories of workers. Following the 1957–58 recession, unions suffered defeats in the steel, railroad, electrical, and other industries. Unionization rates began to decline. But Independent Socialists now failed to see the danger and said, "What has been accomplished cannot be wiped out."[5] Shachtman's faith in the AFL-CIO continued to grow.

He used his followers' rising influence among AFL-CIO officials to promote his strategy for social change. As his influence increased, his strategy shifted. Although he kept to the premises he had adopted in the late 1940s and early 1950s, the practical conclusions he drew from them were different from— or even contrary to—the conclusions he had drawn before.

He still believed that socialists should be a loyal left wing in the democratic labor movement, for example, as he had since 1949. He held to his arguments for strengthening labor's position inside the Democratic Party, preparatory to splitting from the Democrats and creating a labor party. Now he added civil rights activists to his underground Democratic Party constituency. In order to strengthen labor and civil rights forces' clout among Democrats, he decided in 1957 never to oppose union-backed Democratic candidates. Then in 1961 he began advocating participation in Democratic Party organizations, encouraging his socialist followers to join Democratic clubs. He advocated "realignment": mobilizing a progressive network to claim sole ownership of the Democratic Party for the labor, civil rights, liberal, and peace movements and drive out pro-business, segregationist, and urban machine Democrats.

Similarly, Shachtman continued to argue that although socialists should oppose U.S.-backed right-wing dictators in the third world, they should do nothing to facilitate new Communist victories. But from veiled suggestions about preventing Communist victory in the Korean War he moved gradually, almost shamefacedly, in the 1960s toward willingness to rely on U.S. power in the fight against Stalinism. He expressed sympathy for the U.S.-backed Bay of Pigs invasion of Cuba in 1961, which he saw as the only hope for stopping the Castro regime's development toward a "totalitarian climax."

The socialist organization he had previously clung to, the Independent Socialist League, was a casualty of his evolution. The new possibilities he saw later in the 1950s roused him from his partial retreat from politics—and his acceptance of the League's continued existence. By 1957 he decided that the whole idea of organizing Marxists independently of the broader socialist movement had been a mistake. The Communist split from the Socialist Party in 1919 had been a mistake; the Trotskyist split from the Socialist Party in 1937 had been a mistake; the existence of the Workers Party and Independent Socialist League had been a mistake. Dividing socialists into "separate and hostile camps—reformist and revolutionary"—was a mistake. Any attempt to maintain a group that was "independent of the two main historically given movements—socialist and communist"—had been bound to end in political sterility. In 1958 Shachtman dissolved the League into the Socialist Party, the organization in which he would spend the rest of his life.[6]

He was helped in his projects by a new group of young socialists that began clustering around him. The youth group that formed in 1954 grew rapidly, particularly after it returned to the Socialist ranks in 1958. Although the weight Shachtman had gained, the hair he had lost, and his Cold War iconography made him remind young radicals of Nikita Khrushchev, he formed the same kind of close bond with some promising young radicals in the 1950s and early 1960s that he had in the 1930s. "In almost forty years," he said, "I have not seen or worked with a more devoted and enthusiastic group of young socialists."[7] With the acclaim in the early 1960s for his book on poverty, *The Other America*, Mike Harrington in particular became the best known defender of Shachtman's ideas.

But Shachtman's hold over some of his followers, particularly young followers, weakened in the late 1950s and early 1960s. Almost all of them had been recruited and trained, even into the early 1960s, based on some version of his old left-wing politics. About a third of the Young Socialist League refused to follow him into the Socialist Party. About half of the Socialist youth rejected his turn to the Democratic Party. The Young Socialist Alliance (linked to the Socialist Workers Party), the third-camp journal *New Politics,* and the Independent Socialist Clubs were all founded in these years, turning away from Shachtman's social democratic outlook toward the radical impulses of the 1960s.

Shachtman raged against the people who refused to follow his lead and carried on without them. By 1964 he believed that his movement was on the verge of a breakthrough to mass influence and credibility among Democratic Party elites. "The socialist movement," he said in an atypically mystical moment in 1955, *"lives in but is not of this world because the proletariat which is its bearer lives in but at the same time is not of this—that is, of the capitalist—world!"*[8] But by the mid-1960s he was finding a place—in the name of the proletariat—within this capitalist world. His social democratic worldview was beginning to harmonize with the United States of the New Deal, Cold War, and Great Society.

Soviet leader Nikita Khrushchev threw the world Communist movement into disarray in 1956 by admitting that the charges of massive killings, frame-ups, and repression under Stalin's rule had been true. The Hungarian uprising that erupted soon after Khrushchev's admissions, though crushed by Soviet tanks, confirmed Shachtman's faith in Stalinism's decline and democratic socialism's rise. It left heroic images behind of strikes and street battles, of soldiers handing their guns to workers, and of the democracy in action of workers' councils. Shachtman's young admirers "followed these events daily, hourly," feeling that "this was a real revolution in our times"—"our own."[9]

Shachtman saw that social dynamics inside the Soviet Union, as well as resistance by the peoples it dominated, was slowing Soviet rulers' expansionist momentum. Khrushchev pushed forward with "de-Stalinization" even after his leadership was shaken by the Hungarian revolt. In response, Shachtman developed and modified his theory of bureaucratic collectivism. He gave up earlier assumptions that the worst features of Stalin's rule were intrinsic to the system Stalin had created. He referred less to working people's condition under bureaucratic rule as "slavery" once he saw that their living standards and freedom to choose jobs were improving somewhat. But he continued to insist that all the major gains working people had gotten from the Russian Revolution had been lost under Stalin.

He made predictions about the limits to Khrushchev's reform program that Mikhail Gorbachev's later, more drastic, but more short-lived effort at reform largely bore out. He foresaw that a Communist leader who tried to soften single-party rule would face strong opposition from the Soviet military and bureaucracy, be unable or unwilling to devolve power to working-class institutions, and end by concentrating power in his own hands in his doomed attempt to reform the system from above.

Shachtman had no patience with European and U.S. analysts who saw Khrushchev's reforms as a smooth, one-way road to democracy. He saw de-Stalinization as an effort to resolve contradictions that would not go away: contradictions between the bureaucracy and the working class and between different groups of bureaucrats. The attempt to resolve these contradictions was bound to send the regime back and forth between decentralization and recentralization of the economy, appeasement and repression of the people, liberalization and tightening of social life, broadening and concentration of decision-making power. Shachtman predicted that with each swing of the pendulum the bureaucracy would be less able to make the mechanism of its rule work.

A new Soviet working class was emerging, a new force in Soviet society. The working class that had made the Russian Revolution had been decimated in the civil war of 1918–21. The working class that had begun stumbling to its feet in the 1920s had been knocked down again by Stalin's terror and by the mass of proletarianized peasants that had crowded in on it from all sides during the breakneck industrialization. But by the time Stalin died in 1953, the industrial work force, many times larger than ever before, was becoming more cohesive and conscious. It was "a new, vastly more numerous and compact, more self-confident and demanding mass than any working class in Stalin's days," Shachtman said.[10] Many of Khrushchev's reforms, such as efforts to put more and better consumer goods on the market and allow workers more freedom to change jobs, were attempts to appease this more demanding working class. As working people became aware of how much richer Soviet society was than it had been a generation before, they would recognize that Khrushchev was doling out to them only a fraction of the wealth they had created.

Pressure for change from working people was made more effective by pressure from sectors of the ruling bureaucracy that also wanted reforms, Shachtman said. Demands from reform-minded bureaucrats acted as a "transmitting mechanism" for pressures from below. Bureaucratic discontent had its own sources. Bureaucrats too had suffered from Stalin's purges. Their considerable privileges were unconsolidated as long as a dictator's arbitrary action could take any privilege away at a moment's notice. Lower-level bureaucrats yearned for "'normalization'—the right to enjoy their privileges in undisturbed peace and security." The bureaucracy was also grudgingly coming around to Trotsky's argument that some measure of democracy was an economic necessity. Factory managers suffered from "too intensive, too monopolistic, too disruptive intervention in all spheres of economic life" by the secret police. "*The pores of the Russian economy are choking with bureaucracy,*" Shachtman said. Khrushchev fired almost a million officials in 1953–57 and called for firing half a million more in an attempt to clear out the pores.[11]

Efforts to reform the system in a way that would keep workers quiet, bureaucrats satisfied, and the economy running ran into contradictions right away. Keeping bureaucrats happy meant more than anything else making them feel secure. But security for bureaucrats meant a dead weight on the economy and economic stagnation that would fan the flames of working-class discontent. By the late 1950s, Khrushchev's popularity in the ranks of the ruling elite was beginning to fade as his reforms interfered with bureaucratic stability. He responded by making more gestures that would attract popular support against disgruntled bureaucrats.

Economic decentralization fit into his political agenda. "Decentralization and despotism are not mutually exclusive," Shachtman said. "Atomization is often the essential precondition for the preservation of despotism."[12] Khrushchev's liberalization went together with a steady concentration of power in the general secretary's own hands. He eliminated opponents— Beria in 1953, Malenkov in 1955, Molotov in 1957—and strengthened his power throughout the 1950s and early 1960s.

Khrushchev's replacement by Leonid Brezhnev in 1964 flipped the coin of unresolvable contradictions onto its other side. Brezhnev put an end to Khrushchev's purges and gave bureaucrats the security of tenure they wanted. He allowed power to be spread somewhat more widely. But Khrushchev's policies of social liberalization and economic reform were reversed. Censorship and repression of dissent worsened. The Soviet economy went into such a period of decline that after his death, Brezhnev's reign was known as the "period of stagnation." To Shachtman these changes were proof that no bureaucratic regime could represent a genuinely popular alternative for the Soviet Union.

Collective leadership had its limits even under Brezhnev. Shachtman argued that the bureaucracy was forced to limit discussion and democratic decision-making even within its own ranks, because discussion could open "cracks in the monolithic structure through which the masses can so easily pour." Completely collective self-rule for the Soviet bureaucracy was a utopia. Stalin's autocracy was only an extreme manifestation of the system's inherent trend toward concentration of power: The bureaucracy needed a "*supreme arbiter.*" Each time one supreme arbiter died or fell, there was a strong tendency for a new one to emerge. The endless litany of calls for collective leadership from every Soviet leader, including Khrushchev and Brezhnev, did nothing to reverse this tendency. Shachtman pointed out that Stalin in the 1920s, like Khrushchev in the 1950s, had eliminated each of his major adversaries by portraying them as power hungry and himself as "mild, humble, quiet, a simple man" who only wanted collective leadership. Once all rivals were eliminated, the cloak of humility was discarded.[13]

Shachtman was led to exaggerate the permanence and extent of repression and tyranny in Soviet society, partly by a certain one-sidedness in his own theory and partly by his fondness for bloodcurdling images. As late as 1955, he insisted that "incessant warfare" against the people and "police terror" were permanent features of Soviet life. By 1961, he admitted that he had been taken unaware by the extent of Khrushchev's liberalization. "The rule of open and brutal terror, the régime of bloodbaths, has been ended," he said.[14]

But he always said that there were limits beyond which bureaucratic reforms would not go. However many economic concessions the bureaucracy made, however loose its control over intellectual and social life became, it would not willingly give up its hold on power, which was crucial to its privileges and existence. Nothing but a popular upsurge would win genuine democracy from the regime, "because the minute it is granted . . . is the beginning of the end of totalitarian bureaucratic rule." Although economic backwardness had been essential to Stalin's counter-revolution, economic progress would not undo peacefully and legally what had been accomplished by violence. On the contrary, economic progress without political upheaval would strengthen the regime, not weaken it. "An ulcer which may have been produced in the first place by untidy eating habits cannot, after it has developed beyond a certain point, be eliminated merely by changing these habits," Shachtman said. "Surgical methods are required."[15]

"Surgical methods" meant the long-awaited workers' revolution, already given a full dress rehearsal in Hungary. Shachtman imagined that it was approaching in the USSR as well. He thought that it was most likely to begin with uncontrollable conflicts within the bureaucracy: conflicts within a single country, like those that divided Khrushchev from his conservative critics; conflicts between two different national bureaucracies, like the Sino-Soviet split; or a combination of both. The crisis of the regime could be "precipitated by . . . a hard-to-surmount obstacle, which the bureaucracy is unable to face as one man." He thought that deep divisions within the bureaucracy might make the Communist Party useless as an instrument of bureaucratic rule. The party dictatorship might be supplemented or replaced by a military dictatorship. But even naked military force would not save the bureaucracy in the long run once the working class had begun to act on its own. Soviet workers would eventually "speak with the voice of the revolution whose aim it is, in the forgotten but ever-timely words of Marx, to establish democracy."[16]

Shachtman's predictions of workers' uprisings against Stalinism were vindicated several times in the 1960s, 1970s, and 1980s, though not in the USSR itself. In Czechoslovakia in 1968 and China during the Cultural Revolution, uprisings began as Shachtman had foreseen; the accompanying conflicts in Communist leaderships mobilized masses of people outside the party behind one faction or another. In each case the mobilized people were soon making demands that went beyond what any Communist faction would have accepted. Polish workers rose up even in the face of a relatively united Communist Party leadership, posing the clearest working-class challenge of all to bureaucratic rule in 1980-81. In both China and Poland the Communist Party was pushed aside in the confrontations as Shachtman had foreseen, with the quasi-military regimes of Lin Biao and Wojciech Jaruzelski temporarily undertaking the defense of bureaucratic power in place of the weakened parties.

Repeated popular challenges to bureaucratic rule extracted concessions from the regimes greater than Shachtman foresaw, though until the regimes were at death's door the concessions were always granted reluctantly and withdrawn as soon as the back of the popular movement was broken. The Polish regime nominally accepted the existence of independent trade unions in 1980–81 only to crush them; its renewed concessions in 1989 contributed to the Communist Party's disintegration.

In the Soviet Union under Gorbachev in the late 1980s, there was far more latitude for dissent and even organized opposition than at any time since the first years of the Revolution. But sections of the military and bureaucracy resisted to the point of attempting an anti-Gorbachev coup in 1991, whose failure brought down the whole weakened structure of the Soviet Union. Shachtman's prediction of this limit to Communist self-reform, which influenced the thinking of several academic Sovietologists, seems to have been largely vindicated. He would probably have been disappointed that his vindication came through events that, at least in the short run, did not move the Soviet Union or Eastern Europe toward democratic socialism.

In the late 1950s and 1960s, U.S. society was shaken and altered by the African-American movement for civil rights. Beginning with Martin Luther King, Jr.'s Montgomery bus boycott in 1955, the civil rights movement mobilized first African Americans, then white liberals and radicals. By the time of King's 1963 March on Washington, it was the strongest, most dynamic movement in the country. It won passage of the Civil Rights and Voting Rights Acts of 1964 and 1965, ending century-old injustices of Jim Crow. It put on the national agenda issues of full equality for African Americans in education, employment, housing, and political and economic power—issues that remained unresolved and explosive a generation later.

Shachtman was enthusiastic about the civil rights movement from its earliest years. The rhetoric of equality it relied on in the 1950s fit in with the approach to African-American rights he had advocated since the 1930s. Even more important to him, the civil rights movement fit into the strategy he had been developing since 1949 of aggravating contradictions inside the Democratic Party to hasten the emergence of a labor party. The civil rights movement threatened the Democratic Party alliance of northern Cold War liberals, big-city machines, and union leaders with southern segregationist "Dixiecrats." Shachtman began using the word "realignment" to describe the transformation of U.S. politics that he thought could be brought about by uniting the labor and civil rights movements with their liberal allies in a party that labor would dominate.[17]

On the surface, the language of realignment was not a brief for the Democratic Party but an attack on it. It described the Democrats as "a class party bound organizationally and programmatically to capitalism." The Democratic Party talked about peace but "recklessly gambles with nuclear catastrophe." It talked about racial equality but did nothing to bring it about. It consistently betrayed the labor movement.

Shachtman's followers planned to push big business, Cold Warriors, machine politicians, and segregationists out of the Democratic Party so that labor, African Americans, liberals, and the peace movement could take it over. By pushing for progressive programs inside the Democratic Party, above all by aggravating tensions in the Democratic Party over civil rights to the point where the Dixiecrats would walk out, the balance inside it could be shifted decisively to the left so that it became, in effect, a labor party. The civil rights movement was the force "most likely to constitute that catalytic agent capable of forcing realignment." Once Dixiecrats succumbed to the civil rights attack, the scenario went, the Republican Party, covertly linked to Dixiecrats, would be helpless.[18]

Shachtman's main connection with the civil rights movement was through African-American socialist Bayard Rustin. An illegitimate child raised by his grandparents in a rural Pennsylvania town, Rustin had begun his radical career early. He had left the Young Communist League in 1941 when the Communists decided that winning the war was more important than civil rights. He had worked as a youth organizer for the 1943 African-American March on Washington that was organized—and called off at the last minute—by Black labor leader and socialist A. Philip Randolph. Rustin had kept his ties to Randolph ever since. He had gone to jail for his pacifism during the Second World War and become a leader of the pacifist groups Fellowship of Reconciliation and War Resisters League. Both an intellectual and a skilled organizer, Rustin now had "flaring gray hair, high cheekbones, and thin features reflecting part-Indian ancestry, his aristocratic diction shaped by long stays in England."

In 1956, Rustin worked closely with two dynamic Brooklyn College students and Shachtman followers, Tom Kahn and Rochelle Horowitz, to organize a Madison Square Garden rally in support of the Montgomery bus boycott. Unlike the self-consciously Jewish and intellectual teenagers who admired Shachtman in the 1930s, Kahn was the son of a manual laborer and had never given a thought to his ethnic background. But he and Horowitz were energetic and devoted. Thinking of his lost son, Michael, and speaking of Kahn and Horowitz, Shachtman told Benson, "These are my children."[19]

The Madison Square Garden rally helped confirm Rustin's role as a key northern player in a mainly southern civil rights movement. But he was kept in the background because of nervousness about his homosexuality. Although he raised thousands of dollars in the North for the Montgomery bus boycott, helped King formulate his nonviolent philosophy, and played an important role in the 1957 foundation of the Southern Christian Leadership Conference, Rustin's homosexuality barred him from becoming the new organization's executive director. Uneasiness about his sex life among pacifist ministers like King and A. J. Muste, who had been Rustin's mentor, helped pull Rustin away from his earlier pacifist friends, even his close gay socialist and pacifist friend Dave McReynolds. Kahn became Rustin's lover and brought Rustin closer to Shachtman.

Shachtman was not much of a sexual liberationist—anti-gay jokes were part of his repertory—but he was no moralist either. He never let sexual issues interfere with political loyalty or friendship. Under his leadership, Independent Socialists were relatively tolerant of gay members by 1950s standards, as long as gays kept their "private lives" private.[20] Rustin's role in the civil rights movement made him an important person for Shachtman, whatever Rustin's sexuality.

Mike Harrington later remembered that Kahn, Horowitz, and he would take Rustin along with them in the late 1950s to Shachtman's house in Floral Park for drawn-out strategic discussions. Sometimes the five of them would have telephone conference calls to discuss tactical issues that arose.[21] Increasingly, the subject of these meetings and conference calls was events inside the Democratic Party.

Shachtman had gone about as far as he could go in the 1950s in trying to disrupt the Democratic Party from the outside. By the decade's last years, Harrington said, "We had not yet come to the notion of joining the

Democratic Party but we were certainly heading there pretty fast." After Independent Socialists accepted Shachtman's proposal in 1954 to back labor candidates in Democratic primaries, he decided that supporting labor candidates was not enough. There were almost no such candidates, and opposing other Democrats could antagonize union leaders who supported them. He proposed in 1957 that Independent Socialists not oppose labor-endorsed candidates.[22] Since labor routinely endorsed Democrats, after 1957 he would rarely oppose Democrats in general elections. He would continue to root for his kind of Democrats, however—pro-labor and pro-civil rights Democrats—against the rest.

The 1960 election convinced Shachtman and his circle that their kind of Democrat was still on the party's sidelines. In one of their conference calls they decided to organize marches on both parties' conventions to put pressure on both Republicans and Democrats, a tactic that became traditional on the left.[23] They saw the eventual Democratic nominee, John F. Kennedy, as a Cold Warrior who owed his political career to his right-wing millionaire father.

Shachtman decided that more trouble had to be made *inside* the Democratic Party. In 1961 he said that his friends should "immediately get into the Democratic reform clubs." Some of his followers drew back from the consequences of his strategy, but he pushed on. He urged his loyalists to put the policy "*into practice*—and nobody can stop us from doing that."[24] Liberal Democratic reformers battling against Tammany Hall and other old-time Democratic machines welcomed their new allies, who could draw on decades of experience in organizational infighting. Shachtman's followers quickly won influence and offices in the Democratic Party apparatus.

They came to believe that they were creating a political force that would take over the Democratic Party and then the country. They kept making new contacts, new allies, new recruits. As a student at Howard University in Washington in 1961–63, Kahn worked closely with leaders of the Student Nonviolent Coordinating Committee such as Stokely Carmichael, Courtland Cox, and Ivanhoe Donaldson, bringing them at least temporarily close to Shachtman's brand of socialism. In November 1963 he helped organize an SNCC conference that included Rustin, Norman Thomas, and young Socialists as well as a top AFL-CIO official, who called for "democratic central planning" and a "profound reorganization" of the economy. The Shachtmanites thought "our dream of a political realignment in America was about to come true."[25]

Even the Kennedy administration seemed to be crawling in the direction of reform, spurred onward by the civil rights movement and influenced by anti-poverty writers like Harrington. Martin Luther King, Jr.'s 1963 March on Washington was a watershed. Once the administration saw how large the march was bound to be, Kennedy gave it his presidential blessing.

Organizing the march solidified Bayard Rustin's ties to Shachtman's circle. Rustin credited Shachtman's "unwavering support" with persuading him not to resign as march organizer in the face of right-wing attacks on Rustin's homosexuality. When Shachtman heard that Rustin had been entrapped and arrested in a Washington, D.C., men's room, he paused a moment for thought. Then he started sketching out over the phone a statement defending Rustin "with the tones . . . of Southern Baptist ministers. . . . 'We as men of the cloth, as Christians who believe in human redemption. . . .'" A. Philip Randolph, who Kahn doubted had ever "used a bathroom or needed to eat or any of the other things that the rest of us have to do," was also "totally above this foolishness" and would not hear of Rustin's leaving.[26]

The march was the biggest civil rights demonstration that had ever taken place in the United States. It gave Shachtman a chance to lay out his realignment strategy to the civil rights movement at a speech after the march. He spoke of the socialist dream, implicitly likening it to King's dream: "our greatest of all dreams, the dream of a golden age of brotherhood of all men and women marching without fear, with head up, without hunger, without ignorance, without war, with pride in each and pride in all and with the confident dignity that is appropriate to the human animal." He hailed the march as an embodiment of socialists' dream.

> Not because we invented this movement, not because [we] led this movement—we did not; but because its triumph is our triumph, as it is that of all people who cherish freedom, democracy, and human equality. Every achievement in this fight for human rights is, as we see it, a milestone on the road to that complete socialist democracy which is at once our ideal and our political goal.[27]

He explained that achieving the dream would require a labor–civil rights alliance against the Dixiecrat-Republican coalition, "one of the most poisonous roots of the evil in this country." Dixiecrats dependent on the South's one-party, all-white political system were the only reason the Republicans had any power left, he said. An alliance between African Americans and labor could end Dixiecrats' power. Every northern Democrat elected with African-American or labor support, he said, should be asked, "Will you help drive the Dixiecrats out of power? Or are your promises about liberalism . . . just so many nice words?"[28]

Tom Kahn helped create more of a stir than Shachtman, however, through his contributions to a controversial speech delivered at the march by Student Nonviolent Coordinating Committee leader John Lewis. The speech's radicalism upset moderate civil rights leaders so much that they objected to Lewis's delivering it at all. Kahn's most notable contribution was the line, "If any radical social, political and economic changes are to take place in our society, the people, the masses must bring them about." Courtland Cox, another activist close to Kahn and Rustin, added lines that were critical of Johnson's civil rights bill, whose passage moderates saw as the march's whole point.[29] The fight over Lewis's speech kept Rustin furiously busy backstage at the rally, mediating between the two sides and stalling with improvised music until an acceptably bowdlerized speech was agreed on.

The events at the March on Washington seemed to epitomize Shachtman's redefined politics. He was a social democrat now, a Democrat, a person who could speak to the progressive American mainstream; he was, nonetheless, in his own eyes a militant radical. But the next few years would reveal that the progressive unity he hoped to be bringing about was a chimera. By the mid-1960s, fissures over political tactics and foreign policy were appearing among his own followers.

In the late 1950s, Shachtman settled accounts with the Leninist tradition he had defended warmly for thirty years and with qualifications for another ten. In 1949, he and other Independent Socialist leaders had given up the idea that had previously been the touchstone for their Leninist self-conception: that revolution was necessary even in postwar capitalist democracies like the United States. Yet for almost another decade they maintained a left-wing socialist organization.

The new political opportunities of the mid-1950s made Shachtman see the Independent Socialist League less as a political home and more as encumbering political baggage. He was frustrated that he had been a mere bystander to the AFL-CIO merger and the civil rights movement's rise. Independent Socialists might be able to get staff jobs with the tolerant United Auto Workers, but the broader, reunified AFL-CIO was almost pathologically suspicious of organized Marxists. A Christian, pacifist civil rights leader like Martin Luther King, Jr., was not about to identify publicly with Marxists, but he was comfortable with a pacifist Socialist like Bayard Rustin. In other countries, most of Shachtman's co-thinkers had been in member parties of the Socialist International for years.

When Shachtman first urged European Marxists to go into social democratic parties in the mid-1940s, he said that his argument did not apply to the United States. U.S. Socialists were a mere propaganda group like the Trotskyists, he said, and a less effective one. In the early 1950s, he said that the U.S. Socialist Party had never been a real workers' party like European social democratic parties. The pre–First World War Socialist Party had only been an agrarian populist party representing "small freehold farmers against first merchant capital and then industrial capital." The rise of a modern labor movement made it an anachronism. The contemporary Socialist Party was "a mixture of middle class pacifism, 'Christian socialism,' liberalism, 'isolationism,' hostility to revolutionary socialist theory and action, and hero-worship."[30]

But in 1956–57, Shachtman changed his mind. As he made new ties with Socialists like Rustin, he recalled his reluctance to break with the Socialist Party in 1937. He recited Trotsky's original arguments for joining it, saying that they were "more profoundly true than even the most insightful of us ever imagined."[31]

The impetus for Shachtman's new insight came from the crisis that hit the Communist Party in 1956. Khrushchev's secret speech to a Soviet party congress admitting the truth about Stalin's purges sent shock waves through the Communist movement. U.S. Communists, who had been bearing up heroically under McCarthyist attacks, were particularly hard hit. When party leaders supported the Soviet invasion of Hungary, Communists who had argued for transforming the party into a broad, democratic, reformist movement left it in droves.

Shachtman was pleased to see the Communist Party in crisis. He thought that Communist domination of the left had reduced democratic socialism to "virtual impotence." Now he could create a strong new force distinct not only from Stalinism but from every variety of "Stalinoid"—his epithet for people who accommodated to Stalinism or shrank from condemning it. He was willing to write off most of the ex-Communists and most of their whole generation. They had ended up in a state of "utter demoralization," he said.[32] A new generation would have to rebuild the left along new lines.

This frame of mind made Shachtman welcome Socialist Dave McReynolds's suggestion in October 1956 that the Socialist Party and Independent Socialist League merge to take better advantage of the ferment. Shachtman had few illusions about the Socialist organization, which barely functioned. But its anti-Stalinist credentials were in order. Its name and image were less threatening than that of any other socialist organization to leaders in the labor unions, civil rights movement, and Democratic Party. By combining Socialists' respectable image and Independent Socialists' skills, Shachtman hoped to dwarf everyone else on the left.[33]

In preparation for dissolving the Independent Socialist League into the Socialist Party, Shachtman swept out of the way Leninist ideas about organization that made some Socialists reluctant to take him in. Although left-wing Socialists like McReynolds were ready to welcome Independent Socialists into the party, right-wing Socialists were extremely hostile toward Leninism and unwilling to have any kind of Leninists in their organization. They suspected that Shachtman was feigning a friendly, loyal attitude toward the Socialist Party in preparation for a later splitting operation, like the one Trotskyists had carried out in 1937.

In an article for the *New International* in the fall of 1957, Shachtman tried to quiet fears about his followers' future loyalty to the Socialist Party by repudiating the sense of continuity that his followers still felt with the early Communist movement. He argued that the 1919 split between U.S. Socialist and Communists had done far more harm than good. He pointed out how wrong early U.S. Communists' ideas had been: their refusal to work in the AFL, their prejudice against electoral politics, their belief that revolution would be the act of a minority to create the dictatorship of a minority. He pointed out how dependent U.S. Communists had been on guidance from the Communist International, so that the U.S. Communist Party had been easily converted into a Stalinist party. He concluded that founding a separate revolutionary party in 1919 had been a mistake—just as keeping a separate left-wing group in 1957 was a mistake.

As proof of his case against the splits, Shachtman offered in evidence the whole history of Communism. U.S. Communists had done "magnificent" work organizing the unemployed, in the CIO, fighting for African-American rights, he said. But all their achievements could have been made with *"tenfold better results"* by a *"broad, united socialist party."* Since U.S. capitalism was strong and the labor movement had made its peace with capitalism, setting up a small revolutionary group had only emphasized its isolation. Even the Russian Revolution could have been made better with a united socialist party, without the Bolsheviks' ever having split from the Mensheviks, he argued. A situation like that in 1917, in which socialism was a real possibility, was "marked precisely by the rapid decline of the self-confidence, the influence and the power of compromisers of all kinds in the labor movement."[34] Left-wing socialists—those who, like the Bolsheviks, were committed to class struggle and the ultimate socialist objective—could easily have won over a majority of a united movement.

Despite everything that right-wing socialists had done, left-wing socialists could live with them in the same organization, Shachtman concluded. He could even live in the same party with Socialists who supported Democrats—not just labor candidates running as Democrats (whom he had supported for several years himself) but obvious pro-capitalist Democrats. He was ready to build with these right-wingers a new socialist organization based on "the American working class as it really is."[35]

One of Shachtman's key assumptions in this argument was that reformists, after dominating a united party through years of "normal" political life under capitalism, would respect left-wingers' democratic right to take over the party when the approaching prospect of socialism gave leftists a majority. He explained away the experience of the 1919 Socialist split, when reformists would not give up control even when the left wing won a democratic vote. (He half-excused the reformists' "violation of democratic procedure" in 1919 on the grounds of the "reckless provocations of the Left Wing.")[36]

He also assumed that left-wingers who won a majority at a time of revolutionary possibility could organize socialists for victory before the possibility faded away. In earlier years he had pointed to many revolutionary opportunities that were lost because no adequate leadership could be organized in time—Germany in 1919, Catalonia in 1937, Italy and France in 1943–44. He had pointed out that the Bolsheviks could overthrow capitalism in 1917 because they had been organizing independently since 1912, when they split Russian socialism with a substantial mass following but *without* a decisive majority. Marxists learned from the Bolshevik experience that socialists need to prepare in advance for "abnormal" situations, times of crisis and opportunity, when the rulers of society are caught off balance and the ruled are ready to risk radical change. Marxists came to believe that only "abnormal" situations reveal the truth about capitalism's instability and unworkability.

Shachtman was giving up this understanding for the idea that socialism could emerge smoothly from "normal" capitalist life: an idea that has been disproved many times by supposedly socialist governments working by "normal" capitalist rules. François Mitterrand's France is only one recent example: Socialists elected to administer capitalist states naturally tend to preserve the capitalist system on which their administrations rest.

The splits of 1919–21 rested ultimately on the premise that socialism would require every country to get rid of the existing capitalist army, bureaucracy, and parliamentary institutions and replace them with a more truly democratic system created from below. The premise led to the corollary that socialists who saw this necessity had to organize themselves well in advance to prepare for the change, before they had convinced a majority of working people. Shachtman decided by 1949 that the premise no longer applied to the United States: Constitutional, relatively peaceful transitions to socialism had become possible, he said, and the British Labour government pointed the way. Now in 1957 he said that Communists had *always* been "wrong on the dogma of Soviets and armed insurrection as the only road to power."[37] He now saw peaceful, legal politicking as *the* road to power in capitalist democracies.

His willingness to abandon Leninism explicitly and publicly helped make possible his entry into the Socialist Party. He told Norman Thomas, "The Independent Socialist League does not subscribe to any doctrine called Leninism." Although he still said that the Russian Revolution was a socialist revolution and Stalinism was a betrayal of it, these questions were "primarily of historical importance." What mattered for the present was that Independent Socialists belonged in the Socialist Party and Socialist International.[38]

In February 1957, Independent Socialist leaders came out flatly against too broad a unification of the left, which would inevitably "carry the stamp . . . of a re-formed and modified pro-Stalinist movement." Instead they called for unity with the Socialist Party alone.[39] In July 1957, a majority of Independent Socialists agreed. Shachtman openly opposed the American Forum for Socialist Education, an attempt by A. J. Muste, Sidney Lens, and other radicals to bring about a broader regroupment of the left. In June 1958, the Socialists agreed to take Shachtman's followers into membership.

Hal Draper, Gordon Haskell, and many of Shachtman's followers mistrusted his argument that the Socialist Party, "*because* it is right-wing, has prospects denied to us." Draper warned that among Socialists Shachtman's politics would be "bent, fitted, rubbed down, carved, trimmed or cold-storaged so as to ingratiate us as good-dogs with the SP right wing." Once the decision to join the Socialists was made, Draper resigned as *Labor Action* editor and moved to Berkeley. Haskell put out the paper as a biweekly by himself for the last year; he was so frustrated with the job in the end that he became the "most enthusiastic supporter" of joining the Socialists "because obviously we've burnt all our bridges."[40]

Shachtman did his best to reaffirm his political past and principles as he gave up his organization. He still insisted that the Bolsheviks had begun a "new epoch in the socialist movement" in at least one respect: their adherence to class struggle and their practical demonstration that capitalism could be overthrown. One and only one old communist idea remained valid, he said: "the idea of a working class socialist party completely independent of the capitalist class, of capitalist politics and capitalist ideas, with a program and activity based upon the principle of the class struggle. That theory does not die, and it should not die, for if it is not kept alive socialism will never come to life."[41] In hindsight, this was Shachtman's last good-bye to the left-wing socialism he had clung to for a decade.

His lack of clarity about the political transition he was making helped ensure that major political battles would take place not only about joining the Socialist Party (about a third of the Young Socialist League refused to follow Shachtman into the party, instead creating a new Young Socialist Alliance linked to the Socialist Workers Party) but inside the united organization as well. These battles helped make the Socialist Party less of a home than a battleground for the rest of Shachtman's life. Faction fights convulsed the group in the 1960s: first in the early 1960s, over whether to adopt Shachtman's realignment strategy; then in the late 1960s, over how to interpret and implement it.

Several Independent Socialist leaders decided from the beginning that they would have to keep the left-wing third-camp socialist tradition alive outside the Socialist Party. In 1960, Julius and Phyllis Jacobson prepared to publish an independent third-camp magazine, *New Politics*. They assembled a board that included Draper and prominent Socialists such as Norman Thomas. Shachtman viewed the project as a threat to his own project in the Socialist Party. At first he tried to charm them out of the idea, inviting them over to dinner for what Julie Jacobson later described as "one of the strangest evenings we ever experienced," complete with large quantities of food, hugging, cheek-pinching and "bawdy and side-splitting" jokes. When this gambit failed, Shachtman tried to convince Thomas to withdraw as a sponsor of the magazine and convince the Socialist National Committee not to give this suspect publication the Socialist mailing list. One incredulous Socialist pointed out that *New Politics'* founders included not only some of Shachtman's longtime associates but the Socialist Party's Manhattan organizer, Phyllis Jacobson.[42]

Inside the Socialist Party, factional battles undermined the progress that Shachtman had made working in a broader organization with a broader audience. For example, Joel Geier, the University of Chicago student who took over the SP-linked Young People's Socialist League in 1960, was just the kind of quick-witted, theoretically minded follower Shachtman was used to. Geier was "enthralled" when he heard Shachtman speak on the Russian Revolution, saying years later, "I learned more that night than I had any other night in my life." Under Geier's leadership, the YPSL grew to a thousand members by 1962. But Geier could not stomach Shachtman's new social democratic politics. Geier and other YPSL leaders formed a "labor party faction." They denied that Shachtman's forays into Democratic politics were compatible with any genuine independent politics: Being a little involved with Democrats, they said, was like being "a little bit pregnant."[43]

A group of young, Cold War–minded Shachtman loyalists led by Kahn and Horowitz opposed Geier. In the left-wing-led Student Peace Union, which drew more than 5,000 students to its 1962 Washington action against nuclear testing, Shachtman's supporters fought a running battle for control that drove many members out of the group and led to its dissolution in 1964. By 1964, Shachtman's young critics gave up on him and the Socialist Party. Geier left New York and moved to Berkeley, where he joined an Independent Socialist Club led by Draper.[44] The Young People's Socialist League's gains of the early 1960s were almost all lost, and it began virtually from scratch in 1964. Meanwhile, Independent Socialist Clubs grew up in other cities, moved far to the left later in the 1960s, and in 1969 came together to form the third-camp revolutionary socialist group International Socialists.

For the rest of his life, Shachtman insisted that the U.S. Socialist Party and its counterparts abroad were the movement on the left with "real political possibilities," "the sole serious alternative to the futile and future-less parties of the status quo."[45] He and Barsh reaffirmed their allegiance to the Socialist Party in May Day and Labor Day greetings they sent year after year to its newspaper. But he gave little attention to building it as an organization. Instead he used it as a platform to reach the people who commanded his interest—union and civil rights leaders—and to expound his new social democratic outlook.

In 1961 he gathered twenty years' worth of major articles from the *New International* into a book called *The Bureaucratic Revolution*. One of the articles, written in 1950, originally attacked Social Democrats for tolerating the

> dying capitalist regime. . . . That is the particular contribution which the Social Democrats make to the new barbarism! . . . The workers need a lifebuoy to carry them out of danger from the foundering ship of capital-ism and the Social Democrats throw them the anchor. We are revolution-ary socialists; we are democratic socialists; we are not Social Democrats.

Many of the articles in *The Bureaucratic Revolution* were edited to read somewhat differently for publication in 1961, without any hint to readers about the changes. The sentence "That is the particular contribution which the Social Democrats make to the new barbarism!" was omitted, for exam-ple. The phrase "and the Social Democrats throw them the anchor" became simply "and not the anchor." And the phrase "we are not Social Democrats" was, as Draper might have said, "carved, trimmed or cold-storaged."[46] "We" had changed our minds.

Shachtman found himself in sharp disagreement with others in the Social-ist Party over international as well as domestic issues in the 1960s. In 1961 he courted controversy with other Socialists as he faced a new challenge to his worldview: the Cuban revolution. In this controversy, as in others to come, anti-Communist trade unionists had first call on his loyalties and determined his stand.

Unlike any earlier revolution that overthrew capitalism, Fidel Castro's had neither Communist nor trade union roots. His July 26 Movement began as a middle-class democratic movement to get rid of Fulgencio Batista's dictatorship. Yet its victory in January 1959 replaced not only Batista's government but the entire Cuban army and state with a new force born in the guerilla war.

In its first months in power, the movement nationalized 2,000 businesses and expropriated all big landed estates, including the 40 percent of the best sugar land that belonged to U.S. citizens. The Cuban government took over U.S. oil refineries in June—the United States reacted by putting an embargo on Cuban sugar—and all the banks and all remaining U.S.-owned companies in October. It was headed for conflict with the U.S. government, which began preparing an invasion of the island in March 1960.

In 1959 and 1960, Shachtman took no stand on the Cuban revolution. When the Socialist Party discussed it early in 1961 he said nothing.[47] Then on 17 April 1961, 1,400 CIA-armed and -trained Cuban rebels landed at the Bay of Pigs and were crushed by the Cuban revolutionary Militia in three days.

Shachtman arrived in California to give talks to the San Francisco Socialist Party and Berkeley Young People's Socialist League on 18 April, the day after the Bay of Pigs invasion. The fighting was still going on on the beaches. Without knowing how the battle would turn out, he had to take a public stand. He chose to express strong sympathy, if not open support, for the counterrevolutionaries who had invaded Cuba. He suggested more openly than ever before that U.S. power could be used to promote democracy in the third world.

The first assumption Shachtman started from was that there could be no permanent revolution and no socialism in Cuba, just as there could no be socialism in any country without a full-fledged industrial working class. The best possible outcome for Cuba was "a middle-class *democratic* revolution." If this democratic revolution was impossible, he told his listeners, "*I can do nothing and you can do nothing, and the Latin American people can do nothing.*" Fortunately for Cuba, a moderate, democratic revolution had been precisely the program of the July 26 Movement—"land to the peasants, freedom in general for the people," "modernization of the economy," an end to all the "monstrosities" Cubans endured under Batista. Shachtman added that after his 1959 victory, Castro had made a start on this program, making major achievements surprisingly quickly. Castro would be remembered as the July 26 Movement's "hero and leader."[48]

By 1961, however, Castro's conception of a democratic revolution had diverged from Shachtman's in several crucial respects. Castro had not held elections. There had been a "narrowing-down of democratic rights and possibilities." Castro did not share Shachtman's belief that "democracy is not possible in any form—bourgeois democracy . . . or socialist democracy—without free trade unions."[49] Worst of all, Shachtman said, the Cuban government was increasingly in Communist hands. He did not say that Castro was a Communist. But Castro was not a conscious anti-Stalinist, and that was a fatal failing. The Cuban Communists, "a trained, disciplined force which has no other to contest with, instantly and immediately and rapidly occupies the important positions, military, political, cultural, trade-union, everything you want," Shachtman said. The Cuban revolution was moving toward " a totalitarian climax."[50]

If Castro defeated the invasion, the democratic revolution was doomed,

Shachtman concluded. If the Cubans rallied behind Castro because they hated the United States, they would acquiesce in the victory of Communism. But the revolutionary forces were not all on Castro's side. Among the invaders were Cuban trade unionists who had fought the Batista dictatorship but had been ousted from the unions after the revolution. Shachtman had met some of them and thought that they were "good stout working-class fighters." There were also people who had fought with Castro in the July 26 Movement who were opposed to the growth of Communist influence. These dissidents and unionists were not fighting for a dictator like Batista. They were a spontaneous movement made up of "revolutionary democrats, running the gamut from conservative democrats to extreme left-wing democrats."[51] Shachtman's sympathies were with them.

He was not so naive as to picture the invasion force as consisting entirely of good trade unionists and disillusioned democrats. He admitted that the State Department and the CIA were involved with the invasion. He expected them to push for "a turning-back of the wheel" to a dictatorship like Batista's. The president of the invaders' Revolutionary Council, José Cardona, was Washington's man. Shachtman's solution was for Socialists to push the U.S. government for a different kind of foreign policy, a democratic foreign policy. He called for economic aid to Cuba so it would not have to rely on Moscow for help. He called for evacuation of the Guantánamo Bay base. Above all, he called for "hands off Cuba: an absolute refraining from any attempt to dictate to the Cuban people by American force, which is an outrage against democracy."[52]

But "American force" meant to Shachtman "a force that is not Cuban in any way, which is purely mercenary, which reaches the most extreme and obvious form so that even the biggest dunderhead in the world can see it." The Bay of Pigs to him was not "American force." He denied that the rebels had done anything wrong in taking arms from the United States. Revolutionaries had the right to take arms from capitalist governments in a "liberation war," he said. He pointed to the Irish rebels who had accepted German aid in 1916 and the anti-fascist resistance fighters who had accepted U.S. and British aid in 1943–45 with Marxists' approval. He denied that victory for the invasion would necessarily mean another U.S. puppet regime in Cuba. If Cardona had State Department backing, he asked, so what? "You can't buy much beer with that in Cuba." He was willing to bet a nickel that if the invaders overthrew Castro the trade unionists and democrats he favored would have more "inherent power" than "Cardona and the social forces that he represents."[53]

The upshot of Shachtman's analysis was a halfhearted neutrality, weighted toward the unionists and democrats in the Bay of Pigs invasion force. "I hope for their success," he said. But his good wishes were tempered by his fears of the reactionaries and the U.S. administration that the rebels had allied themselves with, just as his hopes in the Castro regime were tempered by fear of Communism. His inclination in the end was "not to approve, not to condemn, so much, but to try to understand how this tragic situation has unfolded."[54] He would not support either side.

Later Shachtman said that he would never endorse an invasion in which the "dirty, stupid, reactionary hand of the CIA was so plainly evident." He thought that the rebels had made a mistake by taking part in it, which they could see for themselves when the CIA "half-imprisoned" them after the invasion failed. Now as during the Korean War, Shachtman saw the U.S. government as an unsavory and unreliable ally against Stalinism. The Eisenhower and Kennedy administrations "couldn't have done a more thorough job" of making sure that Castro's government would both survive and become Communist, he said. "I can still attack American imperialism. . . . That's easy as pie and always has been."[55]

Many of Shachtman's listeners at the San Francisco meeting were disturbed to hear no condemnation of the invasion. Some of his closest allies were uneasy. Hal Draper attacked Shachtman at the 18 April meeting as a "State Department socialist." He said that Shachtman had succumbed to "Stalinophobia"—which "is to Third Camp socialism what the boll weevil is to cotton." Draper denied that the invasion force was independent, casting scorn on Shachtman's analogies. The presence of trade unionists and democrats within it meant nothing: The White armies in Russia in 1918–21 had included trade unionists, democrats, even socialists.[56]

The night after Shachtman's 18 April speech, the Young People's Socialist League disinvited him as their speaker in Berkeley the next day and replaced him with Draper. Shachtman never forgave the Berkeley group and never forgave Draper. His feelings of hurt and betrayal compounded his stubborn defense of his stand. "I did not *condemn* the invasion, and damned happy am I," he said, "that I did not fall into *that* Stalinist-cum-Stalinoid trap."[57]

Shachtman had in fact painted an essentially false portrait of the invasion force. The facts about how it was organized, how it was trained, and where its money came from showed that it was under effective U.S. government control. If the invasion had succeeded, the social weight of Cuban trade unions, on which Shachtman had staked his nickel, would not have counted for much against the enormous military and economic power that enabled U.S. rulers to dominate Cuba for most of the twentieth century.

Shachtman believed that the unionists and democrats among the Bay of Pigs invaders were the best representatives of the Cuban revolution. But popular reaction in Cuba to the invasion showed that a majority of the Cubans who were willing to fight for national independence and against capitalism stood behind the Militia that defeated the invasion. As in Yugoslavia and China, Cuba's anti-capitalist regime was homegrown and therefore less unpopular originally than the Eastern European dictatorships.

Unlike in Yugoslavia or China, no decisive break between bureaucratic and popular forces took place in Cuba in the 1960s, 1970s, or 1980s, despite the regime's repressive measures: purging the trade union leadership, sentencing dissidents to long jail terms, putting gay people in concentration camps. The Castro government showed its continuing confidence in its popular support after 1989 when it responded to loss of Soviet backing and new U.S. threats not only by cracking down on dissent but also by distributing weapons relatively widely (though under strict bureaucratic control) to the Cuban population. By condoning U.S. intervention, Shachtman condoned the imposition in the name of democracy of a solution that most Cubans clearly rejected.

Anti-Communism had become a nonnegotiable condition for being welcome in Shachtman's circle. This overriding anti-Communism would cut him off from the student radicals of the 1960s, who chose to be in solidarity with those in the third world who resisted U.S. power under whatever banner. Students for a Democratic Society leaders Tom Hayden and Al Haber were among the first New Leftists to run up against Shachtman, in 1962.

Hayden and Haber's organization began its spectacular if short existence as the student group of the League for Industrial Democracy, a union-based social democratic organization that had added Shachtman to its board of directors. Mike Harrington represented the parent group at Students for a Democratic Society's 1962 Port Huron convention and found the famous manifesto it adopted there insufficiently anti-Communist. With Shachtman's agreement, the League's board locked Hayden and Haber out of their own group's offices. The incident foreshadowed Students for a Democratic Society's 1965 break with the League for Industrial Democracy and many other battles to come in the 1960s.

Notes

1. ISL PC, "Memorandum on our perspective and orientation in the matter of socialist unity" (2 Feb. 1957), ISM v 12, 2669; Mike Davis, *Prisoners of the American Dream*, 95, 146.
2. ISL PC, "International resolution," ISL bul (1 June 1957), ISM v 12, 2714; Shachtman, "'Co-existence' as a catchphrase," NI v 21 n 1 (Spring 1955), 32; interview with Kahn (7 Apr. 1989), s 4.
3. Shachtman to Harrington (20 Aug. 1963), MSC b 29 f 17 (r 3379).
4. Interview with Harrington by Friend and Hacker (19 Aug. 1988), s 2; interview

with Harrington (19 Nov. 1982), in Maurice Isserman, *If I Had a Hammer*, 228; ISL PC, "Socialist perspectives in the US" (23 May 1957), ISL bul (1 June 1957), ISM v 12, 2696, 2695; interview with Haskell (8 July 1989), s 2.

5. Davis, *Prisoners of the American Dream*, 95, 122–24, 146; "Socialist perspectives in the US," ISM v 12, 2695.
6. Shachtman, "The Independent Socialist League," LA v 22 n 8 (19 May 1958), 3; Shachtman, "Introduction" (1968), *The New International*.
7. Kahn, "Max Shachtman," NA v 10 n 22 (15 Nov. 1972), 4; Wohlforth, "Revolutionaries in the 1950s," *Against the Current* 14 (May–June 1988), 30; Shachtman to Thomas (1 Oct. 1957), ISM v 18, 1118 (also MSC b 15 f 13 [r 3369]).
8. Shachtman, "Socialism in the United States," NI v 21 n 3 (Fall 1955), 140, 150.
9. Wohlforth, "Socialist politics after Hungary '56," *Against the Current* 15 (July–Aug. 1988), 40.
10. Shachtman, "A new stage in the Russian crisis" (May 1957), BR 355 (also NI v 23 n 3 [Summer 1957]).
11. ISL 3rd convention, "The power of the third camp," NI v 20 n 4 (July–Aug. 1954), 186–87 (also ISL bul [July 1954], ISM v 12); ISL PC, "International resolution," ISL bul (1 June 1957), ISM v 12, 2718–19; "A new stage," BR 349.
12. "A new stage," BR 350.
13. Ibid., 348, 342; Shachtman, "The Russian crisis," LA v 20 n 17 (23 Apr. 1956), 5.
14. Shachtman, "'Co-existence' as a catchphrase," NI v 21 n 1 (Spring 1955), 26; Shachtman, "Foreword" (Sept. 1961), BR 3.
15. RMS 497–98; Shachtman, "Stalin on socialism," NI v 18 n 6 (Nov.–Dec. 1952), 292; "Foreword," BR 15.
16. "Foreword," BR 19; "A new stage," BR 350, 355.
17. Walter Reuther called on the CIO in December 1954 to "work within the two-party system of America and bring about within that two-party system a fundamental realignment" (Art Preis, *Labor's Giant Step*, 514). In Shachtman's milieu, the word "realignment" appeared first in Benson, "Why labor needs its own party," LA v 20 n 20 (14 May 1956), 1, but with few of its later connotations. R. M. [Martinson?] and B. S. [?], "Oust the south from the Democratic Party," LA v 20 n 29 (16 July 1956), 3, laid out an early version of Shachtman's strategy.
18. "Statement to party locals on implementation and application of public statement entitled—'Toward political realignment in America'" (1960), MSC b 16 f 34 (r 3373); "Toward political realignment in America" (1960), MSC b 16 f 34 (r 3373); Shachtman, "Draft resolution on the party and the new administration" (1961), MSC b 16 f 35 (r 3373). According to Harrington (interviewed by Friend and Hacker [19 Aug. 1988], s 2), Shachtman's views on the Dixiecrat-Republican alliance were influenced by political scientist James Macgregor Burns.
19. Robert Weisbrot, *Freedom Bound*, 77; interview with Kahn (7 Apr. 1989), s 1, 5; interview with Benson (missing from tape).
20. Interview with Kahn, s 1; interview with Weir by Thompson (14 Aug. 1983), OHAL, tape 4 s 1; interview with Geier (17 Apr. 1989), s 4.
21. Interview with Harrington by Friend and Hacker (19 Aug. 1988), s 1.
22. Interview with Harrington by Friend and Hacker, s 1; ISL 3rd convention, "Growth of American conservatism," NI v 20 n 4 (July–Aug. 1954), 210 (also ISL bul [May 1954], ISM v 12); ISL PC, "Socialist perspectives in the US" (23 May 1957), ISL bul (1 June 1957), ISM v 12, 2699.

23. Interview with Harrington by Friend and Hacker, s 1.
24. Shachtman to Davidson (3 Oct. 1961), MSC b 28 f 26 (r 3377); SP convention (8–10 June 1962), Socialist Party Papers, Duke University Library, r 77; Shachtman to Weinrib (19 Mar. 1962), MSC b 31 f 43 (r 3383).
25. Howard Zinn, SNCC, 229; Michael Harrington, Fragments of the Century, 203–4.
26. "A meeting for Max," NA v 11 n 1 (31 Dec. 1972), 8; interview with Geier, s 3; interview with Kahn, s 1.
27. Shachtman, "Drive out Dixiecrats for jobs and freedom," NA v 3 n 16–17 (24 Sept. 1963), 8, 12.
28. Ibid., 8, 12.
29. Interviews with John Lewis (23 Sept. 1969) and Rochelle Horowitz (8 Nov. 1968) by Archie E. Allen, cited in Taylor Branch, Parting the Waters, 873.
30. Shachtman, "Theses on decline of the American SP" (early 1950s), MSC b 40 f 2 (r 3388); Shachtman, The Fight for Socialism, 161.
31. RMS 301.
32. Shachtman, "Toward a rebirth of socialism," LA v 21 n 19 (13 May 1957), 4–5; Shachtman, "The end of socialism," BR 262–63 (also NI v 20 n 2 [Mar.–Apr. 1954]).
33. Shachtman, "American Communism," NI v 23 n 4 (Fall 1957), 207.
34. Ibid., 221, 240, 236.
35. Ibid., 241–43.
36. Ibid., 218.
37. Ibid., 237.
38. Thomas to Shachtman (20 Sept. 1957), ISM v 18, 1112 (also MSC b 15 f 13 [r 3369]); Shachtman to Thomas (25 Sept. 1957), MSC b 15 f 20 (r 3369); Shachtman to Thomas (1 Oct. 1957), ISM v 18, 1114, 1116–17 (also MSC b 15 f 13 [r 3369]).
39. ISL PC, "Memorandum on our perspective and orientation in the matter of socialist unity" (2 Feb. 1957), ISL bul (Mar. 1957), ISM v 12, 2670–72.
40. Draper, "The meaning of Shachtman's 'socialist unity,'" ISL bul (Mar. 1957), ISM v 12, 2690–91; interview with Haskell (8 July 1989), s 2, 4; interview with Draper (17 Feb. 1989), s 5.
41. Shachtman, "U.S. socialism past and future" (1957), MSC b 18 f 15 (r 3375); "American Communism," NI v 23 n 4, 240–41.
42. Jacobson to Drucker (10 Sept. 1992), 5–7.
43. Interview with Geier (17 Apr. 1989), s 1, 2.
44. Ibid., s 2, 3.
45. Shachtman, "The counsel of despair," NI v 24 n 2–3 (Spring-Summer 1958), 128; Shachtman, "Foreword" (Sept. 1961), BR 20.
46. Shachtman, "Reflections on a decade past," NI v 16 n 3 (May–June 1950), 143; BR 34.
47. Shachtman to Wollod (27 Mar. 1961), MSC b 32 f 6 (r 3384).
48. Max Shachtman and Hal Draper, Two Views of the Cuban Invasion, 5, 1, 6.
49. Ibid., 2, 1.
50. Ibid., 5; Shachtman to Shain (3, 12 May 1961), MSC b 31 f 11 (r 3382).
51. Shachtman and Draper, Two Views, 2, 1, 3; Shachtman to Shain (12 May and 8 June 1961), MSC b 31 f 11 (r 3382).
52. Shachtman to Shain (3 May 1961), MSC b 31 f 11 (r 3382); Shachtman and Draper, Two Views, 1–2.

53. Shachtman and Draper, *Two Views*, 4, 6; Shachtman to Shain (3, 12 May 1961), MSC b 31 f 11 (r 3382).
54. Shachtman and Draper, *Two Views*, 3, 1.
55. Shachtman to Shain (3 May, 12 May, 8 June 1961), MSC b 31 f 11 (r 3382); RMS 516.
56. Shachtman and Draper, *Two Views*, 8, 10, 12.
57. Berkeley YPSL Executive Committee statement (23 Apr. 1961), MSC b 31 f 11 (r 3382); Shachtman to Shain (8 June 1961), MSC b 31 f 11 (r 3382).

9

The "American Century"

Looking back from later decades, people of the most varied outlooks have seen the early and mid-1960s in the United States as a golden age of prosperity and progress. By comparison with the 1980s and 1990s, the country's trade balance in the mid-1960s was favorable, economic growth rates were high, unemployment was low, and economic gaps between rich and poor, Black and white, seemed to be narrowing. Liberals can look back nostalgically to New Frontier and Great Society rhetoric about eliminating poverty and racism; conservatives can point to the prosperity that followed Kennedy's tax cuts as evidence for supply-side economics. But mid-1960s leftists, of all stripes, had a view of their society that was far removed from this retrospective, glowing vision.

Socialists as well as many liberals saw that the progress of the unions and the civil rights movement in the 1950s was running up against a dead end in the 1960s. They saw that the future of working and poor people—white, Black, or brown—depended on the economy's ability to create thousands of new jobs at good wages. They saw that African Americans' hard-won equal rights to be hired for any job and live in any neighborhood would be largely empty if there were no new jobs they could be hired for and they could not afford to live in good neighborhoods. And they saw that the economy's creation of new jobs was slowing, a trend that the artificial Vietnam War boom of the late 1960s would only temporarily conceal before 1970s "stagflation" made it obvious.

In the early 1960s, the urge to find a solution to the problem of jobs and economic growth pulled Max Shachtman and his followers into the Democratic Party. In the late 1960s, the attempt to find a solution through the Democratic Party would first divide them from many of their African-American allies, then pit them against one another. Shachtman and Michael Harrington became the main spokespeople for two different groups of Socialists with two different approaches, two different theoretical perspectives, two different social constituencies, allegiances to two hostile wings of the Democratic Party, and two contrasting attitudes about Marxism's relevance in late capitalist society.

In his own way, Shachtman continued to put the working class at the center of his approach. From the 1920s until the mid-1940s, he had defined the working class as insurgent rank-and-file workers who would push aside the pro-capitalist union bureaucracy, form their own political party, and install a workers' government as steps toward socialist revolution. In the late 1940s, he had turned toward the Reuther wing of the CIO, counting on it to form a labor-based national Liberal Party whose left wing could turn it into an instrument of peaceful, legal, democratic socialist transformation. After the 1955 AFL-CIO merger, he came to see the central AFL-CIO leadership as a force for progressive change and the Democratic Party as the crucible of a future labor-based liberal party.

By 1964 he decided that the Democratic Party was virtually a labor-based liberal party already. He decided that Lyndon Johnson's administration was a force for civil rights and social reform and deserved strong support. At the 1964 Democratic convention he allied with the administration to settle the Mississippi Freedom Democrats' challenge to segregationist Mississippi Democrats through "compromise." He moved from trying to drive moderate, machine, and white southern Democrats out of the party to helping to keep them in. Harrington, by working on Johnson's anti-poverty programs, helped connect Shachtman to the summit of the U.S. political system.

Shachtman began by arguing for involvement in Democratic politics as a means to advance African Americans' interests, but he soon subordinated African-American demands to holding the Democratic Party together and ensuring the AFL-CIO's predominance within it. His strategy for African-American equality diverged from that of many African Americans; he opposed Black Power, broke with its spokespeople such as Stokely Carmichael, and drifted away from Martin Luther King, Jr. He worked instead with African Americans who found niches for themselves in labor's network, particularly Bayard Rustin, who became director of the new union-funded A. Philip Randolph Institute, and A. Philip Randolph himself.

The "Freedom Budget" issued by the Randolph Institute in 1966 and baptized by Shachtman outlined his and his allies' strategy for social change. It said that poverty in the United States could be abolished by 1975, without undue interference with capitalist "responsible free enterprise," simply by keeping the economy growing fast, keeping unemployment rates under 3 percent, raising the minimum wage, and having a guaranteed annual income for those few people who could not find or take jobs. It implicitly assumed that all these desirable outcomes could be brought about by keeping Democrats in the White House and Congress and keeping them in line behind a reinvigorated New Deal coalition led by the AFL-CIO.

Having committed himself to keeping together the coalition that had elected Johnson in 1964, Shachtman found that he could not keep it united around either a leadership or a program. Since Shachtman saw the AFL-CIO apparatus as the incarnation of the U.S. working class, he believed that the AFL-CIO had to lead the Democratic coalition; others refused to accept the AFL-CIO's dictates. Since he saw labor as the key agency of social change, he believed that full employment in unionized jobs was the key to the "Great Society"; others believed that automation was pushing the unions to the economy's sidelines.

Mike Harrington became the leader of ex-Shachtmanite Socialists who refused to concede the dominant role in the Democratic coalition to the AFL-CIO. He looked instead for compromises between labor leaders and representatives of "New Politics," a loose network of progressives, mostly inside the Democratic Party, who were trying to capitalize on the Black, Latino, feminist, youth, countercultural, and anti-war ferment of the 1960s. He drifted away from Shachtman's version of Marxist orthodoxy toward the more freethinking socialism of Irving Howe's magazine *Dissent*.

These differences might never have turned into deep, antagonistic divisions if not for two circumstances. First, the differences among Socialists were enmeshed in divisions in the Democratic Party. The realignment strategy, which Shachtman had imagined would allow Socialists to work together effectively inside the Democratic Party, turned out to be a formula for forcing them to choose between rival Democratic politicians fighting for primary votes and inner-party offices. Second, the differences happened to arise as a popular movement exploded against the Vietnam War.

The U.S. war in Vietnam, which escalated in 1965 after Johnson's reelection, was the dynamite that blew apart the disparate elements of Shachtman's coalition. He chose the year of Johnson's decision to escalate the war to come down firmly, as his 1951 statement on Korea and his 1961 statement on Cuba had foreshadowed, for U.S. power as a lesser evil than Communism in the third world.

At first most Socialists went along with, or at least tolerated, his stand. For his part, after announcing it at a June 1965 forum, he kept quiet about his support for the war and helped work out a series of compromise positions in the Socialist Party. The call for "Negotiations Now" was the fig leaf that allowed Socialists to cover their growing divisions. But in 1970, Shachtman and his allies reaffirmed their continued opposition to U.S. withdrawal from Vietnam in a public statement, which resulted in a public, bitter break with Harrington, Howe, and others.

As Shachtman became an apologist for U.S. global power, Walter Reuther turned against the war, rebelling against George Meany; Stokely

Carmichael and Martin Luther King turned against the war and away from Bayard Rustin and A. Philip Randolph; and Democratic Senators Eugene McCarthy and George McGovern turned against the war, challenging Vice President Hubert Humphrey and Senator Henry Jackson for control of the Democratic Party. The Socialist Party, which had tried to work with almost all these different forces, finally split over the McGovern campaign in 1972–73. Twenty years later, none of its splinters has realized the promise that Shachtman saw in the Socialist Party in 1958.

He had always aimed to build U.S. socialism into a strong movement rooted in forces like the labor and the African-American movements—ones that would have the power to turn society upside down. Once he abandoned his left-wing socialist ghetto in the late 1950s and early 1960s for the mainstream of social democracy, he may well have imagined that he had found his way to a broader, more relevant, less fractious political home. But in the United States of the late 1960s and early 1970s, social democracy proved to be impossible to hold together in a single organization with a single tradition. Shachtman's brand of Marxism helped divide the Socialist Party deeply and kept it from benefiting significantly from either his patient networking or the biggest radical upsurge in the United States in thirty years.

By the time Shachtman died late in 1972, he had helped define a distinctive organizational and ideological strand in U.S. social democracy, one that is almost unique in the world. On international issues—the Middle East and Central America, as well as Vietnam—latter-day Shachtmanites have consistently been on the right wing of international social democracy. But they have combined their right-wing international perspective with a profession of Marxist orthodoxy that is unusual among social democrats, founded on a strong identification with the working class.

In the last months of his life, Shachtman tried to reaffirm his Marxist identity in various ways, some sentimental, some practical. He reached out to Jim Cannon, his old Communist and Trotskyist mentor, visited him in California, and declared his undying loyalty to the ideals and hopes that he and Cannon had shared. At the same time, out of similar emotional impulses, he reached out to people who in the old days had been his and Cannon's most bitter antagonists on the left, the remnant of the pre-1936 Socialist Old Guard. Before he died, he helped unify these old-time, hardline social democrats with what was left of the Socialist Party.

In turning toward these unabashed social democrats, he turned his back on his own political history as a Communist, Trotskyist, and Independent Socialist. Yet paradoxically, at the same time he reaffirmed his identity as a New York Jewish Marxist from immigrant working-class roots.

His death followed four years after the 1968 Tet Offensive against the

United States in Vietnam, an event that some have seen as the beginning of the end of the "American century" that Henry Luce declared in 1945. For most of his political life, Shachtman had worked to bring this American century to an end, supporting movements that resisted the power of U.S. capital in Europe, Asia, Latin America, and inside the United States. Yet as the American century headed toward its end, he aligned himself with forces working to prolong it in Vietnam, in the AFL-CIO, and in the Democratic Party. After a lifetime of resistance, he made his peace with the American century.

The 1964 election pulled Shachtman and his Socialist allies completely into the Democratic Party. The Democratic candidate, Lyndon Johnson, seemed to put forward the core of their agenda: civil rights, full employ-ment, an end to poverty, peace. The Republican, Barry Goldwater, who anticipated both Richard Nixon's "southern strategy" aimed at disgruntled white Democrats and Ronald Reagan's unabashed conservatism, incarnated the Dixiecrat-Republican evil. Shachtman's followers turned the Socialist Party into a virtual Johnson campaign committee.

When Johnson won the 1964 election by a landslide, Shachtman found himself for the first time on the same side with two-thirds of the U.S. electorate. Michael Harrington said, "If the democratic Left rises to the occasion, then the Johnson landslide could provide the basis for a major period of social change."[1] Working almost entirely behind the scenes, where his too-radical past would embarrass no one, Shachtman thought that he could have an impact on the administration's policies. Through Harrington, who worked for a while on Johnson's Great Society anti-poverty programs, Shachtman could even imagine that he had the ear of the president.

Even though Shachtman seemed to have found his way to the corridors of power, he had not become an advocate of the status quo. He still argued for drastic changes in U.S. society, an argument that in the mid-1960s united him not only with other socialists but with many liberals. Many progressives in the mid-1960s thought that the status quo was not only unjust but in trouble.

A spurt in military spending after 1965 concealed the economy's difficul-ties by artificially prolonging the boom and keeping unemployment down. But in fact a quarter century of high profits for U.S. capital ended in 1966–67, and a long period of declining profits, trade deficits, and deindus-trialization began. Danger signs were visible to some even in the early 1960s. Economist Leon Keyserling and AFL-CIO President George Meany warned the League for Industrial Democracy's annual conference in 1961 that unemployment rates were tending to rise in each successive business cycle. Nearly all the new jobs were in either the public or service sector.

Many industrial jobs were dependent on Defense Department contracts, which were threatened (before 1965) by Defense Secretary Robert McNamara's military spending cuts. The benefits of growth were distributed inequitably: The poorest 20 percent of the population received 4.9 percent of the national income in 1944 but only 4.7 percent in 1963.[2]

Shachtman's speech after the 1963 March on Washington connected the future of the civil rights movement to the problematic future of the economy. He focused on the problem of job creation. What the civil rights movement had won so far was "trivial" in comparison with what still needed to be won, he said. The crucial tasks remained: improving African Americans' "abominably low" living standards, education, health, and housing. The way to achieve these goals, he stressed, was to get African Americans good jobs at good wages. There would be no good jobs at good wages, however, as long as the economy was not working efficiently "even to the extent that our dubious prosperity under American capitalism allows it to work" and as long as mass unemployment persisted even in the midst of an economic boom.[3]

Once, Shachtman would have concluded that since mass unemployment was endemic to capitalism, most African Americans would not have good jobs at good wages while capitalism lasted. But now he looked to solve the problem of mass unemployment under capitalism, through the political clout of the AFL-CIO. His confidence in AFL-CIO leaders had grown as his followers became more influential in AFL-CIO councils. By now it was almost boundless.

In the early 1960s, starting from their base in the United Auto Workers, Shachtman's followers had begun getting jobs in the national AFL-CIO. Sammy Fishman became president of the Michigan AFL-CIO. Don Slaiman led the way into AFL-CIO headquarters in Washington by becoming head of the AFL-CIO civil rights department. Through Slaiman Shachtman got the ear of Lane Kirkland, AFL-CIO President Meany's assistant and eventual successor. Shachtman began taking fewer cues from Reuther and more from Meany. United Federation of Teachers President Albert Shanker hired Shachtman's wife Yetta Barsh as his secretary, providing another connection to a national AFL-CIO leader.

Shachtman extended his AFL-CIO network by helping his young followers get union staff jobs. In 1965, following the 1964 collapse of the Young People's Socialist League, he reconstituted it under his right-wing followers' control. The new group had barely a shadow of the independent spirit of Shachtman's earlier youth groups. Even Tom Kahn, who had joined Shachtman's youth group in a livelier time, regretted that the group now had few vigorous debates.[4] But debates were no longer the group's main point. Its main point was to take young people whom the 1960s had begun to radicalize, immunize them against the New Left's subversive appeal, and train them for AFL-CIO or other social democratic careers.

The suspicion of the old AFL and its leaders that Shachtman had grown up with—suspicion that had reinforced his hostility to the LaFollette campaign in 1924, to the Socialists working for Sacco and Vanzetti, and to the Socialist Old Guard that supported Roosevelt after 1936—fell away in the early 1960s. It gave way to an enthusiasm for top AFL-CIO leaders that was sometimes qualified with critical reservations on paper but unconditional in practice. In a letter to Harrington in 1963, Shachtman wrote,

> While my admiration and respect for these trade union–social-democratic movements in the most important countries of the world are under very strict control, I cannot ignore the fact that after three or four decades they have proved to be entirely immune from Stalinism on the one hand and from the often predicted dissolution into purely bourgeois reform movements on the other side. . . . There is something durable and tenacious in these movements . . . a social force of tremendous proportions and power.[5]

His newfound respect for union officialdom made Shachtman look differently at his own past and his old adversaries, particularly old-time social democrats like Morris Hillquit. Shachtman had never had a kind word for Hillquit before Hillquit died in 1933 or for many years afterward. Hillquit had been a die-hard anti-communist, the man who expelled the left wing in 1919, the pillar of the Socialist Party's Old Guard. Yet by 1963, Shachtman praised Hillquit for trying "to bridge the gap . . . between the Socialist movement and the labor movement" that Socialists had opened by opposing the First World War.[6]

The irony of the road Shachtman had taken was brought home when, in January 1971, he was chosen to give a prize named after Hillquit to Charles Zimmerman, an official of the International Ladies Garment Workers Union who had once been a Communist and supporter of Jay Lovestone. Zimmerman jokingly boasted that his "greatest contribution to [the Socialist Party] was that I helped expel Max Shachtman from the Communist Party" in 1928. Shachtman filled his 1971 award speech with praise for Hillquit and calls for new ties between Socialist and AFL-CIO leaders.

> What is in the forefront of our minds and hopes . . . is to restore these old ties, to make them stronger, to make them invincible, in the common struggle for social justice. For us Socialists today, as for Morris Hillquit in his time, the working class and its natural movement, the unions, are the social force and mainspring from which we draw our inspiration [even now,] when every trifler and dilettante finds it fashionable to sneer at it.[7]

Shachtman said that Hillquit's heirs had been right in 1936 to support Franklin Roosevelt, and socialists like Shachtman who opposed Roosevelt had been wrong. The New Deal coalition "worked," Shachtman said. "It did not produce socialism, but then that wasn't Roosevelt's intention." He predicted that the New Deal coalition would be "a decisive element in American politics for a long time to come."[8]

Strengthening the New Deal coalition, and making the AFL-CIO's role within it predominant and hegemonic, was Shachtman's answer to the challenges facing progressive movements in the 1960s. His speech after the 1963 March on Washington was to a large extent a sermon on the importance of a labor–civil rights alliance and the unions' key role. Given the fact that Meany had not even endorsed the march (though Reuther had), he had to put much of the blame for the labor–civil rights alliance's fragility on labor: "It is a wretched labor movement," he said, "miserable on civil rights."

But wretched or not, the labor movement was the force that Shachtman said could win political power. Implicit in his reasoning was the transitional goal he had advocated since 1949–51: a government that, without installing socialism, would be dominated by labor, push through social reforms, and adopt a democratic foreign policy. Only a labor-led government could create full employment in the capitalist United States through a public-works program and massive social spending. Without these policies, he said, "the unions are crippled." With them, the civil rights movement too could achieve its goals.[9] Therefore labor was the civil rights movement's one indispensable ally. Civil rights activists had to push for unity, even bend over backwards to achieve unity, with the AFL-CIO.

Bayard Rustin, with his ties to Martin Luther King, Jr.'s Southern Christian Leadership Conference and the Congress of Racial Equality, became Shachtman's point person for the labor–civil rights alliance. The alliance took on institutional form with the A. Philip Randolph Institute, which promoted civil rights in the unions and linked the two movements together. Rustin directed the Randolph Institute under Randolph's titular authority. The AFL-CIO provided the funding and ultimately set the political parameters (a role reminiscent of white liberal donors' role in the National Association for the Advancement of Colored People as Shachtman had described it in the 1930s).

The Randolph Institute produced the 1966 Freedom Budget, a labor–civil rights agenda for changing national priorities worked out by Rustin, Randolph, and economist Leon Keyserling. Shachtman thought up the name.[10] The Freedom Budget was in fact the most detailed program for domestic social change worked out from Shachtman's final, social democratic perspective.

The Freedom Budget was remarkable for its insistence that "*poverty in America can and therefore must be abolished within ten years*" (by 1975) while leaving the capitalist economy intact. It accepted "our traditional concepts

of a 'mixed economy,' based upon responsible free government and responsible free enterprise." Implicitly assuming that pro-labor Democratic
administrations would be in office throughout the ten years, it mistakenly
foresaw unemployment rates below 3 percent and growth rates of 4.5 to 5
percent at least until 1975. All the social programs by which it proposed to
abolish poverty were to be funded with only a fraction of the resulting
"economic growth dividend."[11]

The Freedom Budget in fact proposed to abolish poverty simply by
raising annual federal social spending from $39.5 billion in 1967 to $67.5
billion in 1975 (in constant dollars).[12] Its wish list of specific programs and
policies consisted mostly of demands that the AFL-CIO had backed for
years: national health insurance, repeal of Taft-Hartley–authorized "right-
to-work" laws, a higher minimum wage ($2 an hour), higher Social Se-
curity and welfare benefits. Its most radical-seeming demand was a
guaranteed annual income, a program whose cost to the federal government
would have been manageable if unemployment had in fact stayed below 3
percent: The private sector would then have provided the guaranteed income to 97 percent of the work force and their families. Though the
Freedom Budget relied on an interventionist government to organize economic growth and redistribute the resulting wealth, it expected the private
sector to provide the great bulk of the money.

If the Freedom Budget was Shachtman's economic prescription for the
civil rights movement's troubles, it presupposed a political strategy that
could keep the Democrats in office and keep Democratic administrations
committed to full employment. Shachtman's political strategy was a New
Deal coalition dominated by the AFL-CIO. This strategy led him to confrontation with some of the African-American leaders he had been close to
earlier in the 1960s. It also began stirring doubts among some of his own
Socialist followers such as Mike Harrington.

Lyndon Johnson's 1964 reelection campaign was a turning point. It
persuaded Shachtman that splitting the Democratic Party was not the best
way to defeat the Dixiecrats and Republicans. He argued instead that a
Democratic Party including most of its current constituencies, though
under a consistently progressive leadership, could be the vehicle for social
change. Socialists should not try to split the Democratic Party, he said now,
but instead turn it into the party the left needed. "If we don't have enough
strength to take over the Democratic Party," he said, "how are we going to
create a labor party with any prospects of winning?"[13] Until the left could
take over the Democratic Party, he decided that the left had to preserve the
Democratic Party.

This conclusion led Shachtman and his friends to try to rein in people on the left who were too confrontational and divisive. At the same time, however, some civil rights leaders who had been close to Shachtman were concluding that they had not been confrontational enough. Stokely Carmichael and other leaders of the Student Nonviolent Coordinating Committee and Congress of Racial Equality were beginning to stress the importance of African Americans organizing and freeing themselves instead of trying to bargain with the white power structure.

Shachtman's new attitude toward the Democratic Party, and the underlying thrust of his approach to African-American issues since the 1930s, went counter to these first stirrings of Black Power. His African-American allies close to the AFL-CIO, particularly Rustin and Randolph, also distrusted the new militancy. Rustin said that Black Power was both "utopian," because "one-tenth of the population cannot accomplish much by itself," and "reactionary," because it took African Americans out of the Democratic Party, "the main arena of political struggle." The Freedom Budget stressed that in order to unite working and poor people behind reforms, "The war against want must be color blind." The gap between advocates of a labor–civil rights alliance and advocates of Black Power widened, until by December 1966 Rustin and Carmichael were debating their opposing strategies in public.[14]

A turning point came with the fight among the Mississippi Democrats at the 1964 Democratic convention. Sixty-eight pro–civil rights Freedom Democrats led by Fannie Lou Hamer challenged the right of sixty-eight white Dixiecrat delegates, elected by a process that excluded African Americans, to represent Mississippi at the convention. The challenge seemed to be exactly what Shachtman had called for at the 1963 March on Washington. But he and his associates no longer favored such uncompromising tactics. They now feared divisions among Democrats because they wanted Johnson to win. Together with a phalanx of civil rights, labor, and liberal leaders, they exerted a "moderating influence" to induce Freedom Democrats to accept an administration-backed "compromise" that seated all sixty-eight Jim Crow delegates and seated two token Freedom Democrats as at-large delegates.

Rustin urged the Freedom Democrats to go along gracefully, saying, "If you are going to engage in politics then you must give up protest." (Later he went back to apologize to them.) After Walter Reuther threatened Martin Luther King with a cutoff of the considerable United Auto Workers funding for the Southern Christian Leadership Conference, King came and told the Freedom Democrats, "The Democratic Party is the best we have." After Reuther threatened the Freedom Democrats' counsel Joseph Rauh with losing his retainer as UAW counsel, Rauh urged his clients to give in. Hubert Humphrey, rumored to have been told that the vice-presidential nomination could hinge on his usefulness in this awkward situation, appealed to Hamer with tears in his eyes.

Michael Harrington later said (citing Democratic Representative Al Lowenstein) that Hamer was willing enough to accept the compromise. But the historical record tells a different story. At one meeting after another, the Freedom Democrats indignantly refused to take the advice that was pushed on them from all sides, and Hamer set the tone: "We didn't come all this way for no two seats!" Many African-American activists shared her sense of outrage and betrayal. Carmichael's and Charles V. Hamilton's 1967 book *Black Power* called the incident proof of liberals' "bankruptcy" and proof that effective coalitions could be built only after African Americans had built "an independent base of political power outside the Democratic Party." James Forman told the 1967 New Politics conference that Black activists had been "victims of the liberal-labor circle's lies." For their part, Shachtman's followers saw the compromise as a "dividing line between an older, more primitive idea of realignment and a more sophisticated one."[15]

The division between the African-American movement and Shachtman's AFL-CIO allies reached its bitterest during the 1968 New York teachers' strike against community control of New York schools. Whatever Shachtman's role in the conflict, his ties through his wife to United Federation of Teachers President Albert Shanker identified him with the striking teachers. Charges of racism against the mostly Jewish teachers, and of anti-Semitism against mostly African-American community activists, flew freely. The strike left a legacy of bitterness and suspicion between white union leaders and the African-American community for decades afterwards.

Shachtman's deepening commitment to an AFL-CIO–Democratic Party network also contributed to the final break in 1965 between Students for a Democratic Society and its parent group, the League for Industrial Democracy. Shachtman's followers rose steadily to prominence in the League under Nathaniel Minkoff's titular presidency. In 1964, Shachtman's young follower Tom Kahn became its executive secretary, and Harrington became chair of its board. It promoted Harrington's *The Other America* and issued influential pamphlets by Kahn ("The Economics of Equality") and Rustin ("From Protest to Politics"). At least one right-wing Republican saw the Socialists in the League as a sinister "idea factory" with "a demonstrated effectiveness in molding public opinion" and close ties to the AFL-CIO's political machine. But the young radicals of Students for a Democratic Society considered the League's social democratic agenda far to their right. At their 1965 national conference in Champaign-Urbana, Illinois, delegates sang a song about the League they were breaking with:

Along came the L.I.D. as fast as it could run,
Going down that S.P. road just forty years behind,
Nathaniel Minkoff at the wheel a-tryin' to make lost time,
Receiving very strict orders from the Shachtman just behind.[16]

In 1964 and 1965, despite growing tensions around Black Power and the
New Left, the great majority of Socialists seemed to go along with Shachtman's support for AFL-CIO leaders, the Johnson administration, and a united
Democratic Party. But in fact, Socialists were beginning to head in different
directions. Subtle differences in approach were beginning to sort them into two
camps, one led by Shachtman and the other by Mike Harrington.

One root of the differences was Harrington's critical attitude toward
Shachtman's Marxist orthodoxy, which went far back in Harrington's
history. Harrington had joined the Socialist Party rather than Shachtman's
Independent Socialist League in 1952, even though the Independent Socialist newspaper *Labor Action* had won him to socialism. The Independent
Socialist League was Marxist, and Harrington believed that as a Catholic he
could not be a Marxist. After he left the Socialist Party and helped found
the Young Socialist League in 1954, he gave up his Catholicism,
decided that he was a Marxist after all, and became a member of Shachtman's group in everything but name.[17] But his unorthodoxy showed itself
again in the 1960s as he distanced himself from Shachtman's understanding
of working-class politics.

Harrington worked in the early 1960s with liberal and leftist intellectuals
who said that the U.S. economy's difficulties in generating jobs were not
due simply to capitalism or the labor movement's lack of power but to the
technological revolution brought about by automation. For many of them,
automation meant that industrial workers were less important now as a
force for social change, and technicians and intellectuals were more important. One 1964 statement called "The Triple Revolution" was signed by
dozens of intellectuals, including Harrington, and included such statements as "Wealth produced by machines rather than by men is still
wealth," which had little in common with Marxism as Shachtman had
always expounded it.[18]

Harrington soon drew explicit political conclusions from his theoretical
unorthodoxy. A nervous breakdown in 1965, which he later attributed to
unease with his newfound prosperity and influence as a popular author and
Democratic Party intellectual, gave him time away from Shachtman to do
his own thinking. The social ferment of the 1960s began to have an impact
on him. He had been as uncomfortable as Shachtman with the emergent
New Left politics of Black Power leaders like Carmichael or student radicals
like Tom Hayden. But with new forms of dissent and resistance springing
up in different parts of U.S. society—a movement against nuclear testing, a

new youth culture, the beginnings of the second wave of feminism—he began looking for ways to converge with them. He looked toward the "New Politics" growing up on the New Left's moderate fringe, mainly inside the Democratic Party at first.

"The theory of the working-class' historical mission has been undermined by the technological revolution," he said in January 1966. "No single class, but a coalition of progressive social forces, is now necessary to achieve a radical democratic transformation of society." He began looking for some kind of merger between New Politics and "the mass left wing of American society" represented by George Meany.[19]

A radically insurgent working-class politics could have converged in many ways with the new African-American, Latino, feminist, and cultural radicalisms of the 1960s. Even if the most prominent spokespeople for these new radicalisms were middle-class, their broad constituencies were to some extent working-class—in fact, they were largely the new working-class sectors that the AFL-CIO was failing to reach. White-collar and service workers, the labor force's fastest growing and least organized sectors, were disproportionately people of color, female, and young. A few rank-and-file insurgencies in the 1960s even among blue-collar workers, such as the Dodge Revolutionary Union Movement, tried to link labor activism with African-American and New Left militancy.

But rank-and-file union insurgencies were relatively rare in the 1960s, and there were few chances for labor and new social movements to connect. New Politics, sometimes completely counterposed to labor, was the most prominent alternative among Democrats and Socialists to an uncritical orientation toward AFL-CIO officials.

Shachtman argued that any genuinely progressive movement would win or lose depending on whether the union movement advanced or retreated. Other movements' demands had to fit into a labor-based strategy. He and his co-thinkers had no interest in diluting their avowedly working-class politics with middle-class liberalism. "In our political 'coalition,' a group of intellectuals and a union of a million members, a department of college professors and a Negro organization of half a million, are not equal in numbers, influence, political experience, tenacity, discipline—in a word, in social weight and durable political power—and they cannot be," Rustin and he said. "We assign more importance to the labor movement than to any other force in the coalition."[20]

Shachtman's and Harrington's different approaches surfaced in the League for Industrial Democracy. As Harrington took office as chair of the League's board in 1964, he proposed that the League should have a "unique, triple constituency of intellectuals, trade unionists and civil rights activists." Kahn's speeches as the League's executive secretary laid less stress on the intellectuals, to whom the League had always had ties, and more on the trade unionists he saw as key. But the League reinforced its ties with leftist intellectuals nonetheless in 1966 by establishing a special working relationship with the socialist magazine *Dissent*; they planned to hold joint forums and publish joint pamphlets.[21] The arrangement helped bring *Dissent* editor Irving Howe closer to Harrington.

Harrington's relationship with Howe, like his unorthodox attitude to Marxism, dated back to the 1950s. In *Dissent*'s first years—out of bitterness at Howe's, Stanley Plastrik's, and Manny Geltman's desertion—Shachtman had the Independent Socialist League prohibit its members from writing for or supporting the new magazine. Harrington, however, proudly and defiantly had the Young Socialist League officially encourage its members to write for and support *Dissent*. At a time when Shachtman's *New International* was eking out its life, putting forward the organizational line of a small and isolated organization, young socialists were bound to find *Dissent*'s more ecumenical and freethinking approach stimulating. Though its editors were to Shachtman's right, they published independent cultural thinkers such as C. Wright Mills, Paul Goodman, Herbert Marcuse, and Norman Mailer. Harrington confirmed his support for *Dissent* by becoming a contributing editor in the fall of 1957.[22]

For a time in the late 1950s and early 1960s, Shachtman, Harrington, and Howe all seemed to work together more closely. Shachtman commented in 1957 that the "icy coldness with the *Dissent*-ers" had thawed somewhat. Howe and Shachtman worked together on an anthology of Trotsky's writings and actually met again in 1961. Howe said, "It was pleasant to meet you again after all these years, Max," and Shachtman answered, "I had the same feeling." But tensions remained. Howe refused to join the Socialist Party, irritating Shachtman with his willingness to speak for socialists without ever affiliating with them. When Shachtman's *Bureaucratic Revolution*, the anthology of his writings on Stalinism over two decades, was published in 1961, Howe reviewed it briefly and not very warmly. Shachtman's one contribution to *Dissent*, a review published in 1964, was a somewhat tired restatement of his views on the Soviet Union.[23]

By late 1966, Harrington was willing to align himself openly with *Dissent*'s intellectual tradition in its pages, in words that could be read as distancing him from Shachtman's tradition. He recalled mockingly his suspicion of *Dissent* in the 1950s, when he said that he thought its editors were "hell-bent for liberalism, a fate worse than death." In hindsight he praised *Dissent* for its decision to "strike out in search of new relevance" instead of continuing to "incant old truths."[24]

Only an insider could have detected any criticism of Shachtman in Harrington's words. To all public appearances, the two men were still close, two leaders of a small socialist movement. They still seemed to agree on basic questions: Both supported liberal Democrats, labor, civil rights, and a democratic foreign policy, and both were disenchanted with Black Power and the campus radicals of Students for a Democratic Society. But the tensions between them were there, waiting to be triggered. The war in Vietnam pulled the trigger.

The last decisive test for Shachtman's worldview came with the U.S. war in Vietnam, which reached its full scale in 1965 and continued on its bloody course until after his death. He extended his devotion to trade unions and union-backed reform movements to the very different context of South Vietnam. Such hopes as he had for Vietnam he pinned on South Vietnam's small anti-Communist opposition; its powerless independent unions and Buddhist dissidents and peace activists aligned with them. Seeing that a Communist victory threatened the anti-Communist opposition as well as the U.S.-backed series of South Vietnamese military dictatorships, he decided that U.S. troops should stay in South Vietnam to defend South Vietnamese democrats. For the first time in his life he openly supported a U.S. war—ironically, picking one of the most unpopular wars the United States ever fought.

Shachtman and his followers had always looked for an anti-Stalinist left to support in conflicts between capitalism and Communism. As early as 1954 the Independent Socialists committed themselves to finding a third force in Vietnam, insisting on neutrality between Communists and the Saigon government even though "French imperialism and its armies are the aggressors."[25] Shachtman stuck to this perspective even after many of his followers gave it up as hopeless.

But his position on the Vietnam War after 1965 contained two major departures from his earlier stands on the Korean War and the Bay of Pigs invasion. First, during the Korean War he had dismissed any idea of coexistence or peace between capitalism and Stalinism. He saw the two systems' warfare as inevitable and overthrow of both as the only way out. By 1965, his closer acquaintance with South Vietnamese trade unionists linked to the AFL-CIO made him see Vietnam differently. He saw the only hope for a Vietnamese third force in a negotiated settlement.

Second, he had never before supported a U.S. military presence anywhere in the world. He never repudiated Independent Socialists' 1950 call for unilateral U.S. withdrawal from Korea. At the time of the Bay of Pigs invasion, he took refuge in the fact that the invaders were technically not U.S. troops. As late as August 1961 he had called publicly for withdrawal of all U.S. forces in Vietnam.[26] But by 1965 he decided that U.S. withdrawal from Vietnam any time soon would doom any negotiated settlement, would ensure a Communist victory, and had to be opposed. He resolved to defend the South Vietnamese anti-Communist left, even if he had to rely on the U.S. government and its South Vietnamese client regime to do it.

The anti-Communist left was never able to stand on its own in Vietnam because, as in Yugoslavia and China, Communists had become the major force fighting for national independence during the Second World War, showing that they could not be defeated or manipulated by the Japanese, French, Americans, Soviets, or Chinese. By defeating the French at Dien Bien Phu in 1954, the Communists made their position as Vietnam's national leadership unassailable. When a national resistance movement grew up in South Vietnam in the early 1960s and was organized into a National Liberation Front, Communists were in firm control.

The United States provided the finances for the French colonial war in the early 1950s and troops, money, and strategy for the war in South Vietnam in the 1960s and 1970s. U.S. military "advisers," limited to 685 under the 1954 Geneva agreement, rose to 16,000 by 1963, 200,000 in 1965, and 500,000 in 1969.

With the number of U.S. troops increasing, the number of U.S. deaths also inevitably rose, and with them the number and anger of protesters. The war in Vietnam, whose brutality further shook people already shocked by white violence against the civil rights movement, helped fuel a new radical upsurge. But the New Left's roots in the labor movement were as feeble as the Old Left's had been strong. Most union officials supported the war, and anti-communism was pervasive even in unions that opposed the war.

The AFL-CIO had Vietnamese trade unionist contacts, some of whom Shachtman met. The South Vietnamese government harassed and jailed these unionists, but they nonetheless felt even more threatened by the prospect of Communist victory than by the status quo. Shachtman was impressed by the fact that the AFL-CIO had enough concern and clout with the administration to get South Vietnamese unionists out of jail on occasion. Apparently it did not occur to him that unionists whose freedom depended on the U.S. government's whim might be poor representatives and fighters for their members' interests.

Mike Harrington remembered one discussion that took place in 1966 in a community room in Bayard Rustin's apartment building. "Of course, the war is horrible and the killing should be stopped as soon as possible," Harrington remembered Shachtman's saying; "of course the United States is involved with dictators, scoundrels, and knaves." But Shachtman insisted that democratic socialists should try to stop the killing and oppose the dictators, scoundrels, and knaves only in ways that contributed to defeating Communism in Vietnam, never in any way that might contribute to its victory. He had decided to back U.S. power in Vietnam as a "shield behind which the democratic revolution could organize itself."[27]

He first expressed his opposition to U.S. withdrawal in June 1965, in front of 250 people at a forum sponsored by *Dissent* and the League for Industrial Democracy. Over the next few years he seemed to avoid restating his position in public in an attempt not to worsen growing divisions over the war among his Socialist followers. But in 1970 he joined in a Statement on Vietnam that reaffirmed his opposition to U.S. withdrawal, took the same basic line of argument as his 1965 speech, and elaborated his analysis at length.[28]

Both Shachtman's 1965 speech and the 1970 Statement on Vietnam reiterated many of the traditional socialist criticisms of U.S. foreign policy that had been part of his position on Korea in 1951 and Cuba in 1961. The 1965 speech repudiated any identification of the South Vietnamese regime as "good"; the 1970 statement opposed any "support for the present Saigon government." The 1965 speech reaffirmed Shachtman's opposition to U.S. intervention wherever—specifically in the Dominican Republic—there was not an immediate danger of a Communist military victory. The Statement on Vietnam attributed the flawed U.S. Vietnam policy to "the capitalist interest in the Cold War." It expressed "solidarity with the millions of Americans who yearn for peace." But in the context of the debate over the war, particularly among socialists, the main thrust of both the speech and the statement was their advocacy of keeping U.S. troops in Vietnam.

The driving inner logic of Shachtman's position, both at the 1965 forum and in the 1970 statement, was that a U.S.-backed semidictatorship was still better for the democratic left than Communism. He said in 1965 that the Saigon regime, although not "good," did "permit the possibility of the people fighting for their rights. . . . In South Vietnam, you can organize a demonstration and get beat on the head," he said. "You can't do that much in North Vietnam." The 1970 statement said that socialists should prefer the capitalist "countries of political democracy" to Communism—"totalitarian despotism"— because a

> non-Communist South Vietnam, even under the Saigon regime, still leaves intact—if only embryonically—a variety of social and political forces that are independent of both the Saigon government and the totalitarians . . . Buddhist and other religious groups, political parties and organizations, trade unions, student organizations.

On the basis of this logic Shachtman, without ever defending the original decision to send U.S. troops, opposed U.S. withdrawal, at least "before the South Vietnamese are in a better position to pursue their own defense." He said in 1965 that U.S. withdrawal would be "monstrous." The 1970 statement argued that withdrawal ending in Communist victory would aid Maoism and Guevaraism ("the most irrational, violence-obsessed, and guerrilla-oriented sections and branches of Communist totalitarianism") as well as "right wing reaction" and "neo-isolationist" forces.

During the Vietnam War, Shachtman consistently—and for the first time—argued for a negotiated peace with the Communists. The Statement on Vietnam demanded free elections in South Vietnam with Communist participation, consistent with Shachtman's past opposition to depriving Communists of their legal, democratic rights. But the statement argued against giving them any place in a South Vietnamese coalition government. It said that such a coalition was "either an illusion for which no precedent can be found anywhere in our time, or a cloak for a more stealthy surrender of the country to the Communists."

The Statement on Vietnam advanced one other key argument: that South Vietnam was fighting for its "national independence." The fact that "the government in the South is dominated by a military or semi-military regime" funded by the United States made no difference, it said.

Shachtman never argued that military victory over North Vietnam was possible, but he said that military defeat would be disastrous. The purpose of waging war should be to win a negotiated settlement, the same trick that the U.S. government ended up trying to pull off. In practice, the idea was full of pitfalls and contradictions. As a result, Shachtman's position on any particular aspect of the war—for example, the U.S. bombing of North Vietnam—was often unclear or changeable. The Socialist Workers Party's newspaper the *Militant* reported that at the 1965 forum Shachtman said that the bombing would compel North Vietnam to negotiate. Harrington later remembered Shachtman's saying in 1966 that "of course the bombing should cease." Tom Kahn said that Shachtman would simply respond to questions about the bombing by saying, "I'm not advising the government on how to carry out this war."[29]

Shachtman did advise the labor and civil rights movements on how to win reforms in the midst of the war. He insisted that "guns and butter" were both possible. The Freedom Budget tried to prove his case. A. Philip Randolph's introduction to the Budget said that the plan took no position on the war, "which is basically a thorny question to be viewed in its own terms." But the Budget foresaw a steadily rising military budget, arguing, in effect, that the government could fight the Vietnam War and still abolish poverty. It even said, "No effort we are making anywhere in the world has any basis except to defend and advance the frontiers of freedom." When *Commentary* editor Norman Podhoretz questioned whether the country could afford the Vietnam War, Shachtman replied, "The country had better be able to afford it."[30]

By 1970, the strategy that the Statement on Vietnam put forward for the war dovetailed with the one Republican President Richard Nixon was carrying out: "Vietnamization" of the war, ending in a peace agreement providing for elections.[31] The strategy turned out to be at least as ineffective

in saving the South Vietnamese regime or the independent South Vietnamese left as U.S. withdrawal would have been. It also took the lives of
about two million people that U.S. withdrawal in 1965 would have
spared—and maimed, poisoned, displaced, and impoverished millions more.

The Statement on Vietnam's evidence that the U.S. war was fostering
democracy in South Vietnam was in fact limited to a virtual handful of
genuine democrats and workers' organizations. The "democracy" that
these stalwart non-Communists were granted by the U.S.-backed South
Vietnamese regime consisted largely of harassment, censorship, imprisonment, and torture.

For thirty years Shachtman had eloquently maintained that only working
and oppressed people could effectively defend or extend the democratic
freedoms that their past struggles had won under capitalism; imperialist
governments would only undermine and make a mockery of those freedoms. South Vietnam was a compelling example of the validity of that
analysis. But by the time this clinching case came along, Shachtman had
changed his mind.

The idea that the South Vietnamese were fighting for independence
presupposed that South Vietnam was a nation rather than a truncated part of
Vietnam set aside at French and U.S. demand in 1954. It ignored the fact
that South Vietnam was defending its "independence" only from other
Vietnamese; the Communists, however undemocratic, were an independent Vietnamese force that resisted Soviet pressure to accept the division of
the country and refused to take sides in the Sino-Soviet conflict in the 1960s.
Shachtman saw his defense of South Vietnam as being in continuity with his
thinking about national liberation going back to the 1940s; but this last
nation that he defended was fictitious.

Shachtman's stand against U.S. withdrawal from Vietnam positioned
him on the right not only of the Socialist Party but of the Democratic Party
as well, during years when massive sections of the U.S. population were
moving to the left. It identified him as an enemy of the New Left that
emerged from the anti-war movement, cut him off from major sections of
the labor and civil rights movements, and helped split his own following in
the Socialist Party.

He was quite willing to be the New Left's enemy. He saw in the New
Left all the apologies for Stalinist crimes he remembered from Communists
in the 1930s. He used Maoist groups' pronouncements (especially the willingness some of them expressed to dispense completely with democracy
and write off the U.S. working class) as an excuse for dismissing the whole
generation of revolutionary socialists that grew up by the early 1970s.

Because some New Leftists saw Ho and Mao as heroes, he wrote off the whole New Left.

"As I watch the New Left, I simply weep," he said. "If somebody set out to take the errors and stupidities of the Old Left and multiplied them to the nth degree, you would have the New Left of today." He saw the New Left as vindication for his belief that a left that turned away from the unions would become "crazier and crazier." He drummed into his remaining followers' heads the need for "permanent vigilance lest the cancer of totalitarianism destroy all that is healthy and promising in the struggle for socialism."[32]

He had to regret much more deeply his alienation from major forces in the unions and the African-American community. He seemed helpless to prevent labor and civil rights leaders from turning against the war and turning away from his AFL-CIO–led coalition. At best he found ways to explain away what he saw as former allies' desertion. Martin Luther King, Jr.'s decision to come out publicly against the war in January 1966 (though Rustin had enlisted UN Ambassador Arthur Goldberg to try to convince King of Johnson's good intentions) was explained away as the softness of a Gandhian pacifist. Rustin and other moderate civil rights leaders countered King's statement with one of their own in November 1966, saying, "For every Negro who tosses a Molotov cocktail, there are a thousand fighting and dying on the battlefields of Vietnam." When Walter Reuther came out against the war, contributing to the United Auto Workers' decision to leave the AFL-CIO, Shachtman and his friends dismissed Reuther's break with Meany as the expression of a frustrated ambition to be AFL-CIO president.[33]

Shachtman's break with the Socialist Party's anti-war left wing led by pacifist Dave McReynolds, who had originally invited him into the party, caused him relatively little pain. Shachtman's followers were still united at the June 1966 Socialist convention in rejecting McReynolds's call for unilateral U.S. withdrawal. The Shachtmanites seemed to stand together behind a vague call for a negotiated solution.[34] Disgusted by the Socialist Party's repeated refusals to call plainly for U.S. withdrawal, McReynolds eventually left it in 1970 with a group of followers.

The apparent unity of Shachtman's group was a façade. His relations with Mike Harrington and Irving Howe were already strained by the end of 1966, with differing attitudes toward the AFL-CIO, New Politics, and Vietnam all contributing to the tension. Slowly and agonizingly, Harrington, Howe, and many of Shachtman's longtime followers were turning against the war.

Shachtman tried to contain the growing tensions over the war by downplaying the issue and minimizing the differences. His most deeply held position about Vietnam seemed to be that it should go away. He "predicted the demise of Vietnam as an issue every year for six or seven years." He tried to avoid debating it in public, to the point where McReynolds said in frustration in February 1967, "Shachtman shall be remembered for his wit, for his singularly important contributions to socialist theory, for his princi- pled and early opposition to Stalinism and—unhappily—for his silence during this time of agony." But the issue would not go away. In the summer of 1967 Harrington, Howe, and others took a public position in *Dissent* that Shachtman would not support, calling for a halt to the bombing as a prelude to a cease-fire.[35]

By the summer and fall of 1968, the war in Vietnam provoked social tremors that shook every corner of the political landscape and threatened to topple governments. Student anti-war protests in Paris led to a nationwide general strike in France; Students for a Democratic Society in New York shut down Columbia University; following his anti-war pronouncements, King was assassinated and inner cities across the United States burned. For Shachtman and his followers, though, what made Vietnam impossible to sidestep was the approach of a presidential election and the fracturing of the Democratic Party. When Senator Eugene McCarthy's strong showing against Lyndon Johnson in the New Hampshire primary prompted Johnson to withdraw from the race in favor of Vice President Hubert Humphrey, Socialists were pulled willy-nilly into a primary campaign that was largely a Democratic referendum on the war.

Shachtman could not believe that anyone trained in his school would support McCarthy over Humphrey. Humphrey's record of support for labor was good. His commitment to civil rights went back twenty years. He had led the fight to drive Communists out of the Minnesota Democratic- Farmer-Labor Party. He would be opposed in November not only by the old McCarthyist Richard Nixon but by George Wallace, the new person- ification of Dixiecrat racism. Realignment in 1968 meant Humphrey.

But Humphrey's identification with Johnson's war meant more to Har- rington and Howe than Shachtman's strategy. Although they reluctantly backed Humphrey over Nixon and Wallace in the end, *Dissent*'s election- eve issue was filled with a debate over whether to vote for Humphrey or abstain. Shachtman called the debate "stupefying."[36] The people who shared his views showed their feelings by having Humphrey receive the League for Industrial Democracy's 1969 annual award. The award cere- mony was bound to provoke a large-scale anti-war protest, and it did.

Shachtman and Harrington continued somehow to work with each other in the Socialist Party. Nonaggression agreements were negotiated repeated- ly, with each side blaming the other when they broke down. New Socialist positions on the war were adopted each year, with Shachtman's allies giving a little ground each time to Harrington's steadily growing reservations. In 1969 the party called for "speedy" if not immediate withdrawal of U.S. troops along with "democratization" of South Vietnam. In a final, hard-fought compromise at the Socialists' 1970 convention, they declared that if democracy and peace remained unattainable in South Vietnam, U.S. support for the South Vietnamese regime should end.[37]

Shachtman and his allies would not let the world think that this stand actually represented them. They issued their public Statement on Vietnam in order to make their stand clear. With the Statement on Vietnam out in public, Harrington would no longer refrain from public debate. He attacked the Statement's signers as advocates of "reactionary anti-Communism," "*supporters of American foreign policy, even at its worst.*" The war was so horrible that a Communist victory would be "a genuine lesser evil," he said now.[38]

The attack from Harrington was as unbearable for Shachtman as the attack from Hal Draper had been earlier. Harrington said later that even when he and Shachtman "hardly spoke to one another . . . I never lost my respect and affection for Max," this "warm, vibrant, utterly serious man who nevertheless sometimes laughed until he cried." But Shachtman did not allow fond memories to interfere with his bitterness when he felt betrayed. He described Harrington's charges as "reckless and irresponsible," "without precedent in what I know of the history of the radical movement." He and Harrington did not speak again.[39]

The dispute over Vietnam also disrupted Shachtman's relationship with Howe, which had already been destroyed and rebuilt once, although both men tried to save it. "What have we learned over all these bitter years if we can't avoid a split?" Howe asked Shachtman. Shachtman responded with unaccustomed softness. "We have known each other for a good three decades and I respect not only your talents but your continuing commitments," he said. He justified his frankness by saying that he had to say "how I really feel": "I do not always have the courage to say it to you face to face."[40]

The Socialist Party began to look like two organizations artificially soldered together—and if Socialists were conceived as a faction within the Democratic Party, they made up two different factions. Harrington could not make anti-war Democrats bow their heads to a labor-imposed yoke—nor did he want to—especially when they were getting stronger within the Democratic Party. As another election year came around in 1972, Harrington's favored candidate, George McGovern, won primary after primary until he had a solid majority of the party convention. The Socialist newspaper *New America* seemed to be torn in two, printing two opposing articles on almost every major topic.

In Shachtman's eyes, New Politics was "a wing of nuts—who aim, not to hold things together, but to bust things apart." He saw no reason to support McGovern, he said: "His foreign policy is a monstrosity, not just as bad as Henry Wallace in 1948 but much worse." McGovern, who advocated withdrawing U.S. troops from Vietnam in six weeks, seemed to Shachtman to favor "turning over all of Vietnam to the Stalinists." Shachtman said that McGovern's campaign ran "entirely against the grain of our realignment policy. He wants an anti-labor machine; I want the opposite."[41]

"I reject of course any sympathy or support for Nixon," Shachtman added. During the primaries he leaned toward Henry Jackson, a Cold War Democratic senator close to the AFL-CIO who hired Tom Kahn for his staff. When McGovern won the Democratic nomination, Shachtman told Kahn that he admired Meany's "guts" in declaring neutrality between Nixon and McGovern. The Socialist Party, with Shachtman's allies in the majority, expressed a preference for McGovern but attacked his supporters for "authoritarian leftist leanings" and "elitist and anti-labor tendencies." Harrington resigned as Socialist Party co-chair in protest.[42] Soon he would leave the organization. The Socialist Party, Shachtman's last hope for building a significant left in the United States, was split.

Shachtman was overcome in his last years years by nostalgia. To all outward appearances, his dedication to his politics never faltered. But the clarity of his mind and firmness of conviction did not protect him from bouts of ill health, particularly heart trouble. He complained about the "medical dictatorship" he sometimes lived under.[43] Besides, many of his old friends and old enemies were dying. People usually have to face this pain in late middle age—those who are lucky enough not to have seen their friends die earlier, in wars or epidemics. Shachtman found it hard to bear.

The emotional difficulties of getting older were compounded for him by the emotional difficulties of having left behind so much of his past and so many people he had been close to. Intellectually, he had largely come to terms with the thought that he had spent decades of his political life on a fundamentally mistaken course. He said that he had been wrong in the 1930s and 1940s to cut himself off from the main body of the labor movement as it integrated into the Democratic Party and acquiesced in U.S. foreign policy. But emotionally, he still could not detach himself from the excitement of old memories, the passion of bygone controversies, and the appeal of Marxist argument and rhetoric.

His sentimental attachment to his revolutionary past found three different, even contradictory, outlets in the late 1960s and early 1970s. As he defined his own distinct version of social democratic politics, he continued to insist that what he was elaborating and defending was Marxism. From time to time he would still lash out at people who disparaged or strayed from Marxism. He also kept to the end a soft spot for the Bolshevik tradition, even though his sympathies were now with latter-day Mensheviks. For years he immersed himself in documents from the old Communist International, without being able to put in writing his own critical rejection of its politics. He continued, finally, to look positively on Trotsky and even Trotskyists, if not young Trotskyists around the New Left then at least the old Trotskyists he had known and worked with. He even renewed a friendship with Jim Cannon, saying that "the distance disputes placed between us did not diminish the feelings and hopes we shared years ago."[44]

Having a long Marxist heritage to draw on helped make up for the fact that in the end his tight Socialist faction was about as small and isolated as his Trotskyist groups had been in the 1930s and 1940s. He used to marvel that despite being "correct on almost every single question," he had so few followers left. There was only one possible explanation, he would joke: "We are cursed!" He tried to make up for his isolation from young radicals by reaching out to old social democrats who, like him, remained attached to Marxist terminology: He pushed for the Socialist Party's reunification with a splinter group of the Socialist Old Guard that had broken away from the party in 1936.[45]

The past he had lived through became for Shachtman a kind of personal property, and he resented other people's interference in putting forward opinions about it that were different from his own. He dismissed Isaac Deutscher's famous biography of Trotsky as "inexcusably dirty-dishonest." He told Theodore Draper, Hal Draper's ex-Communist brother and a major historian of the Communist Party with whom he carried on an otherwise friendly correspondence, "You have handicapped yourself by an abjuration of Marxism." He called ignorance of Marxism "as inexcusable . . . as ignorance of Newton and Darwin" and dismissed "the belief that Marxism is outlived" as outlived itself.[46] Perhaps the violence of his attacks on those who saw Marxism differently betrayed a slight insecurity about the Marxism he had ended up with.

His friendship with Al Glotzer provided one kind of reassurance of continuity with his Marxist past, since Glotzer had traveled the same political road all the way from the Communist Party (and would continue to uphold Shachtman's version of social democracy after Shachtman died). Manny Geltman was a dual link to the past in other ways. He was almost the only remaining friend from the old days who had not shared Shachtman's full political evolution and who was able to tease Shachtman about how far he had come.

Geltman also gave Shachtman an excuse to bury himself in records from the Communist 1920s and 1930s. An editor with Free Press (owned by

Macmillan) as well as *Dissent*, Geltman ate lunch with Shachtman once a week during the 1960s, ostensibly to check on Shachtman's progress on a history of the Communist International for which Free Press had paid him a $15,000 advance. Shachtman's nostalgia showed in the excitement with which he pursued obscure leads and documents, piling up a mountain of paper by 1972. His reluctance to dismiss the whole Communist movement as sweepingly as his latter-day politics would have dictated showed in the fact that he never produced so much as a first draft.[47]

Glotzer said later that Shachtman, "saturated" in bolshevism, "had not reached a focal point where he could do justice to it." Geltman arranged for him to speak at a conference at Stanford and to spend a month as scholar in residence at another university, to no avail. During his scholarship in residence Shachtman gathered a group of intrigued students around him, fed them with revolutionary history, and "never wrote a line."[48]

At least Shachtman and Geltman's lunches gave them a chance to reminisce and joke. Geltman would recall Shachtman's oath that he would support U.S. imperialism on the day he had long hairs growing on the palm of his hand. Increasingly opposed to Shachtman's support for the Vietnam War, Geltman would take Shachtman's hand across the lunch table and cluck reprovingly at the imaginary hairs growing out of Shachtman's palm.[49]

A softness for old Trotskyist memories suggested a barely acknowledged sense of loss behind Shachtman's rejection of his old politics. Natalia Sedova's death from cancer in 1962 particularly saddened him. By becoming Sedova's friend again in the late 1940s Shachtman had, at least in his own mind, received Trotsky's forgiveness, even the acknowledgment that Trotsky had been wrong in their 1939–40 quarrel, which Trotsky's death had denied him. She had broken with the Fourth International in 1951, insisting that only people "obsessed by old and outlived formulas" would uphold Trotsky's view of the Soviet Union as a workers' state.[50] Shachtman's visits to her fed his sense of an unbroken tie to Trotsky.

Shachtman was with Sedova in 1953 when news came of Stalin's death. Her lack of vindictiveness reminded him of Trotsky's sublime indifference to personal injuries.[51] But Shachtman was almost alone in the value he put on her friendship and opinions. Long before she died, most people had forgotten about her existence. Her death seemed to consign her to oblivion.

With hindsight, Shachtman convinced himself that even Trotskyists he had often been at loggerheads with had been wonderful people whom he had always loved. Joe Carter, a Trotskyist since the 1920s and a frequent adversary of Shachtman's in the 1940s, died in 1970. Shachtman had been completely out of touch with him. But he could not reconcile himself to the man's having "gone, silently, unnoticed, unmourned, unGoddamned for, with only a vague memory left behind."[52]

Most remarkably, Shachtman's old affection for Jim Cannon returned. Cannon had gradually become a semiretired elder statesman of the Socialist Workers Party after moving to Los Angeles in 1954. Shachtman and he had occasional, pleasant phone conversations in the 1960s. When Cannon's wife and Shachtman's old friend Rose Karsner died in 1968, Shachtman wrote, "I only wish now that I could put my arms around Jim on this cruel day." In 1972 Shachtman actually visited Cannon in California. Cannon was old and frail and seemed to know that he had only a few years to live. Somehow the two men managed to transcend their differences, which had grown steadily wider, and enjoy each other's company. Shachtman returned from the trip and told Geltman that the reunion had been marvelous.[53]

Shachtman's forgiveness of old enemies did not soften his bitterness toward current enemies. On the contrary, he was angry at the foolish people who had survived while so many better, wiser people had died. He felt himself to be surrounded by detractors who lacked elementary honesty and decency. Kahn saw him cry more than once when people broke with him.[54]

Beneath the anger there was an anguish that Shachtman shrank from. One of his followers from the 1940s and 1950s, Stan Weir, ran into him at a United Auto Workers convention in 1968, where Shachtman was attacking Walter Reuther for opposing the Vietnam War. The two began arguing in the hallway. Soon Weir was explaining that he owed his understanding of why the war was wrong to Shachtman, along with many other things he owed to Shachtman. Shachtman almost ran away. "He said, 'You're killing me,'" Weir remembered, "and I was, because . . . we're both gonna stand there and weep."[55]

The loss of many of the human landmarks of Shachtman's past, through either their deaths or his anger at their deserting his politics, made him cling all the more to those left who remained loyal. Tom Kahn remembered the "bearhug warmth" of Shachtman's friendship in those last years. "Max was always there for advice, for uplift, and for commiseration," Kahn said. "His telephone rang constantly." He enjoyed doing his friends favors, tinkering with their stereo systems.[56]

Set in his convictions, still doing his best to hold together the people and groups he could, Shachtman nonetheless spent much of his time at home in Floral Park, pleased when his loyalists visited him there. On 3 November 1972, Kahn came by and the two talked as usual about their allies and enemies, hopes and setbacks. The next day, 4 November, Shachtman died of heart failure.

Notes

1. NA v 4 n 15 (16 Nov. 1964), 1.
2. League for Industrial Democracy News Bulletin (Summer 1961); Ad Hoc Committee, "The triple revolution," *Liberation* v 9 n 2 (April 1964), 12.
3. Shachtman, "Drive out Dixiecrats for jobs and freedom," NA v 3 n 16–17 (24 Sept. 1963), 8, 12.
4. Interview with Kahn (7 Apr. 1989), s 2.
5. Shachtman to Harrington (20 Aug. 1963), MSC b 29 f 17 (r 3379).
6. RMS 458.
7. Shachtman, "Socialists and the trade unions," NA v 9 n 22 (28 Feb. 1971), 5, 7.
8. Interview with Shachtman by Terkel (1971), NA v 10 n 22 (15 Nov. 1972), 6; Glotzer, "Max Shachtman," NA v 10 n 22, 4.
9. Shachtman, "Drive out Dixiecrats for jobs and freedom," NA v 3 n 16–17 (24 Sept. 1963), 8, 12.
10. "A meeting for Max," NA v 11 n 1 (31 Dec. 1972), 8.
11. *A "Freedom Budget" for All Americans: Budgeting Our Resources, 1966–1975, to Achieve "Freedom from Want"* (New York: A. Philip Randolph Institute, Oct. 1966), 2, 10, 22, 8.
12. *Freedom Budget*, 9.
13. Interview with Kahn (7 Apr. 1989), s 2.
14. Rustin, "Black Power and coalition politics," *Commentary* 42 (Sept. 1966), 35–36; *Freedom Budget*, 2; League for Industrial Democracy News Bulletin (Fall 1966/Winter 1967).
15. Interview with Kahn (7 Apr. 1989) s 3; James Forman, *The Making of Black Revolutionaries*, 392, 500–501; interview with Harrington by Friend and Hacker (19 Aug. 1988), s 2; Claybourne Carson, *In Struggle*, 126; Stokely Carmichael and Charles V. Hamilton, *Black Power*, 93, 96, 97.
16. Philip M. Crane, *The Democrats' Dilemma*, 359. Many thanks to Paul Le Blanc for this quotation, and especially for the lyrics of the song.
17. Interview with Harrington by Friend and Hacker (19 Aug. 1988), s 1.
18. Ad Hoc Committee, "The triple revolution," *Liberation* v 9 n 2 (April 1964), 13. The statement's other signers included Irving Howe and even Bayard Rustin.
19. League for Industrial Democracy News Bulletin (Winter 1966), 2; Harrington, "SP platform draft" (1968), MSC b 18 f 17 (r 3375); Smith, "Novack and Harrington debate," M v 36 n 44 (1 Dec. 1972), 19.
20. Rustin and Shachtman, "Organized labor and coalition politics," NA v 10 n 20 (30 Sept. 1972), 2.
21. League for Industrial Democracy News Bulletin (Fall 1964); League for Industrial Democracy News Bulletin (Winter 1966); *Dissent* v 13 n 1 (Jan.–Feb. 1966).
22. Interview with Harrington by Friend and Hacker (19 Aug. 1988), s 1; *Dissent* v 4 n 4 (Autumn 1957).
23. Shachtman, "On unity with the SP" (1957 convention speech), ISM v 18, 1099; Howe to Shachtman (30 Sept. 1961) and Shachtman to Howe (3 Oct. 1961), MSC b 29 f 26 (r 3379); Shachtman, "Personal and political dimensions," *Dissent* v 11 n 3 (Summer 1964).
24. Harrington, "The tradition of *Dissent*," *Dissent* v 13 n 6 (Nov.–Dec. 1966), 628.
25. "Aftermath of the Korean truce," NI v 19 n 4 (July–Aug. 1953), 17.
26. Farber to Drucker (25 July 1992), 1.

27. Michael Harrington, *Fragments of the Century*, 201.
28. *Dissent* v 12 n 3 (Summer 1965), 290; Ring, "'Socialist' favors bombing N. Vietnam," M v 29 n 23 (7 June 1965), 4; Shachtman et al., "Statement on Vietnam" (1970), MSC b 18 f 14 (r 3375).
29. Ring, M v 29 n 23, 4; Harrington, *Fragments of the Century*, 201; interview with Glotzer (28 Mar. 1989), s 8; interview with Kahn (7 Apr. 1989), s 3.
30. *Freedom Budget*, 2, 9, 10; interview with Kahn (7 Apr. 1989), s 3.
31. "Statement on Vietnam," MSC b 18 f 14 (r 3375).
32. Interview with Shachtman by Terkel, NA v 10 n 22 (15 Nov. 1972), 6; interview with Kahn (7 Apr. 1989), s 2; Glotzer, "Max Shachtman," NA v 10 n 22 (15 Nov. 1972), 4.
33. Interview with Kahn (7 Apr. 1989), s 3, 4; "Crisis and commitment," *Crisis* (Nov. 1966), 474–79, cited in Manning Marable, *Race, Reform and Rebellion*, III.
34. NA v 5 n 22 (30 June 1966).
35. Harrington, *Fragments of the Century*, 209; McReynolds to Feldman (9 Feb. 1967), MSC b 29 f 8 (r 3380); Harrington et al., "What can we do?" *Dissent* v 14 n 4 (July–Aug. 1967), 399.
36. *Dissent* v 15 n 6 (Nov.–Dec. 1968); Shachtman to Howe (11 Nov. 1968), MSC b 29 f 27 (r 3379).
37. SP NC, "Resolution on Vietnam" (13–14 Dec. 1969), MSC b 18 f 14 (r 3375); Harrington, "Draft statement and resolution on Vietnam" (20 Sept. 1971), MSC b 18 f 18 (r 3375).
38. Harrington, "Socialists and reactionary anti-communism" (1970), MSC b 18 f 18 (r 3375).
39. Harrington, *Fragments of the Century*, 196–97; Shachtman to Horowitz (23 Sept. 1970), MSC b 29 f 25 (r 3379).
40. Irving Howe, *A Margin of Hope*, 306; Howe to Shachtman (3 May 1969) and Shachtman to Howe (13 May 1969), MSC b 29 f 27 (r 3379).
41. "Socialists and the trade unions," NA v 9 n 22 (28 Feb. 1971), 7; Shachtman to McIntyre (28 Sept. 1972), MSC b 31 f 19 (r 3382).
42. Shachtman to McIntyre (28 Sept. 1972), MSC b 31 f 19 (r 3382); Kahn, "Max Shachtman," NA v 10 n 22 (15 Nov. 1972), 5; NA v 10 n 20 (30 Sept. 1972), 1–2; NA v 10 n 21 (25 Oct. 1972), 6.
43. Shachtman to Howe (13 Jan. 1964), MSC b 29 f 27 (r 3379).
44. Shachtman to Dobbs (9 Mar. 1968), MSC b 28 f 31A (r 3378).
45. Interview with Kahn (7 Apr. 1989), s 3; Glotzer, "Max Shachtman," NA v 10 n 22 (15 Nov. 1972), 4. One wing of the Old Guard Social Democratic Federation had reunified with the Socialist Party in 1956, so the group that Shachtman joined in 1958 was officially the Socialist Party–Social Democratic Federation. But another die-hard wing of the Old Guard, including the old Yiddish-language federation, had refused to take part in the 1956 reunification, instead forming a separate group called the Democratic Socialist Federation. It was this group that Shachtman's wing united with in 1972–73 to form Social Democrats USA.
46. Shachtman to Howe (13 Jan. 1964), MSC b 29 f 27 (r 3379); Shachtman to T. Draper (11 Mar. 1958), MSC b 28 f 33 (r 3378); Shachtman, "Introduction" (1962), in Franz Mehring, *Karl Marx*, vii.
47. Interview with Geltman (22 Mar. 1989), s 2, 3.
48. Interview with Glotzer (28 Mar. 1989), s 7.
49. Interview with Geltman (22 Mar. 1989), s 2.

50. Shachtman to Jacobs (31 Oct. 1963), MSC b 29 f 30 (r 3379); Sedova to SWP PC (6 June 1951), MSC b 31 f 7 (r 3382).
51. RMS 362.
52. Shachtman to Howe (20 July 1970), MSC b 29 f 27 (r 3379).
53. Kerry to Shachtman (12 Apr. 1964), MSC b 29 f 37 (r 3380); Shachtman to Dobbs (9 Mar. 1968), MSC b 28 f 31A (r 3378); Les Evans, ed., *James P. Cannon as We Knew Him*, 171; interview with Geltman (22 Mar. 1989), s 4.
54. Interview with Kahn (7 Apr. 1989), s 2.
55. Interview with Weir by Thompson (14 Aug. 1983), tape 4 s 2.
56. Kahn, "Max Shachtman," NA v 10 n 22 (15 Nov. 1972), 4.

Conclusion

Of all the outrages against which Shachtman fulminated during a half century well stocked with outrages, the Moscow purge trials of the late 1930s probably horrified him most. That Stalin was capable of great crimes did not shock him too much; he had been indicting Stalin for his crimes for a decade. That the Russian Revolution—the inspiration of his youth and an ideal he was never able to renounce or replace—should have ended in bloody counterrevolution was not too great a surprise; he always said that the Bolsheviks held to power and their communist vision much longer than anyone would have predicted. But he could not stomach the fact that of all those revolutionaries who had made up the Bolshevik leadership, led the revolution, and been Lenin's and Trotsky's companions, only a handful stayed true to their vision and preserved their honor.

The bureaucrats who supported Stalin and did his dirty work were the least of Shachtman's problems. He was not prepared to see so many of the highest-ranking Bolsheviks—men who had towered over U.S. Communists like him in the 1920s—surrender to Stalin, mouth the lies Stalin's flunkies wrote for them, and degrade themselves with abject, repeated self-denunciations. He had known that each of these men had his weaknesses. Somehow in the years of the Bolsheviks' triumph their weaknesses had seemed unimportant, their strengths almost superhuman. Now their strengths were apparently of no use to them or anybody else. Their weaknesses were magnified until these once impressive leaders seemed no longer superhuman but subhuman, groveling and pathetic.

The grinding up of these people impressed Shachtman with the insignificance of individuals within a history that human beings had not yet managed to understand or control. Marx had said a century earlier, "Men make their own history, but they do not make it just as they please." In 1937 Shachtman expanded on Marx's remark, stressing the strength of history's power over individuals.

> While men do make their own history, a multitude of forces combines to produce the great man of each period, and the agglomeration of men not quite so great who compose the general staff. For a period of progress, history kneads its leaders out of one batch of dough; for a period of reaction, a dough of very different ingredients is used.[1]

The Moscow defendants were destroyed in part because they lost the

315

dynamic connection to working people's movements on which all socialists rely. They were major historical figures when they were leaders of movements around the world and enemies of almost every existing government. When the revolutionary movement died down, they were caught between their distaste at what the Communist movement had become and their reluctance to break with it. They were leaders of nothing, involved in nothing, clear about nothing. They seemed insignificant and pitiable.

Shachtman's own peculiar transformation obeyed a similar logic. He was not the great man of any period. But in the ranks of those who built a revolutionary left in the United States in the 1920s and then tried to salvage it from its Stalinist corruption in the 1930s and 1940s, he was a major leader. He had a comprehensive knowledge of Marxism's history and theory and a keen feel for its democratic essence. No one felt more at home with Marxists in Europe or Latin America or Asia or better understood the importance of an international movement for U.S. radicals. No one expressed more eloquently the extent of the tragedy the international left went through in those years, whether its activists were being killed by the Guomindang in China, the Gestapo in Germany, the GPU in the USSR, or the marines in Central America.

He was a creative and original thinker during the years he took part in working-class fights—from Minneapolis in 1934 to Grand Rapids in 1944—and felt an intense solidarity with all those fighting to defeat fascism, win leadership away from Communists, and transform society after the world war. He made a substantial contribution to foreseeing the shape of the postwar world and adapting socialist strategy to it. We can say of him, as he said of the Communists of the 1920s, that he was "painfully beginning to make a rounded conception and practice of revolutionary Marxism a political force in this country—and who had ever done it before?"[2]

For a few years in the 1940s he made one original contribution to Marxist theory and politics after another. The theory of bureaucratic collectivism he developed in 1940 and 1941 was only one highlight. There were also his vision of postwar U.S. world supremacy and his strategy to fight it; his conception of the third camp and its struggle for national liberation and democracy; his explanation of the dual character of Communist parties, which made possible his clear-sighted opposition to the postwar Stalinization of Eastern Europe; his exposition of radical trade union tactics, particularly in his support for the United Auto Workers Rank and File Caucus in 1944 and the GM Program in 1946; and his theory of the all-inclusive revolutionary party and its cadre. Each of these contributions was a breakthrough that has meaning for socialists today.

During the late 1940s and early 1950s, however, Shachtman's ties to labor's rank and file loosened. In the years that followed, he gradually ceased to expect that rank-and-file working people—whether in U.S. unions or third-world countries—would soon speak, act, and take power for themselves. He came to see socialism as a prospect for a future century, not his own. In his own time, he decided, trade union and social democratic leaders would have to act as custodians for the social gains and democratic freedoms that the working class had won. The custodians, in turn, would have to rely on the U.S. government for protection.

Many radicals' admiration for Shachtman's clear-sighted condemnation of the Soviet subjugation of Eastern Europe was diminished, then obliterated, as his opposition to U.S. power faded. Many were shocked when he condoned the U.S.-sponsored invasion of Cuba in 1961 and opposed U.S. withdrawal from Vietnam. In the end, most radicals felt that Shachtman had failed what he himself had called "the real test of the American revolutionist": not "opposition to British, French, or German capitalisms or even to Stalinism, but to the ruling class and its social system in the United States."[3]

As his left and his world were destroyed, his wit seemed gradually more defensive, his loyalties more sentimental or vindictive, his historical and theoretical erudition more tendentiously exploited. His intelligence became ingenuity in rationalizing the decisions that governments would have made anyway. His confidence in his judgment became virtual indifference to others' opinions. Like other socialists of his time, he learned little from the feminist movement's insistence that less intellectual, less articulate, less definite people also deserved to be heard. He and the men he influenced were preoccupied with not being "soft," not giving an inch to a political opponent because of any personal feeling.

As for his eagerness to play an active role in history, it helped ensure that he would journey all the way from the camp of anti-capitalist revolution to the camp of counterrevolution, the one he backed in Vietnam. He would not stop somewhere in the middle, as did his former comrades who rejected the revolutions in progress but stopped short of supporting the suppression of these revolutions by U.S. troops. If he would not be with the guerrillas who were making anti-capitalist revolutions in the third world, then he would be with the Cold Warriors who were opposing revolutions in the name of the labor movement.

Since Shachtman could not find a viable force in the labor movement of the 1950s that was more progressive than Walter Reuther's United Auto Workers leadership, he let loyalty to Reuther pull him toward international social democracy and accommodation to the Cold War. And since he could not find a force in the labor movement of the 1960s that was more powerful than George Meany's AFL-CIO leadership, he let loyalty to Meany pull him into support for the U.S. war in Vietnam.

One theoretical expression of his evolution was the theory he began developing in late 1945; namely, that new bureaucratic ruling classes were being secreted from the pores of decaying capitalism. This theory went together with an underestimation of capitalism's strength and of social democrats' attachment to preserving capitalism. It accelerated his reexamination and rejection of his earlier theoretical work. One after the other, he discarded his earlier theoretical achievements.

He had been an eloquent defender of the Russian Revolution for thirty years, but by the early 1950s he concluded that the Bolsheviks' effort to build socialism in backward Russia had always been doomed to failure. He had been a pioneer in linking national liberation to socialism in the third world, but by the early 1950s he concluded that socialism in the third world would have to wait on socialist transformations elsewhere. He had explained and predicted Western Communists' acquiescence in capitalism after the Second World War, but by the late 1940s he was warning against Communist takeovers in the West that would never come. He had helped create rank-and-file power in the unions, but by the early 1950s the unions were reduced in his thinking to the "politically active officialdom." He had built his Workers Party into an organization where discussion was continuous, free-flowing, and channeled into collective action; by the late 1950s he had dissolved it.

His most enduring legacy, one that all his followers of whatever tendency would continue to affirm after his death, was his appreciation of the inseparability of socialism and democracy. All democratic socialists can rely on his arguments that democratic freedoms and democratic institutions are indispensable to working people who seek to rule and transform society. But even his commitment to democracy changed shape in his last years. He had once criticized U.S. democracy by the standard of the more thoroughgoing, substantive democracy of the Russian soviets and Catalan workers' juntas. He ended by explaining the importance of the crumbs of democracy that existed under the U.S.-backed South Vietnamese regime. The contract between capitalist democracy and socialist democracy faded from his thoughts. Of the Socialists who spoke at his memorial service, not one mentioned the concept of the "third camp" that had been his lodestar.[4]

His orientation to the AFL-CIO did enable him in the mid-1960s to build an alliance between unions and civil rights organizations and to help shape some major Great Society social programs. But in other ways it impelled him to rein in his own radical impulses even on U.S. domestic issues. He subordinated the demands of the civil rights movement to the electoral needs of the Democratic Party. To the extent that there were any stirrings of rank-and-file activism in the unions, he opposed or ignored them.

Sometimes in his last years Shachtman seemed to sense that there had been something finer in his politics in the 1930s and 1940s than in the 1960s. "Many thousands of old radicals, like myself, vote for the goddam Democrats," he said. "And yet, as I look back on that decade, the Thirties, it was for radicals the most exciting period in American history."[5]

The excitement he remembered from the 1930s and early 1940s was the excitement of confrontation: not only confrontation between left and right, labor and capital, but between two different visions of what "America" would be. The excitement came from believing that the United States might become truly his country, a country where an immigrant Jewish Marxist from Harlem could feel fully at home. He believed that his ideals could become the common property of his people. He believed that the unskilled immigrants joining the CIO, the African Americans coming north to work in factories, the rebels against U.S. colonialism in the Philippines, and the heirs of dead Sacco and Vanzetti would be won to his side. He believed that the most powerful capitalist country, the "arsenal of world reaction," could become "the living vindication of Marxism" and an ally of peoples fighting for freedom.

Instead of holding on in his last two decades to his original vision of what the United States could be, he convinced himself that a simulacrum of his vision had already been created. He convinced himself that the AFL-CIO was almost a mass socialist movement, that the Democratic Party was almost a labor party, that Johnson's Great Society had almost made African Americans equal, that the United States had almost saved Vietnam for democracy. He convinced himself that a group of trade union officials incarnated the working-class community into which he had been born, to which he had once been loyal in reality, and to which he was still loyal in imagination.

His adversaries and disillusioned followers sometimes trivialized his tragedy by denying any continuity between his achievements and his end. One Trotskyist said that he died "a firm supporter of the capitalist system." Julius Jacobson called him a man who had already died his "moral and political death," a "renegade" from "his earlier, most fundamental commitment to social justice"; he added, "To say that he died, in any sense at all, a socialist, is to denude the word of all meaning."[6] These comments fail to fully express the paradox of Shachtman's last years. He moved far to the right, but he kept trying to rebuild a socialist movement. Cut off from the rank and file of the labor movement, he kept trying to mend the broken thread that had once tied his politics to the U.S. working class. Straining to reach the thread's lost end, he went rightward to where he imagined it was lying.

No U.S. socialist has managed to mend that thread. But glimmerings of a new radical mood in U.S. labor in the 1980s and 1990s suggest where the lost end might be picked up. It might be where Shachtman saw it in 1938: among those who feel connections between their lives here and working people's lives in Latin America, the Philippines, South Africa, and who recognize the corporate employers they hate as the same ones hated in Southeast Asia and Europe. These working people and today's socialists may meet on a trail that Shachtman helped blaze.

Notes

1. Karl Marx, *The 18th Brumaire of Louis Bonaparte*, 15; Shachtman, "Introduction" (1 May 1937), in Leon Trotsky, *The Stalin School of Falsification*, viii.
2. Shachtman, "In opposite directions," NI v 3 n 3 (June 1936), 65.
3. "Founding principles of the Workers Party," NI v 12 n 4 (Apr. 1946), 124 (also WP bul n 1 [26 Apr. 1940], ISM v 2).
4. Weir, "Requiem for Max Shachtman," *Radical America* v 7 n 1 (1973), 76; "A meeting for Max," NA v 11 n 1 (31 Dec. 1972), 1, 8.
5. Interview with Shachtman by Terkel, NA v 10 n 22 (15 Nov. 1972), 6.
6. Ali, "Introduction," in Max Shachtman, *Genesis of Trotskyism*, 2; Jacobson, "The two deaths of Max Shachtman," *New Politics* v 10 n 2 (Winter 1973), 99.

Bibliography

The main written sources for this book have been the periodicals published by the organizations Shachtman belonged to and the collections of his and his associates' personal papers. These sources are given in the Abbreviations section. Whenever the text contains a direct quotation or paraphrase from a specific article in any of these periodicals or collections, the article is cited. This book has been informed by these periodicals and collections in their entirety, however. I have not included the thousands of articles that I have read or tried to make a comprehensive list of Shachtman's works.

All of Shachtman's books and pamphlets that I am aware of, as well as books and pamphlets for which he wrote introductions, are included in this bibliography. So are books and pamphlets by Lenin, Trotsky, and other socialists that I think contributed to his thinking. Finally, I have listed books and articles that I found particularly useful as background reading. When the relevance of these background readings is not clear from their titles, I have given a brief explanation in brackets.

Altbach, Philip. *Student Politics in America: A Historical Analysis.* New York: McGraw-Hill, 1974 [on the YSL and YPSL].

Anderson, Perry. *Considerations on Western Marxism.* London: Verso, 1979 [on philosophy and national Marxist traditions].

Angus, Ian. *Canadian Bolsheviks: The Early Years of the Communist Party of Canada.* Montreal: Vanguard, 1981 [on Maurice Spector].

Bensaïd, Daniel. *The Formative Years of the Fourth International (1933–1938).* Amsterdam: International Institute for Research and Education, 1988.

Branch, Taylor. *Parting the Waters: America in the King Years, 1954–63.* New York: Simon & Schuster, 1988.

Buhle, Paul. *C. L. R. James: The Artist as Revolutionary.* London: Verso, 1988.

Calverton, V. F. "Bolshevism in Spain." *Modern Monthly* v 10 n 6 (May 1937) [on the Barcelona events].

Cannon, James P. *The First Ten Years of American Communism: Report of a Participant.* New York: Pathfinder Press, 1973.

————. *The History of American Trotskyism: From Its Origins (1928) to the Founding of the Socialist Workers Party (1938): Report of a Participant.* New York: Pathfinder Press, 1972.

————. *James P. Cannon and the Early Years of American Communism: Selected Writings and Speeches, 1920–1928.* New York: Prometheus Research Library, 1992.

————. *Speeches to the Party: The Revolutionary Perspective and the Revolutionary Party.* New York: Pathfinder Press, 1973.

Carlo, Antonio. "Lenin on the party." *Telos* 17 (Fall 1973).

Carmichael, Stokely, and Charles V. Hamilton. *Black Power: The Politics of Liberation in America.* New York: Random House, 1967.

Carr, E. H. *The Comintern and the Spanish Civil War.* New York: Pantheon, 1984.

Carson, Claybourne. *In Struggle: SNCC and the Black Awakening of the 1960s.* Cambridge, MA: Harvard University Press, 1981.

Chester, Eric. *Socialists and the Ballot Box: A Historical Analysis.* New York: Praeger, 1985.

Claudín, Fernando. *The Communist Movement: From Comintern to Cominform.* Trans. Francis MacDonagh. New York: Monthly Review, 1975 [on the Yugoslav and Chinese revolutions].

Cohen, Stephen. *Bukharin and the Bolshevik Revolution: A Political Biography.* Oxford: Oxford University Press, 1980.

Communist International 4th Congress. "Theses on Comintern tactics" [1922]. *Theses, Resolutions and Manifestos of the First Four Congresses of the Third International.* Trans. Alix Holt and Barbara Holland, ed. Alan Adler. London: Ink Links, 1980 [on "workers' governments"].

Crane, Philip M. *The Democrats' Dilemma: How the Liberal Left Captured the Democratic Party.* Chicago: Henry Regnery Co., 1964.

Crouch, Harold. "The trend to authoritarianism: the post-1945 period." *The Development of Indonesian Society: From the Coming of Islam to the Present Day.* Ed. Harry Aveling. New York: St. Martin's Press, 1980.

Davis, Mike. *Prisoners of the American Dream: Politics and Economy in the History of the US Working Class.* London: Verso, 1986.

Deutscher, Isaac. *The Prophet Outcast: Trotsky: 1929–1940.* Oxford: Oxford University Press, 1963.

———. *The Prophet Unarmed: Trotsky: 1921–1929.* Oxford: Oxford University Press, 1959.

Dobbs, Farrell. *Teamster Rebellion.* New York: Monad Press, 1972 [on the Minneapolis strike].

Documents of the Fourth International: The Formative Years (1933–40). New York: Pathfinder Press, 1973.

Draper, Hal. *A Political Guide to the ABC of National Liberation Movements.* Berkeley, 1968 [on the Bay of Pigs and the Vietnam War].

Draper, Theodore. *American Communism and Soviet Russia: The Formative Period.* New York: Random House, 1986.

Drucker, Peter. "The paradoxical Polish state." *Socialist Politics* v 1 n 2 (Oct. 1984) [on Yugoslavia].

Eatwell, Roger. *The 1945–1951 Labour Governments.* London: Batsford Academic, 1979.

Evans, Les, ed. *James P. Cannon as We Knew Him.* New York: Pathfinder Press, 1976.

Feeley, Dianne. "Fighter for the unemployed." *Socialist Action* (Feb. 1984) [on Ernest McKinney].

Fisk, Milton. *Socialism from Below in the United States: The Origins of the International Socialist Organization.* Cleveland: Hera Press, 1977 [on the SWP, WP, and ISL].

Forman, James, *The Making of Black Revolutionaries: A Personal Account.* New York: Macmillan Press, 1972.

Fourth International Conference. "The new imperialist peace and the building of the parties of the Fourth International." *Fourth International* v 7 n 6 (June 1946).

A "Freedom Budget" for All Americans: Budgeting Our Resources, 1966–1975, to Achieve "Freedom from Want." New York: A. Philip Randolph Institute, 1966.

Glaberman, Martin. *Wartime Strikes: The Struggle against the No-Strike Pledge in the UAW during World War II.* Detroit: Bewick, 1980.

Glotzer, Albert. *Trotsky: Memoir and Critique.* Buffalo: Prometheus Books, 1989.

Goldman, Albert. *The Question of Unity.* New York: Workers Party, 1947. Introduction by Shachtman.

Gurock, Jeffrey. *When Harlem Was Jewish, 1870–1930.* New York: Columbia University Press, 1979.

Harrington, Michael. *Fragments of the Century.* New York: Saturday Review Press, 1973.

———. *The Other America: Poverty in the United States.* New York: Macmillan, 1969.

Haskell, Gordon. "Max Shachtman" [unpublished manuscript].

Howe, Irving. *A Margin of Hope: An Intellectual Autobiography.* San Diego: Harcourt Brace, 1982.

Howe, Irving, and Lewis Coser. *The American Communist Party: A Critical History.* New York: Praeger, 1962.

Howe, Irving, and B. J. Widick. *The UAW and Walter Reuther.* New York: Random House, 1949.

International Communist League International Secretariat. *War and the 4th International.* New York: Communist League of America, 1934.

Isserman, Maurice. *If I Had a Hammer . . . : The Death of the Old Left and the Birth of the New Left.* New York: Basic Books, 1987.

Jacobson, Julius. "The two deaths of Max Shachtman." *New Politics* v 10 n 2 (Winter 1973).

Johnpoll, Bernard. *Pacifist's Progress: Norman Thomas and the Decline of American Socialism.* Chicago: Quadrangle Books, 1970.

Kahin, George. *Nationalism and Revolution in Indonesia.* Ithaca, NY: Cornell University Press, 1952.

Kaiser, David, and Francis Russell. "Sacco and Vanzetti: an exchange." *New York Review of Books* v 33 n 9 (29 May 1986).

Klehr, Harvey. *The Heyday of American Communism: The Depression Decade.* New York: Basic Books, 1984.

Kristol, Irving. *Reflections of a Neoconservative: Looking Back, Looking Ahead.* New York: Basic Books, 1983.

Lazitch, Branko, and Milorad Drachkovitch. *Lenin and the Comintern.* Stanford: Hoover Institution, 1972.

Le Blanc, Paul, ed. *Revolutionary Principles and Working Class Democracy.* New York: F. I. T., 1992.

Lenin, V. I., "The discussion on self-determination summed up." *Collected Works.* Vol. 22. Moscow, Progress Publishers, 1964.

———. "The Junius pamphlet." *Collected Works.* Vol. 22. Moscow: Progress Publishers, 1964.

———. "The reorganisation of the party." *Collected Works.* Vol. 10. Moscow: Progress Publishers, 1972.

———. "The socialist revolution and the right of nations to self-determination: theses." *Collected Works.* Vol. 22. Moscow: Progress Publishers, 1964.

———. "Theses and report on bourgeois democracy and the dictatorship of the proletariat." *Theses, Resolutions and Manifestos of the First Four Congresses of the Third International.* Trans. Alix Holt and Barbara Holland, ed. Alan Adler. London: Ink Links, 1980.

———. *What Is to Be Done? Burning Questions of Our Movement* [1902]. New York: International Publishers, 1969.

Lequenne, Michel. "Sur la nature des états bureaucratiques." *Quatrième Internationale* n 13 (1 Apr. 1984).

Lichtenstein, Nelson. *Labor's War at Home: The CIO in World War II.* Cambridge: Cambridge University Press, 1982.

Liebman, Arthur. *Jews and the Left.* New York: John Wiley & Sons, 1979.

Lore, Ludwig. "The challenge of Catalonia." *Modern Monthly* v 10 n 6 (May 1937) [on the Barcelona events].

Löwy, Michael. *The Politics of Combined and Uneven Development: The Theory of Permanent Revolution.* London: Verso, 1981 [on the Yugoslav, Chinese, Vietnamese, and Cuban revolutions].

Lukács, Georg. *Lenin: A Study on the Unity of His Thought* [1924]. Trans. Nicholas Jacobs. Cambridge, MA: MIT Press, 1971.

Luxemburg, Rosa. "What does the Spartacus League want?" *Selected Political Writings.* Ed. Dick Howard. New York: Monthly Review Press, 1971 [on socialist strategy under capitalist democracy].

Mandel, Ernest. "The conflict in Poland: from abstentionism to active intervention in the camp of the class enemy." *Fourth International* v 8 n 2 (Feb. 1947).

———. *Late Capitalism.* Trans. Joris De Bres. London: Verso, 1978 [on post–Second World War capitalist expansion].

———. *The Meaning of the Second World War.* London: Verso, 1986.

———. *Revolutionary Marxism Today.* London: New Left Books, 1979 [on the Second World War and socialist strategy under capitalist democracy].

———. "What should be modified and what should be maintained in the theses of the second World Congress of the Fourth International on the question of Stalinism? (Ten theses)." *The Struggle in the Fourth International: International Secretariat Documents, 1951–54.* New York: SWP, 1974.

Marable, Manning. *Race, Reform and Rebellion: The Second Reconstruction in Black America, 1945–1982.* London: Macmillan Press, 1984.

Marx, Karl. *The 18th Brumaire of Louis Bonaparte.* New York: International Publishers, 1963 [on human beings in history].

———. "General rules of the International Working Men's Association." *Political Writings Volume III: The First International and After.* Ed. David Fernbach. New York: Random House, 1974 [on working-class self-emancipation].

Mehring, Franz. *Karl Marx: The Story of His Life.* Ann Arbor: University of Michigan Press, 1962. Introduction by Shachtman.

Merleau-Ponty, Maurice. *Humanism and Terror: An Essay on the Communist Problem.* Trans. John O'Neill. Boston: Beacon, 1969 [on the Moscow trials].

Miliband, Ralph. *Parliamentary Socialism: A Study in the Politics of Labour.* New York: Monthly Review Press, 1972.

Miller, James. *"Democracy Is in the Streets": From Port Huron to the Siege of Chicago.* New York: Simon & Schuster, 1987 [on SDS].

Morris, Aldon D. *The Origins of the Civil Rights Movement: Black Communities Organizing for Change.* New York: Free Press, 1984.

Morrow, Felix. "It is time to grow up: the infantile sickness of the European Secretariat." *Fourth International* v 7 n 7 (July 1946).

Nedava, Joseph. *Trotsky and the Jews.* Philadelphia: Jewish Publication Society, 1972.

Nelson, Bruce. *Workers on the Waterfront: Seamen, Longshoremen, and Unionism in the 1930s.* Urbana: University of Illinois Press, 1990.

Novack, George. "Max Shachtman: a political portrait." *International Socialist Review* v 34 n 2 (Feb. 1973).

Orwell, George. *Homage to Catalonia.* San Diego: Harcourt Brace, 1980 [on the Spanish Civil War and Barcelona events].

Plastrik, Stanley. *India in Revolt.* New York: Workers Party, 1942. Introduction by Shachtman.

Preis, Art. *Labor's Giant Step: Twenty Years of the CIO.* New York: Pioneer Publishers, 1964.

———. *The Stalinists on the Waterfront.* New York: Pioneer Publishers, 1947.

Raptis, Michel. "Le 3 sept 1938, à Périgny: souvenirs de Michel Pablo." *Sous le drapeau du Socialisme* n 108–9 (Nov.–Dec. 1988).

Reid, Anthony. *The Indonesian National Revolution, 1945–50.* Hawthorn, Australia: Longman, 1974.

Richmond, Al. *A Long View from the Left: Memoirs of an American Revolutionary.* New York: Dell Publishing Co., 1972.

Robbins, Jack. *The Birth of American Trotskyism, 1927–29: The Origins of a Radical Marxist Movement.* N.p., 1973.

Rousset, Pierre. "The peculiarities of Vietnamese Communism." *The Stalinist Legacy: Its Impact on Twentieth-Century World Politics.* Ed. Tariq Ali. Harmondsworth: Penguin, 1984.

Russell, Francis. "Clinching the case." *New York Review of Books* v 33 n 4 (13 Mar. 1986) [on the Sacco-Vanzetti case].

Rustin, Bayard. *Down the Line: The Collected Writings of Bayard Rustin.* Chicago: Quadrange Books, 1971.

Sale, Kirkpatrick. *SDS.* New York: Random House, 1973.

Schneer, Jonathan. *Labour's Conscience: The Labour Left 1945–51.* Boston: Unwin Hyman, 1988.

Seidler, Murray. *Norman Thomas: Respectable Rebel.* Syracuse, NY: Syracuse University Press, 1967.

Serge, Victor. *Memoirs of a Revolutionary.* Trans. Peter Sedgwick. London: Writers and Readers, 1984 [on the Kronstadt uprising].

———. *Russia Twenty Years After.* Trans. Max Shachtman. New York: Hillman-Curl, 1937. Introduction by Shachtman. Also published without introduction as *Destiny of a Revolution.* London: Hutchinson & Co., 1937 [on the Moscow trials].

Shachtman, Max. *Behind the Moscow Trial.* New York: Pioneer Publishers, 1936.

———. *The Bureaucratic Revolution: The Rise of the Stalinist State.* New York: Donald Press, 1962.

———. *The Fight for Socialism: The Principles and Program of the Workers Party.* New York: New International Publishing Co., 1946.

———. *For a Cost-Plus Wage.* New York: Workers Party, 1943.

———. *Genesis of Trotskyism: The First Ten Years of the Left Opposition.* London: IMG 1973. Also published as *The History and Principles of the Left Opposition.* London: New Park, 1974.

———. Introduction to *Karl Marx: The Story of His Life,* by Franz Mehring. Ann Arbor: University of Michigan Press, 1962.

———. Introduction to *The New International.* New York: Greenwood, 1968.

———. Introduction to *Socialist Appeal: An Organ of Revolutionary Marxism.* New York: Greenwood, 1968.

———. *Lenin, Liebknecht, Luxemburg.* Chicago: Young Workers (Communist) League of America, 1924–25.

———. "The Marxists reply to Corey." *The Nation* v 150 n 10 (9 Mar. 1940).

———. "Radicalism in the thirties: the Trotskyist view." *As We Saw the Thirties:*

Essays on Social and Political Movements of a Decade. Ed. Rita James Simon. Urbana: University of Illinois Press, 1967.

————. *Sacco and Vanzetti: Labor's Martyrs.* New York: International Labor Defense, 1927.

————. *Socialism: The Hope of Humanity.* New York: New International Publishing Co., 1945.

————. "The struggle for the new course." In Leon Trotsky, *The New Course* [1923]. Ann Arbor: University of Michigan Press, 1965.

Shachtman, Max, and Hal Draper. *Two Views of the Cuban Invasion.* Oakland: Hal Draper, 1961.

Shannon, David. *The Socialist Party of America: A History.* New York: Macmillan, 1955.

Simon, Rita James, ed. *As We Saw the Thirties: Essays on Social and Political Movements of a Decade.* Urbana: University of Illinois Press, 1967.

Smith, Richard. "The crisis of Maoism—II." *Against the Current* v 1 n 4 (Spring 1982).

Swanberg, W. A. *Norman Thomas: The Last Idealist.* New York: Charles Scribner's Sons, 1976.

Taylor, A. J. P. *The Origins of the Second World War.* Greenwich, CT: Fawcett, 1961.

Trotsky, Leon. *Germany: The Key to the International Situation.* Trans. Sam Gordon and Morris Lewitt. New York: Pioneer Publishers, 1932.

————. *In Defense of Marxism* [1939–40]. New York: Pathfinder Press, 1973.

————. *In Defense of the Soviet Union: A Compilation, 1927–1937.* New York: Pioneer, 1937. Introduction by Shachtman.

————. *Leon Trotsky on Black Nationalism and Self-Determination.* Ed. George Breitman. New York: Merit Publishers, 1967.

————. "Manifesto of the Communist International to the workers of the world." *Theses, Resolutions and Manifestos of the First Four Congresses of the Third International.* Trans. Alix Holt and Barbara Holland, ed. Alan Adler. London: Ink Links, 1980 [on socialist strategy under capitalist democracy].

————. *The New Course* [1923]. Ann Arbor: University of Michigan Press, 1965. Introduction by Shachtman.

————. *The Permanent Revolution.* Trans. Max Shachtman. New York: Pioneer Publishers, 1931.

————. *Problems of the Chinese Revolution.* Ann Arbor: University of Michigan Press, 1967. Introduction by Shachtman.

————. *Problems of the Development of the U.S.S.R.: Draft of the Thesis of the International Left Opposition on the Russian Question.* Trans. Morris Lewitt and Max Shachtman. New York: Communist League of America, 1931.

————. *The Revolution Betrayed: What Is the Soviet Union and Where Is It Going?* [1936]. Trans. Max Eastman. New York: Pathfinder Press, 1972.

————. *The Soviet Union and the Fourth International: The Class Nature of the Soviet State.* Trans. Usick Vanzler. New York: Pioneer Publishers, 1934.

————. *The Stalin School of Falsification.* Trans. John Wright. New York: Pioneer Publishers, 1937. Introduction by Shachtman.

————. *Stalinism and Bolshevism: Concerning the Historical and Theoretical Roots of the Fourth International.* New York: Pioneer Publishers, 1937. Introduction by Shachtman.

————. *The Strategy of the World Revolution* [1928]. Trans. Max Shachtman. New York: Communist League of America, 1930. Introduction by Shachtman.

———. *Terrorism and Communism: A Reply to Karl Kautsky* [1919]. Ann Arbor: University of Michigan Press, 1961. Foreword by Shachtman.

———. *The Third International after Lenin* [1928]. Trans. John Wright. New York: Pioneer Publishers, 1936. Introduction by Shachtman.

———. *Transitional Program for Socialist Revolution: The Death Agony of Capitalism and the Tasks of the Fourth International* [1938]. New York: Pathfinder Press, 1970.

———. *The Turn in the Communist International and the German Situation.* Trans. Morris Lewitt. New York: Communist League, 1930.

———. *Writings.* Ed. George Breitman. New York: Pathfinder, 1979.

Wald, Alan. *The New York Intellectuals: The Rise and Decline of the Anti-Stalinist Left from the 1930s to the 1980s.* Chapel Hill: University of North Carolina Press, 1987.

Weinstein, James. *The Decline of Socialism in America, 1912–1925.* New York: Random House, 1967.

Weir, Stan. "Requiem for Max Shachtman." *Radical America* v 7 n 1 (1973).

Weisbrot, Robert. *Freedom Bound: A History of America's Civil Rights Movement.* New York: W.W. Norton, 1990.

Wohlforth, Tim. "Revolutionaries in the 1950s." *Against the Current* 14 (n.s. v 3 n 2, May–June 1988).

———. "Socialist politics after Hungary '56." *Against the Current* 15 (n.s. v 3 n 3, July–Aug. 1988).

Workers Party Campaign Committee. *How to Get Jobs for All* [1945]. WP Records b 1 f 1, Bancroft Library, University of California, Berkeley.

Zeluck, Steve. "The evolution of Lenin's views on the party, or, Lenin on regroupment." *Against the Current* v 3 n 3 (Winter 1985).

Zinn, Howard. *Postwar America: 1945–1971.* Indianapolis: Bobbs-Merrill, 1973 [on the Bay of Pigs and the Vietnam War].

———. *SNCC: The New Abolitionists.* Boston: Beacon Press, 1965.

Index

INDEX